One of the most striking features of late medieval and early modern Germany was the countless feuds carried out by nobles. A constant threat to law and order, these feuds have commonly been regarded as a manifestation of the decline – economic and otherwise – of the nobility.

This study shows that the nobility was not in crisis at this time. Nor were feuds merely banditry by another name. Rather, they were the result of an interplay between two fundamental processes: princely state building, and social stratification among the nobility. Offering a new paradigm for understanding the German nobility, this book argues that the development of the state made proximity to princes the single most decisive factor in determining the fortune of a family. The result was a violent competition among the nobility over resources which were crucial to the princes. Feuds played a central role in this struggle that eventually led to the formation of an elite of noble families on whose power and wealth the princely state depended.

CAMBRIDGE STUDIES IN EARLY MODERN HISTORY

State and nobility in early modern Germany

CAMBRIDGE STUDIES IN EARLY MODERN HISTORY

Edited by Professor Sir John Elliott, University of Oxford
Professor Olwen Hufton, University of Oxford
Professor H. G. Koenigsberger, University of London
Dr H. M. Scott, University of St Andrews

The idea of an 'early modern' period of European history from the fifteenth to the late eighteenth century is now widely accepted among historians. The purpose of Cambridge Studies in Early Modern History is to publish monographs and studies which illuminate the character of the period as a whole, and in particular focus attention on a dominant theme within it, the interplay of continuity and change as they are presented by the continuity of medieval ideas, political and social organization, and by the impact of new ideas, new methods and new demands on the traditional structure.

For a list of titles published in the series, please see end of book

State and nobility in early modern Germany

The knightly feud in Franconia, 1440–1567

HILLAY ZMORA
St Catharine's College, Cambridge

CAMBRIDGE
UNIVERSITY PRESS

PUBLISHED BY THE PRESS SYNDICATE OF THE UNIVERSITY OF CAMBRIDGE
The Pitt Building, Trumpington Street, Cambridge CB2 1RP, United Kingdom

CAMBRIDGE UNIVERSITY PRESS
The Edinburgh Building, Cambridge, CB2 2RU, United Kingdom
40 West 20th Street, New York, NY 10011–4211, USA
10 Stamford Road, Oakleigh, Melbourne 3166, Australia

First published 1997

Printed in the United Kingdom at the University Press, Cambridge

Typeset in Ehrhardt 10/12 [CE]

A catalogue record for this book is available from the British Library

Library of Congress Cataloguing in Publication data

Zmora, Hillay, 1964–
State and nobility in early modern Germany: the knightly feud in Franconia, 1440–1567
/ Hillay Zmora.
p.   c. – (Cambridge studies in early modern history)
Includes bibliographical references.
ISBN 0 521 56179 5
1. Nobility – Germany – Franconia – History.
2. Knights and knighthood – Germany – Franconia – History.
3. Feudal law – Germany – Franconia.
4. Landfriede.   5. Franconia (Germany) – Politics and government.
I. Title.   II. Series.
DD801.F566Z57   1997
929.7′33–dc21   97–1834   CIP

ISBN 0 521 56179 5 hardback

DD801
.F566
Z57
1997

Contents

List of figures	*page*	ix
List of tables		x
Preface		xi
List of abbreviations		xiii

1	The problem of the feud	1
	Historiography	1
	Method and sources	11
2	The politics of violence: feuding in late medieval Franconia	16
	Vestenberg versus Vestenberg	16
	Schott versus Nuremberg	26
3	The Franconian nobility	36
	Office	38
	The pledge, creditors, and guarantors	42
	Marriage	62
4	Prosopography of feuding noblemen	68
	Method	68
	Individual parameters	78
	Family parameters	80
5	State, nobility, and lordship: the feud interpreted	87
	From aristocracy to nobility	88
	Territorialising princes and feuding noblemen	92
	Wars and feuds	96
	Lordship, 'protection', and the feud	102
	State-making and the feud	111
	Conclusion	118
6	The decline of the feud	122
	The formation of the Knighthood	123
	The Common Penny of 1495	129
	The end of the feud	132

Contents

A note on Appendixes   147

Appendix A: Creditors and guarantors of the margraves of   148
    Brandenburg

Appendix B: Sample of intermarriages among the noble élite   155

Appendix C: Individual parameters of feuders (Sample-I)   157

Appendix D: Family parameters of feuders (Sample-I)   164

Appendix E: Individual parameters of feuders (Sample-II)   171

Appendix F: Family parameters of feuders (Sample-II)   173

Sources of information for Appendix A   175

Sources of Information for Appendixes C and D   183

Sources of Information for Appendixes E and F   200

Selected bibliography   204

Index   229

Figures

4.1 Genealogy of the Fuchs von Bimbach in Wallburg, 1404–36   *page* 70

4.2 Genealogy of the Fuchs von Bimbach in Wallburg, 1404–54   71

4.3 Genealogy of the Fuchs von Bimbach in Wallburg, 1404–1522   74

Map: The Holy Roman Empire (first half of sixteenth century)   xiv

Tables

3.1   Sample of debts (in gulden) of German princes, 1472–1559   *page* 43

3.2   Creditors of the margraves of Brandenburg in 1529   50

3.3   Noble creditors and guarantors of the margraves of Brandenburg   52
(mainly 1520s and 1530s)

4.1   Distribution of feuders in Sample-I across individual parameters   79

4.2   Distribution of feuders in Sample-II across individual parameters   80

4.3   Distribution of feuders and their families across family parameters   84

Preface

Late medieval and early modern Germans often accused noblemen of using the feud as a legal mantle with which to cloak their real purpose: banditry. Modern historians, believing that the nobility of this period was in economic crisis, have not taken exception to this view. A somewhat similar charge of ulterior motives can be made against the book that follows. For the feud, albeit forming its focus, serves as a 'pretext' for exploring other, larger themes. However interesting a subject the knightly feud may be in its own right, its real value lies elsewhere: in what it reveals about polity and society; more specifically, about state and nobility and the relationship between them. Together, these two formations constitute the core of the book. Indeed, the essence of the interpretation it offers is that the feud both resulted from, and helped to shape, an interplay between princely state building and social stratification among the aristocracy. An analysis of the feud thus illuminates both processes as few other phenomena can.

This interplay was probably already at work before 1440. But it is then that the links become apparent in the extant documentation. The year 1440 is therefore the temporal point of departure of the present study. However, the choice of this date is not entirely arbitrary: the years around 1440 saw a significant upsurge in the intensity of the territorial conflicts between the Franconian princes. And it was mainly for this reason that the role which noblemen's feuds played in these struggles became both more important and more transparent. Feuds continued unabated until the second half of the sixteenth century. The book closes with the execution of Wilhelm von Grumbach in 1567, which brought an end to the last feud on Franconian soil.

The research on which this book is based spanned nearly seven years. It could not have been undertaken and completed but for the help of numerous people and institutions. The potential of the feud as a subject of historical inquiry was impressed on me by Bob Scribner, and I have profited from his enlightening guidance ever since. I am in equally great debt to Dr Sheilagh Ogilvie upon whose wisdom and benevolence I have been allowed to draw. Dr Henry J. Cohn, Dr Tom Scott and Dr Scott Dixon provided acute readings and careful, constructive criticisms. My former teacher Professor Zvi Razi constantly monitored the progress of my research, intervening every now and then with characteristically eye-opening advice. I should like to state firmly, however, that I reserve to myself all rights to the errors, of judgement and otherwise, which this book may contain.

I am particularly grateful to the Master and Fellows of St Catharine's College, Cambridge, who elected me to a Research Fellowship. The College has provided me with a rare combination of three years of sheltered existence and an intellectually stimulating environment. Special thanks are due to the historians at St Catharine's: Professor Christopher Bayly, Dr John Thompson and Dr Christopher Clark. They have been an inexhaustible source of support and encouragement.

A protracted research, especially in and on a foreign country, requires considerable financial resources. It would have been impossible without the generous support of the Prince Consort and Thirlwall Fund, Cambridge University, Clare College, the Overseas Research Students Scheme, the German Academic Exchange Service (DAAD) and the Horodisch Foundation.

I am deeply indebted to the staffs and owners of the archives I consulted for their keen assistance, especially to Dr Gerhard Rechter of the Staatsarchiv Nürnberg who shared with me his unmatched knowledge of the local nobility; to Mr Wagenhöfer and Dr Heeg-Engelhart of the Staatsarchiv Würzburg; and to Monica von Deuster and her family who looked after me during the chilly days I worked in their castle in Burgpreppach. I should also like to register my thanks to Professor Rolf Sprandel and Dr Joachim Schneider of the Institut für Geschichte of the University of Würzburg for their help and hospitality.

Finally, I am most grateful to five members of my family: Mira and David Molchadsky for their essential support; Yaël Molchadsky-Zmora for her un-wavering companionship and some positive distractions; and Zohara and Ohad Zmora: their love of learning made this project possible in the first place, their parental love sustained me through the thick and the thin of it.

Abbreviations

AO	*Archiv des Historischen Vereins für Oberfranken*
AU	*Archiv des Historischen Vereins für Unterfranken und Aschaffenburg*
Bb	Reichsstadt Nürnberg, Briefbücher des Inneren Rates
BK	Beamtenkartei
BL	British Library
FA	Freiherrlich Fuchs'sches Archiv, Schloß Burgpreppach
Fstm.Ansb.	Fürstentum Ansbach
GNM	Bibliothek des Germanischen Nationalmuseums
Jb.Mfr.	*Jahrbuch des Historischen Vereins für Mittelfranken*
JffL	*Jahrbuch für fränkische Landesforschung*
Ldf	Libri diversarum formarum
MJfGK	*Mainfräkisches Jahrbuch für Geschichte und Kunst*
Prod.	Produkt
Rep.	Repertorium
RTA, jR	*Deutsche Reichstagsakten, jüngere Reihe*
RTA, mR	*Deutsche Reichstagsakten, mittlere Reihe*
StAA	Staatsarchiv Amberg
StAB	Staatsarchiv Bamberg
StAN	Staatsarchiv Nürnberg
StAW	Staatsarchiv Würzburg
Stb	Standbücher
VSWG	*Vierteljahrschrift für Sozial- und Wirtschaftsgeschichte*
WFr	*Württembergisch Franken*
ZbLG	*Zeitschrift für bayerische Landesgeschichte*
ZGO	*Zeitschrift für die Geschichte des Oberrheins*
ZHF	*Zeitschrift für Historische Forschung*

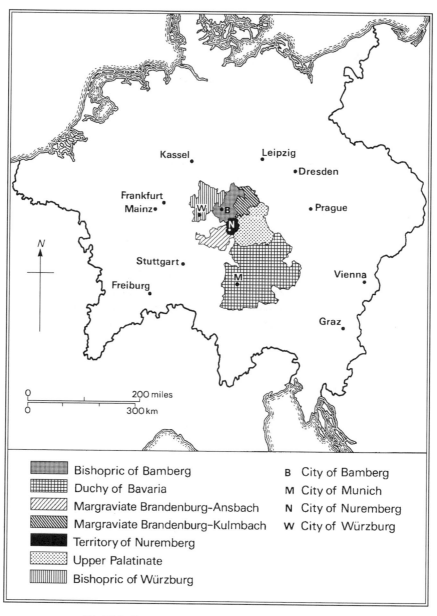

The Holy Roman Empire (first half of sixteenth century)

The problem of the feud

HISTORIOGRAPHY

'All Germany is a gang of bandits and, among the nobles, the more grasping the more glorious' – a Roman cardinal thus summed up the state of the German nation in the late Middle Ages.[1] There was more to this remark than curial hauteur: complaints about the bad manners and violence of German noblemen were a commonplace among German literati as well.[2] The latter were wont to base their criticism on an old European tradition which equated nobility with personal virtue rather than genetic qualities.[3] This was a conviction to which aristocratic authors, too, were willing to subscribe. At the same time, they gave it a different interpretation. In his dialogue 'The Robbers' (1521), the Franconian noble and humanist Ulrich von Hutten made one of the characters, Franz von Sickingen, say that

I am of the opinion that virtue is not hereditary and that he who has to reproach himself with ignominious deeds should in no way be counted among the nobility, even if he were a prince . . . [I]f there was in our family one who, albeit descending from this lineage, still displayed in his life only sordid baseness – such a one I would not recognise as a relation or a kinsman, nor as a noble, and never have anything in common with him.[4]

It is noteworthy that this harangue is delivered in the context of an argument between the three dramatis personae – Franz von Sickingen, Ulrich von Hutten, and a nameless merchant – over the right of noblemen to feud. The merchant denies that nobles have a self-contained authority to declare feuds. Indeed, virtue is to him incompatible with feuding: 'how can you give yourself out as so upright', he asks Franz, 'and yet you have robbed so many, also killed some, out

[1] 'Germania tota unum latrocinium est, et ille inter nobiles gloriosor, qui rapacior.' Quoted by Johann Kamann, *Die Fehde des Götz von Berlichingen mit der Reichsstadt Nürnberg und dem Hochstifte Bamberg 1512–1514* (Nuremberg, 1893), 103 n. 2.

[2] Will-Erich Peuckert, *Die grosse Wende: Das apokalyptische Saeculum und Luther. Geistesgeschichte und Volkskunde* (Hamburg, 1948), 351–5.

[3] For the tension and changing balance between these two strands of thought see Claudio Donati, *L'idea di nobiltà in Italia: Secoli XIV–XVIII* (Bari, 1988), esp. chaps. 1–4; Maurice Keen, *Chivalry* (New Haven, 1984), 156–61.

[4] Ulrich von Hutten, 'Die Räuber', in *Gespräche von Ulrich von Hutten*, ed. and trans. David Friedrich Strauß (Leipzig, 1860), 315–89, at 318–19.

of flimsy causes and without any right'. This invective infuriates his interlocutors; it amounts in their eyes to a negation of the nobility. They then put him right: nobles' principal virtue is chivalric fortitude. Their nobility rests on their ability to safeguard justice, to help the downtrodden, to avenge the ill-treated, to protect widows and orphans. And it is only by force of arms that they are able to fulfil this social obligation that defines them. Hence they have not only the right, but also the duty to carry out feuds.[5]

This justification by Hutten echoed criticisms of the nobility that were widespread at the time.[6] These shared Hutten's assumption about the nobility's social role, but not his conclusion about the feud. On the contrary, feuds provided the very grist to the mill of the nobility's detractors. They were construed as *la trahison des nobles*. The noblemen, lamented Sebastian Franck, plunder the very widows and orphans they are supposed to defend; 'and those who should be the sheep-dogs at the enclosure are often the wolves themselves, seizing with violence whatever they can, so that it is necessary to be protected and guarded from the protectors and guards'.[7]

Another commentator on these matters wrote in 1524 that 'to quash robbery and murders, to keep the roads pacified, to prove oneself courageous in all just deeds – this would be noble'. But in this respect, too, noblemen dismally failed to live up to the functional ideal of virtue. Both Johannes Trithemius and Matthias Widmann, alias von Kemnat, describe how in 1469–70 three princes of the Empire, Archbishop Adolf of Mainz, Bishop Rudolf of Würzburg and Count Palatine Friedrich, joined forces in order to lay siege to castle Boxberg. Held by the Franconian noble family von Rosenberg, the fortress served as a refuge for highway robbers who were 'despisers of imperial mandates and breakers of the General Peace'. From the Odenwald down to the river Neckar, the roads had become desolate and no one could travel them safely. Trithemius was particularly appalled by these brigands' habit of castrating God's ministers.[8]

Indignant reports like this were made not only by the commoners among the learned. Count Froben Christoph of Zimmern, that voluble talebearer, was also critical of his peers. He tells the story of how a discalced friar preached before the duke of Württemberg against highway robbers. The friar recommended that they should be prosecuted and, if found guilty, executed, adding: '"ho, ho, this would be an amusing sight"'. He barely got away with his sermon, for 'the duke had at

[5] Ibid., 319–20. That the protection of widows and orphans was not just a literary convention, but a concrete element in the self-perception of noblemen, is documented in StAW, Stb, no. 892, fol. 147ᵛ (1511).

[6] See H. C. Erik Midelfort, 'Adeliges Landleben und die Legitimationskrise des deutschen Adels im 16. Jahrhundert', in *Stände und Gesellschaft im Alten Reich*, ed. Georg Schmidt (Stuttgart, 1989), 245–64.

[7] This and the next quotation are from Peuckert, *Die grosse Wende*, 352.

[8] Johannes Trithemius, *Annales Hirsaugienses*, vol. II (St Gall, 1690), 470; Conrad Hofmann (ed.), *Des Matthias von Kemnat Chronik Friedrich I. des Siegreichen* (Munich, 1862), 51.

his court . . . many Franconians who on the basis of an alleged old privilege thought it permissible to plunder on the highways with impunity'. Those Franconian noblemen were so outraged that one of them planned to kill the friar. Count Froben Christoph ended the story by noting that 'such an unchristian and unbecoming view about robbing was moreover upheld by the Big Jacks (*hochen Hannsen*) and great families in the *tenebroso seculo*'.[9]

Zimmern's disapproving, self-distancing attitude toward feuds is understandable yet quite prejudiced. He was writing at a time when the feud was fast becoming a thing of the past, being replaced by what he considered as new, finer mores. But in the fifteenth and first half of the sixteenth century feuds still were – and not only metaphorically – a burning issue. One writer who made an effort to go beyond the usual diatribes and to account empathically for noblemen's violence was the Carthusian Werner Rolevinck. In 1474 he produced the first 'sociological' explanation of feuding noblemen:

> they are of great bodily power, of active disposition, and naturally benevolent . . . It is only in times of need that they are violent . . . Unfortunate poverty teaches them many evils . . . You cannot look at these handsome squires without shedding a tear, struggling daily for little food and clothing, risking the gallows in order to overcome hunger.[10]

Rolevinck has become a *locus classicus* for every student of the knightly feud (*Ritterfehde*). That he has been elevated to this status represents a significant historiographical development. Elaborating on his observations, historians have since argued that the German nobility had experienced a general crisis in the late Middle Ages and that impoverished noblemen, seeking to alleviate their financial difficulties, had taken to banditry cloaked with the legal mantle of the feud. These noblemen have come to be known in modern historiography as robber-knights (*Raubritter*).

The term 'Raubritter' was used for the first time probably as late as 1810 by Friedrich Gottschalk.[11] It was given particularly strong currency when, in 1847, it was applied to feuding noblemen by Friedrich C. Schlosser. He mentioned in his multi-volume world history that the 'numerous robber-knights of Thuringia . . . earned their living on the highways by [robbing] cities of their goods'.[12] The phrase had quickly come to be used uncritically. In 1880, for instance, a German history textbook reproduced an illustration from the *Soester Nequambuch*

---

[9] Hansmartin Decker-Hauff (ed.), *Die Chronik der Grafen von Zimmern*, vol. II (Sigmaringen, 1967), 184–5.

[10] Werner Rolevinck, *De Westphalorum sive Antiquorum Saxonum Situ, Moribus, Virtutibus, et Laudibus Libri III* (Cologne, 1602), 190–1.

[11] Klaus Graf, 'Feindbild und Vorbild: Bemerkungen zur städtischen Wahrnehmung des Adels', *ZGO* 141 (1993), 121–54, at 138. This date roughly corresponds to a period of renewed literary interest in the feud. See A. Maier, 'Das Wiederaufleben von "Fehde" im 18. Jahrhundert', *Zeitschrift für deutsche Wortforschung* 10 (1908/9), 181–7.

[12] Friedrich Christoph Schlosser, *Weltgeschichte für das deutsche Volk*, vol. VII (Frankfurt am Main, 1847), 452.

depicting four armed horsemen engaged in some bellicose activity. Whereas the original caption is 'These ambushed the town of Barenbrok and robbed afterwards. . .', the modern one reads 'Contemporary depiction of robber-knights'.[13]

The year 1939 saw a radical break in the by then nearly five hundred years old historical perception of the late-medieval feud as banditry by another name. The most incisive criticism of the term robber-knight and of the intellectual convictions it embodied was made by the Austrian historian Otto Brunner. Brunner had reappraised the feud already in 1929.[14] But it was the incorporation of this study into his monumental *'Land' and Lordship*, dubbed 'one of the century's most important works of German history',[15] that made it the canonical exposition of the feud to date.[16]

Brunner did not study the feud for its own sake.[17] Rather, it served the purpose of addressing much larger questions concerning the relation between the past and the present, and between history proper and the historical methods appropriate for its comprehension. Brunner used the feud both as the touchstone of his censure of the historiography of his day, and as the bedrock of a new one. Together, these two aspects of his work formed Brunner's 'Old Europe', a concept he borrowed from Jakob Burckhardt.[18]

'Old Europe' offers a model of the history of Western civilisation, of its underlying structures and constituent elements, from the eleventh to the

---

[13] Respectively: 'Isti fecerunt insidias civitati in barenbroke et postea spoliaverunt. . .'; 'Zeitgenössische Darstellung von Raubrittern': Ludwig Stacke, *Deutsche Geschichte*, vol. I, *Von der ältesten Zeit bis zu Maximilian* (Bielefeld, 1880), 640.

[14] Otto Brunner, 'Beiträge zur Geschichte des Fehdewesens im spätmittelalterlichen Oesterreich', *Jahrbuch für Landeskunde von Niederösterreich* 22 (1929), 431–507.

[15] Peter Blickle, 'Otto Brunner (1898–1982)', *Historische Zeitschrift* 236 (1983), 779–81, at 779.

[16] All subsequent citations are from the English translation of the fifth edition: Otto Brunner, *'Land' and Lordship: Structures of Governance in Medieval Austria*, trans. Howard Kaminsky and James Van Horn Melton (Philadelphia, 1992).

[17] Given Brunner's enormous breadth of intent, the following discussion of his work cannot possibly do full justice to the coherence and persuasiveness of his interpretation. But I believe that I give the essential points of it, so far as they concern the feud. A fuller assessment of Brunner's work can be pieced together from Otto Gerhard Oexle, 'Sozialgeschichte – Begriffsgeschichte – Wissenschaftsgeschichte: Anmerkungen zum Werk Otto Brunners', *VSWG* 71 (1984), 305–41; Pierangelo Schiera, 'Otto Brunner, uno storico della crisi', *Annali dell'Istituto storico italo-germanico in Trento* 13 (1987), 19–37; Hans Boldt, 'Otto Brunner: Zur Theorie der Verfassungsgeschichte', *Annali dell'Istituto storico italo-germanico in Trento* 13 (1987), 39–61; James Van Horn Melton, 'From Folk History to Structural History: Otto Brunner (1898–1982) and the Radical-Conservative Roots of German Social History', in *Paths of Continuity: Central European Historiography from the 1930s to the 1950s*, ed. Hartmut Lehmann and James Van Horn Melton (Cambridge, 1994), 263–92; Edgar Melton, 'Comment: Hermann Aubin', in *Paths of Continuity*, 251–61, at 256–61; Michael Borgolte, 'Das soziale Ganze als Thema deutscher Mittelalterforschung vor und nach der Wende', *Francia* 22, no. 1 (1995), 155–71.

[18] Otto Brunner, 'Inneres Gefüge des Abendlandes', *Historia Mundi* 6 (1958), 319–85, at 319; Wolfgang Hardtwig, *Geschichtsschreibung zwischen Alteuropa und moderner Welt: Jacob Burckhardt in seiner Zeit* (Göttingen, 1974), 299–310.

eighteenth century.[19] The period is treated as having had a temporal unity, structural consistency and identity all of its own, setting it apart from other epochs. This unorthodox periodisation, straddling what are commonly regarded as the Middle Ages and the early modern era, is the logical consequence of an idiosyncratic approach predicated on the tension between 'real' history and the history of concepts (*Begriffsgeschichte*).[20] The dissonance Brunner detected between the two was, in his view, the outcome of the sudden demise of Old Europe in the wake of the Industrial and French Revolutions, the rise of the market economy and the bureaucratic state. The modern world is thus the result not of an evolutionary process, but of a radical break with the past. Hence historians confront profound methodological difficulties in describing Old Europe. For the central concepts they employ – state, society, and economy – presuppose that very caesura which occurred in the eighteenth century.[21]

Brunner accused historians of foisting these modern, anachronistic concepts on a pre-modern past. Indeed, their scholarly reconstructions of it seemed to him little more than a reification of the bourgeois-liberal world they inhabited and its characteristic positivist 'disjunctive thought' (*Trennungsdenken*).[22] This resulted in a dualistic image of Old Europe, a set of dichotomies reflecting 'the inner fragmentation of the modern world – the polarity of state and society, individual and group, Is and Ought, nature and mind, Right and Might'.[23] But Old Europe was, according to Brunner, organised around principles fundamentally different from the modern ones of the separate yet mutually assuming state, civil society, and market economy. Neither Thomas Aquinas (d. 1274) nor Francisco Suarez (d. 1617) would have been able to make sense of these distinctions; both experienced the sociopolitical order of their day as an integral whole: 'respublica sive societas civilis sive populus'.[24] A public sphere hived off from the state was a phenomenon destined to emerge only with the modern bourgeoisie. Old Europe could therefore be reconstructed by the historian only from within, studied only on its own terms.

It is here that Brunner's explication of the feud comes into its own. Indeed, occupying the opening chapter of *'Land' and Lordship*, the study of the feud is the

---

[19] The fullest presentation of the model is in Otto Brunner, *Adeliges Landleben und europäischer Geist: Leben und Werk Wolf Helmhards von Hohberg 1612–1688* (Salzburg, 1949). For a concise presentation see Brunner, 'Inneres Gefüge des Abendlandes'.

[20] Christof Dipper, 'Otto Brunner aus der Sicht der frühneuzeitlichen Historiographie', *Annali dell'Istituto storico italo-germanico in Trento* 13 (1987), 73–96, at 75; Fernand Braudel, 'On a Concept of Social History', in his *On History*, trans. Sarah Matthews (London, 1980), 120–31, at 128.

[21] Otto Brunner, 'Das Zeitalter der Ideologien: Anfang und Ende', in his *Neue Wege der Verfassungs- und Sozialgeschichte*, 3rd edn (Göttingen, 1980), 45–63.

[22] Otto Brunner, 'Moderner Verfassungsbegriff und mittelalterliche Verfassungsgeschichte', *Mitteilungen des österreichischen Instituts für Geschichtsforschung. Erg.-Band* 14 (1939), 513–28, at 514.

[23] Brunner, *'Land' and Lordship*, 137.

[24] Ibid., 98; Brunner, 'Das Zeitalter der Ideologien', 54–5.

showpiece of Brunner's method of juxtaposing 'real' history and the history of concepts, thereby transcending the dichotomies of 'disjunctive thought'. Brunner's *cheval de bataille* is that the feud was not, as historians contended, a criminal use of naked power which the deplorably weak state was unable to quell. It was a lawful practice, provided the feuders carried it out in accordance with the accepted rules of conduct. These ranged from a preliminary attempt to settle differences peacefully to – if this failed – a delivery of a 'challenge' well before opening hostilities.[25] The feud, however, was not only lawful. More importantly, it was the

> juridical form of all medieval politics, in so far as it resorts, internally as well as externally, to the force of arms. Only from the perspective of the feud, which is simultaneously Right and Might, can one understand the relationship between these two factors in the Middle Ages. A world in which the feud is always a possibility, of necessity has a structure altogether completely different from the civil world of an absolute state which claims the monopoly of the legitimate use of force.[26]

This point is hammered in most forcefully by four examples of noblemen's feuds against kings and emperors.[27] That these could be considered lawful and not high treason reveals, according to Brunner, the 'otherness' of Old Europe. A dramatically alien practice, the feud illustrates a historical problem which defies explanations based on modern preconceptions. Its incompatibility with the state, at least in the latter's classic, Weberian definition, puts paid to the historians' cherished prepossessions about the nature of medieval 'sovereignty'.[28]

That the feud and the state were mutually exclusive still did not make the medieval secular order one of 'disorder, chaos, anarchy – a non-state or the "law of the fist"'.[29] There existed a different form of polity in which law and order subsisted: the *Land*, a 'judicial district in which territorial law applied'. This law unified the people of the *Land* into a legal, territorial community (*Landgemeinde, Landschaft*). Sovereignty had no place in it, for the final and absolute authority did not lie with the body politic. Rather, it resided in the concept of Right (*Recht*) which corresponded to an overarching system of moral and religious tenets embodied in the '"good and old law", good custom, and in short, justice'. It was on this system that Old European civilisation rested.[30]

Unlike the modern state, this sociopolitical order was not only consistent with the feud, but was actually shaped by it. For the exercise of one's right to feud was the chief means of upholding Right. If a conflict could not be composed either

---

[25] Brunner, *'Land' and Lordship*, 36–86.
[26] Brunner, 'Moderner Verfassungsbegriff', 527.
[27] Brunner, *'Land' and Lordship*, 9–14.
[28] For his criticism of Max Weber see Otto Brunner, 'Bemerkungen zu den Begriffen "Herrschaft" und "Legitimität"', in his *Neue Wege*, 64–79.
[29] Brunner, *'Land' and Lordship*, 95.
[30] Ibid., 192, 195–6.

through 'love' (*Minne*) or through judicial procedure, then the *Land* provided the legal framework within which the contestants could legitimately resolve their dispute through force. Hence the feud was 'at heart a struggle for Right that aimed at retribution and reparation for a violation of one's right'.[31] With no state authority to enforce the law, the defense of their rights was left to the opposing parties. And only those able to rise to this challenge, those with the capacity to bear arms, counted as full members of the *Land*-community. These were the seigneurs, those in possession of a 'house of residence in the land that served as the organisational centre of the noble's estate, his lordship'. The rest 'required a lord or advocate who could grant them protection and safeguard . . .'.[32] In this way, the ubiquitous feud and the consequently unmitigated need people had for protection shaped the *Land* as a commonwealth of aristocratic houses regulated by the conventions of lordship.[33] It was the noble house and its lordship, then, as the primary sociopolitical unit, that undergirded Old Europe, making it an aristocratic world (*Adelswelt*).[34]

In appraising Brunner's theory it is necessary to distinguish between the problems he posed and the solutions he proposed. Brunner's emphasis on the historical singularity of the past, and the resulting unbridgeable conceptual gap between it and the present, was not new.[35] Yet his unprecedentedly pointed and vigorous arguments to this effect helped turn this methodological problem into the common property of critical German history.[36] By the same token, Brunner also 'rehabilitated' the feud in historical judgement. Now an integral and constitutive part of the social order, rather than an aberration, it stood to reason that the feud would become a worthy object of research and controversy. On the other hand, it is debatable whether the same historiographical value can be attached to the solutions Brunner offered to the very problems he raised. Indeed, most of the central ideas around which Brunner constructed his Old Europe have suffered greatly at the hands of historians. These have shown that Brunner, quite tendentiously, took his sources at face value, and consistently mistook normative prescriptions for descriptions of reality. The result is that his 'Old Europe' is as unhistorical an outline as those which he took to task.[37]

---

[31] Ibid., 36, 81, 196–7.
[32] Ibid., 197–9.
[33] This point is the crux of Brunner's interpretation of the feud. For the sake of coherence, the more specific critique of his concepts of the house and lordship in their relation to the feud is deferred to chap. 5.
[34] Brunner, *Adeliges Landleben*, 248–50, 286, 288; Brunner, 'Inneres Gefüge des Abendlandes', 328, 364; Otto Brunner, 'Das "ganze Haus" und die alteuropäische "Ökonomik"', in his *Neue Wege*, 103–27, at 116–17; Otto Brunner, 'Europäisches Bauerntum', in his *Neue Wege*, 199–212.
[35] Giovanni Tabacco, 'La dissoluzione medievale dello stato nella recente storiografia', *Studi medievali*, 3rd ser., 1 (1960), 397–446, at 428.
[36] Oexle, 'Sozialgeschichte – Begriffsgeschichte – Wissenschaftsgeschichte', 328; Melton, 'From Folk History to Structural History', 278.
[37] Werner Trossbach, 'Das "ganze Haus" – Basiskategorie für das Verständnis der ländlichen

Inevitably, this bent is reflected also in Brunner's discussion of the feud. In the first place, he largely equated the norms which allegedly governed and legitimated feuds with motives and causes. This is most transparent in his conceptualisation of the feud as essentially a mechanism for restoring Right and consequently harmony in the *Land* by rectifying injustice: 'for every violation of a man's rights, his "honour",' wrote Brunner, 'demands retribution; this was the aim of the feud . . .'.[38] This formulation all but obliterates the contrast which he himself had set out to draw between the feud as prosecuted by German noblemen and the vendetta. As he himself put it, 'however precise the distinction between blood vengeance and the feud, both constituted enmity, the feud, in the broadest sense'.[39]

The point is crucial, for the sanctioning of the blood-feud is indeed a defining attribute of acephalous, stateless societies.[40] But this was evidently not the case with the knightly feud in late medieval and early modern Germany. German society had political centres which mattered a great deal. Attempts were continually made to set measures to feuding. In Westphalia the law forbade nobles from waging feuds against their territorial princes.[41] And in 1495 the Imperial Diet of Worms outlawed the feud unconditionally and indefinitely.[42] Indeed, there was generally a strong movement to criminalise the feud.[43] Nobles went on feuding all the same, but they could not altogether ignore these forces. The records they left are replete with references to imperial restrictions and prohibitions of the feud.[44] As these examples indicate, Brunner's view that the feud was legal was not uniformly shared by contemporaries. Precisely this, however, is what Brunner's indiscriminate definition of the feud serves to insinuate in order

Gesellschaft deutscher Territorien in der Frühen Neuzeit?' *Blätter für deutsche Landesgeschichte* 129 (1993), 277–314; David Warren Sabean, *Property, Production, and Family in Neckarhausen, 1700–1870* (Cambridge, 1990), 90–5; Gadi Algazi, *Herrengewalt und Gewalt der Herren im späten Mittelalter: Herrschaft, Gegenseitigkeit und Sprachgebrauch* (Frankfurt am Main, 1996), 51–127; Wolfgang Neuber, 'Adeliges Landleben in Österreich und die Literatur im 16. und im 17. Jahrhundert', in *Adel im Wandel: Politik, Kultur, Konfession 1500–1700*, ed. Herbert Knittler, Gottfried Stangler, and Renate Zedlinger (Vienna, 1990), 543–53.

[38] Brunner, *'Land' and Lordship*, 19, 36.

[39] Ibid., 16.

[40] Max Gluckman, 'The Peace in the Feud', in *Custom and Conflict in Africa* (Oxford, 1963), 1–26; Jacob Black-Michaud, *Cohesive Force: Feud in the Mediterranean and the Middle East* (Oxford, 1975), passim; William Ian Miller, *Bloodtaking and Peacemaking: Feud, Law, and Society in Saga Iceland* (Chicago, 1990), passim. See also Edward Muir, *Mad Blood Stirring: Vendetta & Factions in Friuli during the Renaissance* (Baltimore, 1993).

[41] Friedrich von Klocke, 'Beiträge zur Geschichte von Faustrecht und Fehdewesen in Westfalen', *Westfälische Zeitschrift* 94 (1938), 3–56, at 18–19.

[42] *RTA, mR*, v, 359–73, no. 334.

[43] Ulrich Andermann, *Ritterliche Gewalt und bürgerliche Selbstbehauptung: Untersuchungen zur Kriminalisierung und Bekämpfung des spätmittelalterlichen Raubrittertums am Beispiel norddeutscher Hansestädte* (Frankfurt am Main, 1991).

[44] See, for example, StAN, Amts- und Standbücher, no. 146, fol. 6ʳ: 'Auch umb solichenn mutwilligen unverschuldten unverhörtenn hanndel, alles unnenntsagt, uber unnd zuverbrechunng des kaiserlichenn und konigklichenn des heiligen Reichs lanndtfridenn geubt.'

to bear out his notion of 'Old Europe'. The feud is presented by him as a custom so primordially rooted in 'Old European' mentality in general, and in the Germanic community in particular, that it entirely transcends its historical conditions. Brunner was aware that feuds were also conflicts over various tangible rights; but the elusive ghost of the timeless Right casts an impenetrable shadow over the feud, screening it from historical scrutiny.

This, finally, raises the problem of historical change. Expectedly, Brunner's handling of it is awkward; it betrays an unresolved tension between the feud in its legal framework, the *Land*, and the feud in its relation to central authorities. For Brunner postulated that for the feud to have declined 'what was needed was a structural transformation of the state itself', 'the elimination of the legitimate use of armed force in the feud and in resistance to the ruler'.[45] This was not achieved before the sixteenth century because princes were until then bound by the 'sphere of Right'. Here the contradiction inherent in Brunner's understanding of the feud manifests itself: if the feud structurally negated the state, then its 'elimination' cannot possibly be clarified by summoning the rising state as a *deus ex machina*.[46]

The first serious challenge to Brunner came in 1982 with a systematic effort to identify the social location of the feud.[47] In a seminal article on the problem of robber-knighthood in the late Middle Ages, Werner Rösener has dismissed Brunner's view of the lawfulness of the feud.[48] Instead, he considers noblemen's feuds to have been mere attempts to legitimate what was otherwise unjust violence. His hypothesis is founded mainly on an examination of the economic situation of the German nobility in this period. Rösener argues that the lesser nobility was badly hit by the general demographic decline of the late Middle Ages which entailed a crisis of seigneurial revenues. In his support he cites a number of specialised studies that point out that the income sources of the nobility had

---

[45] Brunner, *'Land' and Lordship*, 30, 323.

[46] 'What then occurred [*scil.* sixteenth century] was not a "constitutional" change in the modern sense, but rather a growth in the prince's real power . . . that made resistance by individuals impossible': ibid., 323.

[47] For earlier criticisms of Brunner, which were made, however, mainly within the conceptual framework set by him, see Hermann Rothert, 'Das mittelalterliche Fehdewesen in Westfalen', *Westfälische Forschungen* 3 (1940), 145–55; Heinrich Mitteis, 'Land und Herrschaft: Bemerkungen zu dem gleichnamigen Buch Otto Brunners', parts 1 and 2, *Historische Zeitschrift* 163 (1941), 255–81; 471–89; Karl Siegfried Bader, 'Herrschaft und Staat im deutschen Mittelalter', *Historisches Jahrbuch* 62–9 (1949), 618–46, at 627–34; Herbert Asmus, 'Rechtsprobleme des mittelalterlichen Fehdewesens: Dargestellt an Hand südhannoverscher Quellen vornehmlich des Archives der Stadt Göttingen' (PhD thesis, University of Göttingen, 1951), 13–15, 79–80; Herbert Obenaus, *Recht und Verfassung der Gesellschaft mit St. Jörgenschild in Schwaben: Untersuchungen über Adel, Einung, Schiedsgericht und Fehde im fünfzehnten Jahrhundert* (Göttingen, 1961), passim; Elsbet Orth, *Die Fehden der Reichsstadt Frankfurt am Main im Spätmittelalter: Fehderecht und Fehdepraxis im 14. und 15. Jahrhundert* (Wiesbaden, 1973), 54–7, 65.

[48] Werner Rösener, 'Zur Problematik des spätmittelalterlichen Raubrittertums', in *Festschrift für Berent Schwineköper zu seinem siebzigsten Geburtstag*, ed. Helmut Maurer and Hans Patze (Sigmaringen, 1982), 469–88.

stagnated since the late thirteenth century and tapered off in the fourteenth and fifteenth centuries.[49] Moreover, noblemen's economic predicament was further aggravated by new cultural trends of conspicuous consumption.[50] The competition with town patriciates exerted an intensified pressure on noblemen to live sumptuously. On the other hand, outlets were largely unavailable. Lucrative positions in princely administration were inaccessible to the bulk of the knightly class and were increasingly occupied by learned men of urban extraction.

It is in this context, according to Rösener, that the robber-knighthood is to be understood: 'The knight, his existence having been threatened, angrily protested against the general development and took to actions, operating in the grey area between a just feud and flagrant robbery.'[51] The term robber-knighthood, then, despite being an anachronism, is none the less an apposite description of the reality behind the feuds of German nobles. Since Rösener's interpretation is the classic statement of the so-called 'robber-knighthood thesis', it merits a detailed examination. Its underlying assumptions can be challenged from three perspectives: factual, theoretical and methodological.

Rösener's argument for nobles' economic vulnerability hinges on the premise that their most important sources of income in this period were agrarian and that a main segment of these were nominally fixed feudal rent payments due from peasants. Hence the general inflationary tendencies and diminishing purchasing power of the late Middle Ages struck at the heart of noblemen's seigneurial economy. However, a growing body of evidence indicates that feudal rents in Western Germany were predominantly in kind and not in cash, and thus less at the mercy of inflation and debasement of currency.[52] This evidence also suggests that noblemen stood to profit from the rise in the price of grain in Franconia in the fifteenth century.[53] A second, perhaps related, factual problem is that the economic studies of the nobility on which Rösener relies are inconclusive. The more sophisticated among them describe a complex and diversified situation which the robber-knighthood thesis cannot accommodate:[54] examples of

---

[49] Ibid., esp. 482–4.

[50] Rösener's article, like most versions of this model, suggests a decadence of the nobility in the later Middle Ages. See Bernd Moeller, *Deutschland im Zeitalter der Reformation*, 3rd edn (Göttingen, 1988), 27; Rothert, 'Das mittelalterliche Fehdewesen in Westfalen', 154. For a corrective criticism of this approach see Maurice Keen, 'Huizinga, Kilgour and the Decline of Chivalry', *Medievalia et Humanistica*, n.s., 8 (1978), 1–20.

[51] Rösener, 'Zur Problematik des spätmittelalterlichen Raubrittertums', 487–8.

[52] For a detailed discussion see chap. 3.

[53] Rolf Sprandel, 'Die spätmittelalterliche Wirtschaftskonjunktur und ihre regionalen Determinanten: Forschungsüberblick und neue Perspektiven', in *Historia Socialis et Oeconomica: Festschrift für Wolfgang Zorn zum 65. Geburtstag*, ed. Hermann Kellenbenz and Hans Pohl (Stuttgart, 1987), 168–79, at 177.

[54] Roger Sablonier, *Adel im Wandel: Eine Untersuchung zur sozialen Situation des ostschweizerischen Adels um 1300* (Göttingen, 1979); Hans-Peter Sattler, 'Die Ritterschaft der Ortenau in der spätmittelalterlichen Wirtschaftskrise', parts 1–4, *Die Ortenau* 42 (1962), 220–58; 44 (1964), 22–39; 45 (1965), 32–57; 46 (1966), 32–58. For a criticism of Sattler's and other works see Joseph

economic failure are regularly offset by examples of prosperity. Moreover, one of the works adduced by Rösener came to a positive estimation of noblemen's economic condition and it is difficult to see how exactly it substantiates his contentions.[55]

On a theoretical plane, the robber-knighthood thesis operates with a demographic-economic supply-and-demand model which does not address questions of power relations either between lords and peasants or within the nobility itself.[56] The point is crucial, for the heavy emphasis on the nobility's dependence on agrarian seigneurial resources results in disregarding whole areas of noblemen's activity. As a later chapter will show, some of the more important of these areas were opened up in precisely this period, mainly by the growth of the state. Thus, the thesis fails to account for intervening and mediating strategies noblemen could have used in adjusting to social and economic change.[57]

Thirdly and perhaps most important is that the very methodology invariably employed by advocates of this model is flawed. One can charitably assume that what really is being implied is that only certain sections of the German nobility were impoverished. But it is precisely here that the questionable formulation of the thesis becomes evident, since a direct link is supposed to have existed between penury and feud violence. The thesis fails to consider the possibility that wealthy noblemen feuded as well, nor does it ask whether every poor nobleman took to feuding. In short, investigation concludes at the exact point at which it becomes of serious sociological interest.

METHOD AND SOURCES

The method made use of in this study is designed to deal with the problems just described. It takes the individual noble feuder, rather than his class, as its point of departure. And, complementarily, it proceeds from the premise that the late medieval German nobility, due to its relationship with the budding princely territorial state, was a deeply stratified group.[58] This stratification was determined by social, economic and political statuses at once. It found expression in, among other things, the quality of matrimonial alliances, financial transactions with rulers, and patterns of office-holding. None of these spheres was either exclusively social or economic or political. They incessantly fed back into each other. A

Morsel, 'Crise? Quel crise? Remarques à propos de la prétendue crise de la noblesse allemande à la fin du Moyen Age', *Sources. Travaux historique* 14 (1988), 17–42.

[55] Karl Otto Müller, 'Zur wirtschaftlichen Lage des schwäbischen Adels am Ausgang des Mittelalters', *Zeitschrift für württembergische Landesgeschichte* 3 (1939), 285–328.

[56] Cf. Robert Brenner, 'Agrarian Class Structure and the Economic Development of Pre-Industrial Europe', in *The Brenner Debate: Agrarian Class Structure and Economic Development in Pre-Industrial Europe*, ed. T. H. Aston and C. H. E. Philpin (Cambridge, 1985), 10–63.

[57] See chap. 3.

[58] For a detailed discussion see chap. 3.

complex of interlocking status-determining and status-reflecting elements is therefore quite transparent to the observer. Hence comprehensive information on the overall situation, economic or otherwise, of the nobility is unnecessary for an evaluation of a nobleman and his family. Instead, a number of specific and economical parameters have been formulated to subserve this evaluation. The rationale and analytical content of these parameters will be discussed in chapter 3 which examines the foundations of aristocratic existence.

The second stage (chapter 4) is a prosopographical analysis of feuding noblemen. Based on the parameters devised in chapter 3, its purpose is to demarcate the social location of the feud within the nobility. By definition it entails also an identification of the economic and political conditions of the feud. One important advantage of this prosopographical procedure is that it can manage with scrappy documents. It is not an impediment that what many feud records reveal are merely the names of the feuders. Additional biographical particulars can be culled from a wide array of other sources: registers of fiefs, genealogies, family histories, and so on. By the same token, documents containing fragmentary economic data are also useful. An example is the lists of noble creditors of princes. Whereas they do not lend themselves to a quantitative economic analysis of the nobility as a whole, it is highly valuable that an individual feuder can be ascertained to have been a moneylender.

Another advantage of prosopography is its indifference to the blame parties to feuds were seeking to lay on each other. That a Konrad von Schaumberg was accused of handing the mandatory cartel of defiance to his rival upon surprising the latter in bed[59] – a rude awakening if there ever was one – is of no consequence for prosopography. The only indispensable facts are the names of the rivals and that violence was exercised. Indeed, the methodological problem in this regard is, ironically, diametrically opposed to that of Rösener's: it is not to verify that those noblemen incriminated in the sources as 'robbers' were indeed poor noblemen; it is rather to establish that these sources are not simply the scandalised accounts of the sins of the great and illustrious among noblemen. This and other of prosopography's perils and limitations are well known.[60] They and the specific prosopographical technique adapted to minimise them are discussed in chapter 4. In any case, prosopography in itself is not an interpretation of the facts. Rather, it generates new facts, albeit of a different order. The prosopography of feuding

---

[59] Felix Priebatsch (ed.), *Politische Correspondenz des Kurfürsten Albrecht Achilles*, vol. II (Leipzig, 1897), 545–6 n. 3, no. 586.

[60] Lawrence Stone, 'Prosopography', in his *The Past and the Present Revisited* (London, 1981), 45–73; Claude Nicolet, 'Prosopographie et histoire sociale: Rome et l'Italie à l'époque républicaine', *Annales: E.S.C.* 25 (1970), 1209–28; Neithard Bulst, 'Zum Gegenstand und zur Methode von Prosopographie', in *Medieval Lives and the Historian: Studies in Medieval Prosopography*, ed. Neithard Bulst and Jean-Philippe Genet (Kalamazoo, 1986), 1–16; T. F. Carney, 'Prosopography: Payoffs and Pitfalls', *Phoenix* 27 (1973), 156–79.

noblemen intends merely to create a new set of matrices for an interpretation that will follow (chapter 5).[61]

The interpretation of the feud in terms of noblemen's relationship with the princes is well reflected in the sources: most of the archival material on feuds among the nobility comes from former princely archives (now housed in state archives). One main – and by far the most instructive – form these records take is of correspondence either between nobles and princes or between the latter themselves. Another form is of documents produced by the chancelleries for internal purposes, particularly to enable the princes better to meet the problems of law and order created by feuds: registers of feuders, oaths to keep the peace (*Urfehden*), memoranda and expert opinions, protocols of arbitration sessions, injunctions to administrative officials, and so on. With some variations, due chiefly to a different type of political relations, the sources for feuds between nobles and cities are generically similar. And indeed, since these feuds could not but engage the princes as well, many of them are reported on in princely papers too.[62]

An altogether different case is noble family archives. Few of them have been consulted for this study. One reason is that those of them which are in private hands are not readily accessible. Another is that those which were called on turned out discouragingly little material on feuds.[63] Indeed, in the archive of the Fuchs family, as ardent feuders as any, there is only one account of a conflict resembling a feud. The file is tellingly titled 'all sorts of old articles of no importance'.[64] To judge from the edited sources, most other family archives are not much better in this respect.[65] Moreover, what they did yield is even less in a

---

[61] This approach, applied to feuding noblemen in Westphalia, has already produced new facts which stand the 'robber-knighthood thesis' on its head. See Regina Görner, *Raubritter: Untersuchungen zur Lage des spätmittelalterlichen Niederadels, besonders im südlichen Westfalen* (Münster in Westfalen, 1987). Görner's work is not discussed here mainly because the factual results of her prosopography are very similar to mine. However, my methodology and interpretation of the data are different. For a criticism of her methodology see Kurt Andermann, 'Review of *Raubritter: Untersuchungen zur Lage des spätmittelalterlichen Niederadels, besonders im südlichen Westfalen*, by Regina Görner', *ZHF* 19 (1992), 243–45. See also p. 101 n. 79 below.

[62] See chap. 2. For a further discussion of the sources see chap. 4.

[63] StAN, Herrschaft Pappenheim; ibid., Reichsgrafschaft Geyer; ibid., Herrschaft Sugenheim. According to their administrators, no material on the feud is stored in the archives of the von Gebsattel, von Stein and von Rotenhan families.

[64] FA, Schrank 3.

[65] Karl Hannakam and Ludwig Veit (eds.), *Archiv der Freiherrn Schenk von Geyern auf Schloß Syburg* (Munich, 1958); Michael Renner (ed.), *Archiv der Grafen Wolffskeel von Reichenberg* (Munich, 1961); Rudolf M. Kloos (ed.), *Nachlass Marschalk von Ostheim: Urkunden* (Neustadt a.d. Aisch, 1974); Gerhard Rechter (ed.), *Die Archive der Grafen und Freiherren von Seckendorff: Die Unrkundenbestände der Schloßarchive Obernzenn, Sugenheim, Trautskirchen und Unternzenn*, 3 vols. (Munich, 1993); Fritz Luckhard, 'Das Archiv der Ritter von Mörlau zu Steinau an der Haun', parts 1–3, *Fuldaer Geschichtsblätter* 40 (1964), 107–26; 151–70; 187–96; Pius Wittmann (ed.), *Monumenta Castellana: Urkundenbuch zur Geschichte des fränkischen Dynastengeschlechtes der Grafen und Herren zu Castell, 1057–1546* (Munich, 1890); Ehrensberger, 'Freiherrlich von Zobel'sches Archiv zu Messelhausen', *ZGO* 52 (1898), m121–m150; Otto Hagmaier, 'Gräflich von Berlichin-

way of entirely new evidence, that is feuds unknown from parallel documents in erstwhile princely or urban archives.

Once the sources have been garnered, actual feuds have to be sifted out. Identifying feuds is not always a simple matter. Unlike their Burgundian counterparts,[66] German nobles lacked the sophisticated technical vocabulary necessary for a scrupulous classification of types of military engagement. Although most sources do differentiate feuds from other forms of violence, they do not do this invariably. Not all conflicts that display the recognisable features of a feud are indeed so termed in the sources.[67] Other expressions – dispute, strife, enmity, and the like – were also used to denote what were knightly feuds to all intents and purposes. Hence it is occasionally impossible to tell between feuds and, for example, duels. In the absence of complementary evidence, it cannot be determined whether or not a duel was the culmination of a preceding feud.[68] At the other extreme of the continuum, the sources sometimes apply the term feud to wars. This is not a problem when 'feud' is used to designate a major war;[69] it is when 'feud' refers to a small-scale 'war' made up of a sequence of feud-like campaigns led by noblemen.

The conceptual difficulties surrounding the feud are also the result of its protean nature, its malleability to being put to multiple, albeit interconnected, uses. In order to do justice to the richness of experience divulged by the sources, one has to settle for practical compromises. One such compromise concerns the boundary drawn between feud and war. For this purpose, a working definition of war treats it as a military confrontation between two or more political entities which *practically* did not recognise any lord other than the emperor. A belligerence between, say, the duke of Bavaria and the margrave of Brandenburg, or between the latter and the imperial city of Nuremberg, was not by this definition a feud, however limited its scope may have been. Hence princes are excluded from the prosopographical sample, even in cases of feuds against nobles. Conversely, conflicts involving the Franconian counts do not qualify as wars.

---

gen'sches Archiv in Neunstetten', *ZGO* 60 (1906), m47–m110; Johann Gustav Weiss, 'Freiherrlich Rüdt'sches Archiv zu Bödigheim', *ZGO* 50 (1896), m32–m46.

[66] C. A. J. Armstrong, 'La Toison d'Or et la loi des armes', in his *England, France and Burgundy in the Fifteenth Century* (London, 1983), 375–81.

[67] For common features of the feud see chaps. 2 and 5.

[68] Duels, however, were rare in this period. For the few that took place see Constantin Höfler (ed.), *Des Ritters Ludwig von Eyb zu Eybburg Denkwürdigkeiten brandenburgischer (hohenzollerischer) Fürsten* (Bayreuth, 1849), 139–40; Joseph Aschbach, *Geschichte der Grafen von Wertheim von den ältesten Zeiten bis zu ihrem Erlöschen im Mannsstamme im Jahre 1556* (Frankfurt am Main, 1843), 284–6; Joseph Aschbach, *Wertheimisches Urkundenbuch*, part 2 of his *Geschichte der Grafen von Wertheim*, 311–13, no. 205; Karl von Weber, 'Ueber Turniere und Kampfspiele', *Archiv für die sächsische Geschichte* 4 (1866), 337–84, at 375–81.

[69] Friedrich von Weech (ed.), 'Das Reissbuch anno 1504: Die Vorbereitungen der Kurpfalz zum bairischen Erbfolgekriege', *ZGO* 26 (1874), 137–264, at 143; Friedrich Stein (ed.), *Monumenta Suinfurtensia historica inde ab anno DCCXCI usque ad annum MDC: Denkmäler der Schweinfurter Geschichte bis zum Ende des 16. Jahrhundert* (Schweinfurt, 1875), 357.

Although they were of the titular nobility and had their own territorial administration and noble vassals, none of them reached the actual power position of the counts (from 1495 dukes) of Württemberg. The Franconian comital houses lacked the resources and the political independence to wage wars. Their conflicts too were of the order of feuds.

A more haphazard compromise concerns discerning feuds from 'lower' forms of violence: duels, scuffles, murders, and the like. In such incidents feuds had to be either distinguished by the conduct of the rivals,[70] or disqualified from the sample altogether. Flexible criteria for inclusion in, and exclusion from, the sample of feuds thus seem justified. This will do for most instances. A positive definition of the feud is better avoided.[71] It is preferred here to let the sense of what a feud was like emerge from a description in the next chapter of two 'typical' feuds.

---

[70] For an example see Adalbert von Keller (ed.), *Die Geschichten und Taten Wilwolts von Schaumburg* (Stuttgart, 1859), 70: 'Darnach begab sich, das [sie] . . . mit einander auf stießen und unwillig wurden . . . *Und wiewoll kainer des andern abgesagter veint, dennochtn,* wo sie aber ir knecht zusamen kamen, schlugen si sich, stachen an einander under die pfert' (italics added).

[71] For definitional essays see Ekkehard Kaufmann, 'Fehde', in *Handwörterbuch zur deutschen Rechtsgeschichte*, ed. Adalbert Erler and Ekkehard Kaufmann, vol. I (Berlin, 1971), cols. 1083–93; A. Boockmann, 'Fehde, Fehdewesen', in *Lexikon des Mittelalters*, ed. Robert-Henri Bautier et al., vol. IV (Munich, 1989), cols. 331–4.

2

The politics of violence: feuding in
late medieval Franconia

The two feuds – one between noblemen, the other between noblemen and a city – whose stories are told in this chapter are 'normal exceptions'. That is to say that they are unusual only in that they are well documented. Whereas most other feud records, being fragmentary, highlight different, disjointed aspects of the phenomenon, here its salient features appear concurrently. This will facilitate putting the feud in context. To impart in this way a concrete sense of what a feud was like and, by extension, a preliminary interpretation, is the main aim of what follows.

VESTENBERG VERSUS VESTENBERG

The starting point of Veit von Vestenberg's career was relatively auspicious. His father Hans was most probably well off.[1] His mother Margaretha came from an illustrious Franconian lineage, the von Thüngen.[2] Yet from youth to old age Veit had to struggle hard for everything he wished to attain or even retain. In 1456 he had differences with one noble, and in 1463 he was in feud with another.[3] The year 1466 brought new, more intimate enemies to the fore: members of his own family. This feud was over castle Haslach, one of the lineage's seats. It was resolved by Margrave Albrecht of Brandenburg.[4] The settlement was, however, a short-lived one. In 1471 a feud broke out once again.[5] It assumed, as far as Veit was concerned, a much more menacing aspect than the previous one: Margrave Albrecht sided with Veit's relations. Veit reacted harshly. He captured a margravial servitor, stormed the castle of another, and burned and caused extensive damage to property of other vassals of the prince.[6] As a response, the margrave impounded Veit's property.

In 1473 a compromise was reached, and Veit was reinstated in his patrimony. The price was high. Veit had to take two irrevocable oaths: one compelled him to

---

[1] Hans was creditor of the bishop of Würzburg for 600 gulden: StAW, Ldf, no. 13, pp. 343–5.
[2] Rudolf Karl Reinhard Freiherr von Thüngen, 'Zur Genealogie der Familie derer von Thüngen', *AU* 54 (1912), 1–180, at 98.
[3] StAN, AA-Akten, no. 808, fol. 46; ibid., Fstm.Ansb., Urfehden, Fehdesachen, Urkunden, no. 25.
[4] StAB, Hofrat Ansbach-Bayreuth, no. 522; StAN, AA-Akten, no. 580, prod. 2.
[5] StAN, Fstm.Ansb., Fehdeakten, no. 42.
[6] Sigmund Haenle, 'Urkunden und Nachweise zur Geschichte des Schwanen-Ordens', *Jb.Mfr.* 39 (1873/74), 1–178, at 169.

keep his peace with the margrave in any circumstances, the other to become a servitor of the margrave. This agreement, as the prince explained, ruled out the possibility of Veit ever again turning against him in the future.[7] Interestingly, and quite uncommonly, the official resolution of the feud was signed also by Veit's wife, Magdalena née von Lentersheim. The reasons are not very far to seek: Veit was Magdalena's second husband; her previous one was Lienhard von Vestenberg. The latter appears to have died in or shortly before 1466, that is the very year in which a rift in the lute occurred among the Vestenbergs. All this, together with the fact that Magdalena had three sons from Lienhard, suggests that her remarriage to Veit was largely responsible for the family quarrels.[8]

This fateful marriage may have been the turning point of Veit's career in another respect as well. Magdalena's family were staunch supporters of the margravial dynasty, providing the Hohenzollern princes with some of their leading courtiers, office-holders and diplomats.[9] And indeed, Magdalena's brother Sigmund and Wilhelm von Lentersheim were instrumental in reconciling the margrave with Veit.[10] Presumably, it was also the Lentersheims' influence that carried Veit forward in the following years, until he was able to stand on his own two feet. Already in 1482 Veit was margravial marshall, and a year later he was awarded 50 gulden by Margrave Albrecht for his help in arranging the betrothal of Margravine Anastasia to Landgrave Wilhelm III of Hesse.[11] Veit was by now a trusted councillor. So when he began his next feud in 1484, once again against members of his lineage, his rivals were to learn the hard way that his position now was very different from a decade earlier.

On 5 October 1484 Veit reported to the margrave that Eukarius von Vestenberg had abducted two of his subject peasants, and asked, he of all people, for advice on how to act in this matter. The margrave responded by ordering Eukarius to release the two captives. Eukarius did not deny that he was holding the two men. He explained, however, that

---

[7] StAN, Fstm.Ansb., Urfehden, Fehdesachen, Urkunden, nos. 30, 32; ibid., Fstm.Ansb., Fehdeakten, no. 42, prod. 13, 15. See also Carl August Hugo Burkhardt (ed.), *Das funfft merkisch Buech des Churfuersten Albrecht Achilles* (Jena, 1857), 56, no. 25.

[8] Veit is first mentioned as the husband of Magdalena von Lentersheim, widow of Lienhard von Vestenberg and mother of Kaspar, in 1467 (StAW, Stb, no. 865, fols. 113ʳ, 334ʳ). In the same year Kaspar is said to have two brothers, Eukarius and Heinz (ibid., fol. 143ʳ). Veit, according to his own testimony, married Magdalena more than 366 days after the death of Lienhard (StAN, Ansbacher Historica, no. 210, prod. of Samstag nach Auffahrtstag [17 May] 1488).

[9] Otto Rohn, 'Die Herren von Lentersheim im Mittelalter', *Alt-Gunzenhausen* 37 (1977), 31–47; Otto Rohn, 'Die Herren von Lentersheim. Zweiter Teil: Vom Erwerb des Schlosses Altenmuhr im Jahr 1430 bis zum Erlöschen des Stammes im Jahr 1799', *Alt-Gunzenhausen* 38 (1979), 108–45.

[10] StAN, Fstm.Ansb., Fehdeakten, no. 42. prod. 12, 13.

[11] Gerhard Rechter (ed.), *Die Archive der Grafen und Freiherren von Seckendorff: Die Urkundenbestände der Schloßarchive Obernzenn, Sugenheim, Trautskirchen und Unternzenn*, vol. I (Munich, 1993), 225, no. 609; Felix Priebatsch (ed.), *Die politische Correspondenz des Kurfürsten Albrecht Achilles*, vol. III (Leipzig, 1898), 254, no. 949.

My mother [Veit's wife] had requested me to lend her one of my peasants to run her to Ansbach. As he was running her to Ansbach, Sir Veit fell on and incarcerated him. So in return I captured two of his peasants. When he has released my and my brother's man, then I would release his men. Your Grace, Sir Veit has undertaken to build [a castle] and he builds on, and digs through, my land. I request Your Princely Grace as my gracious lord, considering that I am Your Grace's retainer and court servitor [*Hofgesind*], to help me be spared this violence.[12]

Eukarius and his brother Kaspar proceeded to inundate the margrave and other Franconian powers with letters presenting their case against Veit. They made a number of charges and employed various strategies, most of which were, in one form or another, common to disputes between noblemen. Apart from the specific accusations of building on Kaspar's land, of attempting to shoot down Eukarius, and of usurping property left to the brothers by their mother, they alleged that Veit had hindered a planned loveday between the parties.[13] Although platitudinous, this reproach was serious. It was meant to imply that Veit's feud was unjust. Unless some attempt was made to reach a peaceful settlement, a feud would have been open to the charge of being mere banditry.[14] Accusations like this were made with 'public opinion' in mind, the desired effect being to make princes and nobles concerned with their good reputation pause before openly supporting one's rival.[15]

Another stratagem was even more politically transparent: Kaspar wrote to the bishop of Würzburg informing him that Veit had undertaken to build a castle above Haslach and had made it over to the margrave of Brandenburg from whom he would then hold it in fee. Now 'since Haslach is held in fee from the counts of Castell . . . and, furthermore, since Your Grace is the feudal overlord of the counts . . . I trust that Veit von Vestenberg had acted against his duty [as a vassal] and I request Your Princely Grace to make Veit cease building without delay'.[16]

The brothers also encouraged the count of Castell himself to take steps against Veit's alarming project. Compliantly, Count Friedrich reminded Veit that he was building on a comital fief, and threatened to spread the word that Veit had

---

[12] StAN, Ansbacher Historica, no. 210, prod. of Dienstag nach Michaelis [5 October]; prod. of Freitag nach Francisci [8 October]; prod. of Dienstag nach Dionysii [12 October] 1484.

[13] Ibid., prod. of Martini [11 November]; prod. of Samstag nach Martini [13 November] 1484. For lovedays see Michael Clanchy, 'Law and Love in the Middle Ages', in *Disputes and Settlements: Law and Human Relations in the West*, ed. John Bossy (Cambridge, 1983), 47–67.

[14] Herbert Obenaus, *Recht und Verfassung der Gesellschaft mit St.Jörgenschild in Schwaben: Untersuchungen über Adel, Einung, Schiedsgericht und Fehde im fünfzehnten Jahrhundert* (Göttingen, 1961), 50, 72; Elsbeth Orth, *Die Fehden der Reichsstadt Frankfurt am Main im Spätmittelalter: Fehderecht und Fehdepraxis im 14. und 15. Jahrhundert* (Wiesbaden, 1973), 54–6; Otto Brunner, *'Land' and Lordship: Structures of Governance in Medieval Austria*, trans. Howard Kaminsky and James Van Horn Melton (Philadelphia, 1992), 63–7.

[15] Obenaus, *Recht und Verfassung*, 67–9, 84.

[16] StAN, Ansbacher Historica, no. 210, prod. of Mittwoch vor Elisabeth [12 November] 1484.

become 'disloyal and perjured' if he did not desist forthwith.[17] This was the commonest ploy to which noblemen resorted in feuds. In a fragmented *territorium non clausum* such as Franconia, almost every point was of strategic significance in the ongoing competition between the local princes. This state of affairs enabled noblemen to play off one prince against the other and provided them with considerable room for manoeuvre. In explaining why sentences passed by Franconian law-courts were difficult to enforce, one margravial noble councillor wrote that 'the knighthood . . . are provided with many princes; when one is not pleased with a prince's or a lord's judgement, he goes over to another prince or lord'.[18] It was this situation that Kaspar and Eukarius von Vestenberg were trying to manipulate in order to bring Veit's enterprise to a halt, couching their letters in the legal and normative idiom of the loyalty vassals were expected to display to their feudal lords.

Veit rejected all his kinsmen's charges one by one, and tried to lay the guilt at their door.[19] But he knew full well that words were not enough and that concrete measures were necessary to countervail Kaspar's and Eukarius's machinations. The previous feud was an object lesson. He now waived proprietorship over the – according to him – precious allodial property on which he was constructing his new stronghold, and made it over to the margrave.[20] Not only that, it was also laid down that his new castle, Fürstenforst, would be an 'open house' for the margraves of Brandenburg; that is, they would have the right to use it in wartime. In exchange Veit was expressly granted the margrave's 'especially gracious protection and safeguard' (*Schutz und Schirm*).[21] In taking these steps, which, by compromising its autonomy, were against the best interests of the larger lineage, Veit too was exploiting the tense political situation in Franconia.

The margrave's interest in these arrangements is plain. He obtained two valuable rights. The first was overlordship of the new castle which would escheat to his principality once the line of the von Vestenberg in Fürstenforst died out. The second, and much more significant in the short run, was the acquisition of the right to operate from the castle. This entitlement was not only a military utility, but also a very important means of territorial consolidation.[22] This was especially true in the case of the von Vestenberg. Their seat in Haslach lay at the border between the margraviate of Ansbach-Brandenburg and the diocese of

[17] Ibid., prod. of Mittwoch nach dem heiligen Jarestag [5 January] 1485.

[18] Wilhelm Vogel (ed.), *Des Ritters Ludwig von Eyb des Aelteren Aufzeichnung über das kaiserliche Landgericht des Burggrafthums Nürnberg* (Erlangen, 1867), 62.

[19] StAN, Ansbacher Historica, no. 210, prod. of Freitag Elisabeth [19 November] 1484.

[20] Ibid., prod. of Dienstag nach dem Sonntag Jubilate [11 May] 1484; StAN, Lehensurkunden, no. 609.

[21] StAN, Ansbacher Historica, no. 210, prod. of Dienstag nach dem Sonntag Jubilate [11 May] 1484; ibid., Lehensurkunden, nos. 1276–7; ibid., Brandenburg-Ansbachische Lehenbücher, no. 11, fol. 29ᵛ; ibid., Fstm.Ansb., Gemeinbücher, Tom. 5, fols. 54–5.

[22] Rolf Sprandel, *Verfassung und Gesellschaft im Mittelalter*, 4th edn (Paderborn, 1991), 162–3.

Würzburg. And indeed, there was a long-running dispute between the two principalities over jurisdiction in the area in general, and over the Vestenbergs in particular.[23] The latter thus found themselves caught up in a relentless territorial contestation in which every conflict invited the intervention of princes eager to take advantage of it.

The collusion between the margrave and Veit von Vestenberg emerges unmistakeably from the hectic correspondence between the different parties. Had the count of Castell and the bishop of Würzburg shown each other the letters they received from Veit von Vestenberg and from the margrave they would have marvelled at their similarity. Veit wrote to the bishop that it was an old and laudable tradition that the nobility in Franconia built on the land, and 'that each of the Franconian princes should wish that the land of Franconia would be well developed'. Margrave Albrecht told Castell that even if it turned out that Veit had built on his [the count's] fief, he [Veit] would in fact deserve thanks and not abuse for improving comital property.[24] Significantly, the joint effort of the margrave and Veit dated back to a few days before the feud erupted, when the margrave presciently instructed a number of his district governors to protect Veit if someone undertook to harm him.[25]

As letters were being exchanged between the parties, Kaspar and Eukarius, as well as Konrad von Vestenberg, gradually came to understand that all their attempts to bring Veit's project to a standstill would be in vain, mainly because the margrave himself had an axe to grind. Konrad bemoaned the fact that Veit was able to wheedle the prince into assisting him against other Vestenbergs. Veit's rapidly rising new keep just above his own dwelling was intolerably threatening, he asserted. The margrave could understand that, as God had blessed him [Konrad] with nine children, it would be a calamity if he were to be ousted from Haslach. He implored the margrave to consider 'with what great application and devotion Your Grace had taken care of Your Grace's children . . . and how would Your Grace feel if someone wanted to harm them'. Kaspar, less vulnerable than Konrad, was blunter. He told the margrave that were it not for his support of Veit, he [Kaspar] would not have had to endure Veit's unfair undertaking.[26] Upon this realisation he and his brother Eukarius took the drastic step of renouncing their service obligations to the margrave. Eukarius also informed the prince that he had become a servitor of the (Wittelsbach) Count Palatine instead.[27]

---

[23] StAW, Adel, no. 1114, passim.

[24] StAN, Ansbacher Historica, no. 210, prod. of 22 November 1484; prod. of Dienstag nach Trium regum [11 January] 1485.

[25] Ibid., prod. of Samstag nach Matthei [25 September] 1484.

[26] Ibid., prod. of Samstag vor Antonii [15 January]; prod. of Mittwoch Petri et Pauli [29 June]; prod. of Viti [15 June] 1485.

[27] Ibid., prod. of Sonntag nach Catharine [28 November] 1484; prod. of Sonntag nach dem heiligen Jarestag [2 January] 1485. In 1497 Eukarius was district governor and councillor of the bishop of Eichstätt: Theodor Neuhofer, *Gabriel von Eyb, Fürstbischof von Eichstätt 1455–1535: Ein Lebensbild*

In the middle of 1485, while still trying to keep up the façade of an impartial feudal lord,[28] the margrave had at least 120 craftsmen sent to Veit von Vestenberg to expedite the building of the castle in Fürstenforst.[29] It is noteworthy that the first directive to this effect was issued less than two weeks after castle Stein, a fief of the prince-bishop of Bamberg but lying in margravial territory, was captured by Otto of Mosbach, the Wittelsbach Count of the Upper Palatinate. The latter, moreover, made half of it over to another, more powerful Wittelsbach prince, Duke Georg of Bavaria.[30] At the same time a larger conflict was brewing as Duke Georg began from early 1485 to beleaguer the imperial city of Nördlingen, an ally of the margrave. These events threatened to fan the smouldering strife between the Hohenzollern and Wittelsbach houses.[31] Now Kaspar von Vestenberg was not only an official of the duke of Bavaria, but also one of the commanders in the campaign against Nördlingen.[32] Margrave Albrecht had some misgivings about Kaspar's activities in this capacity.[33] It is possible that these larger events precipitated and hardened the margrave's by now almost undisguised support of Veit von Vestenberg.

Kaspar and Eukarius, if they had any illusion about the margrave, were by now completely disabused of it. In a letter to the margrave, Kaspar regretted that the prince was allowing and even helping Veit to dispossess him [Kaspar] violently.[34] He came to the conclusion that even 'if my cousins and I are absolutely right and [Veit] is wrong, still we must be wrong and [Veit] right'.[35] Even the cautious Konrad could not contain himself any longer and explained to the margrave that Veit 'uses Your Grace for the sake of his malice which he has long had in his treacherous heart'.[36] The dispute was well on the way to escalation.

aus der Wende vom Mittelalter zur Neuzeit (Eichstätt, 1934), 35, 41. In 1501 he became district governor in the service of the bishop of Würzburg: StAW, Stb, no. 790, fols. 4ᵛ–5ʳ.

[28] StAN, Ansbacher Historica, no. 210, prod. of Freitag nach Viti [17 June] 1485.

[29] Ibid., prod. of Montag nach Reminiscere [1 March]; prod. of Mittwoch nach Reminiscere [2 March]; prod. of Fronleichnamstag [2 June]; prod. of Freitag nach Corpus Christi [3 June]; prod. of Dienstag nach Corpus Christi [7 June] 1485.

[30] Julius von Minutoli (ed.), *Das kaiserliche Buch des Markgrafen Albrecht Achilles: Kurfürstliche Periode von 1470–1486* (Berlin, 1850), 99–101, no. 86.

[31] Reinhard Seyboth, *Die Markgraftümer Ansbach und Kulmbach unter der Regierung Markgraf Friedrichs des Älteren (1486–1515)* (Göttingen, 1985), 117; Matthias Thumser, *Hertnidt vom Stein (ca. 1427–1491): Bamberger Domdekan und markgräflich-brandenburgischer Rat. Karriere zwischen Kirche und Fürstendienst* (Neustadt a.d. Aisch, 1989), 167–70.

[32] Reinhard Stauber, *Herzog Georg von Bayern-Landshut und seine Reichspolitik: Möglichkeiten und Grenzen reichsfürstlicher Politik im wittelsbachisch-habsburgischen Spannungsfeld zwischen 1470 und 1505* (Kallmünz, 1993), 261.

[33] StAN, Ansbacher Historica, no. 210, prod. of Freitag nach Viti [17 June] 1485.

[34] Ibid., prod. of Montag nach [?] Viti [20 (?) June] 1485.

[35] 'dar bey ich abnemen musse wann mein vetern und ich gantz Recht und er unrecht so müssen wir dannoch unrecht und Er recht haben': ibid., prod. of Sonntag nach Johannis baptiste [26 June] 1485. For the margarve's angry answer to Kaspar see ibid., prod. of Dienastag nach Johannis baptiste [28 June] 1485.

[36] Ibid., prod. of Petri et Pauli [29 June] 1485.

21

Veit and his attendants intensified their attacks on the subjects of Kaspar, Eukarius and Konrad. They imposed an oath on the latter's shepherds to avoid grazing the sheep, shot at other shepherds with crossbows, laid pastures waste, knocked down fences, felled trees, slaughtered poultry, destroyed fishponds, and shelled Haslach with cannonballs to boot. Finally, they nominated as a chaplain of the local church a certain 'mendacious knave' from among their ranks, and arranged for two other excommunicates to mock the priests 'in their face' during Mass. In concluding this list of Veit's offences which was delivered to the margrave, Konrad remarked that 'Your Grace can see that if Your Grace did not help building [the castle] I would have been spared all this damage and wanton violence.'[37]

In 1486 Margrave Albrecht died. The immediate concern of his sons, Friedrich and Sigmund, was to ensure as smooth a succession to power as possible. The tense 'foreign' relations required quiet on the 'home' front. The feud of the Vestenbergs was in these circumstances irksome. Veit was now asked to co-operate with the margraves in a way different than he had with their father. Feud violence was unwelcome, 'since we are, at this time of our coming into rule, encumbered with numerous affairs'.[38] Otherwise in trouble, Veit was helped out unintentionally, but by no means unexpectedly, by the bishop of Würzburg. The latter could not help testing the young princes' political resolve. He argued that Veit, in building a new castle on episcopal land without his express consent, was violating his spiritual and temporal jurisdiction in the area. The margraves answered with a divergent conception of 'sovereignty': they denied that clearly demarcated territories were the primary units of rule; instead, they took as a frame of reference the entire Land of Franconia in which they, too, enjoyed princely rights and privileges similar to the bishop.[39] Veit's feudal and other personal ties to the margrave were, in this possibly ad hoc view, more binding than the geographical location of his castle.

The bishop was not convinced: he made his point by forbidding the subjects of his nearby governorship of Schlüsselfeld to trade with Fürstenforst. Action taken, there now was no need to mince words: in a letter dealing with the economic blockade the bishop made out the margraves, not Veit, to be the true architects of the castle. In a sense, he was right. The margraves, like their father two years earlier, ordered the monasteries under their sway to provide Veit with building materials. They themselves sent supplies and men-at-arms to Fürsten-

---

[37] Ibid. [n.d. (= 1485)].   [38] Ibid., prod. of Sonntag Cantate [23 April] 1486.
[39] Ibid., prod. of Dienstag Vincula Petri [1 August] 1486. For the dynastic-historical legitimation schemes employed by the margraves of Brandenburg see Jean-Marie Moeglin, '"Toi, Burgrave de Nuremberg, misérable gentilhomme dont la grandeur est si récente . . .": Essai sur la conscience dynastique des Hohenzollern de Franconie au xve siècle', *Journal des Savants* (1991), 91–131, esp. 123–5.

forst.[40] It was not too long before some nasty clashes occurred between the creatures of the margrave (under Veit's command) and the retainers of Konrad von Vestenberg. As usual, it was the subject peasants of the two sides that bore the brunt of the attacks.[41]

Thus, the higher the political tension rose, the more inextricably entangled became the agendas of the opposing princes with those of the rival nobles.[42] And it became definitively clear that, whatever else was in question, Veit's new fortress was the central issue, the point of convergence of all conflicting interests. Indeed, so much so, that it determined the outcome of the feud. Whereas the margraves were prepared to press concessions on Veit energetically with regard to other disputed points, they held back with respect to the castle: 'It does not become us', they explained, 'to force anything on Veit'.[43] Konrad was to suffer the consequences of this approach, for it was to him that Fürstenforst posed the greatest threat. The brothers Kaspar and Eukarius were more tractable on this score, and were made to concern themselves chiefly with their differences with their mother.[44] A wedge was thus driven between them and Konrad. As Veit himself told the margraves, Konrad had become the main hindrance to a peaceful settlement.[45] This enabled the margraves to impose a solution, albeit a – in both senses of the word – partial one: the scope of the legal resolution of the conflict was narrowed down to deal only with the dower of Veit's wife. It was divided between her and Veit on the one hand, and her sons Kaspar and Eukarius on the other.[46] Konrad, judging from the absence of relevant documents, was left to fend for himself.

What the feud was all about was made clear by the antagonists themselves: property rights. Eukarius stated its importance in the most unequivocal terms: 'it is proper for me to defend myself when one unjustly takes away my property . . . I have always heard that one should fight and die for one's paternal inheritance before one allows it to be taken away.'[47] Straightforward self-defence, however,

---

[40] StAN, Ansbacher Historica, no. 210, prod. of Mittwoch nach Bartholomei [30 August]; prod. of Dienstag nach Egidii [5 September]; prod. of Montag nach Marien geburt [11 September]; prod. of Montag nach Nativitatis Marie [11 September]; prod. of Mathei [21 September] 1486.

[41] Ibid., prod. of Dienstag nach dem Sonntag Judica [3 April]; prod. of vierten Ostertag [19 April] 1487.

[42] An incident indicative of this situation is related in ibid., prod. of Dienstag nach dem Sonntag Judica [3 April] 1487.

[43] Ibid., prod. of Mittwoch Presentatio Marie [21 November] 1487.

[44] Ibid., prod. of Dienstag nach Vocem jocunditatis [22 May] 1487; prod. of Samstag nach dem Sonntag Letare [22 March]; prod. of Palmtag Abend [29 March]; prod. of Montag nach Palmtag [31 March] 1488.

[45] Ibid., prod. of Mittwoch nach Palmtag [2 April] 1488; see also ibid., prod. of Samstag vor dem Christtag [22 December] 1487: 'wil dan Contz sich von caspar rittern und kargeß [*scil.* Eukarius] sein bruder thun und sein geprechen die er zu mir vermaint zu haben, an sie mit mir vor e g zu ende lassen lauffen wie sich gepurt'.

[46] Ibid., prod. of Dienstag nach Matthei [22 September] 1489.

[47] 'zimpt mir so mir einer das meyn an recht nymt zu weren . . . wan ich albeg gehort habe, einer soll umb sein vetterich [*sic*] erbe streyten und sterben ee und er im das nemen laße': ibid., prod. of Montag Antonii [17 June] 1485.

cannot have been more than half of the truth about the drive to violence. It was a stock argument of all parties to feuds. A more cogent explanation of the purpose of using force is provided by Kaspar's protestation that Veit 'now undertakes to deal with my subject peasants [*armen lewten*] in order to coerce them into unjust duties, aiming at making them tributary and subservient to his advocacy [*gultpar und vogtpar*]'. Veit made a similar accusation against his relations.[48] Seizing peasants, imposing duties and exacting tributes, as well as causing them material damage – these actions were an important part of a repertoire of techniques of violence on which all feuding noblemen drew.[49] The Vestenbergs' eloquent explicitness reveals the internal logic of such actions.

As a residence Veit's new castle was of little value. It was the use to which it could be put to command resources – fishponds, sheep-runs, woodland – and human labour that alarmed Veit's kinsmen. Veit used violence mainly in order to cow their subject peasants into entering into personal ties of dependence on him. Presumably, the desired and expected result was intensified extraction of tributes, the maximisation of rents, and the consolidation of his estates. In short, Veit was busy expanding his lordship, and that at the expense of his neighbours, inferiors and equals alike.[50] Peasants were as much the objects of as the unfortunate pawns in a brutal game noblemen played against each other. 'By tightening their hold on peasants, securing their legal rights over them', noblemen could, as Thomas Robisheaux has pointed out, 'extend or round off their control over their territories'.[51] It was mainly for this reason that a feud could scarcely go unnoticed by the regional princes.[52]

As far as Veit was concerned, a feud was probably the best possible means to win a dispute over property to which legal claims were many, mixed up and moot. Indeed, the parties could not even agree on which legal instance should hear the case.[53] But once Veit was able to secure the margraves' support, he had to worry less about justice than otherwise. He now had good prospects of prevailing, by hook or by crook, over his kinsmen. In the end this is what appears to have happened. Veit did compromise over his wife's dower, but in return he was able to establish himself firmly in his new seat. In all subsequent documents the toponym Fürstenforst was attached to his name, and to the names of his nephews, as well as of their progeny.[54]

---

[48] Ibid., prod. of Viti [15 June] 1485; prod. of Dienstag nach Dionisii [19 October] 1486; prod. of Sonntag nach Martini [18 November] 1487.

[49] Brunner, *'Land' and Lordship*, 67–81.

[50] In the process Veit distrained upon property of some peasants over whom the right to bid and forbid (*gepot und verpot*) was disputed: StAN, Ansbacher Historica, no. 210, prod. of Dionisii Abend [8 October] 1486.

[51] Thomas Robisheaux, *Rural Society and the Search for Order in Early Modern Germany* (Cambridge, 1989), 35.

[52] See chap. 5.   [53] StAN, Ansbacher Historica, no. 210, passim.

[54] StAN, Lehensurkunden, nos. 1274–7, 1280, 1282–3, 1285, 4287, 5738; ibid., Brandenburg-Ansbachische Lehenbücher, no. 11, fols. 53ᵛ–54ʳ.

Veit grew increasingly powerful. In 1496 he was one of three councillors called upon to compose differences between the margrave and the dukes of Saxony.[55] In 1499 he was one of the small coterie of six noblemen who advised Margrave Friedrich on a particularly delicate matter of dynastic policy.[56] His success was translated into concrete gains on his landed estates. In 1495 Emperor Maximilian granted him the right to fortify his castle, and the right to hold an annual fair in Fürstenforst.[57] His crowning achievement was to influence the margrave in 1503 to transform Fürstenforst into a margravial district governorship and nominate his namesake nephew to the post.[58] Veit's other nephew, Philipp, became margravial councillor in 1497.[59] The nephews' close relationship with the prince came in handy since they were by no means any less grasping than their uncle. In 1500 they had been requested by Wolf Gottsmann to be the custodians of his castle Lauffenburg when he left Franconia to serve Emperor Maximilian for several years. It was the last time Gottsmann saw his castle from within. His many entreaties to the margrave to help him regain the castle were of no avail. It was to remain in the Vestenbergs' sure hands for a long time to come.[60]

The rise of Veit von Vestenberg and through him of the line he set up in Fürstenforst was remarkable, although in no way atypical for the untitled nobility. It surely was too complex a process to be reduced to a monocausal explanation. But at least a good part of it may lie in Veit's numerous feuds.[61] Ironically, it was his feud against the margrave in the early 1470s that brought him into proximity to the prince as his servitor. How exactly he then made the leap from this status to that of an important figure in the prince's court can only be speculated about. In any case, from this power position he moved against his siblings. This feud, beginning in 1484, was a well-thought-out enterprise. Veit shrewdly enlisted the margrave's backing in advance by making his new castle available to him. In other words, Veit took advantage of the political conditions then prevalent in the region to mesh his interests with those of a powerful princely dynasty and thus to mobilise its superior resources. This was the single most crucial factor which enabled him to intensify his lordship in the area to the detriment of his relations. It is likely that it was also this political moment that generated the 'critical mass' necessary for Veit's further ascent.

---

[55] Adolph Friedrich Riedel (ed.), *Codex diplomaticus Brandenburgensis: Sammlung der Urkunden, Chroniken und sonstigen Quellenschriften für die Geschichte der Mark Brandenburg und ihrer Regenten*, part 2, *Urkunden-Sammlung zur Geschichte der auswärtigen Verhältnisse der Mark Brandenburg und ihrer Regenten*, vol. VI (Berlin, 1858), 139, no. 2344.

[56] Eberhard Freiherr von Eyb, *Das reichsritterliche Geschlecht der Freiherren von Eyb* (Neustadt a.d. Aisch, 1984), 105.

[57] *RTA, mR*, v, 698, no. 659. [58] StAN, AA-Akten, no. 808, fol. 58. [59] StAN, BK, F/V, 20.

[60] StAN, Akten des siebenfarbigen Alphabets, no. 35; StAN, Lehensurkunden, nos. 1277, 1282–3, 2222.

[61] Between 1473 and 1500 Veit conducted four other feuds: StAW, Adel, no. 1114, prod. of Donnerstag nach Francisci [7 October] 1473; StAB, Hofrat Ansbach-Bayreuth, no. 535; StAN, Fstm.Ansb., Fehdeakten, nos. 10, 69; StAN, AA-Akten, no. 1733 (unpaginated, n.d. [= 1500]).

Veit's eventful career was not unique. Quite a few other German noblemen owed their rise to prominence to a timely prosecution of feuds. This, in fact, is one of the most salient traits of the feud in this period of intense princely territorialisation.[62] It was the unfailing intervention of princes that lent feuds much of their strong political colouring. This feature of the feud was even more apparent in conflicts between nobles and imperial cities. Indeed, in these cases the ingrained political element of the feud could gather such momentum as to radicalise the camps to a degree rarely experienced in feuds among the aristocracy.

SCHOTT VERSUS NUREMBERG

Konrad Schott was certainly one of the most violent and, almost as certainly, one of the most hated noblemen in Franconia. A 'soulless man' was the epithet by which he came to be known to citizens of the imperial city of Nuremberg.[63] A local songster recommended roasting this 'wild nobleman' alive.[64] He may not have had too many well-wishers among the aristocracy either. Accused of dishonourable conduct in a feud against a fellow noble, Schott found that none of his peers was prepared to speak for him when his case came before the duke of Saxony. Unable to justify his 'misdeeds, [he] wept like a child' and begged for the prince's mercy.[65] Konrad Schott was not, however, an obscure, marginal nobleman. His father Lutz was district governor and marshal of the Count Palatine.[66] And in 1497 at the latest Konrad was considered sufficiently prestigious to be elected burgrave of the Rothenberg co-heirship (*Ganerbschaft*).[67]

In 1498 Schott, in collaboration with Christoph von Giech, opened a feud against Nuremberg. The feud provoked furore across Germany and elicited massive correspondence, each party seeking to inculpate the other.

According to Nuremberg,[68] their retainer Hans Herzog, on his way from the city to Gräfenberg, was stopped by Christoph von Giech and his followers.

---

[62] See chap. 5.

[63] Joseph Baader (ed.), *Verhandlungen über Thomas von Absberg und seine Fehden gegen den Schwäbischen Bund 1519 bis 1530* (Tübingen, 1873), 71 n. 1.

[64] Rochus Freiherr von Liliencron (ed.), *Die historischen Volkslieder der Deutschen vom 13. bis 16. Jahrhundert*, 4 vols. (Leipzig, 1865–69), II, 351–3, no. 193.

[65] Adalbert von Keller (ed.), *Die Geschichten und Taten Wilwolts von Schaumburg* (Stuttgart, 1859), 74.

[66] Cf. Liliencron (ed.), *Die historischen Volkslieder der Deutschen*, II, 351–3, no. 193 and Karl Hofmann, 'Das pfälzische Amt Boxberg zur Zeit des Bauernaufstands 1525', *ZGO* 97 (1949), 467–97, at 467.

[67] StAA, Ganerbschaft Rothenberg, no. 2538a, anno 1497; Martin Schütz, 'Die Ganerbschaft vom Rothenberg in ihrer politischen, juristischen und wirtschaftlichen Bedeutung' (PhD thesis, University of Erlangen, 1924), 9.

[68] Nuremberg's detailed accounts of the events leading to the feud are reproduced in Johann Joachim Müller, *Des Heil. Römischen Reichs Teutscher Nation ReichsTags Theatrum, wie selbiges unter Keyser Maximilians I. allerhöchsten Regierung gestanden, und was auf selbigem in Geist- und Weltlichen Reichs-Händeln berahtschlaget, tractiret und geschlossen worden*, part 2 (Jena, 1719), 699–702, 712–19. See

Learning that Hans was in Nuremberg's service, they cried out 'it is the right one, stab him to death! stab him to death!' and cut him to pieces. A few hours later, there occurred another bloody engagement, as twenty-four mounted retainers of the city were patrolling the countryside.[69] One of them, who was sent forward to Eschenau 'in order to find out certain things', chanced upon fifteen or sixteen threatening horsemen and took to his heels. In coming to his rescue, his twenty-three companions fell into an ambush of about a hundred cavalrymen. The captain of this troop was Konrad Schott.[70] They killed two of Nuremberg's men and wounded many others.

Christoph von Giech and Konrad Schott had a slightly different story to tell.[71] It so transpired, Christoph related, that he and his men were recruited by another nobleman to serve a certain prince. On their way, near Eschenau, their vanguard was attacked by Nuremberg's 'staghounds' (*hetzrüden*), yelling 'stab them to death! it is the right ones' (*sic*). They came to the help of their friends, and in the skirmish that followed some Nuremberg men may have been killed, others wounded.[72] Whereas their actions were legitimate self-defence, those of Nuremberg were a breach of the General Peace (*Landfrieden*). The attack on Hans Herzog is missing from Giech's account, as indeed Nuremberg pointed out.[73]

That the city's 'bloodhounds' failed in their task to 'shed noblemen's blood' was, according to Giech, a blow to Nuremberg's pride and vanity, 'in which they wallow as an old Jew in his usury'.[74] So they fell back on their cherished tradition of perfidy, and put money on his and Schott's heads. When he learned of this, he wrote to the city council trying to explain what had taken place and to demonstrate his innocence – in vain. The council gave credence to their 'blood merchants'' version of the affair, despite their being of ignoble origins. Nuremberg's response to Giech's and Schott's self-justification was to suggest that each of the noblemen involved in the mêlée near Eschenau should appear before the city council and purge himself of all suspicion under oath. However, 'as noblemen this answer seemed to us so arrogant and haughty, that for several reasons it would have been humiliating and disadvantageous for us [to put up with such] a

---

also Georg Wolfgang Karl Lochner (ed.), *Das deutsche Mittelalter in den wesentlichsten Zeugnissen seiner geschichtlichen Urkunden, Chroniken und Rechtsdenkmäler*, part 2 (Nuremberg, 1851), 302–10.

[69] Nuremberg emphasised that there was no connection between the attack on Hans Herzog and this patrol: Müller, *ReichsTags Theatrum*, 713.

[70] *Die Chroniken der fränkischen Städte, Nürnberg*, 5 vols. (Leipzig, 1862–74), V, 603.

[71] The following account is based mainly on von Giech's letter to an unnamed prince, printed in *Verhandlungen zwischen der Stadt Nürnberg und der fränkischen Ritterschaft wegen Christoph von Giech und Contz Schott* (Nuremberg, 1500). I have used the copy GNM, Inc. 1872. Another copy of this letter is in BL, cat. no. I.B.8243. A similar letter to Elector Friedrich of Saxony and his brother Duke Johann is in Müller, *ReichsTags Theatrum*, 702–4.

[72] Cf. StAN, Bb, no. 45, fol. 34ʳ.   [73] Lochner (ed.), *Das deutsche Mittelalter*, part 2, 306.

[74] Karl Klüpfel (ed.), *Urkunden zur Geschichte des Schwäbischen Bundes (1488–1533)*, 2 vols. (Stuttgart, 1846–53), I, 403.

piece of impudence, to appear before them at their pleasure, and to take an oath'.[75]

Instead, Schott and Giech proposed to bring the case before either the emperor or the electors or the Knighthood (*Ritterschaft*). Nuremberg declined and showed their real face, or 'as the proverb has it, "when one asks the peasant [for something] his stomach belches" . . . that is, they consider their law-court as worthier than that of a laudable prince'.[76] Since Nuremberg refused to negotiate and to 'release me from danger . . . necessity demanded . . . that I would not bear the anxiety for nothing and unmerited, and that I make those of Nuremberg pay for [my] fear with fear'. So he became their enemy, that is he officially proclaimed feud on Nuremberg by sending them a cartel of defiance.[77]

Christoph von Giech glossed over another incident, the one that probably earned Schott his reputation as a 'soulless man'. On 6 April 1499 Schott captured Wilhelm Derrer, a Nuremberg city councillor. He tried to force Derrer to lay his right hand on a block so that he could chop it off. When Derrer refused, Schott threatened to run him through with a sword. Derrer beseeched Schott to consider that he had three children. The supplication cut no ice with Schott, who ordered Derrer to hurry up and lay his hand on the block. Derrer extended his left, but Schott insisted on the right hand, explaining to Derrer that it was 'so . . . you would write me no more letters', and thrust down his sword. Derrer recoiled and the sword met his fingers. Schott took out an axe and tried again; Derrer flinched again. The blow struck home nevertheless. Schott placed the severed hand at Derrer's lap, uttering 'carry it home to your masters'.[78]

This brutal assault was outside the gamut of the ordinary means of feuding, and Schott and Giech knew it full well. They justified themselves by arguing that it was merely a reaction to an equally abnormal manhunt launched by Nuremberg immediately after the clash near Eschenau. Nuremberg disagreed and claimed that it was because of the attack on Derrer that they put a price on Schott's and Giech's heads.[79] Whatever the order of events, Derrer's mutilation gave the feud a new turn. It steeled Nuremberg against Schott and Giech, and made them adopt an intransigent 'anti-terrorist' stance which precluded any negotiations.[80] The incident also sparked off a battle for 'public opinion' in which each side sought to undermine the legitimacy of the other's actions.

To produce this effect, the city maintained that Christoph von Giech had begun his feud against them, committing murders, robberies, and arson, before sending them a cartel of defiance.[81] As such cartels had been since 1186 a

---

[75] *Verhandlungen zwischen der Stadt Nürnberg und der fränkischen Ritterschaft.*
[76] 'wann man den pauwren pit, so groltz im der pauch': ibid. The proverb means 'a rude refusal'.
[77] Ibid.; StAN, Bb, no. 45, fol. 188ᵛ.   [78] *Die Chroniken der fränkischen Städte, Nürnberg*, V, 605.
[79] StAN, Bb, no. 45, fols. 30ʳ–31ᵛ.   [80] Ibid., fols. 28ᵛ, 190ʳ, 218ᵛ–220ᵛ.   [81] Ibid., fol. 188ᵛ.

precondition for a lawful feud,[82] this would have made it difficult for Giech to enlist the support of honourable noblemen and princes. Giech, on the other hand, attempted to secure sympathy by capitalising on resentments against Nuremberg. In a letter to an unnamed prince he compared Nuremberg to Venice in that both cities endeavoured to suppress their surrounding princes and nobility by using their commercial wealth. 'A poor, hunted nobleman', he asked for princely assistance and – anticipating Montesquieu[83] – observed that a prince without nobility was not a prince at all. To drive the message home, of his own accord he proclaimed Nuremberg a breaker of the General Peace.[84]

However, it was he and Schott who were placed under the imperial ban (*Acht*).[85] Instrumental in procuring it was the royal secretary Sixt Ölhafen, known to be also in Nuremberg's pay.[86] Nuremberg went on to urge almost every conceivable political power in Germany to make the ban public by posting a notice in central locations and to assist in its execution.[87] The ban created a dangerous situation for the nobles, because it provided the city with a licence to use whatever means were necessary to clamp down on them. It comes as no surprise, therefore, that Nuremberg city council soon received reports that, 'at the instigation of some persons', the ban on Konrad Schott was about to be lifted. The city council directed the learned humanist Willibald Pirckheimer, its emissary to the emperor, to try to delay the repealing of the ban until they had prepared a new document to be presented to His Majesty detailing Schott's fresh atrocities.[88]

The attempt failed, the ban was suspended,[89] and Konrad Schott was soon back at his bellicose work. He fell upon Nuremberg's villages, burning and looting. On one occasion he and his men slyly used women to wheedle villagers out of shelter, pretending they wished to have an amicable chat with them. They captured one villager and 'vented all of their anger on him', shooting at him point-blank with a crossbow, so that he 'uttered neither "wee" nor "ach"', and at once dropped down dead'. Forensic investigation revealed that on two sides of the arrow was engraved '"for a Nuremberger"'.[90]

The feud entered its second and more dangerous phase, as Schott and Giech won over a large following. With bands numbering fifty to a hundred horsemen

---

82 Karl Zeumer (ed.), *Quellensammlung zur Geschichte der deutschen Reichsverfassung in Mittelalter und Neuzeit* (Tübingen, 1907), 21.
83 'no monarch, no nobility; no nobility, no monarch': Charles de Secondat, Baron de Montesquieu, *The Spirit of the Laws*, ed. and trans. by Anne M. Cohler, Basia Carolyn Miller, and Harold Samuel Stone (Cambridge, 1989), 18.
84 *Verhandlungen zwischen der Stadt Nürnberg und der fränkischen Ritterschaft*; StAN, Bb, no. 45, fol. 188ᵛ.
85 StAN, Bb, no. 45, fols. 31ʳ⁻ᵛ.
86 Emil Reicke (ed.), *Willibald Pirckheimers Briefwechsel*, 2 vols. (Munich, 1940–56), I, 85 n. 3.
87 StAN, Bb, no. 45, fols. 31ʳ, 188ʳ, 244ʳ–245ʳ.
88 Ibid., fols. 39ʳ⁻ᵛ; Reicke (ed.), *Pirckheimers Briefwechsel*, I, 85–6.
89 Schütz, 'Ganerbschaft vom Rothenberg', 10.   90 StAN, Bb, no. 45, fol. 196ᵛ.

they were roaming the roads leading to and from Nuremberg, blocking commerce. The city council made a desperate appeal to princes of the Empire not to give credence to nobles' letters which besmirched the city, and to provide its merchants with Safe Conduct (*Geleit*), reminding them that the imperial ban had been renewed.[91] It was too late. A new, albeit still inchoate force was at work tipping the scale against Nuremberg: the Franconian Knighthood.

The knights were precisely in these years laying the foundations of their political organisation.[92] Like so many previous and subsequent conflicts of various sorts, Schott's and Giech's feud against Nuremberg gave the Franconian Knighthood another impetus to work out a common policy. In early 1500, counts, barons (*Herren*) and knights gathered a number of times in various locations. Nuremberg tried to persuade the assembled nobles to see in Schott and Giech peace-breakers, and to this effect sent them a copy of the imperial ban.[93] Unimpressed, the knights responded by giving the city an ultimatum to release the nobles from danger within eight days. They told the city council that they would give their full support to Schott if their request was refused.[94] The noblemen regarded the matter as so serious that they took a solemn oath to stand by each other.[95]

Nuremberg countered the threat by the usual method of proposing to bring the case before a third party such as the emperor or a prince. This time the city council sent the assembled noblemen two copies of the imperial ban.[96] Rather irritated, the knights replied that it simply would not do 'to go to law with us, to go to war against Schott' – these two methods were incompatible.[97] Tempers began to run high, and the city charged the knights with 'conspiracy and rebellion', and told them they had placed themselves outside the body politic of the Empire and proved disobedient to the emperor.[98] A similar conclusion was reached, probably with some encouragement from Nuremberg,[99] by Emperor Maximilian. He characterised the knights' assemblies as an 'alliance against us', that is a 'crimen conspiracionis und rebellionis'. He also reminded several princes and counts of their co-operation in formulating the statutes of the General Peace of 1495 so as to prevent them from lending the knights a helping hand.[100] The knights, who like their 'forefathers . . . had always been loyal to the emperors and kings and to the Empire', were enraged by these allegations, and put the blame

[91] Ibid., fols. 196ᵛ, 244ʳ–245ʳ; Müller, *ReichsTags Theatrum*, 709–12, 719–20, 727.
[92] See chap. 6.   [93] StAN, Bb, no. 45, fol. 245ᵛ.
[94] *Verhandlungen zwischen der Stadt Nürnberg und der fränkischen Ritterschaft*; BL, cat. no. I.B.8244.
[95] StAN, Fstm.Ansb., Fehdeakten, no. 26, prod. 3.
[96] StAN, Bb, no. 46, fols. 3ᵛ–5ʳ.
[97] *Verhandlungen zwischen der Stadt Nürnberg und der fränkischen Ritterschaft*; BL, cat. no. I.B.8244.
[98] *Verhandlungen zwischen der Stadt Nürnberg und der fränkischen Ritterschaft*; StAN, Bb, no. 46, fols. 13ʳ, 15ᵛ–16ᵛ.
[99] StAN, Bb, no. 46, fols. 25ᵛ–26ᵛ.
[100] Seyboth, *Die Markgraftümer Ansbach und Kulmbach*, 248.

on Nuremberg's easy access to the imperial ear. For them it was a clear if unnecessary proof of the city's 'spiteful disposition toward the noble race'.[101] They appear to have carried out their threats and to have taken sporadic military action against Nuremberg.[102]

In the end, the mounting pressure on both sides resulted in a peace treaty mediated by the bishops of Bamberg and Würzburg. The feud was proclaimed over, the bounty on Schott's and Giech's heads revoked, and the imperial ban probably lifted.[103] It is difficult to claim victory for Schott and Giech, since it is unknown what the objective of their feud was in the first place, though it probably originated from a territorial dispute between the city and the Rothenberg co-heirs.[104] It is certain, however, that Nuremberg got the worst of it, not only because it succumbed to the pressure of the Knighthood and made peace with feuders who caused it considerable damage with impunity; nor even because it had to give up its claim for compensation for Wilhelm Derrer's dismembered hand.[105] Rather, the compelling reason is that the real winner of the feud was the Peacock. The Peacock was the code-name used by Nuremberg to denote Margrave Friedrich of Branden-burg in its by now paranoic correspondence with its envoys and allies.[106] At least with regard to the margrave, Nuremberg was one of those few paranoids who really did have enemies. Precisely at the time of Schott's and Giech's feud a serious conflict was building up between the city and the prince.

A brief interim of rapprochement in an otherwise hostile relationship between Brandenburg and Nuremberg was ended in late 1496 by a revived conflict over 'sovereign' rights. Differences over the jurisdiction of the Territorial Court (*Landgericht*) of the prince followed. In March 1498 Nuremberg renewed its alliance with Count Palatine Philipp, Duke Albrecht and Duke Georg of Bavaria, all Wittelsbachs and traditional opponents of the Hohenzollern margraves of Brandenburg.[107] In the summer of 1499, as Margrave Friedrich was leading the imperial army against the Swiss Confederacy, Nuremberg had a number of watchtowers erected outside its walls. The margrave immediately protested that this was an outright violation of his overlordship (*Fraisch*).

This development gave a dangerous twist to the contention between the city

---

[101] *Verhandlungen zwischen der Stadt Nürnberg und der fränkischen Ritterschaft*; BL, cat. no. I.B.8245.

[102] StAN, Bb, no. 46, fols. 148^r–149^v.

[103] The knights made the lifting of the ban a condition for negotiations with Nuremberg: *Verhandlungen zwischen der Stadt Nürnberg und der fränkischen Ritterschaft*.

[104] StAN, Bb, no. 45, fols. 26^v, 151^r–153^r, 169^r–170^v. Christoph von Giech, too, was a member of the *Ganerbschaft* and in 1502 acted as its *Baumeister*: StAA, Ganerbschaft Rothenberg, no. 2538a, anno 1502.

[105] StAN, Reichsstadt Nürnberg, 35 neue Laden der unteren Losungsstube, V 93/1 3026; StAN, Bb, no. 46, fols. 152^{r-v}.

[106] Heinz Dannenbauer, *Die Entstehung des Territoriums der Reichsstadt Nürnberg* (Stuttgart, 1928), 178 n. 1080; Friedrich Wagner, 'Nürnbergische Geheimschrift im 15. und zu Anfang des 16. Jahrhunderts', *Archivalische Zeitschrift* 9 (1884), 14–62.

[107] Seyboth, *Die Markgraftümer Ansbach und Kulmbach*, 229–30.

and the margrave. In mid-June 1499 the city council reported to Willibald Pirckheimer that two margravial emissaries, 'who were perhaps slightly tipsy', taunted the workers constructing the towers by asking them '"what were these shit-fountains they were building"'. A fracas followed. The council instructed Pirckheimer that if complaints were made to Emperor Maximilian and explanations demanded, he should point out that the source of this conflict was the feud with Konrad Schott.[108] A letter to the same effect was sent to the Swabian League, explaining that the towers were erected to defend the *contado* against the ravaging feuders, and that they infringed on none of the margrave's rights in the area.[109] With the end of the war against the Swiss in sight, both sides began to prepare for a showdown.[110]

The connection between Nuremberg's conflict with the margrave and its feud with the nobles was possibly tighter than the city council gave out. Whatever Schott's and Giech's personal motives may have been, it is likely that their feud was fomented by the margrave. Indeed, that the latter often assumed the role of *éminence grise* in noblemen's feuds against cities was not lost upon contemporaries. Count Froben Christoph of Zimmern wrote in his chronicle that he

heard that Margrave Friedrich of Brandenburg many times addressed his nobles, saying: "it is all right to shake the wallets of merchants so long as you do not endanger their lives". This was a suitable precept for these fellows. For this reason it was advanced as a criticism that no punishment was to be expected of him. Apart from this, he was a God-fearing, just prince.[111]

Although this was not an empty conspiracy theory,[112] there is no direct evidence for the margrave's involvement in Schott's and Giech's feud. Yet it is difficult to overlook the general context in which the feud occurred, and the coincidence of events. This is not to say that it was an operation hatched at the margrave's court in Ansbach; in the political atmosphere then prevailing in Franconia, tacit complicity would have sufficed. The tension between Nuremberg and Brandenburg gave Schott and Giech a good opportunity to open a feud. They could count on at least the passive support of the margrave, for example on free passage through his territories. Moreover, it is not inconceivable that one incentive for their feud was the hope of finding favour in the prince's eyes. It is perhaps significant that shortly after the feud had terminated, in 1501, Konrad Schott officially entered upon margravial service for five years. Christoph von Giech was already a margravial servitor in 1490.[113]

---

[108] Reicke (ed.), *Pirckheimers Briefwechsel*, I, 87.
[109] Klüpfel (ed.), *Urkunden zur Geschichte des Schwäbischen Bundes*, I, 392–6.
[110] Reicke (ed.), *Pirckheimers Briefwechsel*, I, 116–17.
[111] Hansmartin Decker-Hauff (ed.), *Die Chronik der Grafen von Zimmern*, vol. II (Sigmaringen, 1967), 185.
[112] See chap. 5.
[113] StAN, BK, S, 85; 'Urkunden und Aktenprodukte im Königlichen Archive zu Nürnberg das Hochgräfliche Geschlecht Giech betreffend', *Jb.Mfr.* 9 (1839), 99–106, at 102.

For the prince the feud certainly came in handy. It rendered Nuremberg more vulnerable than otherwise and was also likely to provoke the city to excesses and hence provide him with a respectable casus belli. Perhaps a fear of playing into his hands is what explains the otherwise very curious reticence of Nuremberg's correspondence regarding the margrave. The city council went about this feud as if the margrave did not exist at all: on the one hand he was not among the princes whose co-operation they courted; on the other hand, not even once in their official correspondence did they impute to him sponsorship of the feuders.

In practice, however, the city did make a link between their feud with the nobles and their territorial conflict with the margrave. They did it by the construction of the towers. The city council could not have failed to predict Margrave Friedrich's reaction. Only a few years earlier he had violently had the towers built by the imperial city of Windsheim demolished.[114] Nuremberg had every reason not to take a step that was bound to aggravate the situation, unless they thought escalation was inevitable. According to this scenario, the feud was used by the city against the margrave as much as it was used by him against the city. It provided the city with a pretext for putting up defences necessary for an armed confrontation with the margrave, a confrontation that was expected anyway, with or without towers. And this pretext was needed also in order to provide the margrave's allies with a much-sought-after excuse not to bring into effect provisions of military aid. Hence Nuremberg's elaborate letter of self-justification to the Swabian League.[115] As one of its most important members, the margrave was taking advantage of the imminent expiry of the League and the negotiations over its extension to make his re-entry conditional on military assistance against Nuremberg.[116]

If it is true that the Nuremberg city council's premonitions were that war was unavoidable, then they were proved right two years later. The city's compliance with Emperor Maximilian's mandate to raze the towers to the ground did not avert it. Nor did efforts to settle the territorial differences peacefully. The margrave's son, prince Kasimir, exploited the first opportunity, the annual church anniversary festival of 1502 in Affalterbach, the protection of which was a disputed 'sovereign' right, to force a battle on Nuremberg. Many Franconian nobles fought on his side and helped him to defeat the city.[117] Those nobles with a penchant for special effects knew where they would find the action, with Christoph von Giech '[who] would take the sow by the ears, for he was not sweet on those of Nuremberg, and recently has become their enemy once again'.[118]

[114] Elisabeth Fuchshuber, *Uffenheim* (Munich, 1982), 223.
[115] Klüpfel (ed.), *Urkunden zur Geschichte des Schwäbischen Bundes*, I, 392–6.
[116] Seyboth, *Die Markgraftümer Ansbach und Kulmbach*, 232–46.
[117] Ibid., 252–3, 265–6.
[118] Helgard Ulmschneider (ed.), *Götz von Berlichingen: Mein Fehd und Handlung* (Sigmaringen, 1981), 66.

33

The two tales told in this chapter provide 'typical' examples of the structured conflict over various rights that is called the 'feud'. On a descriptive level the feud was, fundamentally, a series of sporadic yet organised, usually small-scale raids involving burning, looting, abductions, and causing all sorts of material damage. It was carried out not by kin groups, but by two principal feuders and their bands of followers. The main victims were normally the rivals' subjects. These violent attacks, however, were by and large restrained. They were regulated by accepted rules of conduct and by a more or less fixed repertoire of sanctioned methods, which in theory, and often in practice, precluded flagrant brutality. This was especially the case of feuds between noblemen. The fact that the Franconian noble families were closely interrelated militated against to-the-bitter-end feuds. Another factor which may have raised the threshold of violence was a shared chivalric ethos. In the case of feuds against cities these constraints were largely absent. Moreover, an explosive ideology was at hand that could be superimposed on disputes which were otherwise generically similar. Christoph von Giech's comparison of Nuremberg to Venice is a good example of the rhetoric of class conflict noblemen were apt to deploy. Accordingly, feuds could be conducted more viciously. But even here, virulent feuds like that of Schott were rather exceptional. In most cases, feuds displayed a surprising degree of moderation. Unlike vendettas, killings were rare.

Yet all these differences and similarities are overshadowed by one predominant feature which all kinds of feuds had in common: they were ineluctably linked to larger political conflicts. The practices and ideologies of the feud were manipulated to facilitate the process by which contending powers tried to consolidate authority and lordship and to dominate neighbours. Feuds were a particularly effective instrument of political contestation, and this was taken advantage of both by the feuding parties themselves and by those powers which were quick to become involved in them. One very striking example is the feud of Albrecht von Rosenberg against members of the erstwhile Swabian League. The feud became politically so volatile that Emperor Charles V and his brother Ferdinand almost succeeded in using it to detonate the Protestant Schmalkaldic League.[119] This sort of intervention was especially the territory of princes. They seldom failed to meddle in feuds, if they did not instigate them in the first place. Feuds were nearly always part of the political process by which they were in turn regulated. Hence they were often as much ethical as violent. The opposing parties invariably set much store on 'public opinion' and legitimacy: they used ink no less than sword and torch. Naked power was by and large inconceivable.

These salient features of the feud suggest also what it was not. Above all, they

---

[119] Joseph Frey, 'Die Fehde der Herren von Rosenberg auf Boxberg mit dem Schwäbischen Bund und ihre Nachwirkungen (1523–1555)' (PhD thesis, University of Tübingen, 1924), 80–95.

make it difficult to accept the view that feuds were robberies by another name. This is not to deny that many feuds were acted out on the anyway faintly marked boundary between respectability and criminality. But on the whole it takes either a considerable stretch of the imagination or strong ideological convictions to label 'criminal' or 'robber-knighthood' something as open, as public, and above all as political as the feud. Indeed, neither Veit von Vestenberg nor Konrad Schott fits the stereotype of the impoverished nobleman turned 'robber-knight'.[120] Both were established nobles and held important offices in princely administrations.[121] Konrad Schott was also one of the wealthiest nobles in Franconia: in 1524 he was creditor of the margraves of Brandenburg for the colossal sum of 11,000 gulden.[122] As the next chapters will show, most feuding noblemen had a similar social and political profile.

---

[120] Konrad Schott is considered an archetypal 'robber-knight', 'one of the pillars of Franconian hedge-knighthood': Ulmschneider (ed.), *Mein Fehd und Handlung*, 24.

[121] Schott was district governor in the service of the duke of Württemberg (1510–15) and later in the service of the margraves of Brandenburg: Moritz von Rauch (ed.), *Urkundenbuch der Stadt Heilbronn*, vol. III (Stuttgart, 1916), 262, 330, 421; StAN, AA-Akten, 1402, fols. 169^v–171^v.

[122] StAN, Brandenburger Literalien, no. 582, fol. 1^r.

3

The Franconian nobility

> We have concluded that no knight should display gold or embroidered velvet, be it a frock or a mantle; no woman or maiden should have more than four dresses with which to adorn herself . . . [and] no more than two of [these dresses] should be of velvet . . . so that poor noblemen could visit tournaments together with their wives and daughters and sisters.

With these sartorial sumptuary regulations, laid down in 1478, the Franconian nobility recognised, and gave articulate expression to, the social and economic fissures within their ranks that threatened to 'destroy and ruin the nobility'.[1]

To establish the nature of social stratification within the nobility is a project fraught with problems. On the one hand, direct access to nobles' views on this matter is hampered by ideology. Indeed, what elicited the ordinance just quoted was that social reality alarmingly failed to match up to the very ideal tournaments were supposed to celebrate: the solidarity and intrinsic equality of all nobles.[2] As a venerable dictum has it, noblemen get to know each other in one evening better than bourgeois in one month.[3] One can therefore expect nobles to have said either too little or too much about this subject. On the other hand, the validity of the views of modern scholars is also debatable. The main difficulty here is with the analytical categories appropriate for an enquiry into stratification. Although the range of variables is limited, there is no agreement among historians on the relative weight of each. Nor is the character of the relation between these variables clear. As a result, one cannot be certain whether the lines one draws between different social strata are real, or whether they are figments of the intellect.[4]

---

[1] Heide Stamm (ed.), *Das Turnierbuch des Ludwig von Eyb (cgm 961). Edition und Untersuchung mit einem Anhang: Die Turnierchronik des Jörg Rugen (Textabdruck)* (Stuttgart, 1986), 215–17. See also William H. Jackson, 'The Tournament and Chivalry in German Tournament Books of the Sixteenth Century and in the Literary Works of Emperor Maximilian I', in *The Ideals and Practice of Medieval Knighthood: Papers from the first and second Strawberry Hill Conferences*, ed. Christopher Harper-Bill and Ruth Harvey (Woodbridge, 1986), 49–73, at 55–6.

[2] Joseph Morsel, 'Le tournoi, mode d'éducation politique en Allemagne à la fin du Moyen Age', in *Éducation, apprentissages, initiation au Moyen Age: Actes du premier colloque international de Montpellier*, vol. II (Montpellier, 1993), 309–31, at 316.

[3] Georg Simmel, *Soziologie: Untersuchungen über die Formen der Vergesellschaftung* (Leipzig, 1908), 737. A similar view is to be found in an elegant novel by Irene Dische, *Ein fremdes Gefühl oder Veränderungen über einen Deutschen* (Berlin: Rowohlt, 1993), 11.

[4] What is meant by strata is primarily the social boundaries between noblemen of equal legal rank. See

A related problem is the identity of the elementary unit of stratification among the nobility. Was it the entire lineage, the line, or perhaps the individual? The main difficulty involved in answering this question is that the extent and importance of aristocratic kinship ties varied according to circumstances. In the realm of remembrance, for instance, it is the lineage which appears dominant, as in the chronicle composed by Michael von Ehenheim in 1515.[5] However, when property and succession were at issue, the lineage could easily recede into the background. Only a few years after Michael's death, his childless relation Georg von Ehenheim set out to prepare a will. It was of little assistance to him that he held in trust Michael's family 'history'.[6] The von Ehenheim lineage being very large and widely ramified, he said, he did not know who his next of kin and heir was. Nor did the other Ehenheims, or so he claimed. This gave rise to an ugly dispute between them.[7] The noble lineage was perhaps less comprised of lines than divided into them. Indeed, as a number of works have shown, the fortunes of different lines of the same lineage could differ greatly.[8]

Yet the line, too, cannot be assumed to have been nobles' uncontested focus of loyalty. A strong drive among the nobility toward personal autonomy is unmistakeable.[9] This was closely linked to the practice of partible inheritance. Following the father's death, the sons would sooner or later divide the patrimony and become each a lord in his own right. Such fragmentations, which were often the first step toward the establishment of new lines, strongly suggest that the primary element of stratification was the individual. This is a necessary working assumption, but in itself is not entirely satisfactory, if only because no nobleman

Michael Mitterauer, 'Probleme der Stratifikation in mittelalterlichen Gesellschaftssystemen', in *Theorien in der Praxis des Historikers*, ed. Jürgen Kocka (Göttingen, 1977), 13–43, at 20.

[5] Christian Meyer (ed.), 'Die Familienchronik des Ritters Michel von Ehenheim', *Hohenzollerische Forschungen* 5 (1897), 369–419.

[6] Cf. ibid., 370, 372 and Otto Puchner, 'Zur Geschichte der Schenk von Geyern und ihres Territoriums', in *Archiv der Freiherrn Schenk von Geyern auf Schloß Syburg*, ed. Karl Hannakam and Ludwig Veit (Munich, 1958), 1–15, at 7 n. 39.

[7] 'Vor jharen Seind deren von Ehenheim vill gewest derhalben sie unter einander Mancherley zu Namen gehabt . . . Nun ist jorg von Ehenheim zu Geyern seins zu Namens ein Wilde und derselbenn linien der letzt gewest, und hat nit wissen mögen, welcher unter allen von Ehenheim So nach im selben gewest, sein Nechster Erb oder freundt sei, so habens die von Ehenheim unter einander auch nit gewust': StAW, Literaliensammlung des Historischen Vereins von Unterfranken und Aschaffenburg, Ms f. 1044 (unpaginated). See also Hannakam and Veit (eds.), *Archiv der Freiherrn Schenk von Geyern*, 40–4, U 49, U 54, U 57.

[8] Harold H. Kehrer, 'The von Sickingen and the German Princes 1262–1523' (PhD thesis, Boston University Graduate School, 1977), 91; Peter-Michael Hahn, *Struktur und Funktion des brandenburgischen Adels im 16. Jahrhundert* (Berlin, 1979), 230; Kurt Andermann, *Studien zur Geschichte des pfälzischen Niederadels im Mittelalter: Eine vergleichende Untersuchung an ausgewählten Beispielen* (Speyer, 1982), passim; Wieland Held, 'Das Adelsgeschlecht der Brandenstein im 16. Jahrhundert: Seine wirtschaftliche und soziale Position im ernestinisch-sächsischen Territorialstaat', *VSWG* 80 (1993), 175–96, at 182–4; Klaus Rupprecht, *Ritterschaftliche Herrschaftswahrung in Franken: Die Geschichte der von Guttenberg im Spätmittelalter und zu Beginn der Frühen Neuzeit* (Neustadt a.d. Aisch, 1994), 59, 213.

[9] Rupprecht, *Ritterschaftliche Herrschaftswahrung in Franken*, 69 and passim.

was truly a self-made man. Unfortunately, still too little is known about the relationship between all these units in determining each other's social position. As long as the precise boundaries and workings of the noble kinship remain opaque, so does the nature of social inequality among the nobility. To give a hypothetical example: it is not clear what warrants regarding a poor noble from a prominent family as of higher or lower status than a rich noble from an undistinguished one.

Given these open questions, the criteria proposed in this study for an analysis of social stratification cannot be taken as definitive. However, the purpose is not to construct a general model of stratification of the Franconian nobility. Rather, it is to draw a dividing line between high-status and low-status noblemen. This it will do by setting up three evaluative parameters, which will then serve the prosopographical investigation of feuding noblemen:[10] (1) holding of high offices in princely administration; (2) financial transactions with princes as either a creditor or a guarantor or both; and (3) the quality of individual matrimonial alliances, which is judged according to the two preceding parameters. These indicators can be subsumed under the historiographical paradigm of Proximity to Rule (*Herrschaftsnähe*).[11] This paradigm contains of course the theoretical danger of favouring the rulers' perspective. But it appears as the single most credible framework into which the crucial moments of noblemen's experience can be fitted. Evidence will later be cited which shows that the noblemen themselves would not have taken exception to this view.

OFFICE

In 1547 Prince-Bishop Melchior Zobel von Giebelstadt of Würzburg was deeply concerned about the threat posed to his authority by the formation of the Free Imperial Knighthood. In an attempt to foil a political alliance between the Franconian knights and the emperor, he explained to the latter that

The diocese of Würzburg daily nourishes 54 noblemen as canons in the cathedral chapter; 18 in the chapter of St. Burkhard; approximately 10 in the two chapters of Haug and Neu-Münster . . . 7 as assessors at the Territorial Court; 45 as district governors on the country; 40 daily at the court as councillors, courtiers, servitors and pages; approximately 10 or 15 who perform indentured services (*von Haus aus*) and enjoy a yearly payment; altogether approximately 178. In addition, the number of those who hold property in fee from the diocese is more than twice as high. The greater part of the Franconian Knighthood, then, is supported by the prince . . .[12]

---

[10] See chap. 4.
[11] Waltraud Hörsch, 'Adel im Bannkreis Österreichs: Strukturen der Herrschaftsnähe im Raum Aargau-Luzern,' in Guy P. Marchal, *Sempach 1386: Von den Anfängen des Territorialstaates Luzern. Beitrag zur Frühgeschichte des Kantons Luzern* (Basel, 1986), 353–402.
[12] Andreas Sebastian Stumpf, *Denkwürdigkeiten der teutschen besonders fränkischen Geschichte*, 3 parts (Erfurt and Würzburg, 1802–4), I, 14–15.

Zobel, it seems, meant to intimate to Charles V that his policy regarding the knights was unviable. Zobel's princely authority over the knights rested on the sort of tangible powers which the emperor lacked: the Franconian nobility simply depended on him for their livelihood. The listing of these positions, and the economic dependence they allegedly entailed, raise questions about the foundations of aristocratic power which are central to the arguments of this study: the criteria for appointments to these offices, the economic benefits accruing to their incumbents, the actual political influence they conferred.

The executive and political powers of office-holders are often difficult to assess. The structure of princely administration was in the late Middle Ages still labile, precise assignments and duties were not clearly prescribed. Relatively transparent, though, is the nature of court offices. The master of the household (*Hofmeister*) was usually the highest court functionary. In Würzburg he presided over the prince's Aulic Court of justice (*Hofgericht*) and supervised the noble councillors.[13] In wartime, he was the commandant of the Marienberg, the imposing princely castle perched on a precipice overlooking the city of Würzburg. He was very well paid, his yearly salary normally being 400 gulden in addition to perquisites.[14] His deputy and surrogate, the marshal, managed financial matters at court and served as a court magistrate. In battle he was the commander-in-chief of the bishop's forces. Around 1500 he was paid 200 gulden a year. Moreover, most masters of the household and marshals were simultaneously councillors.[15]

The duties of the noble councillors were of a more general constitution. Apart from the obligation to attend the daily sessions of the council, they had to perform military services. Their salary was substantially lower than those of the master of the household and the marshal. Lists of payments due to councillors of the bishop of Würzburg between 1515 and 1531 indicate that their emoluments ranged from as little as 19 gulden to 71 gulden.[16] But, like the masters of the household and marshals, most councillors supplemented their income from other offices.[17] Moreover, councillors were frequently appointed for life as a recognition

---

[13] Sebastian Zeißner, 'Zwei Mitarbeiter des Fürstbishofs Rudolf von Scherenberg', *MJfGK* 3 (1951), 127–38, at 127.

[14] Heinzjürgen N. Reuschling, *Die Regierung des Hochstifts Würzburg 1495–1642: Zentralbehörden und führende Gruppen eines geistlichen Staates* (Würzburg, 1984), 43–5.

[15] Ibid., 161–5, 182–7, 221, 234–6, 278–81. The same was the case in the Brandenburg margraviate of Ansbach-Kulmbach: StAN, Ansbacher Historica, no. 340, fols. 25^r–33^r, 68^r–73^v. For the margravial court see Karin Plodeck, 'Hofstruktur und Hofzeremoniell in Brandenburg-Ansbach vom 16. bis zum 18. Jahrhundert: Zur Rolle des Herrschaftskultes im absolutistischen Gesellschafts- und Herrschaftssystem', *Jb.Mfr.* 86 (1971/72), 1–257, esp. 99–105.

[16] C. G. Scharold, 'Hof- und Staatshaushalt unter einigen Fürstbischöfen von Würzburg im sechzehnten Jahrhundert', *AU* 6, no. 1 (1840), 25–67, at 52–4. See also Reuschling, *Die Regierung des Hochstifts Würzburg*, 37.

[17] Reuschling, *Die Regierung des Hochstifts Würzburg*, passim. For Brandenburg–Ansbach–Kulmbach see StAN, Ansbacher Historica, no. 340. See also Dieter Kerber, *Herrschaftsmittelpunkte im Erzstift Trier: Hof und Residenz im späten Mittelalter* (Sigmaringen, 1995), 369–420.

of their service.[18] That this post, too, was financially lucrative is thus beyond doubt.

The political power of noble councillors varied from one territory to another. Since they tended to represent themselves and fellow nobles as much as they did their prince, one factor determining the degree of their influence must have been their numerical strength relative to non-noble councillors. A number of German princely councils underwent a rapid process of 'de-nobilisation' in the late Middle Ages and early modern period. In Bavaria the ratio of noble councillors fell from 63.8 per cent in 1511–50 to 47.8 per cent in 1579–98. In Württemberg it declined from 31 per cent in 1520–50 to 15 per cent in 1550–68. But in Franconia, as only befitted a stronghold of the nobility, this process was resisted and retarded with greater success. In Würzburg in 1495–1519 the nobles predominated over the council with a ratio of approximately 87 per cent. In 1544–58 they still had a solid majority of 65.5 per cent.[19] Similar statistics are available neither for Bamberg nor for margravial Brandenburg. Yet a document listing margravial councillors between 1449 and 1528 makes it sufficiently clear that the council was as blue-blooded as that of Würzburg.[20] Moreover, in contrast to other principalities, the trend in the margraviate appears to have been the reverse. After the death of Margrave Albrecht Achilles in 1486 the noble element in the council grew ever more powerful.[21]

A dim light on the actual influence councillors had is shed by a letter sent to councillor Hans von Seckendorff-Aberdar by Prince Friedrich of Brandenburg, prior of the cathedral chapter of Würzburg.[22] Friedrich expressed concern about the erratic rule of his reigning brother Margrave Georg, which he described as 'April weather'. He attributed the latter's inconsistent decisions to the evil influence of two other councillors, the baron (*Freiherr*) of Schwarzenberg and the villainous commoner Georg Vogler. Nothing can be done against their will, he complained. It was not for nothing that Prince Friedrich sought in Seckendorff a counterpoise against the Schwarzenberg–Vogler faction. The career of this towering figure illustrates how predominant a councillor might become. In 1500 he received the spectacular privilege of a supreme penal court – otherwise the source of much contention between princes and noblemen – in his own territory

---

[18] Reuschling, *Die Regierung des Hochstifts Würzburg*, 37.

[19] Maximilian Lanzinner, *Fürst, Räte und Landstände: Die Entstehung der Zentralbehörden in Bayern 1511–1598* (Göttingen, 1980), 187–8; Irmgard Lange-Kothe, 'Zur Sozialgeschichte des fürstlichen Rates in Württemberg im 15. und 16. Jahrhundert', *VSWG* 34 (1941), 237–67; Reuschling, *Die Regierung des Hochstifts Würzburg*, 398–9.

[20] StAN, Ansbacher Historica, no. 340, fols. 68ʳ–73ᵛ.

[21] Reinhard Seyboth, *Die Markgraftümer Ansbach und Kulmbach unter der Regierung Markgraf Friedrichs des Älteren (1486–1515)* (Göttingen, 1985), 352–66.

[22] Johann Heinrich von Falckenstein (ed.), *Urkunden und Zeugnisse vom achten Seculo bis auf gegenwärtige Zeiten worinnen . . . das hochfürstl. Burggrafthum Nürnberg . . . betreffende hohe Vorrechte, Freiheiten, Begnadungen, Concessiones und desgleichen mehr enthalten . . .*, 2 vols. (Neustadt a.d. Aisch, 1789), II, 525–6, no. 427.

of Sugenheim.[23] In 1507 he was also nominated master of the household. Around these years hardly any major policy decision was taken without first sounding him out. One also suspects – despite an understandable *omertà* of the sources – that he helped to stage-manage the dethronement of Margrave Friedrich by his sons in 1515.[24]

Seckendorff was not splendidly alone; favourites of the kind of Don Alvaro de Luna in mid-fifteenth-century Castile or of the duke of Buckingham in seventeenth-century England did not exist in Germany around 1500. Some of his colleagues enjoyed comparable political clout, which likewise was amplified by their fulfilling other important functions simultaneously. Of twenty-eight margravial councillors between 1487 and 1528, twenty-one also occupied other offices; at least fourteen of these were district governors (*Amtleute*).[25] District governorships (*Ämter*) were the building-blocks of the late medieval and early modern German princely states.[26] The territory of Würzburg was composed of forty-four such governorships, that of Bamberg of fifty-four.[27] Their evolution everywhere took the same course: they emerged from complexes of princely seigneuries at the centre of which stood a castle which served as the governor's seat. Governorships were fundamentally jurisdictional and financial units of territorial lordship.[28] However, they were rarely fully consolidated. Neighbouring powers had rights in one another's district governorships, and the local nobility created enclaves as

---

[23] Ibid., 450, no. 383; Gerhard Rechter (ed.), *Die Archive der Grafen und Freiherren von Seckendorff: Die Unrkundenbestände der Schloßarchive Obernzenn, Sugenheim, Trautskirchen und Unternzenn*, 3 vols. (Munich, 1993), I, 242, no. 655.

[24] Seyboth, *Die Markgraftümer Ansbach und Kulmbach*, 360.

[25] StAN, Ansbacher Historica, no. 340, fols. 70ʳ–73ᵛ. Not all councillors who held other offices are mentioned in this document in their other capacities. For them cf. ibid. and H. Wilhelm, 'Die Edeln von und zum Absberg: Ein Beitrag zur fränkischen Geschichte,' *Alt-Gunzenhausen* 8 (1931), 3–197, at 119; Hans Hofner, 'Zur Geschichte des vogtländischen Adels: Die Herren von Feilitzsch auf Feilitzsch', *AO* 54 (1974), 257–317, at 284; Seyboth, *Die Markgraftümer Ansbach und Kulmbach*, 356 n. 73, 360 n. 90; Eberhard Freiherr von Eyb, *Das reichsritterliche Geschlecht der Freiherren von Eyb* (Neustadt a.d. Aisch, 1984), 160; Otto Freiherr von Waldenfels, *Die Freiherrn von Waldenfels: Stammfolgen mit urkundlichen Belegen*, 5 vols. (Munich, 1952–70), I, 258 and II, 37; Alban Freiherr von Dobeneck, 'Zur Geschichte des erloschenen Geschlechtes der Rabensteiner von Doehlau', *AO* 25, no. 3 (1914), 37–145, at 109; Frank Baron Freytag von Loringhoven, *Europäische Stammtafeln: Stammtafeln zur Geschichte der europäischen Staaten*, n.s., ed. Detlev Schwennicke (Marburg, 1980–), V, tables 104, 110.

[26] Ernst Schubert, *Fürstliche Herrschaft und Territorium im späten Mittelalter* (Munich, 1996), 14–19; Michel Hofmann, 'Die Außenbehörden des Hochstifts Bamberg und der Markgrafschaft Bayreuth', *JffL* 3 (1937), 52–96, at 61; Rolf Sprandel, 'Mittelalterliche Verfassungs- und Sozialgeschichte vom Blickpunkt einer Landschaft: Mainfranken', *ZHF* 7 (1980), 401–22, at 410.

[27] Lore Muehlon, 'Johann III. von Grumbach, Bischof von Würzburg und Herzog zu Franken (1455–1466)' (PhD thesis, University of Würzburg, 1935), 170; Wilhelm Schwemmer, *Burg und Amt Veldenstein-Neuhaus* (Nuremberg, 1961), 96.

[28] Rolf Sprandel, 'Die territorialen Ämter des Fürstentums Würzburg im Spätmittelalter,' *JffL* 37 (1977), 45–64, at 45–7; Wolfgang Leiser, 'Das hohenzollerische Amt Dachsbach/Aisch bis zum Forchheimer Rezeß 1538', *JffL* 34/35 (1974/75), 725–50, at 740; Inge-Maren Peters, 'Amt', in *Lexikon des Mittelalters*, Robert-Henri Bautier et al., vol. I (Munich, 1980), cols. 551–3.

well.[29] Hence district governorships were frequently at the cutting edge of princely territorial expansion.[30] Indeed, the eighteen border districts of the diocese of Bamberg enjoyed a special status and were run by a high governor (*Oberamtmann*).[31]

The governors represented the territorial prince in the country. Their executive purview was as a result extensive. Their duties ranged from policing the population, administering justice and enforcing princely economic policies, to performing various kinds of military service against the prince's internal and external enemies. That such a large portfolio could invite abuse of authority was not lost on the princes. As a proverb had it, 'the governorships are of God, the governors of the Devil'.[32] Princes therefore reserved to themselves the right to remove from office governors who did not comply with orders. Patents of appointment invariably express the princely will to monitor the governors closely and to narrow their scope for pursuing an independent course of action.[33] Clearly, the office of governor subjected its holder to strict control by the prince. One could not even travel to a spa without first being granted leave of absence.[34] Even more inconveniently, governors were automatically placed under the prince's exclusive jurisdiction.[35] Court officers were of course under equally obtrusive surveillance, if not more of it.[36] If, as is often argued, noblemen's mainstay of power was the autonomous exercise of lordship on their estates, then they must have had strong incentives not to limit themselves to it and to assume the burdens of office. As will become evident, it was not the high salaries that primarily induced nobles to enter into princely service. Nor was it the political prestige attached to state offices as such. The compelling motives lay deeper, in the very workings of the system of governance and its implications for noblemen's existence *qua* noblemen.

THE PLEDGE, CREDITORS AND GUARANTORS

The creation of centralised territorial states required, among other things, enormous amounts of capital which were beyond the independent means of the

---

[29] Schubert, *Fürstliche Herrschaft*, 17.
[30] Hofmann, 'Die Außenbehörden des Hochstifts Bamberg und der Markgrafschaft Bayreuth,' 64; Henry J. Cohn, *The Government of the Rhine Palatinate in the Fifteenth Century* (Oxford, 1965), 235–7; Regina Görner, *Raubritter: Untersuchungen zur Lage des spätmittelalterlichen Niederadels, besonders im südlichen Westfalen* (Münster in Westfalen, 1987), passim.
[31] Schwemmer, *Veldenstein-Neuhaus*, 96.
[32] Eduard Graf and Mathias Dietherr (eds.), *Deutsche Rechtssprichwörter* (Nördlingen, 1864), 516, no. 227.
[33] E.g. StAW, Stb, nos. 790–2.
[34] Felix Priebatsch (ed.), *Politische Correspondenz des Kurfürsten Albrecht Achilles*, vol. I (Leipzig, 1894), 335, no. 306.
[35] Carl August Hugo Burkhardt (ed.), *Das funfft merkisch Buech des Churfuersten Albrecht Achilles* (Jena, 1857), 124–5, no. 63; Rupprecht, *Ritterschaftliche Herrschaftswahrung in Franken*, 135, 307.
[36] Seyboth, *Die Markgraftümer Ansbach und Kulmbach*, 354.

Table 3.1. *Sample of debts (in gulden) of German princes, 1472–1559*

Prince	Date	Debt
Dukes of Saxony	1472	190,598
Counts Palatine	1476	500,000
Counts of Württemberg	1480	213,358
Bishops of Constance	1491	150,000
Dukes of Bavaria	1514	741,953
Margraves of Brandenburg	1515	233,514
Margraves of Brandenburg	1542	708,299
Landgraves of Hesse	1520–9	159,225
Landgraves of Hesse	1550–9	992,092

Sources: dukes of Saxony: Johannes Falke, 'Die Finanzwirthschaft im Kurfürstenthum Sachsen um das Jahr 1470', *Mittheilungen des Königlich Sächsischen Vereins für Erforschung und Erhaltung vaterländischer Geschichts- und Kunstdenkmale* 20 (1870), 78–106, at 102; Electors Palatine: Henry J. Cohn, *The Government of the Rhine Palatinate in the Fifteenth Century*, (Oxford, 1965), 116; counts of Württemberg: Fritz Ernst, *Eberhard im Bart: Die Politik eines deutschen Landesherrn am Ende des Mittelalters* (1933; reprint, Darmstadt, 1970), 74; bishops of Constance: Franz Keller, 'Die Verschuldung des Hochstifts Konstanz im 14. und 15. Jahrhundert', *Freiburger Diözesan-Archiv*, n.s., 3 (1902), 1–104, at 42; dukes of Bavaria: Helmut Rankl, *Staatshaushalt, Stände und 'Gemeiner Nutzen' in Bayern 1500–1516* (Munich, 1976), 64–5; margraves of Brandenburg: Uwe Müller, *Die ständische Vertretung in den fränkischen Markgraftümern in der ersten Hälfte des 16. Jahrhunderts* (Neustadt a.d. Aisch, 1984), 261; landgraves of Hesse: Kersten Krüger, *Finanzstaat Hessen 1500–1567: Staatsbildung im Übergang vom Domänenstaat zum Steuerstaat* (Marburg, 1980), 243.

princes. Indeed, what characterises all German rulers in the axial period between the fourteenth and sixteenth centuries is an insatiable craving for credit. And they were, as Table 3.1 displays, heavily indebted in this period.[37]

The enormous size of these debts becomes evident when one considers the revenues rulers regularly drew from their territories. The yearly income of the count of Württemberg between 1483 and 1486 ranged from 44,339 to 48,451 gulden. But at the same time he was borrowing between 25,000 and 35,200

---

[37] It is noteworthy that the German word used in this period to denote 'budget' was *stat*: Gerhard Oestreich, 'The Estates of Germany and the Formation of the State', in his *Neostoicism and the Early Modern State*, ed. Brigitta Oestreich and H. G. Koenigsberger, trans. David McLintock (Cambridge, 1982), 187–98, at 191. An earlier example than the one given by Oestreich (1520) is to be found in Julius von Minutoli (ed.), *Das kaiserliche Buch des Markgrafen Albrecht Achilles: Kurfürstliche Periode 1470–1486* (Bayreuth, 1850), 286, no. 236: 'Wir haben auch gekrigt und grossen korfurstlichen stat gehalten, das wir wol rechin wolten, ober sechs oder sibenmal hundert tausent gulden vorzert haben' (1470).

gulden annually.[38] The annual receipts of the proverbially rich duke of Bavaria from his domanial estates in 1511–13 came to approximately 132,200 gulden, in other words around 18 per cent of his debts in 1514.[39] The income of the margrave of Brandenburg between 1533 and 1539 was 75,755 gulden a year,[40] that is between 10.5 per cent and 13.3 per cent of his debts around the same time.

As a rule, most of the loans taken up by German princes were extended by noblemen. Of the 213,358-gulden debt of the counts of Württemberg, 176,250 gulden (or 82.6 per cent) were provided by the nobility. And out of a total of 131 creditors, 98 (or 74.8 per cent) were nobles, which means that the average loan of a noble was larger than that of a commoner or an ecclesiastic.[41] For the Rhine Palatinate, Henry J. Cohn has suggested that loans advanced by the nobility to the Electors made up a much larger proportion than the recorded 24.2 per cent.[42] A similar picture emerges from Peter-Michael Hahn's study of the nobility of electoral Brandenburg: 60 of the Elector's 103 creditors between 1507 and 1564 were nobles, and their loans were on average remarkably higher than those made by burghers.[43] The same pattern holds true for the rents due from the bishops of Speyer and the counts and (from 1495) dukes of Württemberg: compared with other social groups, both noblemen's absolute share in the payments and their average rent were the largest. The case of the house of Württemberg is particularly striking: more than 80 per cent of the rent obligations were toward nobles.[44]

With this recurring motif of princely debtors and noble creditors the theme is introduced of a particular historical phase in the development of the early modern state, of an idiosyncratic configuration of politics and economy.[45] The financial and administrative problems of the developing territorial state required flexible, extra-feudal solutions. They were found in the institution of the pledge (*Pfandschaft*). This institution was based on the claim raised by German princes since the fourteenth century to a free disposition of their regalian and other supreme rights. Its pervasiveness is a salient feature of the German late Middle

---

[38] Fritz Ernst, *Eberhard im Bart: Die Politik eines deutschen Landesherrn am Ende des Mittelalters* (1933; reprint Darmstadt, 1970), 71.

[39] Helmut Rankl, *Staatshaushalt, Stände und 'Gemeiner Nutzen' in Bayern 1500–1516* (Munich, 1976), 24–8. For the dukes' proverbial wealth see Reinhard Stauber, *Herzog Georg von Bayern-Landshut und seine Reichspolitik: Möglichkeiten und Grenzen reichsfürstlicher Politik im mittelbachisch-habsburgischen Spannungsfeld zwischen 1470 und 1505* (Kallmünz, 1993), 54–7.

[40] Computed according to Bernhard Sicken, 'Landesherrliche Einnahmen und Territorialstruktur: Die Fürstentümer Ansbach und Kulmbach zu Beginn der Neuzeit', *JffL* 42 (1982), 153–248, at 245, 247–8.

[41] Ernst, *Eberhard im Bart*, 75.   [42] Cohn, *Rhine Palatinate*, 163.

[43] Hahn, *Struktur und Funktion des brandenburgischen Adels*, 194.

[44] Kurt Andermann, 'Zu den Einkommensverhältnissen des Kraichgauer Adels an der Wende vom Mittelalter zur Neuzeit', in *Die Kraichgauer Ritterschaft in der frühen Neuzeit*, ed. Stefan Rhein (Sigmaringen, 1993), 65–121, at 103–8.

[45] Wolfgang Reinhard, 'Staatsmacht als Kreditproblem: Zur Struktur und Funktion des frühneuzeitlichen Ämterhandels', *VSWG* 61 (1974), 289–319.

Ages. Entire territories, district governorships and advocacies (*Vogteien*), towns and castles, market boroughs and villages, forests and vineyards, mines and mints, tolls, taxes, and tithes – all became in the late Middle Ages objects of pledge transactions.[46] In Hesse, for instance, around 600 pledges were granted by the landgraves in the fourteenth and fifteenth centuries.[47] For the diocese of Würzburg, the chronicler Lorenz Fries observed that around 1450 most of the episcopal towns and castles were pledged.[48] In 1463 all district governorships and jurisdictional rights of the Archbishopric of Cologne were pledged for the impressive sum of 600,000 gulden.[49]

In a pledge agreement the pledge-grantor turned over the pledge object to the recipient for a specified amount. According to an older school of legal history, the pledge object served as collateral for a debt corresponding to the pledge sum. The debt was paid when the pledge object was redeemed. This formulation was successfully challenged by Götz Landwehr, who demonstrated that, unlike the Roman *pignus*, the pledge was a discharge transaction: the conveyance of the pledge object itself, not its redemption, was payment for the debt.[50] By handing over a pledge to the creditor, the debtor was freed from his original liabilities toward the creditor; in return, the creditor forfeited his right to sue the debtor on a plea of debt for recovery of the amount due to him or her. A contractual lien replaced a pecuniary obligation. This new relationship gave the erstwhile debtor and now pledge-grantor the right to recover the pledge object eventually by reimbursing the grantee.[51] The juridical character of the pledge reflected its purposes and uses. For the grantor, the traffic in pledges subserved the commodification and mobilisation of lordship rights to meet his financial requirements. From the angle of the pledge receiver, the goal of the transaction was control over the pledge object.[52]

A distinction has to be made between rent pledges (*Rentenpfänder*) and pledge-lordships (*Pfandherrschaften*). The former, which made up a minority of all pledges, were exclusively a financial bargain, and frequently involved com-

---

[46] Götz Landwehr, 'Mobilisierung und Konsolidierung der Herrschaftsordnung im 14. Jahrhundert', in *Der deutsche Territorialstaat im 14. Jahrhundert*, ed. Hans Patze, 2 vols. (Sigmaringen, 1970–1), II, 484–505.

[47] Horst Bitsch, *Die Verpfändungen der Landgrafen von Hessen während des späten Mittelalters* (Göttingen, 1974), 52–4.

[48] Lorenz Fries, *Historie, Nahmen, Geschlecht, Wesen, Thaten, gantz Leben und Sterben des gewesenen Bischoffen zu Wirtzburg und Hertzogen zu Francken* [1544], in *Geschicht-Schreiber von dem Bischoffthum Wirtzbürg*, ed. Johann Peter Ludewig (Frankfurt am Main, 1713), 804.

[49] Georg Droege, 'Spätmittelalterliche Staatsfinanzen in Westdeutschland', in *Öffentliche Finanzen und privates Kapital im späten Mittelalter und in der ersten Hälfte des 19. Jahrhunderts*, ed. Hermann Kellenbenz (Stuttgart, 1971), 5–13, at 8.

[50] Götz Landwehr, *Die Verpfändung der deutschen Reichsstädte im Mittelalter* (Cologne, 1967), 373–87.

[51] Götz Landwehr, 'Die rechtshistorische Einordnung der Reichspfandschaften', in *Der deutsche Territorialstaat im 14. Jahrhundert*, I, 97–116, at 109–11.

[52] Hans-Georg Krause, 'Pfandherrschaften als verfassungsgeschichtliches Problem', parts 1 and 2, *Der Staat* 9 (1970), 387–404; 515–32, at 390.

moners.[53] The latter type entailed the transference or delegation of lordship rights originally held by the prince to the pledge receiver. It was these arrangements which were most attractive and crucial for noblemen.[54] They were of two basic kinds: (1) the so-called Older Statute (*Ältere Satzung*), according to which the pledge-holder enjoyed the usufruct from, and the plenipotentiary authority over, the pledge; and (2) the so-called Newer Statute (*Jüngere Satzung*), according to which the grantor retained full proprietary rights over the pledge. The second category of the pledge grew increasingly common during the fifteenth century. A prevalent form of this contract was pledge in office-wise (*in amtsweise*). Under the terms of such a contract the pledge remained within the territorial ambit ruled by the pledge-grantor, and the pledge-holder served simultaneously as an administrative official.[55]

The institution of the pledge in general and of the pledge *in amtsweise* in particular had some significant economic, administrative and political advantages for princes. First, it provided them with the possibility of either raising money or rewarding followers for services rendered or expected, without having to bear cash expenses. Secondly, and by the same token, it was a way of recruiting for local administration men trained to exercise leadership and military command in their own right. Thirdly, and an allied consideration, the pledge was an effective means of drawing local noblemen into closer association and identification with their territories. For example, the margraves of Brandenburg regularly pledged the governorships Hohenberg and Thierstein, which bordered on Bohemia, to the neighbouring von Schirnding family, drawing them in this way into their clientele.[56] At the same time, the pledge *in amtsweise* obviated the danger of complete alienation of princes' property and authority.

Indeed, as far as princes were concerned, noblemen were the most suitable pledge-holders: only they were sufficiently wealthy to hold a pledge without at the same time being sufficiently powerful to usurp it. No prince was willing, in normal circumstances, to pledge property to other princes or to imperial cities. Such independent political powers were sure to compromise the authority of the grantor over the pledge at best, and likely to appropriate it altogether at worst. Hence princes regularly made provisions for the sale of pledges by their holders to a third party, provided the latter was not a prince or a city.[57]

The benefits accruing to noble pledge-holders were also considerable. Receiving important pledge-lordships, especially district governorships, meant exercising such supreme rights as criminal justice, tax, toll, and Safe Conduct –

---

[53] Ibid.   [54] Marchal, *Sempach 1386*, 71–4.

[55] Markus Bittmann, *Kreditwirtschaft und Finanzierungsmethoden: Studien zu den Verhältnissen des Adels im westlichen Bodenseeraum* (Stuttgart, 1991), 116–23; Marchal, *Sempach 1386*, 80, 91.

[56] Rupprecht, *Ritterschaftliche Herrschaftswahrung in Franken*, 292.

[57] Marchal, *Sempach 1386*, 72 n. 56; Sprandel, 'Die territorialen Ämter des Fürstentums Würzburg,' 52; Kehrer, 'The von Sickingen', 70.

rights rarely held, or rarely held uncontestedly, by untitled noblemen. It brought a momentous increase in their authority. Significantly, many of these governors had their family estates in the very districts they headed.[58] This may have been one important criterion for nominating particular noblemen to the office. Presumably, governors' rule was more effective where they could, as local traditional lords, operate networks of patronage and fidelity. Another important consideration was possibly that they were in a good position to provide the prince with that precious commodity, information.[59] In any case, integrating the authority of governorship into his local lordship, and vice versa, was bound to consolidate a nobleman's power to a degree otherwise unattainable. The von Guttenberg family provide an illuminating example. For much of the fifteenth century they held in pledge three adjacent district governorships of the prince-bishop of Bamberg. Throughout this time the prince did not challenge the family's own supreme penal court. Their rights as governors and as feudal lords were apparently so interwoven as to render a distinction almost hopeless. Indeed, Georg von Guttenberg, the governor in Marktleugast, used this authority to have one of his own 'private' tenants executed there. Serious disputes over capital jurisdiction between the family and the bishop broke out only in 1486, when the latter redeemed his governorships.[60] Noblemen's enthusiasm for such blending of state and seigneurial authority was manifest in the efforts of margravial councillor Veit von Vestenberg to arrange for his nephew and namesake to become district governor of Fürstenforst in 1503. Both the attempt and its success are remarkable, since Fürstenforst was not previously a governorship; it was merely one of the family seats. The achievement meant artificially creating an administrative unit out of the family estates and its castle, and backing its lordship over its dependent peasants with state power.[61] It is upon this (con)fusion of the public domain and the private that the early modern state was built.[62]

The full impact of pledge-holding on noble families has been demonstrated by Harold Kehrer's superb work on the von Sickingen family. Pledges were the principal element in the family's economic and political vigour during the late Middle Ages. Up to 1523 the Sickingens held thirteen castles or fractions of castles in allodial tenure, and received a further sixteen castles or fractions in fief.

[58] Joseph Morsel, 'Une société politique en Franconie à la fin du Moyen Age: Les Thüngen, leurs princes, leurs pairs et leurs hommes (1275–1525)' (PhD thesis, University of Paris-IV Sorbonne, 1993), 831–2; Wilhelm Störmer, 'Der Adel im herzoglichen und kurfürstlichen Bayern der Neuzeit: Fragen der adeligen Grundherrschaft und Ständemacht', in *Adel im Wandel*, ed. Helmuth Feigl and Willibald Rosner (Vienna, 1991), 47–71, at 70.
[59] Heinz Quirin, 'Landesherrschaft und Adel im wettinischen Bereich während des späteren Mittelalters', in *Festschrift für Hermann Heimpel zum 70. Geburtstag am 19. September 1971*, vol. II (Göttingen, 1972), 80–109, at 97.
[60] Rupprecht, *Ritterschaftliche Herrschaftswahrung in Franken*, 255, 262–3.
[61] StAN, AA-Akten, no. 808, fol. 58.
[62] Robert R. Harding, *Anatomy of a Power Elite: The Provincial Governors of Early Modern France* (New Haven, 1978), 167.

On the other hand, they held forty-seven castles or fractions in pledge. And whereas they had no town as their allodial property, and only two as fiefs, they held twenty-one towns or fractions in pledge. These acquisitions were also what made the great difference between the prosperous main line of the family and the Hofwart line which was never able to secure a strong economic or political base.[63] The strength of the Sickingens lay in pledges, but it was inextricably linked to the development of the principalities in the middle and upper Rhine region. Their spectacularly extensive acquisitions were the consequence of close association with territorial princes. The same is true of a number of Franconian noble families. In the case of the von Bibra, one of the most prominent local lineages, pledges constituted some 40 per cent of their property in 1400.[64]

Yet the relations between noble office-bearers and princes were not of one-sided dependence of the former on the latter. There are many positive indications of the substantial power of noblemen relative to princes. The latter's right to relieve nobles of office was frequently an empty formula. If the prince was indeed capable of dismissing individual governors by redeeming pledges, he was scarcely in a position to buy out the entire noble officiary. The cash required to recover a particular pledge was often raised from another noble who might then be installed in office.[65] To be sure, Bishop Rudolf von Scherenberg of Würzburg's campaign of freeing pledges was an exceptional success – 'more to wonder at than to believe in'.[66] But – as one of his successors was to discover some fifty years later – the achievement was precarious.[67]

Moreover, a built-in contradiction was also at work: the higher the value of the pledge – which was in the prince's interest but against that of noblemen – the more difficult it was to redeem – which was in noblemen's interest but against that of the prince.[68] It is no surprise, therefore, that there are numerous instances of district governorships and other important pledges running in the same family

---

[63] Kehrer, 'The von Sickingen', 89–97.

[64] Morsel, 'Une société politique en Franconie', 1407 n. 55. Another example is the Voit von Salzburg family. Around 1400, pledges constituted 19 per cent of their property, declining to 8 per cent around 1450, and rising to 13 per cent around 1500: Günter Fäth, 'Der Grundbesitz der Voite von Salzburg im 14. und 15. Jahrhundert' (*Zulassungsarbeit*, University of Würzburg, 1976), 96–7.

[65] StAW, Stb, no. 1012, fols. 462ʳ, 499ᵛ; Franz Nikolaus Wolf, 'Geschichtliche Beschreibung der Burg Hohenburg ob der Werrn', *AU* 6, no. 2 (1840), 83–114, at 104; Otto Schnell, 'Geschichte der Salzburg an der fränkischen Saale: Mit besonderer Rücksicht auf die Zeit von der Uebergabe der Burg an Bischof Heinrich von Würzburg bis auf den heutigen Tag', *AU* 29 (1886), 1–128, at 36; Erich Freiherr von Guttenberg, *Das Bistum Bamberg*, part 1 (Berlin, 1937), 275; Paul Schlitzer, 'Die Herren von Lüder: Ein Beitrag zur Ortsgeschichte von Großlüder', *Fuldischer Geschichtsblätter* 36 (1960), 178–90, at 184.

[66] Sebastian Zeißner, *Rudolf II. von Scherenberg: Fürstbischof von Würzburg 1466–1495*, 2nd edn (Würzburg, 1952), 36–45. Citation from Wilhelm Engel (ed.), *Die Würzburger Bischofschronik des Grafen Wilhelm Werner von Zimmern und die Würzburger Geschichtsschreibung des 16. Jahrhunderts* (Würzburg, 1952), 127.

[67] See p. 65 below.

[68] For a striking example see Richard von Steinau-Steinrück, 'Abriß aus der Geschichte des fränkischen Geschlechtes von Steinau genannt Steinrück in bezug auf seine Zugehörigkeit zu dem

for generations.[69] In like manner, pledges occasionally served as stepping-stones to the definitive takeover of the objects in question, to their permanent alienation from the princely fisc.[70]

Another, derivative expression of the power of noble pledge-lords and district governors was their frequent abuse of their offices. With state power at hand, and the prospects of losing it in mind, many of them attempted to exploit the pledge and its subject population as much as possible. Complaints about the novelties introduced by pledge-holders and their oppressive rule are legion.[71] In 1457 the inhabitants of Schwarzach remonstrated with the bishop of Würzburg that they were being exploited by Lamprecht von Seckendorff, to whom the town had been pledged for 2000 gulden. Lamprecht resented the inhabitants going above his head and, to teach them a lesson, seized the town councillors who then had to buy their freedom.[72] More spectacular were the events of 1460 in the lordship of Hewen. The arbitrary and predatory rule of the counts of Lupfen as its pledge-holders led to a *Bundschuh*, or rural uprising, by the subjects of the pledge.[73] It was perhaps not a coincidence that the Peasants' War broke out in the counts' lordship of Stühlingen in 1524.[74] Another compelling case is that of Herbolzheim. In 1524 the inhabitants were so desperate as to suggest to the archbishop of

Hochstifte Würzburg und im besonderen auf seine Desitzungen daselbst', *AU* 49 (1907), 1–134, at 43. See also StAW, Stb, no. 790, fols. 65ᵛ–66ᵛ.

[69] StAW, Ldf, no. 13, pp. 81–2, 177–9; Steinau-Steinrück, 'Geschichte des fränkischen Geschlechtes von Steinau genannt Steinrück', 59; Gerd Wunder, 'Die Ritter von Vellberg', in *Vellberg in Geschichte und Gegenwart*, ed. Hansmartin Decker-Hauff, vol. I, *Darstellungen* (Sigmaringen, 1984), 129–96, at 167; Hans Körner, 'Die Familie von Hutten: Genealogie und Besitz bis zum Ende des Alten Reiches', in *Ulrich von Hutten: Ritter, Humanist, Publizist. Katalog zur Ausstellung des Landes Hessen anläßlich des 500. Geburtstages*, ed. Peter Laub (Kassel, 1988), 57–78, at 63; Zeißner, *Rudolf II. von Scherenberg*, 44; Kehrer, 'The von Sickingen', 75. See also Rolf Sprandel, 'Die Ritterschaft und das Hochstift Würzburg im Spätmittelalter', *JffL* 36 (1976), 117–43, at 138–43.

[70] Johann Adolph Schultes, *Diplomatische Geschichte des Gräflichen Hauses Henneberg*, 2 vols. (Hildburghausen, 1788–91), I, 361; Morsel, 'Une société politique en Franconie', 839; Rolf Köhn, 'Die Abrechnungen der Landvögte in den österreichischen Vorlanden um 1400. Mit einer Edition des *raitregisters* Friedrichs von Hattstatt für 1399–1404', *Blätter für deutsche Landesgeschichte* 128 (1992), 117–78, at 138; Hahn, *Struktur und Funktion des brandenburgischen Adels*, 223.

[71] Marchal, *Sempach 1386*, 92–8; Bittmann, *Kreditwirtschaft und Finanzierungsmethoden*, passim; Rankl, *Staatshaushalt, Stände und 'Gemeiner Nutzen'*, 69; Hermann Freiherr von Reitzenstein-Reuth, *Geschichte der Familie von Reitzenstein*, part 1, *Geschichte der Linie zu Wildenau* (Munich, 1882), 3–4, 11; Hanns Freiherr von Hessberg, 'Über die Truchsesse zu Wildberg', *MJfGK* 10 (1958), 42–69, at 52; Hermann Rebel, *Peasant Classes: The Bureaucratization of Property and Family Relations under Early Habsburg Absolutism 1511–1636* (Princeton, 1983), 3; Georges Bischoff, 'Les grèves anti-seigneuriales de Ferrette: Les habitants d'un baillage du Sundgau et leur seigneur au début du xviᵉ siècle', *Revue d'Alsace* 105 (1979), 35–52. I am grateful to Dr Tom Scott for kindly making the last reference available to me.

[72] Fries, *Historie*, 814–15.

[73] Rolf Köhn, 'Der Hegauer Bundschuh (Oktober 1460) – ein Aufstandsversuch in der Herrschaft Hewen gegen die Grafen von Lupfen', *ZGO* 138 (1990), 99–141.

[74] This view was expressed some forty years after the event by Count Froben Christoph of Zimmern: Hansmartin Decker-Hauff (ed.), *Die Chronik der Grafen von Zimmern*, vol. II (Sigmaringen, 1967), 268.

Table 3.2. *Creditors of the margraves of Brandenburg in 1529*

	Noble	%	Non-noble	%	Total	%
Creditors	116	72.5	44	27.5	160	100.0
Total amount						
loaned (in gulden)	303,975	83.8	58,825	16.2	362,800	100.0
Average loan	2,620.5	115.5	1,336.9	59.0	2,267.5	100.0

Source: Müller, *Die ständische Vertretung*, 238.

Mainz, the pledge-grantor, that they finance the repossession of the pledge in order to rid themselves of its holder, Philipp von Sickingen.[75] Here too, the date cannot have been a mere accident. The implication of these examples is that until the pledge was finally regained, there was little the prince could do to restrain Verres-like governors. It is an intriguing question to what degree the system of pledges, with its concomitant intensification of lordship and exploitation, was responsible for the Peasants' War.[76] In any case, one should not repeat the mistake of Archbishop Ruprecht of Cologne, who failed to appreciate the power of his district governors and pledge-holders: in 1463, having tried to remove his noble creditors from their offices without indemnifying them for their losses, he was forced to resign.[77] Indeed, so ubiquitous was the pledge and so strong the position of the pledge-holders that one historian suggested characterising the late Middle Ages in Germany as the age of pledge-holding following that of feudalism.[78]

The strength of pledge-holders' position in general, and of district governors in particular, both in absolute terms and relative to the prince, is well reflected in the structure of the debts of the Franconian margraves of Brandenburg. As Uwe Müller has shown (see Table 3.2), noblemen predominated among the margraves' creditors. He has further stressed two points: the first concerns the proportional contribution of the district governors to the loans taken up by the margraves. Of the 116 noble creditors, 19 were district governors, that is 16.4 per cent of the noble creditors and 11.9 per cent of all creditors. The loans they extended, however, made up 26.2 per cent of the sum lent by the nobility and 22 per cent of the total amount. The average loan of district governors was as high as 4,200

[75] Kehrer, 'The von Sickingen', 75.
[76] See ibid., 77. Rudolf Endres, 'Franken,' in *Der deutsche Bauernkrieg*, ed. Horst Buszello, Peter Blickle, and Rudolf Endres (Paderborn, 1984), 134–53, has emphasised the development of the state as the decisive factor in the Peasants' War in Franconia, but overlooked the problem of pledges.
[77] Görner, *Raubritter*, 69.
[78] Krause, 'Pfandherrschaften als verfassungsgeschichtliches Problem', 515–16, 532. See also Landwehr, 'Einordnung der Reichspfandschaften', 116.

gulden.[79] Some of them advanced loans of extraordinary size: Moritz Marschall von Ostheim lent the margraves 10,000 gulden, and Konrad Schott lent 11,000;[80] Wolf von Crailsheim's 14,000-gulden loan came close to the 15,600 gulden drawn yearly from taxes in the two Franconian margraviates of Ansbach and Kulmbach taken together.[81] The second point made by Müller is that only three of the nineteen noble creditors who held high office did not stipulate that their loans were subject to recall. It is likely that this proviso was used as an instrument of 'credit politics' designed to put pressure on the prince. Indeed, Margrave Georg expressed himself to this very effect. For his part, he warned that if his request for financial aid were to be turned down, 'it is to be feared that His Princely Grace would take charge of the governorships and man them with valets (*Knechte*), so that he would have more than 8000 gulden a year, which would otherwise go to the nobility'. But the threat failed to bring the nobility round to the prince's position. As the margravial lieutenants (*Statthalter*) reported, some noblemen were prepared to lend him money only in return for district governorships or other gainful pledges such as towns.[82] A combination of wealth and the political use to which it was put is thus rather evident in the case of this group.

Müller's illuminating analysis is, however, incomplete. He considered only those district governors who served the margraves during – and to some extent also between – the two years in which the lists of creditors he examined were composed, 1529 and 1539. Yet many of the noble creditors served as margravial district governors intermittently and happened not to officiate in these particular years. Others occupied equally high offices at the court. Still other noble creditors of the margraves were district governors and high officials in the service of other princes in and around this period. As a result, quite a few noblemen who were actually incumbents of high offices are not so designated in these lists. And even this fact does not fully indicate these noblemen's economic situation, since extending loans was not the only financial service they performed for the margraves.

A more realistic picture emerges from a register of the loans taken up by the margraves of Brandenburg mainly in the 1520s and 1530s.[83] The creditors enumerated in this document are, with few exceptions, those recorded in the

---

[79] Uwe Müller, *Die ständische Vertretung in den fränkischen Markgraftümern in der ersten Hälfte des 16. Jahrhunderts* (Neustadt a.d. Aisch, 1984), 240–1.

[80] StAN, AA-Akten, no. 1402, fols. 79ʳ, 106ʳ–107ʳ; ibid., Fstm.Ansb., Brandenburger Literalien, no. 582.

[81] Cf. StAN, Landtagsakten, Tom. 8, no. 36, fol. 148ʳ and Sicken, 'Landesherrliche Einnahmen und Territorialstruktur', 245.

[82] Müller, *Die ständische Vertretung*, 224, 240–1, 243–4.

[83] StAN, AA-Akten, no. 1402. Complementary sources are StAB, Hofrat Ansbach-Bayreuth, nos. 95, 166ⁱ; Günther Schuhmann (ed.), *Stadtarchiv Ansbach* (Munich, 1956). Not all creditors and guarantors who were office-holders are named as such. Biographical data for all creditors and guarantors were culled from other sources. Not included here is the small number of women creditors.

Table 3.3. *Noble creditors and guarantors of the margraves of Brandenburg*
(mainly 1520s and 1530s)

Function	No.	%
(1) Creditors only	29	15.4
(2) Guarantors only	35	18.6
(3) Creditors/guarantors	5	2.7
(4) Creditors/officials	33	17.5
(5) Guarantors/officials	53	28.2
(6) Creditors/guarantors/officials	33	17.5
Total	188	99.9

Source: Appendix A.

deeds of the Provincial Diet (*Landtagsakten*) analysed by Müller.[84] An important variation, however, is that this register, by specifying the formalities of the transactions, also names the guarantors. It thus complements the *Landtagsakten* in two important ways: first, it reveals the multiplicity of, and the relation between, functions noblemen performed for the margraves; secondly, by recording the guarantors, it provides what is probably a nearly complete roster of 188 noblemen who financially backed the princes during these decades. Table 3.3 demonstrates the various combinations between services rendered by noblemen as creditors and as guarantors, and their relation to office-holding. It classifies the 188 noblemen into 6 mutually exclusive groups.

Of the 100 creditors (rows 1, 3, 4 and 6), 66 were high officials (rows 4 and 6). This is a remarkably high proportion, especially in comparison with Müller's finding that district governors made up 16.4 per cent of the noble creditors of the margraves. The ratio of high office-holders among the guarantors is almost the same: 86 out of 126 (68.2 per cent; rows 5 and 6). Guarantors must also have been financially viable, since standing surety was not a mere formality: it was an obligation that entailed serious risks and the economic situation of guarantors was taken into account. In 1521 the guarantor Konrad von Rosenberg was replaced by another nobleman because 'his circumstances at present are such that if it came to unpaid debts [he] would not be able to guarantee'.[85] In 1543 Hans Christoph von Eyb was replaced because 'his wits have become damaged'.[86] And when guarantors died, both the prince and his noble creditors took pains to name new

---

[84] Müller, *Die ständische Vertretung*, 333–51.

[85] StAN, AA-Akten, no. 1402, fol. 29ᵛ. However, in 1535 he became district governor in the diocese of Würzburg: StAW, Stb, no. 792, fols. 21ʳ–22ᵛ.

[86] StAN, AA-Akten, no. 1402, fol. 264ʳ.

ones.[87] Lastly, the total of 119 high officials constitutes an impressive 63.3 per cent of the 188 creditors and/or guarantors (rows 4, 5, and 6). The economic potency of this group is conspicuous.

The sixty-nine nobles who were not high officials (rows 1, 2, and 3) make an interesting case: twenty-nine functioned only as creditors, thirty-five only as guarantors. Only five nobles who both lent money to and stood surety for the margraves were not officials (row 3). On the other hand, the number of those creditors-cum-guarantors who did hold office was thirty-three (row 6), that is, more than six times higher. In other words, the odds that a nobleman who was both creditor and guarantor would also be a high office-holder were nearly 9:10. Clearly, ability to support the princes financially and political prominence were inextricably intertwined.

That quite a few nobles had such large sums of money at their disposal is striking, particularly given the prevalent historiographical view of an impecunious nobility. Underlying this view is the theory of an agrarian crisis in the late Middle Ages. According to the causal chain forged by Wilhelm Abel, the onslaught of a general demographic decline in the early fourteenth century resulted in slumping prices of farm produce and feudal rents. On the other hand, no comparable fall in the prices of manufactured goods occurred. The outcome was a 'price scissors'. The nobility, the argument goes, was a main casualty of these developments, since rent revenues formed the basis of their sustenance.[88] Moreover, an aggravating factor was that the feudal rent payments due from peasants had become nominally fixed and therefore prey to monetary devaluations and inflationary tendencies.[89] As a consequence, seigneurial incomes dwindled.[90] For the same reason, nobles could not profit from periodically favourable market opportunities.[91] Hence the nobility fell into poverty.[92] Abel himself drew the ultimate

---

[87] Ibid., passim; Schuhmann (ed.), *Stadtarchiv Ansbach*, 11, U 36; 12, U 39; 13, U 44; 14, U 47–8.

[88] Wilhelm Abel, *Geschichte der deutschen Landwirtschaft vom frühen Mittelalter bis zum 19. Jahrhundert*, 2nd edn (Stuttgart, 1967), 128–42. For a discussion of Abel's theory see Peter Kriedte, 'Spätmittelalterliche Agrarkrise oder Krise des Feudalismus?' *Geschichte und Gesellschaft* 7 (1981), 42–68.

[89] Wilhelm Abel, *Agricultural Fluctuations in Europe: From the Thirteenth to the Twentieth Centuries*, trans. Olive Ordish (London, 1980), 36; Werner Rösener, *Agrarwirtschaft, Agrarverfassung und ländliche Gesellschaft im Mittelalter* (Munich, 1992), 106–7.

[90] Hans-Peter Sattler, 'Die Ritterschaft der Ortenau in der spätmittelalterlichen Wirtschaftskrise', parts 1–4, *Die Ortenau* 42 (1962), 220–58; 44 (1964), 22–39; 45 (1965), 32–57; 46 (1966), 32–58; Werner Rösener, 'Zur Problematik des spätmittelalterlichen Raubrittertums', in *Festschrift für Berent Schwineköper zu seinem siebzigsten Geburtstag*, ed. Helmut Maurer and Hans Patze (Sigmaringen, 1982), 469–88, at 482–4; Peter Blickle, *Die Revolution von 1525*, 2nd edn (Munich, 1981), 46, 113; Rolf Köhn, 'Einkommensquellen des Adels im ausgehenden Mittelalter, illustriert an südwestdeutschen Beispielen', *Schriften des Vereins für Geschichte des Bodensees und seiner Umgebung* 103 (1985), 33–62, at 36.

[91] Hans-Jürgen Goertz, *Pfaffenhaß und groß Geschrei: Die reformatorischen Bewegungen in Deutschland 1517–1529* (Munich, 1987), 35.

[92] This view is to be found in virtually all text-books as well as in many monographs. The most important work on the alleged economic crisis of the Franconian nobility is by Rudolf Endres,

conclusion: those noblemen who failed to secure employment in princely service – the implicit assumption being that this was a mere outlet – took to feuds – the explicit assumption being that feuders were poor noblemen.[93]

A serious weakness of these arguments is that they are theoretical inferences from a model constructed largely on the basis of data collected from other sections of medieval society and economy.[94] When applied to the nobility, the model is often inconsistent with the facts. The works of Kurt Andermann on the nobility of south-western Germany have demonstrated that the structure of nobles' income was different from what had been assumed. Rents due from peasants were predominantly in kind and not in cash.[95] The nobles he describes might commute for cash payments insignificant articles such as poultry, eggs, oil and the like, but seldom, if at all, valuable produce such as grains and wine. The same pattern emerges from researches into various Franconian lordships.[96] Indeed, in some cases noble lords increased rather than reduced their demands for rents in kind.[97] Moreover, the 'agrarian crisis' model does not take into account one important sector of the nobles' economic regime: those parts of the lordship, usually in the immediate vicinity of its centre, which were not leased out but administered by the lords themselves. The proceeds of the Schenk von Schenkenstein family from managing estates on their own made up between 19 per cent and 25.5 per cent of their total income around the middle of the fifteenth

'Adelige Lebensformen in Franken zur Zeit des Bauernkrieges', *Neujahrsblätter der Gesellschaft für fränkische Geschichte* 35 (1974), 5–43. See also Hanns Hubert Hofmann, 'Der Adel in Franken', in *Deutscher Adel 1430–1555*, ed. Hellmuth Rößler (Darmstadt, 1965), 95–126. For a critical discussion of the 'Crisis of the aristocracy' literature see Joseph Morsel, 'Crise? Quelle crise? Remarques à propos de la prétendue crise de la noblesse allemande à la fin du Moyen Age', *Sources. Travaux historiques* 14 (1988), 17–42.

93 Wilhelm Abel, *Strukturen und Krisen der spätmittelalterlichen Wirtschaft* (Stuttgart, 1980), 10; Abel, *Geschichte der deutschen Landwirtschaft*, 140. See also Rösener, *Agrarwirtschaft, Agrarverfassung und ländliche Gesellschaft*, 108; Rudolf Endres, *Adel in der Frühen Neuzeit* (Munich, 1993), 9.

94 For other weaknesses see the devastating general criticism by Ernst Schubert, *Einführung in die Grundprobleme der deutschen Geschichte im Spätmittelalter* (Darmstadt, 1992), 5–9.

95 Kurt Andermann, 'Grundherrschaften des spätmittelalterlichen Niederadels in Südwestdeutschland: Zur Frage der Gewichtung von Geld- und Naturaleinkünften', *Blätter für deutsche Landesgeschichte* 127 (1991), 145–90; Andermann, 'Einkommensverhältnissen des Kraichgauer Adels', 74–86. Some of the families whose archives Andermann studied were Franconian. See also Willi A. Boelcke, 'Die Einkünfte Lausitzer Adelsherrschaften in Mittelalter und Neuzeit', in *Wirtschaft, Geschichte und Wirtschaftsgeschichte: Festschrift zum 65. Geburtstag von Friedrich Lütge*, ed. Wilhelm Abel et al. (Stuttgart, 1966), 183–205, at 193 n. 33.

96 Rainer Braun, *Das Benediktinerkloster Michelsberg, 1015–1525: Eine Untersuchung zur Gründung, Rechtsstellung und Wirtschaftsgeschichte*, vol. I (Kulmbach, 1978), 282–8; Klaus Arnold, *Niklashausen 1476: Quellen und Untersuchungen zur sozialreligiösen Bewegung des Hans Behem und zur Agrarstruktur eines spätmittelalterlichen Dorfes* (Baden-Baden, 1980), 161, 175; Walter Scherzer, 'Siedlungs- und Wüstungsbewegung, Bevölkerungsfluktuation und Inforestierung im Bereich des Guttenberger und Irtenberger Forstes', in Helmut Jäger and Walter Scherzer, *Territorienbildung, Forsthoheit und Wüstungsbewegung im Waldgebiet westlich von Würzburg* (Würzburg, 1984), 80–235, at 204, 212–13, 222; Richard Schmitt, *Frankenberg: Besitz- und Wirtschaftsgeschichte einer reichsritterschaftlichen Herrschaft in Franken, 1528–1806 (1848)* (Ansbach, 1986), 173, 175, 381–2.

97 Scherzer, 'Siedlungs- und Wüstungsbewegung', 213.

century.[98] And around 1530 the Frankenberg line of the von Hutten family derived more than one third of their annual grain yield from their demesne lands. Using also the rents delivered in this kind by the tenants, their revenues from the sale of grains between 1528 and 1550 reached the impressive yearly average of 860 gulden. This constituted more than half of their total income of 1,649 gulden. Their takings from rents in cash, on the other hand, amounted to 209 gulden annually (12.5 per cent).[99] Another example is provided by the Fuchs von Bimbach family. In 1572–3 their income from one of their manors was slightly over 3,000 gulden. But whereas rents in cash brought in approximately 280 gulden, the sale of grains yielded 970 gulden, wine 864, oats 177.5, sheep 166, fish 117, wool 103, and oxen 67.[100] As this evidence suggests, some nobles were in a position to become active in the market economy by selling surplus. Precisely this possibility must have been one of the factors which made office-holding crucial for noblemen.

The solidifaction of peasant communal organisation in the late Middle Ages must have made the extraction by seigneurs of surplus value an ever more difficult task. As Peter Blickle has pointed out, there were no peasant revolts prior to the formation of peasant communities, and very many afterward. 'With the help of the communal organisation – and only in this way – did peasants and the burghers learn to say no, to protest, to question the demands of lordship and the claims of the authorities.'[101] As a result, a wide discrepancy could develop between what the lords declared and recorded as their due and what they actually got.[102] Particularly vulnerable to this eventuality were monastic lordships.[103] Their ability to enforce their rights was for obvious reasons limited. On the other hand, those lords who disposed of means of coercion other than seigneurial had better prospects than otherwise of succeeding in carrying through their claims.[104] The regalian and other superior rights exercised by pledge-holders and high

---

[98] Gerhard Rechter, 'Das Verhältnis der Reichsstädte Windsheim und Rothenburg ob der Tauber zum niederen Adel ihrer Umgebung im Spätmittelalter', *JffL* 41 (1981), 45–87, at 56.

[99] Schmitt, *Frankenberg*, 248, 256–7, 311–13.

[100] FA, Schrank 5, Rechnung Georgen Pfannenstils vogts zu Binbach [*sic*] alles seines Einnemens, unnd auss gebens, ann Geldt und Getreidt und allen andern des Ritterguts Binbach Gefellen, und Ein kommens, von Petri Cathedra im 1572 Biss wider uff Petri des 1573 Jars.

[101] Peter Blickle, *Communal Reformation: The Quest for Salvation in Sixteenth-Century Germany*, trans. Thomas Dunlap (New Jersey, 1992), 169–70. See also Schubert, *Einführung in die Grundprobleme der deutschen Geschichte*, 82–96.

[102] Andermann, 'Grundherrschaften des spätmittelalterlichen Niederadels', 153–4; Friedhelm Langendörfer, 'Die Landschaden von Steinach: Zur Geschichte einer Familie des niederen Adels im Mittelalter und der frühen Neuzeit' (PhD thesis, University of Heidelberg, 1971), 92.

[103] Braun, *Das Benediktinerkloster Michelsberg*, 233–9; Kurt Andermann, 'Klösterliche Grundherrschaft und niederadelige Herrschaftsbildung: Das Beispiel Amorbach', in *Siedlungsentwicklung und Herrschaftsbildung im Hinteren Odenwald*, ed. Hermann Ehmer (Buchen, 1988), 29–50, at 47.

[104] Roger Sablonier, *Adel im Wandel: Eine Untersuchung zur sozialen Situation des ostschweizerischen Adels um 1300* (Göttingen, 1979), 240, 254–5; Rolf Sprandel, 'Review of *Die Grundherrschaft im späten Mittelalter*, 2 vols. (Sigmaringen, 1983), ed. Hans Patze', *Göttingische Gelehrte Anzeigen* 235 (1983), 315–21, at 321.

officials, the 'state power' they wielded, could be harnessed by them in their seigneurial capacity to the ruthless collection of rents, dues and tithes. Not unrelated is the fact that the centres of many district governorships in Franconia and elsewhere were market towns of local or even regional importance. Farm produce obtained from peasants could be easily sold by district governors in the towns under their 'protection'. And the same applies to their salaries, which were often paid, wholly or partly, in kind.[105] It is significant in this regard that noble pledge-holders also proved able to intensify forced labour by flying in the face of both custom and the contracts they signed themselves.[106] Another possible economic benefit for district governors was their control of the large tithe granaries of the prince. This may have enabled them to store large quantities of grain and to profiteer in times of poor harvests.[107] Thus, the superior quality of the rights associated with offices and pledges gave their holders access to sources of wealth which were unavailable to simple seigneurs.[108] From this to economic viability it was presumably only a short step.

The evidence for Franconia, albeit impressionistic, confirms this assumption. Much of it relates to sheep-farming. The business prosperity of the local cloth industry was a strong stimulant for nobles to take particular interest in this branch of the economy.[109] There can hardly be a clearer testimony to the relentless concern of nobles with sheep-farming than the numerous conflicts to which it gave rise.[110] Other, related manifestations are the acreage occupied by sheep-runs and the size of flocks owned by noblemen.[111] Philipp von Guttenberg, for example, had at least 800 sheep. During a dispute over jurisdiction they were

---

[105] Reuschling, *Die Regierung des Hochstifts Würzburg*, 45; Zeißner, 'Zwei Mitarbeiter', 134.

[106] Schmitt, *Frankenberg*, 189–90, 193; Köhn, 'Der Hegauer Bundschuh'; Kehrer, 'The von Sickingen', 214.

[107] Rudolf Endres, 'Die wirtschaftlichen Grundlagen des niederen Adels in der frühen Neuzeit', *JffL* 36 (1976), 215–37, at 220; Rupprecht, *Ritterschaftliche Herrschaftswahrung in Franken*, 215.

[108] For the greater profitability of these rights in comparison with simple feudal rents see Wilhelm Störmer, 'Grundherrschaften des höheren und niederen Adels im Main-Tauber-Raum,' in *Die Grundherrschaft im späten Mittelalter*, ed. Hans Patze, vol. II (Sigmaringen, 1983), 25–45, at 36–7; Walter Scherzer, 'Das Henneberger Schloss und Amt Mainberg bei Schweinfurt (bis 1542)', in *Thüringische Forschungen: Festschrift für Hans Eberhardt zum 85. Geburtstag am 25. September 1993*, ed. Michael Gockel and Volker Wahl (Cologne, 1993), 111–29, at 126–7; Herbert Knittler, 'Zur Einkommensstruktur niederösterreicher Adelsherrschaften 1550–1750', in *Adel in der Frühneuzeit: Ein regionaler Vergleich*, ed. Rudolf Endres (Cologne, 1991), 99–118, at 106.

[109] Endres, 'Die wirtschaftlichen Grundlagen des niederen Adels', 221; Rudolf Endres, 'Der Bauernkrieg in Franken', *Blätter für deutsche Landesgeschichte* 109 (1973), 31–68, at 40. The most important trade in Bayreuth was weaving: Karl Heinrich Lang, *Neuere Geschichte des Fürstenthums Baireuth*, part 1, *Vom Jahr 1486 bis zum Jahr 1527* (Göttingen, 1798), 57.

[110] For a few examples see StAN, Bb, no. 120, fols. 27^{r-v}; no. 134, fols. 94^r–95^v; ibid., Ansbacher Historica, no. 210, passim; ibid., Fstm.Ansb., Verträge mit dem Adel, Truchsesse von Baldersheim, no. 1; StAW, Stb, no. 892, fol. 99^v; no. 1012, fols. 515^v–516^r; FA, Schrank 3, prod. of Samstag nach Pfingsten [25 May] 1521; Gerhard Rechter (ed.), *Die Archive der Grafen und Freiherren von Seckendorff*, passim. See also Rupprecht, *Ritterschaftliche Herrschaftswahrung in Franken*, 191.

[111] Winfried Wackerfuß, *Kultur-, Wirtschafts- und Sozialgeschichte des Odenwaldes im 15. Jahrhundert:*

confiscated by Margrave Friedrich, who went on to have some of them sold. Thanks to the intercession of Duke Georg of Bavaria, whose district governor he was, Philipp was permitted to fetch the remaining head. If the reports of the margrave's proxy in waging the feud, the local governor Konrad von Wirsberg, are anything to go by, then the heated confrontation had done nothing to break Philipp's calculating spirit: as he was slow to recover his sheep, Wirsberg remarked that Philipp wanted to let the margrave carry the expenses of fodder for a little longer.[112]

There are also indications that noblemen were encroaching on common land.[113] One of the flashpoints in the 1494 feud between Christoph von Giech, a margravial servitor,[114] and the bishop of Bamberg was a sheep-run. The bishop maintained that Christoph's mother was farming sheep on lands to which she had no legal claim. This threatened to lay waste a number of villages, for the peasants were prevented from grazing their cattle. The bishop was anxious about the direct economic loss he himself might suffer from an eviction of tribute-raising peasants.[115] In 1509 the bishop had another feud for a similar reason with councillor Eukarius von Aufseß.[116]

It is notable that the evidence for noblemen's sheep-farming comes mostly from district governors, pledge-holders, and other princely servitors.[117] This would seem to support the assumption that office-holding opened up opportunities for some market-oriented activities and for economic success in general. Unfortunately, the sources divulge nothing beyond the existence of this conjunction. The degree to which the capital required for these activities was the cause or the effect of office-holding must ultimately remain an open question.[118]

Die ältesten Rechnungen für die Grafen von Wertheim in der Herrschaft Breuberg (1409–1484) (Breuberg-Neustadt, 1991), 375–82; Schmitt, *Frankenberg*, 224–5.

[112] StAN, AA-Akten, no. 1831.

[113] StAN, AA-Akten, no. 132/1, prod. of Donnerstag nach Lauerntii [11 August] 1496 and prod. of 1496 [n.d.]; Veit Leo von Seckendorff-Gutend, *Quellenbände [zur seckendorffischen Familiengeschichte]*, vol. IV, 2741 (private papers of the family). See also Minutoli (ed.), *Das kaiserliche Buch des Markgrafen Albrecht Achilles*, 477–9, no. 354.

[114] 'Urkunden und Aktenprodukte im Königlichen Archive zu Nürnberg das Hochgräfliche Geschlecht Giech betreffend', *Jb.Mfr.* 9 (1839), 99–106, at 102.

[115] 'wan sein mutter hat furgenomen auss Bucha einen schafftribe uff etlich dorffer auch unser grunt und poden zu unserm Ambt und Casten weismein gehorend, dahin sie kein gerechtikeit hat noch ire gestanden wurdt in solicher massen zwuben woe ir des stat geben und zugeseen, so wurdt dadurch mere dan eins solicher unser dorffer und gutter verodigt und verwust vermochten die armen leutt irs vihs nit zuweiden oder zuerneren und daraus uns unser ziens und gerechtikeit nit zu geben oder zureichen': StAB, Hofrat Ansbach-Bayreuth, no. 545, prod. 6.

[116] Otto Freiherr von Aufseß, *Geschichte des uradelichen Aufseß'schen Geschlechtes in Franken* (Berlin, 1888), 187–8.

[117] It has been observed also for Austria that what characterised those entrepreneurial noble families involved in pisciculture was that they occupied influential offices and engaged in pledge and other financial transactions: Herbert Knittler, 'Adel und landwirtschaftliches Unternehmen im 16. und 17. Jahrhundert', in *Adel im Wandel: Politik, Kultur, Konfession 1500–1700*, ed. Herbert Knittler, Gottfried Stangler, and Renate Zedlinger (Vienna, 1990), 45–55, at 46, 49–50.

[118] Cf. Rupprecht, *Ritterschaftliche Herrschaftswahrung in Franken*, 214, 224, 226.

Yet it is sufficiently clear that the conclusions drawn from the model of an agrarian crisis are not readily applicable to the late medieval and early modern German nobility *en bloc*. Registers of debts left by nobles show that the most active creditor of the nobility was the nobility itself.[119] And large-scale financial and property transactions involving nobles demonstrate that it was principally nobles who stood to profit from the financial problems of fellow nobles.[120] Konrad von Lentersheim, for instance, bought in 1430 castle Altenmuhr from the twelve noble creditors of Georg von Buttendorf for 4,000 gulden.[121] Another, particularly telling example is provided by the von Absberg family. During the second half of the fifteenth century they were enjoying economic prosperity. Dr Georg von Absberg, an eminent margravial councillor, district governor and master of the household, bought castle Hallerndorf for 6000 gulden.[122] His brother Hans, a margravial governor, purchased three fourths of castle and lordship Vorderfrankenberg from the perhaps financially troubled von Heßberg for 9480 gulden.[123] However, in the early sixteenth century the Absbergs found themselves in dire economic straits. Hans's son, Hans Georg, also a margravial governor, owed 24,584 gulden to different creditors. When the margraves stepped in and took it upon themselves to sort out his finances, a list of all his creditors was drawn up. Apart from 2000 gulden lent to him by the margraves themselves, Hans Georg owed at least 15,088 gulden to fellow nobles,[124] including 5000 gulden to his son Hans Christoph. The Absbergs had to sell Vorderfrankenberg. The buyers were three members of the von Hutten family, who paid the proud

---

[119] Eighty-three per cent of Anstand von Seckendorff's 20,000-gulden debt (1537): Gerhard Rechter, *Die Seckendorff: Quellen und Studien zur Genealogie und Besitzgeschichte*, 2 vols. (Neustadt a.d. Aisch, 1987–90), I, 210–11; 79.5 per cent of Hans Dietrich Fuchs von Bimbach's 2925-gulden debt (1577): FA, Schrank 1, Füchsische vormundschaftliche Acta, fols. 127–9; 95 per cent of Georg Fuchs von Bimbach's 62,280-gulden debt (*c.* 1590): FA, unnumbered bookshelf (unnumbered file). Also revealing in this regard are the account-books of those noblemen who acted as 'professional' moneylenders: StAN, Reichsgrafschaft Geyer, Akten, no. 49; Joseph Albrecht (ed.), *Conrads von Weinsberg, des Reichs-Erbkämmerers, Einnahmen- und Ausgaben-Register von 1437 und 1438* (Stuttgart, 1850); Alfred Wendehorst and Gerhard Rechter, 'Ein Geldverleiher im spätmittelalterlichen Franken: Philipp von Seckendorff-Gutend', in *Hochfinanz, Wirtschaftsräume, Innovationen: Festschrift für Wolfgang von Stromer*, ed. Uwe Bestmann, Franz Irsigler, and Jürgen Schneider, 3 vols. (Trier, 1987), I, 487–529; Schmitt, *Frankenberg*, 386 n. 1.

[120] The same is probably true also of small-scale transactions: Morsel, 'Une société politique en Franconie', 866–70; Hans-Peter Baum, 'Der Lehenhof des Hochstifts Würzburg im Spätmittelalter (1303–1519): Eine rechts- und sozialgeschichtliche Studie', 3 vols. (*Habilitationsschrift*, University of Würzburg, 1990), I, 121, 125–7.

[121] Otto Rohn, 'Die Herren von Lentersheim. Zweiter Teil: Vom Erwerb des Schlosses Altenmuhr im Jahr 1430 bis zum Erlöschen des Stammes im Jahr 1799', *Alt-Gunzenhausen* 38 (1979), 108–45, at 108.

[122] Johann Looshorn, *Die Geschichte des Bisthums Bamberg*, vol. IV, *Das Bisthum Bamberg von 1400–1556* (Munich, 1900), 347; Wilhelm, 'Die Edeln von und zum Absberg', 107–8, 112.

[123] Wilhelm Engel, Walter Janssen, and Hellmut Kunstmann, *Die Burgen Frankenberg über Uffenheim* (Würzburg, 1956), 37–8.

[124] Uncertain identifications are not included.

58

price of 28,000 gulden.[125] It is noteworthy that two of the Huttens were governors.[126]

Many of their colleagues displayed a similar acquisitiveness: between 1540 and 1550 Wolf von Crailsheim, a margravial district governor, bought Walsdorf from Georg von Thüngfeld for 7000 gulden; Fröhstockheim from Wolf von Heßberg for 4300; castle Neuhaus from Sigmund von Heßberg for 24,000; Altenschönbach from the von Esel family for 12,100; Sommersdorf from Hans Christoph von Eyb for 20,000 – expending altogether 67,400 gulden.[127] Some time before 1560, district governor Sebastian Neustetter-Stürmer purchased castle Unterhohenried and other property from Georg Fuchs von Wonfurt for 41,700 gulden.[128] In 1549 district governor Ludwig von Eyb bought castle Runding from the Nothaffts for 34,000 gulden. Veit Asmus von Eyb, a master of the household, paid Martin Wolf von Redwitz 10,000 gulden for castle Vogelsburg.[129] These examples are but a small fraction of the extensive acquisitions by nobles from nobles. It seems to have been the rule that the buyers in transactions of such magnitude were seldom non-nobles and usually noble high officials. The overall impression is that property not only was not alienated from the nobility, but was rather being concentrated in the hands of families of noble office-holders.

That the nobility was not a socio economically homogeneous group is not in doubt. Studies of various European nobilities have established that, even among nobles of equal legal condition, there were pronounced disparities in terms of wealth and social standing.[130] Particularly relevant here is Hans-Peter Baum's research into the Court of Fiefs (*Lehenhof*) of the diocese of Würzburg between 1303 and 1519. This has shown that by the end of this period a group of 51 lineages (out of 182) had come to control just over a half of the pool of high-quality, lordship-conferring fiefs to be held from the prince-bishop. All but one of these fifty-one families were noble.[131] Now thirty of them were around the same time among the most persistent creditors and high officials in the service of the prince-bishops of Würzburg and Bamberg and of the margraves of Branden-

[125] StAN, AA-Akten, no. 1402, fols. 126ʳ–129ʳ.   [126] Körner, 'Die Familie von Hutten', 69.
[127] Sigmund Freiherr von Crailsheim, *Die Reichsfreiherrn von Crailsheim*, vol. II (Munich, 1905), 145–6.
[128] FA, Schrank 4, 'copia der kauffsabrede uber das schloß unterhöhrith'.
[129] Eyb, *Freiherren von Eyb*, 176, 197.
[130] Edouard Perroy, 'Social Mobility among the French *Noblesse* in the Later Middle Ages', *Past and Present* 21 (1962), 25–38; C. A. J. Armstrong, 'Had the Burgundian Government a Policy for the Nobility?' in *Britain and the Netherlands*, vol. II, ed. J. S. Bromley and E. H. Kossmann (Groningen, 1964), 9–32, at 29; Peter Feldbauer, 'Rangprobleme und Konnubium österreichischer Landherrenfamilien', *ZbLG* 35 (1972), 571–90; Sablonier, *Adel im Wandel*, 108–11, 138; Hahn, *Struktur und Funktion des brandenburgischen Adels*, 207; James B. Wood, *The Nobility of the 'Election' of Bayeux, 1463–1666: Continuity through Change* (Princeton, 1980), 95–7, 122–6; H. K. F. van Nierop, *The Nobility of Holland: From Knights to Regents, 1500–1650*, trans. M. Ultee (Cambridge, 1993), 42–5.
[131] Baum, 'Der Lehenhof des Hochstifts Würzburg', I, esp. 171; II, 90–1.

burg.[132] At least a further five lineages, having had their main seats and interests in other, neighbouring territories, were leading office-holders mainly of other princes.[133] Given this overlap, it seems safe to conclude that by the late Middle Ages an élite had formed among the Franconian nobility, set apart from those who were otherwise their peers by a combination of significant and extensive landed property and distinguished careers in princely service.

The main point that all this evidence makes is that rather than a general crisis, it was a process of social stratification which the Franconian nobility underwent in the wake of the consolidation of the territorial states. The impact of the economic changes of the late Middle Ages, however fundamental they may have been, was differential according to the group of nobles in question.[134] Some noble families, having for various reasons failed to adapt to the new circumstances, certainly experienced acute financial difficulties, which in turn imperilled their noble status.[135] Families of noble office-holders, on the other hand, bid fair to survival and success. Their position enabled them both to minimise the losses of

---

[132] The main sources used are: StAW, Stb, no. 788, fols. 26^v–27^v, 72$^{r–v}$, 74$^{r–v}$; nos. 790–92; no. 892, fol. 120^v; no. 1012, fols. 499^v–500^r, 502^r; 546^r; ibid., Literaliensammlung des Historischen Vereins von Unterfranken und Aschaffenburg, Ms f. no. 1044, passim; ibid., Ldf, no. 15, passim; StAN, AA-Akten, nos. 838 and 1402, passim; ibid., Ansbacher Historica, no. 340; FA (unnumbered bookshelf); Lorenz Fries, *Die Geschichte des Bauernkrieges in Ostfranken*, ed. August Schäffler and Theodor Henner, vol. II (Aalen, 1978), passim; Stumpf, *Denkwürdigkeiten der teutschen besonders fränkischen Geschichte*, III, 118–23; Schuhmann (ed.), *Stadtarchiv Ansbach*, passim; Rudolf M. Kloos (ed.), *Die Inschriften des Landkreises Bamberg bis 1650* (Munich, 1980), passim; Müller, *Die ständische Vertretung*, 333–5, 338–44, 347–51; Sprandel, 'Die Ritterschaft und das Hochstift Würzburg,' 138–43; Reuschling, *Die Regierung des Hochstifts Würzburg*, 182–95, 221–8, 234–44; Sebastian Zeißner, 'Beiträge zur Geschichte mainfränkischer Burgen,' *MJfGK* 6 (1954), 106–28; Gottfried Freiherr von Rotenhan, *Die Rotenhan: Genealogie einer fränkischen Familie von 1229 bis zum Dreißigjährigen Krieg* (Neustadt a.d. Aisch, 1985), passim; Freytag von Loringhoven, *Europäische Stammtafeln*, n.s., V, tables 22–6; Eberhard Graf von Fugger, *Die Seinsheim und ihre Zeit: Eine Familien- und Kulturgeschichte von 1155–1890* (Munich, 1893), passim; Fritz Luckhard (ed.), *Die Regesten der Herren von Ebersberg genannt Weyhers in der Röhn (1170–1518)* (Fulda, 1963), passim.

[133] Wilhelm Störmer, *Miltenberg: Die Ämter Amorbach und Miltenberg des Mainzer Oberstifts als Modelle geistlicher Territorialität und Herrschaftsintensivierung* (Munich, 1979), 173; FA, Schrank 5 (unnumbered files); *Genealogisches Handbuch des Adels*, vol. 37 (Limburg an der Lahn, 1966), 126–7, 132, 157–8; Freytag von Loringhoven, *Europäische Stammtafeln*, n.s., V, tables 74–6; Walther Möller, *Stamm-Tafeln westdeutscher Adels-Geschlechter im Mittelalter*, vol. III (Darmstadt, 1936), tables 135–7; Walther Pfeilsticker (ed.) *Neues Württembergisches Dienerbuch*, 2 vols. (Stuttgart, 1957–63), nos. 1134, 2616; Jürgen Rauser, 'Die Ahnen der Herren von Stetten 1166–1966', *Hohenloher Historische Hefte* 17 (1967), 1–66, at 33, 40 and StAN, Brandenburg-Ansbachische Lehenbücher, no. 9, fol. 70.

[134] Roger Sablonier, 'Zur wirtschaftlichen Situation des Adels im Spätmittelalter', in *Adelige Sachkultur des Spätmittelalters* (Vienna, 1982), 9–34, at 20–1.

[135] Klaus Freiherr von Andrian-Werburg, 'Die niederadeligen Kemnater im Coburgischen: Zur politischen und wirtschaftlichen Existenz der mittelalterlichen adeligen Unterschicht', *Jahrbuch der Coburger Landesstiftung*, 30 (1985), 97–136. It is noteworthy that during the 400 years of its history only two members of this family were high officials. See also Gerhard Rechter, *Das Land zwischen Aisch und Rezat: Die Kommende Virnsberg Deutschen Ordens und die Rittergüter im oberen Zenngrund* (Neustadt a.d. Aisch, 1981), 215–18, 260.

economic crises and to maximise profits in better times. It seems that in Franconia, as in electoral Brandenburg and Austria,[136] the accumulation of wealth had two preconditions: a nobleman had to be involved in commercial and credit business, and had to occupy high office, each activity backing up the other. The princely territorial state was a powerful generator of social inequality.

Hence princely service – contrary to the frequently made claim that it was an indication of economic frailty and political submission[137] – was hardly scorned by the nobility.[138] It was at the heart of their self-perception as a ruling class. Even the most notable and wealthy nobles did not consider it beneath them to wait on a prince or a princess at a ceremonial dinner, carving the meat and serving the wine.[139] To interpret this as a surrender of one's liberty and of weakness is to misconceive the essence of the nobility. By performing such services noblemen were of course recognising the prince's superiority, but at the same time they were basking in his honour and power, thereby confirming their own. Some nobles, indeed, expressed their positive evaluation of princely service, and of the sense of identity it gave them, in an unequivocal manner.

In his autobiography, the fifteenth-century knight Jörg von Ehingen described how, as a young lad, he wanted to 'bring himself forward' with the prince and his court. On his father's advice he approached Duke Albrecht of Austria, telling him that 'I have learnt that my gracious lord Duke Sigismund is about to visit your court. If he were to see that I have deserved no post, be it never so small, in your Grace's service, I shall be looked down upon as one of no account . . .' Having found the duke in high spirits, he was given keys to the prince's apartment and was attached to the service of his bedchamber. With evident satisfaction he wrote that when 'my lord Duke Sigismund arrived I provided myself with a number of keys and waited diligently as a chamberlain on my gracious master Duke [Albrecht], so that Duke Sigismund and his train could see that I had earned a post at court'.[140] At the other end of life, one margravial district governor carried the memories of princely service to his deathbed. In his testament he instructed

---

136 Hahn, *Struktur und Funktion des brandenburgischen Adels*, 231; Otto Brunner, 'Zwei Studien zum Verhältnis von Bürgertum und Adel', in his *Neue Wege der Verfassungs- und Sozialgeschichte*, 3rd edn (Göttingen, 1980), 242–80, at 271–9.

137 Norbert Schindler, 'Habitus und Herrschaft: Zum Wandel der aristokratischen Herrschaftspraxis im 16. Jahrhundert', in his *Widerspenstige Leute: Studien zur Volkskultur in der frühen Neuzeit* (Frankfurt am Main, 1992), 47–77, at 52–4; Werner Rösener, 'Adelige Herrschaft in einer alten Königslandschaft: Herrschaftspraktiken und Lebensformen des oberschwäbischen Adels im Spätmittelalter', in *Politische Kultur in Oberschwaben*, ed. Peter Blickle (Tübingen, 1993), 119–46, at 136–7.

138 This holds good for comital dynasties as well: Schultes, *Geschichte des Gräflichen Hauses Henneberg*, I, 387.

139 StAN, Landtagsakten, Tom. 7, no. 107, fols. 8^r–12^r. In this regard see the comment by Norbert Elias, *The Civilizing Process*, trans. Edmund Jephcott (Oxford, 1994), 97–8.

140 Malcolm Letts (ed.), *The Diary of Jörg von Ehingen*, trans. Malcolm Letts (London, 1929), 19–21.

his two sons to 'serve princes and counts'.[141] Other noblemen displayed the ultimate fervency: they had the official position they had held inscribed on their tombstones.[142]

MARRIAGE

The last parameter of status and stratification to be examined here is the marriage alliance. Connubium was in late medieval Germany both a mark of social standing and a means of advancement, and was amply acknowledged as such by contemporaries.[143] Noblemen, for their part, used it to protect or reinforce the exclusivity of their order. Tournament regulations laid down in 1485 debarred from participation noblemen who married artisans' daughters. Those who married town patricians were admitted into the games on condition that their dowries exceeded 4000 gulden, or even 10,000 gulden when one's family had only been tourneying during the previous fifty years. It was stipulated, however, that they should still reckon with a punishment in the form of thrashing with truncheons administered by the other jousters.[144]

This conscious instrumentalisation suggests that matrimonial alliances could also be used to raise or maintain barriers between different social ranks of the nobility itself. A strong inclination to endogamous marriages was certainly a fundamental characteristic of aristocratic ruling groups in late medieval and early modern Europe.[145] In Germany this tendency reached extremes: 87.5 per cent of the counts and barons married their equals in the period between the thirteenth and sixteenth centuries; only 6 per cent married below their station.[146] Yet within the bounds of each rank – titled and untitled nobility – no such deep chasms could evolve as did between them. There were many considerations shaping the

---

[141] Sven-Uwe Bürger, 'Burg Amlishagen – Anmerkungen zur Besitzgeschichte', *WFr* 76 (1992), 39–60, at 48.

[142] Isolde Maierhofer (ed.), *Die Inschriften des Landkreises Hassberge* (Munich, 1979), passim; Karl Borchardt (ed.), *Die Würzburger Inschriften bis 1525* (Wiesbaden, 1988), passim; Kloos (ed.), *Die Inschriften des Landkreises Bamberg*, passim.

[143] Ulf Dirlmeier, 'Merkmale des sozialen Aufstiegs und der Zuordnung zur Führungsschicht in süddeutschen Städten des Spätmittelalters', in *Pforzheim im Mittelalter: Studien zur Geschichte einer landesherrlichen Stadt*, ed. Hans-Peter Becht (Sigmaringen, 1983), 77–106, at 87–8, 93–4; Mitterauer, 'Probleme der Stratifikation', 17.

[144] Christian Meyer (ed.), *Aus dem Gedenkbuch des Ritters Ludwig des Älteren von Eyb, Hofmeister und Rath des Markgrafen Albrecht Achilles von Ansbach* (Ansbach, 1890), 67. See also William H. Jackson, 'Tournaments and the German Chivalric *renovatio*: Tournament Discipline and the Myth of Origins', in *Chivalry in the Renaissance*, ed. Sydney Anglo (Woodbridge, 1990), 77–91.

[145] Anthony Molho, *Marriage Alliance in Late Medieval Florence* (Cambridge, Mass., 1994), passim; Nierop, *The Nobility of Holland*, 74; Wood, *The Nobility of the 'Election' of Bayeux*, 108–9, 116–18.

[146] Karl-Heinz Spieß, *Familie und Verwandtschaft im deutschen Hochadel des Spätmittelalters: 13. bis Anfang des 16. Jahrhunderts* (Stuttgart, 1993), 398–400.

choice of spouse, and they were not all compatible. As one noble advised his nephews:

for your own and your children's good, marry into a respectable, eminent family and not into a family of which only wealth but no relations (*Freundschaft*) are to be expected, so that you would not cause the time-honoured noble family von Flersheim to sink into unimportance.[147]

Beside these sometimes conflicting social and economic pressures, politics, demographics and geography also played an important role in informing nobles' matrimonial practices.[148]

Considering these various factors, whose diversity mitigated against consummate oligarchisation, the rate of homogamous marriages among Franconian noble office-holders was remarkably high. This conclusion is based on two samples. The first comprises those thirty-three nobles who were both princely high officials and creditors and guarantors.[149] It has been assumed that they enjoyed both substantial wealth and particularly close relations with princes, and that they therefore occupied the apex of their class. However, the difficulties of identifying their wives and then the wives' fathers have resulted in a smaller sample of twenty-two noblemen. Hence a second statistical group of noblemen was created. This is composed of noblemen found to have served as masters of the household – the most elevated office – of the Franconian princes between 1440 and 1567. The initial sample of forty-one nobles has encountered the same technical problems and consequently shrunk to include only twenty-two. Now of the forty-four nobles in the combined sample, twenty-eight (63.6 per cent) were married to daughters of high officials.[150] It is noteworthy that this figure conforms closely to the rates of in-marriages established for the ruling class of Renaissance Florence, the French *noblesse d'épée* of Bayeux between 1430 and 1669, and the English peerage in the seventeenth and eighteenth centuries.[151] Of the latter, John Cannon remarked that 'it is difficult to see how a much higher proportion of endogamous marriage could be achieved in a free society'.[152]

Beyond this proportion, the significance of intermarriages of office-holding families lay also in their pattern and particular qualities. This can be illustrated by examining the marital connections between two of the families most closely associated with the margraves of Brandenburg: the von Eyb and the von

---

[147] Quoted by Harold H. Kehrer, 'Die Familie von Sickingen und die deutschen Fürsten 1262–1523', *ZGO* 127 (1979), 73–158, at 88.

[148] The fundamental work on this and allied themes is Spieß, *Familie und Verwandtschaft im deutschen Hochadel.*

[149] See Appendix A.   [150] See Appendix B.

[151] Molho, *Marriage Alliance in Late Medieval Florence*, 289; Wood, *The Nobility of the 'Election' of Bayeux*, 108; John Cannon, *Aristocratic Century: The Peerage of Eighteenth-Century England* (Cambridge, 1984), 90–1.

[152] Cannon, *Aristocratic Century*, 90.

Seckendorff. Between the middle of the fifteenth century and the middle of the sixteenth, they contracted between them eleven marriages. The fathers of the brides all occupied high posts in princely administrations. Of the eleven husbands, seven were high office-holders, one was a margravial creditor, and two who held no office were sons of officials. The greatly uneven distribution of these marriages both among the various lines of the von Eyb and across time betrays the careful planning that preceded them. Margravial master of the household Hans von Eyb alone married off three of his nubile daughters and one of his sons to Seckendorffs. His niece and two of his grandchildren went the same way.[153]

The marriage of his daughter, Anna, and Hans von Seckendorff, a margravial lieutenant and district governor, displays another salient feature of these unions: the involvement in them of the prince and his noble entourage. It was arranged by Margrave Friedrich of Brandenburg in 1505. He also granted the couple a 100-gulden 'court-contribution' (*Hofgabe*). The other four matchmakers and guarantors for the dowry were all high office-holders.[154] The couple's daughter, Anna von Seckendorff, was married off to Adam von Thüngen, district governor in the diocese of Würzburg. Of her 2,000-gulden dowry, 1,000 were paid in cash and 1,000 taken from a loan of 5,000 gulden her father had made to the margraves and now assigned to the groom. The latter, too, became a margravial creditor.[155] It is hard to imagine relations between the princely state and noble officials' families more tightly knit than that.[156] The princes thus mediated a process of partial oligarchisation within the nobility. Their administrations represented a select marriage market. Conversely, matrimonial alliances with officials' families were, among other things, a route to proximity to princes.[157]

Proximity to, or distance from, princes was the single most decisive factor in determining the social position of a nobleman. The examination of the group of noblemen in princely service leaves no doubt that they were potent both economically and politically. These two attributes were bound up with each other. Unfortunately, the existing evidence does not allow us to be more specific about this connection. It does, however, make quite plain that the connection was

---

[153] Eyb, *Freiherren von Eyb*, 60, 83–4, 114, 124, 137, 149–50, 153, 160, 162, 170, 179, 189, 205–6; Rechter, *Die Seckendorff*, I, 131, 138; II, 164, 200, 213, 215; Rechter (ed.), *Die Archive der Grafen und Freiherren von Seckendorff*, I, 297, no. 792; II, 498, 526, nos. 1226, 1291.

[154] Rechter (ed.), *Die Archive der Grafen und Freiherren von Seckendorff*, I, 254, no. 684. For the matchmaker Georg Adelmann von Adelmannsfelden, who is not mentioned here in his official capacity, see Georg Sigmund Graf Adelmann von Adelmannsfelden, *Das Geschlecht der Adelmann von Adelmannsfelden* (Ellwangen, 1948), 10, no. 47.

[155] StAN, AA-Akten, no. 1402, fols. 81ʳ–83ʳ, 85ʳ⁻ᵛ; Rechter (ed.), *Die Archive der Grafen und Freiherren von Seckendorff*, I, 273–4, nos. 728–9.

[156] For other examples of the interweaving of 'public' and 'private' finance see StAN, AA-Akten, no. 1402, fols. 67ʳ–68ʳ, 78ʳ–79ᵛ, 164ᵛ–169ᵛ, 183ᵛ–184ʳ.

[157] Kurt Andermann, 'Ritter – Edelknechte – Amtleute: Aspekte pfälzischer Adelsgeschichte im späten Mittelalter, skizziert am Beispiel der Familien von Mühlhofen und von Otterbach', *Pfälzer Heimat* 36 (1985), 1–8, at 6; Spieß, *Familie und Verwandtschaft im deutschen Hochadel*, 96–113.

mainly the outcome of the growth of the territorial state. For this growth relied to an appreciable extent on the resources of the nobility. Bishop Melchior Zobel's assertion to the contrary was not only grossly partisan,[158] it proved also painfully wrong: only a few years later his principality went bankrupt as a result of wars in the 1550s, and Zobel had to raise more than 500,000 gulden by pledging and selling episcopal property. At least 300,000 gulden of this sum came from the nobility in general and from high office-holders in particular.[159]

This sort of support cannot be classified as 'purely' financial, testifying only to economic well-being. The loans made by noblemen were as much political undertakings with far-reaching consequences. Margrave Friedrich once told his son Albrecht that 'I am not worried about my own debts . . . Rather, I am more concerned that the diocese of Würzburg might extricate itself from its debts. If this occurred, I would be in trouble.'[160] To put it in another way, large-scale credit transactions lent themselves to being used as a political strategy in the chronic conflict among the Franconian territorial powers.[161] In these circumstances, it was prudent for each prince to try to entice affluent noblemen from competing princes and to draw them into his own orbit of influence. Indeed, Margrave Albrecht took advantage of the bishop of Würzburg's debts to four noble pledge-holders to exercise pressure on him, and in 1443 was able to acquire from the bishop the important district governorship of Kitzingen.[162] A few years later, the margrave entrusted his noble councillor Martin von Eyb with making good his own miserable financial situation. In the process, Martin discovered that Count Michael of Maidburg had put up for sale valuable rights and assets, and that Wilhelm von Rechberg wanted to buy them. A margravial master of the household, Rechberg could be prevailed upon to withdraw his offer, and the property was sold to the margrave for 24,000 gulden.[163]

Princes, as these examples show, depended on those noblemen who could help them realise their political designs. In return, the system of pledge-lordships and district governorships upon which the princely territorial state was built provided the noblemen with a whole gamut of means of exercising authority, of intensifying their control over the subject population, and of enriching themselves: 'If you want to make money', taught a contemporary adage, 'become a district gover-

[158] See pp. 38–9 above.
[159] Computed according to Stumpf, *Denkwürdigkeiten der teutschen besonders fränkischen Geschichte*, III, 118–24.
[160] Quoted by Heinz Quirin, 'Markgraf Albrecht Achilles von Brandenburg-Ansbach als Politiker: Ein Beitrag zur Vorgeschichte des süddeutschen Städtekriegs', *JffL* 31 (1971), 261–308, at 288.
[161] Cf. Wolfgang von Stromer, *Oberdeutsche Hochfinanz 1350–1450*, part 2 (Wiesbaden, 1970), 219–94.
[162] Falckenstein (ed.), *Urkunden und Zeugnisse*, I, 284–7, no. 257. See also Quirin, 'Markgraf Albrecht Achilles', 288–9.
[163] Constantin Höfler (ed.), *Des Ritters Ludwig von Eyb zu Eybburg Denkwürdigkeiten brandenburgischer (hohenzollerischer) Fürsten* (Bayreuth, 1849), 134–5.

nor'.[164] These noblemen emerged from the crucible of state formation as winners, rising above all the rest of their class. They formed what one historian has called a 'pledge aristocracy'.[165]

The members of this group stood between aristocratic political power and bourgeois high finances. They represented a peculiar type of nobleman: the *financiers gentilshommes*.[166] They owed their elevated position to a conflation of political and economic developments in the wake of the 'finance state' – a term coined by Gerhard Oestreich to demarcate the intermediate phase between the 'domain state' and the 'tax state'.[167] No longer able to 'live of their own', not yet able to live off universal taxation, princes resorted to funded debt to pay for their state-building activities. They commercialised their regalian rights. As a result, the territorial state came to resemble an enterprise, opening up new opportunities for noblemen capable of investing in it. Apparently with other people in mind, Marx pointed out that public debt was one of the most powerful levers of primitive accumulation.[168] In the case of the German late medieval nobility, this led to the formation of a plutocratic élite of office-holding families.

Another symptom of the intimate link between princely state-building and the formation of this élite was the inclination of office-holding families to intermarry. The part played by princes in effecting such alliances indicates the great store they set by a cohesive clientele of strong families. The interconnections between these families functioned to bolster the social and economic basis of the rulers. Here, as in so many other areas, the princes' interests accorded, at least in large part, with those of the nobles: for marriage into leading families was critical in gaining proximity to princes. The status value of these marriages is further underscored by their costs.[169] The dowries accompanying noble officials' daughters greatly exceeded those brought by noblewomen from humbler families. On the other hand, they were by no means put to shame by the dotal prestations offered with daughters of rich town patricians.[170]

Thus, directly and indirectly, princes exercised profound influence on the

---

[164] Sander L. Gilman (ed.), *Johannes Agricola: Die Sprichwörtersammlungen*, vol. I (Berlin, 1971), 233.

[165] Sablonier, *Adel im Wandel*, 163.

[166] Franz Irsigler, 'Reinhard von Schönau und die Finanzierung der Königswahl Karls IV. im Jahre 1346: Ein Beitrag zur Geschichte der Hochfinanzbeziehungen zwischen Rhein und Maas', in *Hochfinanz, Wirtschaftsräume, Innovationen*, I, 357–81, at 357.

[167] Kersten Krüger, 'Gerhard Oestreich und der Finanzstaat: Entstehung und Deutung eines Epochenbegriffs der frühneuzeitlichen Verfassungs- und Sozialgeschichte', *Hessisches Jahrbuch für Landesgeschichte* 33 (1983), 333–46.

[168] Karl Marx, *Capital: A Critique of Political Economy*, trans. Ben Fowkes, vol. I (Harmondsworth, 1976), 919.

[169] For dowries as status symbols see Spieß, *Familie und Verwandtschaft im deutschen Hochadel*, 344–69.

[170] Cf. the references in nn. 153–6 above and Andrian-Werburg, 'Die niederadeligen Kemnater im Coburgischen', 116–18. For patricians' dowries see Dirlmeier, 'Merkmale des sozialen Aufstiegs', 93; Lyndal Roper, *The Holy Household: Women and Morals in Reformation Augsburg* (Oxford, 1989), 148–9.

creation and calibration of a noble élite. This carries three implications which are significant for the following analyses of feuds and feuders. First, there was no general crisis, let alone decline, of the late medieval nobility which can serve to explain the phenomenon of the feud. Rather, what took place was a process of social differentiation stimulated by the consolidation of the territorial state. Secondly, offices, as the wealth of their holders makes clear, were no mere outlets for noblemen in financial embarrassment. Rather, they and the credit transaction they usually involved were principal factors in that process of stratification. Hence both can safely be regarded as indications of high status. The same applies – though perhaps to a diminished degree – to marriages to daughters of these high-status noblemen. But, thirdly, the very fact that offices and credit transactions with princes were so indispensable to noblemen's social standing points up the fundamentally unsettled nature of their situation in that period. For failure to win them was in the long run likely to result in social degradation. One would expect this precariousness to have produced pervasive tensions in the nobility, especially in its upper ranks.

4

Prosopography of feuding noblemen

The group of feuding noblemen under discussion is a fictitious one. It is made up for, and depends upon, research procedures. Necessarily, an analysis of it has another goal than prosopography in the classic, Symian sense of uncovering the dark reality behind the façade of political rhetoric.[1] The aim of this prosopographical study is merely to identify the social lineaments of the feuders. This will serve to create a frame of reference for an interpretation of the feud.

METHOD

The composition of the group of feuding noblemen hinges ultimately on the definition of a 'feuder'. Unlike 'feud', the term 'feuder' does not involve conceptual difficulties, and it is safe to follow contemporary nomenclature. Whether war or feud, late medieval Germans usually distinguished between the principal foes or feuders on the one hand and their helpers on the other.[2] This distinction was a fundamental juristic tenet of the feud. The principals represented and were responsible for their workforce. The duration and conclusion of a feud rested solely with them.[3]

This discrimination between principals and helpers underlies the constitution of the sample of feuding noblemen. It is the primary principle of selection, and the only one against which there can be no appeal, if the sample is to have the basic coherence essential for its interpretation. This is so because the helpers' motives often had little affinity with those of the principals. Some joined for booty, others because they were bound by service, still others 'out of kinship and tradition'.[4] Whether siblings, underlings or hirelings, the helpers' reasons for supporting the principal feuder were ancillary to his. They reveal much about the dynamics of the feud, next to nothing about its causes and aims.

The principal feuders having been listed, the next step was to build a data base for prosopographical analysis. In many cases the feud records themselves give

---

[1] Ronald Syme, *The Roman Revolution* (1939; reprint, Oxford, 1985), 7.
[2] See, e.g., GNM, Hs 22 547 (Fehdebuch der Reichsstadt Nürnberg 1381–1513).
[3] Elsbet Orth, *Die Fehden der Reichsstadt Frankfurt am Main im Spätmittelalter: Fehderecht und Fehdepraxis im 14. und 15. Jahrhundert* (Wiesbaden, 1973), 28.
[4] StAN, Bb, no. 81, fol. 61ᵛ.

away enough biographical information; in many others they disclose no more than names of persons and places. Additional data have to be collected from an array of primary sources and secondary literature. It is true that, the nobility being the nobility, this array is almost inexhaustible. However, one then has to be able to relate all the available facts to the right person, the feuder. At this point one usually comes up against that abominable *bête noire* of genealogists: the custom of transmitting the same Christian names in the family. Consequently, it is difficult to distinguish between different members of the same family. And the larger the family was, the more troublesome is identification.

This problem is greatly diminished, or altogether nonexistent, in cases where the family of the feuder in question has been subject to a modern, detailed study. Yet the genealogical literature on the Franconian nobility, rich as it is, does not cover more than a substantial minority of the local families.[5] Identification of feuders from the 'silent majority' of lineages has had to take a different, longer route. The raw data gathered for them have been refined in four progressive stages: (1) registration; (2) differentiation; (3) segmental lineage reconstruction; (4) final identification. A feud which exemplifies this process is the one which pitted Christoph Fuchs against Bishop Georg of Bamberg.

(1) Christoph opened his feud against the bishop in 1462. In his cartel of defiance he called himself just 'Cristoffel Fuchs'.[6] According to the Würzburg episcopal secretary, archivist and chronicler Lorenz Fries (1491–1550), Christoph was of the Bimbach line. He is also said to have held in pledge portions of the Würzburg district governorship of Wallburg. The other parts belonged to Christoph's 'cousins' (*Vettern*), who are not named in this particular context. Later Fries mentions a Heinz (i.e. Heinrich) and a Hans Fuchs as sharing with Christoph the lordship over a village that was damaged in the hostilities. As a result, they too became active in the feud. Lastly, Fries speaks of a Christoph Fuchs who was the bishop's bailiff (*Schultheiß*) of the town of Würzburg. He was accused by the bishop of Bamberg of having assisted his feuding 'Vetter' Heinz.[7]

---

[5] The comprehensive genealogical work of Johann Gottfried Biedermann is at many points unreliable and has to be used with caution. See Johann Gottfried Biedermann, *Geschlechtsregister der Reichsfrey unmittelbaren Ritterschaft Landes zu Franken löblichen Orts Baunach* (Bayreuth, 1747); *Geschlechtsregister der Reichsfrey unmittelbaren Ritterschaft Landes zu Franken löblichen Orts Gebürg* (Bamberg, 1747); *Geschlechtsregister der Reichsfrey unmittelbaren Ritterschaft Landes zu Franken löblichen Orts Altmühl* (Bamberg, 1748); *Geschlechtsregister der Reichsfrey unmittelbaren Ritterschaft Landes zu Franken löblichen Orts Steigerwald* (Nuremberg, 1748); *Geschlechtsregister der Reichsfrey unmittelbaren Ritterschaft Landes zu Franken löblichen Orts Rhön und Werra* (Bayreuth, 1749); *Geschlechtsregister der Reichsfrey unmittelbaren Ritterschaft Landes zu Franken löblichen Orts Ottenwald* (Kulmbach, 1751); *Geschlechs Register der löblichen Ritterschafft im Voigtlande* (Kulmbach, 1752). For Biedermann see Gerhard Hirschmann, 'Johann Gottfried Biedermann zum 200. Todestag', *Blätter für fränkische Familienkunde* 9, no. 1 (1966), 2–9.

[6] StAW, Stb, no. 717, fols. 257^{r-v}.

[7] Lorenz Fries, *Historie, Nahmen, Geschlecht, Wesen, Thaten, gantz Leben und Sterben des gewesenen Bischoffen zu Wirtzburg und Hertzogen zu Francken* [1544], in *Geschicht-Schreiber von dem Bischoffthum Wirtzbürg*, ed. Johann Peter Ludewig (Frankfurt am Main, 1713), 838–43.

Whether Christoph the bailiff and Christoph the feuder were one and the same person is not spelled out.

(2) The word 'Vetter' as used by Fries cannot be taken at face value to mean cousins. In the language of the time it could refer to a variety of agnates. But the names and spatial locations he relates provide a number of important leads. Above all, the fact that Christoph, Heinz, and Hans shared property suggests that they were of the same line of the Fuchs family. And, indeed, various sources touching on the feud not only confirm this assumption, but make clear that they were also of the same branch: Heinz appears in these documents as 'zu Wallburg' or 'governor in Wallburg'.[8] That Heinz, Hans and the feuder Christoph Fuchs were all of the Wallburg branch of the Bimbach line of the family should help distinguish Christoph from any other namesakes living around those years.

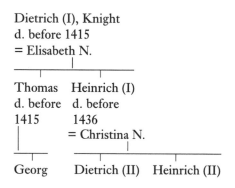

Figure 4.1: Genealogy of the Fuchs von Bimbach in Wallburg, 1404–36.

(3) The next stage was to reconstitute the Wallburg segment of the family. Like most aristocratic bynames, 'Wallburg' was taken from the main seat: the castle, town and governorship of Wallburg (near Eltmann). It was continuously held in pledge by the family until 1477, when it was redeemed by Bishop Rudolf of Würzburg from Hans. The document recording this transaction also traces the early history of the pledge:[9] in 1404, Dietrich Fuchs, a Knight, and his son Thomas received the governorship of Wallburg/Eltmann for 7,000 gulden. In

---

8 StAW, Stb, no. 717, fols. 142ᵛ, 192ᵛ; no. 865, fol. 331ᵛ; C. A. Schweitzer, 'Auszüge der Urkunden aus der Chronik des Michaelsberger Abtes Eberhard', *Bericht des Historischen Vereins Bamberg* 17 (1854), 1–175, at 87, 88, 90–1, 104; Adolf Bachmann (ed.), *Briefe und Acten zur österreichisch-deutschen Geschichte im Zeitalter Kaiser Friedrich III.* (Vienna, 1885), 460, no. 367; Theodor J. Scherg, 'Franconica aus dem Vatican 1462–1492', *Archivalische Zeitschrift*, n.s., 16 (1909), 1–156, at 73, no. 131; Johannes Linnebron, 'Ein 50jähriger Kampf (1417–ca.1467) um die Reform und ihr Sieg im Kloster ad sanctum Michaelem bei Bamberg', parts 1–6, *Studien und Mitteilungen aus dem Benediktiner- und dem Zisterzienser-Orden* 25 (1904), 252–65; 579–89; 718–29; 26 (1905), 55–68; 247–54; 534–45: esp. part 4, 63–8 and part 6, 541: 'Heinric[us] Fuchs, tunc prefect[us] in Walpurg'.
9 StAW, Ldf, no. 13, pp. 81–2, 177–9.

1406 this Dietrich and his wife Elisabeth acquired also the governorship of Haßfurt. In 1415 the governorship of Stollberg was pledged to Elisabeth, Dietrich's widow, as well as to her son Heinrich and to Georg, the son of the late Thomas. In 1436 the bishop came to an agreement regarding his debts to Christina, widow of Heinrich Fuchs, and her sons Dietrich and Heinrich.

As for most noble families, the further descent of the Fuchs in Wallburg can be reconstructed by using one of the most accessible kinds of sources: registers of fiefs (*Lehenbücher*) and feudal title deeds (*Lehensurkunden*). These indicate that Dietrich (II) must have died in or shortly before 1454. For in this year his brother Heinrich (II) was enfeoffed in trust for the late Dietrich (II)'s minor sons, Heinrich (III) and Hans (the 'Vettern' of the feuder Christoph Fuchs von Bimbach).[10]

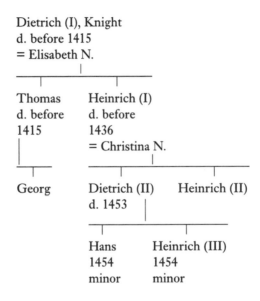

Figure 4.2: Genealogy of the Fuchs von Bimbach in Wallburg, 1404–54

From the *Lehenbücher* it also emerges that at the time of the feud Christoph was not the only Fuchs to carry this Christian name. In 1454 a Christoph Fuchs von Preppach was enfeoffed by the bishop of Würzburg with property held by his father Georg.[11] That he was of the Preppach line suggests that he was not the

---

[10] StAW, Würzburger Lehenbücher, no. 18, fol. 67ᵛ. A similar enfeoffment occurred in 1457: ibid., no. 21, fol. 20ʳ. For Dietrich's precise date of death (1453) see Alfred Wendehorst (ed.), *Urkundenbuch der Marienkapelle am Markt zu Würzburg 1317–1530* (Würzburg, 1974), 77.

[11] StAW, Adelsarchiv Fuchs von Bimbach, no. 5 [part 2, 'Würzburgisches Lehen'], fol. 48ʳ. This source is the family's *Lehenbuch*. It consists of extracts from the *Lehenbücher* of Bamberg and Würzburg.

feuder, but as yet does not rule this out. It was not rare for members of one line to inherit parts in the castles of another and then call themselves after their new habitation.[12] Moreover, in terms of dates and possible succession, this Christoph would have fit in nicely as Georg's son and Thomas's grandson (see Figure 4.2). But other facts to do with inheritance and descent finally eliminate him as a candidate.

Georg Fuchs von Bimbach died childless in 1472. This emerges from the fact that he was inherited by, among others, Hans Fuchs for himself and for Adam, the minor son of the late Heinrich (III).[13] And whereas part of Georg's property went also to a Christoph Fuchs in 1473, the other Christoph Fuchs, the one 'von Preppach', had already died in or shortly before 1466. He too left no male children: his feudal property was divided not only between members of his own line, but also between some of the other lines.[14] Among the latter was Christoph Fuchs, 'bailiff in Würzburg'.[15] Unfortunately, the *Lehenbücher* do not name his father. They do, however, name his line: Leuzendorf (*sic*).

Leuzendorf was not one of the Fuchs family's main, constant lines. Christoph, it seems, moved to Leuzendorf seeking to set up a new branch.[16] Three documents read conjointly indicate that this Christoph was the one who formerly resided in Wallburg: (a) a 'Christoph Fuchs zu Leuzendorf' is mentioned as already dead by 1508;[17] (b) in 1520 another Christoph Fuchs, of unspecified line, received his father's, Christoph's, feudal possessions;[18] (c) in 1522 a 'Christoph Fuchs zu Leuzendorf, a Knight', obtained the governorship of Bramberg in pledge.[19] His father must have been Christoph the bailiff, for, as has been said, the Christoph who died in 1466 had left no male issue.[20] This could be verified by consulting another type of serial documentation: ancestry proofs of canons of cathedral chapters.

---

[12] Thomas Beyer, 'Zu Familienstruktur und Konnubium des niederadeligen Geschlechtes von Grumbach im Spätmittelalter' (*Zulassungsarbeit*, University of Würzburg, 1977), 35–6.

[13] StAW, Adelsarchiv Fuchs von Bimbach, no. 5 [part 2], fols. 64^{r-v}. The book of the Society of the Clasp (*Gesellschaft mit der Fürspang*) records the burial of Georg Fuchs von Bimbach in 1472: StAN, Reichsstadt Nürnberg, Amts- und Standbücher, no. 340, fol. 60^v. For another indication that Georg died childless see Joseph Widemann (ed.), *Urkunden der Benediktiner-Abtei St. Stephan in Würzburg. Ergänzungsheft* (Erlangen, 1983), 55–6, no. 101.

[14] StAW, Adelsarchiv Fuchs von Bimbach, no. 5 [part 1, 'Bambergisches Lehen'], fols. 14^{r-v}; ibid. [part 2], fols. 60^r–61^r.

[15] Ibid. [part 2], fols. 61^v–62^r. It is probably this enfeoffment which led Sebastian Zeißner, 'Zwei Mitarbeiter des Fürstbischofs Rudolf von Scherenberg', *MJfGK* 3 (1951), 127–38, to mistake Christoph the bailiff for Christoph Fuchs von Preppach.

[16] Zeißner, 'Zwei Mitarbeiter', explains this move to have been the result of a conflict between Christoph and his relations of the Preppach line.

[17] StAW, Würzburger Lehenbücher, no. 29, fol. 152^v.

[18] StAW, Adelsarchiv Fuchs von Bimbach, no. 5 [part 2], fols. 96^r–97^v.

[19] StAW, Stb, no. 791, fols. 38^v–41^r.

[20] Another Christoph Fuchs von Bimbach living around this time could be excluded, because he was the son of Hans and brother of Dietrich (III), Hans (II), Wolf, and Veit: StAW, Adelsarchiv Fuchs von Bimbach, no. 5 [part 1], fols. 27^r–28^v. See Figure 4.3.

A necessary condition of eligibility to chapters was a noble pedigree of three generations.[21] Not only the canon himself, the deponents on his behalf too, had to prove that their parents and grandparents were of noble stock. So if Christoph the bailiff had a son or a grandson who either was a canon or testified for a postulant, this can be expected to reveal further particulars regarding this Christoph's identity. It turns out that he had two sons, Andreas and Jakob, who were canons in both Bamberg and Würzburg.[22] Andreas was later the guardian of the sons of his deceased brother 'Christoph Fuchs zu Leuzendorf, a Knight, of the lines Wallburg and Eltmann'.[23] In the oaths he performed before taking up his benefices he named himself Andreas Fuchs zu Leuzendorf, son of Christoph Fuchs von Wallburg.[24]

(4) This segmental lineage reconstitution has made identification certain. Christoph the feuder could be none other than the one who was the bailiff in Würzburg in 1466. And although no document has been uncovered that proves this directly, he must have been the son of Heinrich (II) and indeed the cousin of Heinrich (III) and Hans.

From this identification flow a number of important prosopographical details about Christoph the feuder. He was not only a bailiff. Since his son Christoph could not have been born prior to 1468,[25] it was he who was district governor of Gemünden in 1470; of Ebern and Seßlach in 1475; of Bramberg in 1492; and marshall of the bishop of Würzburg in 1479 and 1492.[26] Thus, in spite – or perhaps because – of his feud, Christoph made a brilliant career. He was a nobleman of the highest standing.

The same technique was employed whenever the identity of a feuder was in doubt. It has not always worked out: either pieces of evidence crucial to clinching identification were missing, or there was not enough material to go on in the first place. Whereas the initial list comprised 313 principals, 71 (22.7 per cent) were disqualified on the ground of uncertainty. That the sources may reflect differential statuses of noblemen is obvious. That is, whatever feud and other relevant

---

[21] Sigmund Freiherr von Pölnitz, 'Stiftsfähigkeit und Ahnenprobe im Bistum Würzburg', in *Herbipolis Jubilans: 1200 Jahre Bistum Würzburg. Festschrift zur Säkularfeier der Erhebung der Kiliansreliquien* (Würzburg, 1952), 349–55.

[22] Cf. StAW, Stb, no. 46, fol. 24ʳ and Johannes Kist, *Das Bamberger Domkapitel von 1399 bis 1556: Ein Beitrag zur Geschichte seiner Verfassung, seines Wirkens und seiner Mitglieder* (Weimar, 1943), 181, 185, nos. 58, 63.

[23] StAW, Lehensachen, no. 1948.

[24] StAW, Stb, no. 46, fol. 24ʳ; Kist, *Das Bamberger Domkapitel*, 181, no. 58.

[25] 'Christoph Fuchs, bailiff', married Anna N. in 1468: StAW, Würzburger Lehenbücher, no. 24, fol. 117ʳ. His son Christoph was from a second or subsequent marriage to Elisabeth von der Kere: cf. StAW, Stb, no. 46, fol. 24ʳ and Kist, *Das Bamberger Domkapitel*, 181, 185, nos. 58, 63.

[26] StAW, Adelsarchiv Fuchs von Bimbach, no. 5 [part 2], fols. 62ᵛ–63ᵛ; ibid., Ldf, no. 12, pp. 826, 1002–3; ibid., Ldf, no. 15, pp. 414–15; ibid., Würzburger Lehenbücher, no. 27, fol. 242ᵛ. See also Zeißner, 'Zwei Mitarbeiter'. In his nomination to the governorship of Ebern and Seßlach he is called 'Christoph Fuchs von Burgpreppach'. This, it will be recalled, is because he inherited property there from the Christoph Fuchs von Preppach who died in 1466.

records have come down to us may simply be the outcome of an inherent contemporary bias to commit to writing the deeds of the great. Allowance must therefore be made for a certain skew in the sample in favour of noblemen of mark.

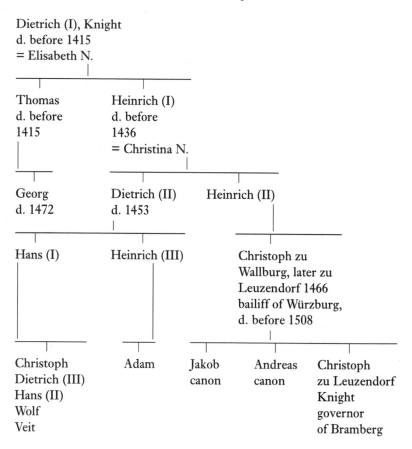

Figure 4.3: Genealogy of the Fuchs von Bimbach in Wallburg, 1404–1522

However, for a number of reasons it seems that the effect of possible distortions on the argument is not overwhelming. These reasons all revolve around the implications feuds carried for the political order in Franconia. First, all noblemen were vassals and servitors of one, usually of several, of the local princes. It was a prince's duty to attend to his vassals and servitors of whatever rank. As the feud of the Vestenbergs shows,[27] the expectations entailed by a lord-vassal bond were still sufficiently strong to be deployed rhetorically as normative referents in the

---

[27] See chap. 2.

context of dispute. Hence petty noblemen were also likely to be the subject of documents generated by princely chancelleries. An example is offered by the conflict between Christoph von Hetzelsdorf and Karl Schütz von Hagenbach. He cannot afford to engage scribes and lawyers, Christoph complained to the margrave, and would therefore like to forego legal instruments altogether. Apparently realising that this was unacceptable, he proposed that each party to the dispute be allowed to submit no more than two statements of claim.[28] Thus, even a feud of a professedly small-time nobleman was documented. His rival, too, was a modest noble. But his letters to the margraves have been preserved as well.[29] The most probable reason is that, apart from being a margravial vassal,[30] Schütz asserted rights to a fief which was a bone of contention between the margrave and the bishop of Bamberg.

Here another factor presents itself which was conducive to the maintenance of formal equality between noblemen: Franconia's territorial fragmentation. This was so extreme, and the ensuing competition between the princes so fierce, that vassals' feuds were bound to take on bright political colouring. It was in the princes' interest not to alienate noble vassals by failing to give them their due attention, for this would have pushed them into a competing prince's camp. As a result, princes rarely neglected to take part in feuds, either as backers of this or that feuder, or as arbiters between them.[31] Their stature brought feuds into the limelight. Thirdly, the princes' traditional role as keepers of law and order was central to both their legitimacy and self-understanding.[32] That they often – sometimes deliberately – failed to live up to the ideal did nothing to subdue their official concern about it. The efficacy of feuds in disturbing the peace ensured that they were meticulously recorded. Indeed, even commoners' feuds were entered into the books next to noblemen's.[33]

The same lively interest in feuds was shown, with a vengeance, by towns – but for somewhat dissimilar reasons. The structure of noblemen's relationship with cities was different from that with princes. Cities were neither noblemen's feudal lords nor their main employers. Instead, they were most of the time at odds with the latter.[34] There was therefore little to draw nobles and cities together, and a lot to set them against each other. This is where feuds repeatedly came in.[35] As hubs of trade, cities were the more vulnerable side; their merchants, especially when moving about, were 'sitting ducks'. Urban prosperity depended to a desperate

---

[28] StAB, Hofrat Ansbach-Bayreuth, no. 565, prod. 2.   [29] Ibid., no. 552.
[30] StAN, Ansbacher Lehensurkunden, nos. 552, 2116.   [31] See chaps. 2 and 5.
[32] See Margrave Albrecht's injunctions to his lieutenants to keep the peace and avert robbery ('Behalt frid, weret rauberey'): Carl August Hugo Burkhardt (ed.), *Das funfft merkisch Buech des Churfuersten Albrecht Achilles* (Jena, 1857), passim. See also StAN, AA-Akten, no. 392.
[33] StAW, Stb, no. 788, part 3; ibid., Ldf, no. 15, pp. 395–6, 435.
[34] Thomas A. Brady, *Turning Swiss: Cities and Empire, 1450–1550* (Cambridge, 1985), 14–15, 94, 99, 110, 125, 216.
[35] See chap. 5.

extent on the containment, if not suppression, of noblemen's feuds.[36] No method was deemed too foul in this running battle. Turncoats from among nobles' domestics were hired. So was, in one instance, a Jewish ad hoc hitman, who was charged with dispatching a particularly troublous nobleman.[37] Writing was another weapon townsfolk were good at plying. Nuremberg kept from a very early date obsessively tidy registers of its enemies.[38] They served a number of related purposes. One was to facilitate the prosecution and penalising of the city's foes.[39] Another was to gather information useful in protecting trade routes. Certain cases of feud give the impression that no detail was too minute not to be noted down. Reports dealing with the feuds of Mangold von Eberstein and Hans Thomas von Absberg describe the feuders' movements across the region; their horses' salient traits; what they and their helpers wore when they were last seen; who provided them with shelter and food, and so on.[40] Spies were employed on a regular basis, sending their accounts coded and written in milk on the back of an order of purchase.[41] Some of the reports and correspondence regarding feuds against Nuremberg were later collected and bound in separate, occasionally exquisite, volumes.[42] Here the purpose was to instruct future generations in overcoming difficult political situations.[43] Thus, whether against cities, princes, or fellow noblemen, it is hard to imagine how a feud could have escaped documentation.

Differential status, however, might have affected identification. For example, to identify feuders from the titular nobility, i.e. counts and barons, is seldom a

---

[36] Brady, *Turning Swiss*, 242–5.

[37] Peter Ritzmann, '"Plackerey in teutschen Landen"': Untersuchungen zur Fehdetätigkeit des fränkischen Adels im frühen 16. Jahrhundert und ihrer Bekämpfung durch den Schwäbischen Bund und die Reichsstadt Nürnberg, insbesondere am Beispiel des Hans Thomas von Absberg und seiner Auseinandersetzung mit den Grafen von Oettingen (1520–31)' (PhD thesis, University of Munich, 1993), 255–6, 516–17.

[38] Werner Schultheiß (ed.), *Die Acht-, Verbots- und Fehdebücher Nürnbergs von 1285–1400. Mit einer Einführung in die Rechts- und Sozialgeschichte und das Kanzlei- und Urkundenwesen Nürnbergs im 13. und 14. Jahrhundert* (Nuremberg, 1960). See also GNM, Hs 22 547 (Fehdebuch der Reichsstadt Nürnberg 1381–1513).

[39] Schultheiß (ed.), *Die Acht-, Verbots- und Fehdebücher Nürnbergs*, 224*–5*.

[40] Louis Ferdinand Freiherr von Eberstein (ed.), *'Dem Landfrieden ist nicht zu trauen': Fehde Mangold's von Eberstein zum Brandenstein gegen die Reichsstadt Nürnberg 1516–1522. Charakterbild der rechtlichen und wirtschaftlichen Zustände im deutschen Reiche unmittelbar vor dem grossen Bauernkriege* (Nordhausen, 1868), passim; Joseph Baader (ed.), *Verhandlungen über Thomas von Absberg und seine Fehden gegen den Schwäbischen Bund 1519 bis 1530* (Tübingen, 1873), passim; Ritzmann, '"Plackerey in teutschen Landen"', passim.

[41] Joseph Morsel, 'Une société politique en Franconie à la fin du Moyen Age: Les Thüngen, leurs princes, leurs pairs et leurs hommes (1275–1525)' (PhD thesis, University of Paris-IV Sorbonne, 1993), 1359–60 n. 554. See also StAN, Bb, no. 69, fol. 137ᵛ.

[42] StAN, Nürnbergs Amts- und Standbücher, nos. 146, 150. A volume describing the feud of Konrad Schott is also supposed to have existed, but is not to be found anywhere: Emil Reicke (ed.), *Willibald Pirckheimers Briefwechsel*, vol. I (Munich, 1940), 85–6 n. 3.

[43] Gerhard Pfeiffer, 'Hans Thomas von Absberg (ca. 1480?–1531)', *Fränkische Lebensbilder* 13 (1990), 17–32, at 17.

complicated business. Conversely, the seventy-one disqualifications on the ground of uncertainty might be assumed to reflect low status. In some cases this is certainly true. But abortive identifications might equally betoken high status. A growing body of ethological and anthropological literature indicates a positive correlation between status or wealth and reproductive success in preindustrial societies.[44] Research into various European aristocracies has adduced similar evidence. Roger Sablonier has found that the most successful families among the Swiss nobility around 1300 had the greatest number of children.[45] James Boone's demographic analysis of the Portuguese nobility has demonstrated that reproductivity increased with rank.[46] A similar picture has emerged from an examination of the ruling class of Renaissance Florence.[47] For the late medieval Franconian nobility, this has been confirmed by Hans-Peter Baum's study of the *Lehenhof* of the bishops of Würzburg.[48] It has already been noted that problematic identifications are most common with large families. Hence they might be as much a sign of high as of low status.

One Franconian lineage, the von Schaumberg, can serve as an example. The Schaumbergs were counted among the wealthiest and most influential noble families in the region. They boasted one cardinal, four prince-bishops, three abbots, twenty-six canons in cathedral chapters, and numerous high office-holders between 1400 and 1550. Throughout this period the family was teeming with offspring (some 230 males). The example of this 'tribe' shows that identification can still be a problem even when a complete and accurate modern genealogy is available.[49] One member of the family, Georg, feuded against Nuremberg in 1449. Unfortunately, the chronicler of this event left out of the narrative all relevant facts about Georg which would have facilitated identification.[50] The result is that the number of possible candidates for the person of the feuder is five, and Georg has to be disqualified. The elevated position of the

---

[44] J. Hill, 'Prestige and Reproductive Success in Man', *Ethology and Sociobiology* 5 (1984), 77–95; Paul W. Turke and L. L. Betzig, 'Those Who Can Do: Wealth, Status, and Reproductive Success on Ifaluk', *Ethology and Sociobiology* 6 (1985), 79–87; Hillard Kaplan and Kim Hill, 'Hunting Ability and Reproductive Success among Male Ache Foragers: Preliminary Results', *Current Anthropology* 26, no. 1 (1985), 131–3.

[45] Roger Sablonier, *Adel im Wandel: Eine Untersuchung zur sozialen Situation des ostschweizerischen Adels um 1300* (Göttingen, 1979), 194.

[46] James L. Boone, 'Paternal Investment and Elite Family Structure in Preindustrial States: A Case Study of Late Medieval–Early Modern Portuguese Genealogies', *American Anthropologist* 88 (1986), 859–78.

[47] Anthony Molho, *Marriage Alliance in Late Medieval Florence* (Cambridge, Mass., 1994), 211–12.

[48] Hans-Peter Baum, 'Der Lehenhof des Hochstifts Würzburg im Spätmittelalter (1303–1519): Eine rechts- und sozialgeschichtliche Studie', vol. I (*Habilitationsschrift*, University of Würzburg, 1990), 171.

[49] Oskar Freiherr von Schaumberg, *Neuaufstellungen der Stammtafeln des uradelig fränkischen Geschlechts von Schaumberg* (Bamberg, 1953).

[50] Johannes Müllner, *Die Annalen der Reichsstadt Nürnberg von 1623*, ed. Gerhard Hirschmann, vol. II (Nuremberg, 1984), 407.

Schaumbergs is of course not a guarantee that Georg was as noteworthy as his family. It is equally true, on the other hand, that one should not automatically see a causal link between failed identification and obscurity. In any case, such indeterminacies are inevitable side-effects of prosopography. Some controls intended to test the sample for lopsidedness will be injected into the analysis as it progresses.

INDIVIDUAL PARAMETERS

The 242 identified principal feuders are analysed on the basis of the parameters discussed earlier as determinants of noblemen's social status: (1) office-holding: only the most prestigious and lucrative offices are considered – district governors, councillors, masters of the household, marshals, and major-domos. (2) Marriage alliances: for the sake of brevity and coherence, a matrimonial alliance was valued as conferring high status only if the bride's father was himself a high office-holder and/or a creditor or guarantor to princes. In the case of counts, the same value was attached also to marriages with princesses. Such rare affairs were not just marriages above one's station. They were coups with usually positive consequences for one's political and economic position.[51] (3) Money-lending or standing surety: both indicate economic strength and all too often political power as well.

These three parameters are not intended to lead to a social stratification analysis in the strict sense. Their aim is rather to create an ad hoc distinction between two categories. One is of feuding noblemen whose personal circumstances were remarkably positive, even if their families did not belong to the élite. The other is of feuding noblemen who cannot be said to have been well off or politically influential, even if their families were. Arguably, the condition of some of the feuders appraised as lesser nobles might in reality have been better than allowed here. Leaving out as important a parameter as property probably underestimates the social profile of the group. A further distortion in this direction should be allowed for, since low rank is being argued, in many cases, from silence. Data for marriages, for instance, are extremely difficult to come by. On the other hand, the advantage of employing a small number of variables is twofold. The result is straightforward; and it would necessarily be more conservative and cautious than if numerous variables were used. By setting up a few demanding parameters there is less risk of giving undue weight to feuders.

Throughout most of the following analysis, two samples of feuders will be examined separately but in juxtaposition. The first consists of noblemen who feuded against other noblemen, including princes; the second of noblemen who

---

[51] Karl-Heinz Spieß, *Familie und Verwandtschaft im deutschen Hochadel des Spätmittelalters: 13. bis Anfang des 16. Jahrhunderts* (Stuttgart, 1993), 101, 111, 404–7.

Prosopography of feuding noblemen

Table 4.1. *Distribution of feuders in Sample-I across individual parameters*

	Parameters	No.	%
(1)	Officials only	76	38.2
(2)	Highly married only	6	3.0
(3)	Creditors/guarantors only	7	3.5
(4)	Officials/highly married	16	8.0
(5)	Officials/creditors/guarantors	27	13.6
(6)	Highly married/creditors/guarantors	6	3.0
(7)	Officials/highly married/creditors/guarantors	14	7.0
	(High-status)	(152)	(76.3)
(8)	Low-status	47	23.6
	Total	199	99.9

Source: Appendix C.

feuded against cities and commoners (henceforward Sample-I and Sample-II, respectively). This division accords with what has earlier been observed on the different sets of relations obtaining among the nobility on the one hand and between nobles and cities on the other. Given that the guidelines for recording feuds were as a result also different, this is one way of testing by comparison the representativeness of each sample.

Of the 199 noblemen listed as having feuded against other noblemen, 152 (76.3 per cent) belonged to the upper echelons of the nobility. The solidity of this result is underscored by the fact that of these 152, 133 (87.5 per cent) were high office-holders – the most direct and safest indicator. Table 4.1, which classifies the 199 principals into eight mutually exclusive groups, provides further indications of the soundness of the sample. It shows that only six of the forty-two highly-married feuders (rows 2, 4, 6, 7) were neither office-holders nor creditors or guarantors; and that only seven of the fifty-four creditors and/or guarantors in the sample (rows 3, 5, 6, 7) were neither officials nor highly married. These figures square well with the argument made in chapter 3 that there was considerable overlap between criteria of high status. This inter-crossing of variables suggests another significant figure: 57 of the 133 officials among the feuders were also either highly married or creditors (or guarantors) or both (rows 4, 5, 7). Thus, more than one-fourth of the feuders enjoyed a degree of status crystallisation that places them at the very pinnacle of the nobility.

The social composition of the group of noblemen who took on cities was, as Table 4.2 shows, quite similar: thirty-one of the forty-three feuders (72 per cent) possessed high status. And of these thirty-one, twenty-eight (90.3 per cent) were high office-holders. Sample-II is certainly too small, and its range of variation too wide, to be able to claim unerring verisimilitude for its figures. Yet the fact that

79

Table 4.2. *Distribution of feuders in Sample-II across individual parameters*

Parameters	No.	%
(1) Officials only	14	32.6
(2) Highly married only	1	2.3
(3) Creditors/guarantors only	1	2.3
(4) Officials/highly married	5	11.6
(5) Officials/creditors/guarantors	5	11.6
(6) Highly married/creditors/guarantors	1	2.3
(7) Officials/highly married/creditors/guarantors	4	9.3
(High-status)	(31)	(72.0)
(8) Low-status	12	27.9
Total	43	99.9

Source: Appendix E.

the percentage of high-status feuders is almost the same in both samples suggests that it is at least a representative indication. Moreover, the fact that Sample-II is based mainly on feuds against imperial cities, Nuremberg in particular, seems to substantiate this indication. For if an undeserved share in urban wealth was the purpose of feuds of destitute noblemen against cities,[52] then Nuremberg and its Franconian sisters would certainly have been the ideal target. That such a high proportion of Nuremberg's enemies was made up of anything but poor, marginal noblemen makes at least the broad contours of the high social profile of feuders sufficiently visible.

FAMILY PARAMETERS

It has already been argued that to deduce the status of a nobleman from that of his family is a dangerous operation. Stratification did not stop at the threshold of the aristocratic house; it cut deep into the lineage, creating sharp disparities between lines.[53] Yet it is none the less highly plausible that nobles from a leading lineage had greater chances to be of high status than nobles from a minor one. Family parameters, despite their shortcomings, are therefore essential for a full prosopographical study of feuders. They can at least serve to control the analysis carried out on the basis of individual parameters.

The first family parameter is the status of the feuders' fathers. The fact that all sons had equal claim to inheritance makes the father's status relevant to theirs.

[52] Hermann Wiesflecker, *Kaiser Maximilian I: Das Reich, Österreich und Europa an der Wende zur Neuzeit*, vol. V, *Der Kaiser und seine Umwelt: Hof, Staat, Wirtschaft, Gesellschaft und Kultur* (Vienna, 1986), 99.
[53] See pp. 37–8 above.

Judging fathers by the individual parameters reveals that, in Sample-I, at least 109 (54.8 per cent) of them were high-status noblemen.[54] As might be expected, ninety-three (85.3 per cent) of these passed on their status to their feuding sons. The figures in Sample-II are quite similar: twenty-four of the fathers (55.8 per cent) were themselves eminent noblemen. Nineteen (79.2 per cent) of these were fathers of feuders of the same standing.[55] Most feuders, then, came from established lines.

The second family parameter is access to cathedral chapters. Its importance was derived from, among other things, the critical role it played in nobles' familial strategies. Underlying these was the desire to secure the continuity of the lineage. In view of the low life-expectancy and high mortality rate, perhaps all the more so in the nobility, the realisation of this objective called for a large number of male children. Birth control was therefore normally out of the question.[56] But at the same time, given the prevalent practice of partible inheritance, a large number of sons threatened the economic viability of the family. A succession of prolific generations would have resulted in too many divisions of property, each too small to support its holder.[57] Thus, numerous progeny would sooner or later have jeopardised the very continuity of the lineage they were supposed to ensure. One way to prevent the gradual disintegration of landed estates was the imposition of ecclesiastical celibacy on children. Yet claustration did not provide a perfect solution. If the noble monk's secular brothers died heirless the line would come to an abrupt end. An ecclesiastical institution that offered a life-return ticket, and much else, was the cathedral chapter.

In order to gain access to a cathedral chapter one needed more than just to qualify as a noble, or as the formula ran: *de militari ab utroque parente*. Even the prerequisite wealth and princely patronage were not enough, for cathedral chapters were effectively 'closed shops'. Most of the member families were tightly interrelated, forming a sort of clan that dominated the chapter.[58] This caste-like exclusivity was echoed in criticisms levelled against it, more often than not by frustrated applicants. One of these, the humanist Jakob Wimpfeling, complains in his *Mirror of Princes* that in allocating prebends young lads still

---

[54] See Appendix D.   [55] See Appendix F.

[56] Spieß, *Familie und Verwandtschaft im deutschen Hochadel*, 442–53; Gregory W. Pedlow, 'Marriage, Family Size, and Inheritance among Hessian Nobles, 1650–1900', *Journal of Family History* 7 (1982), 333–52.

[57] A marvellously graphic example is in StAW, Lehensachen, no. 2636 (Succession der Truchsessen zu Wetzhausen unnd Buntdorff im Forstmapt uff dem haßberg).

[58] Gerhard Fouquet, *Das Speyerer Domkapitel im späten Mittelalter (ca. 1350–1540): Adlige Freundschaft, fürstliche Patronage und päpstliche Klientel*, 2 vols. (Mainz, 1987), I, passim; Gerhard Fouquet, 'Reichskirche und Adel: Ursachen und Mechanismen des Aufstiegs der Kraichgauer Niederadelsfamilie v. Helmstatt im Speyerer Domkapitel zu Beginn des 15. Jahrhunderts', *ZGO* 129 (1981), 190–233; Rolf Sprandel, 'Die Ritterschaft und das Hochstift Würzburg', *JffL* 36 (1976), 117–43, at 118; Helmut Hartmann, 'Der Stiftsadel an den alten Domkapiteln zu Mainz, Trier, Bamberg und Würzburg', *Mainzer Zeitschrift* 73, no. 4 (1978/79), 99–138.

incapable of blowing their nose are preferred to real scholars.[59] More good-humoured was Erasmus. The story went round in aristocratic circles that, having been familiarised with the lofty cathedral chapter of Strasbourg, Erasmus quipped that it would not have admitted even Christ himself.[60]

Not for nothing was admission made difficult. Members of cathedral chapters drew impressive income and exercised political authority into the bargain.[61] Each member had also the at least theoretical chance of becoming a bishop, that is a prince of the Empire (or – in Mainz, Trier, and Cologne – an Elector). In such a case he would be in a position to further his family's interests by promoting the careers of some relations in the cathedral chapter, by installing others in offices, by providing still others with new fiefs. Bishop Lorenz von Bibra of Würzburg went to extremes, appointing nine members of his family to the offices of councillor or district governor, three of them to both. His successor, Konrad von Thüngen, went further, placing thirteen of his relations in high posts.[62] The imposition of celibacy by claustration was a far cry, then, from the imposition of celibacy by procurement of prebends in cathedral chapters. The latter's value extended far beyond the economic.

The 199 feuders in Sample-I came from 72 families. Forty-seven (65.3 per cent) of these had canons in the Franconian cathedral chapters of Würzburg, Bamberg, Eichstätt, and elsewhere.[63] But taking heed of the number of feuders that chapter families yielded, the result is once again above 70 per cent (see Table 4.3). The figures of Sample-II are notably higher. Here the forty-three feuders come from twenty-eight families. Twenty-five (89.3 per cent) of these had canons in cathedral chapters. The proportion of feuders made up by individuals from

---

[59] Bruno Singer, *Die Fürstenspiegel in Deutschland im Zeitalter des Humanismus und der Reformation: Bibliographische Grundlagen und ausgewählte Interpretationen. Jakob Wimpfeling, Wolfgang Seidel, Johann Sturm, Urban Rieger* (Munich, 1981), 239.

[60] Hansmartin Decker-Hauff (ed.), *Die Chronik der Grafen von Zimmern*, vol. III (Sigmaringen, 1972), 72. See on this point also Aloys Schulte, *Der Adel und die deutsche Kirche im Mittelalter*, 2nd edn (Stuttgart, 1922), 248.

[61] Fouquet, *Das Speyerer Domkapitel*, I, 28 and passim; Ernst Schubert, *Die Landstände des Hochstifts Würzburg* (Würzburg, 1967), passim.

[62] Heinzjürgen N. Reuschling, *Die Regierung des Hochstifts Würzburg 1495–1642: Zentralbehörden und führende Gruppen eines geistlichen Staates* (Würzburg, 1984), 435.

[63] See Appendixes D and F. The data for these Appendixes are from August Amrhein, 'Reihenfolge der Mitglieder des adeligen Domstifts zu Wirzburg, St. Kilian-Brüder genannt von seiner Gründung bis zur Säkularisation 741–1803', parts 1 and 2, *AU* 32 (1889), 1–314; 33 (1890), 1–380; Johannes Kist, *Das Bamberger Domkapitel*; Hugo A. Braun, *Das Domkapitel zu Eichstätt: Von der Reformationszeit bis zur Säkularisation (1535–1806). Verfassung und Presonalgeschichte* (Stuttgart, 1991); Fouquet, *Das Speyerer Domkapitel*, II; Albert Haemmerle, *Die Canoniker der Chorherrnstifte St. Moritz, St. Peter und St. Gertrud in Augsburg bis zur Saecularisation* (n.p., 1938); Wilhelm Kisky, *Die Domkapitel der geistlichen Kurfürsten in ihrer persönlichen Zusammensetzung im vierzehnten und fünfzehnten Jahrhundert* (Weimar, 1906); Rudolf Holbach, *Stiftsgeistlichkeit im Spannungsfeld von Kirche und Welt: Studien zur Geschichte des Trierer Domkapitels und Domklerus im Spätmittelalter*, part 2 (Trier, 1982). Also used were various family histories and genealogies. They are not being referred to here for reasons of space.

these families is a striking 90.7 per cent (see Table 4.3). These figures corroborate the previous results to the effect that the bulk of feuding noblemen were of high status and came from distinguished families.

The third parameter is continuity. The link between wealth or status and reproductive success has already been noted. A logical inference is a positive correlation between these elements and continuity. Hans-Peter Baum's research into the *Lehenhof* of Würzburg has come up with significant evidence supporting this assumption. According to his calculations, the chances of a noble family which survived from 1400 to the sixteenth century having belonged to the upper stratum in terms of property were 1 : 8. On the other hand, the probability ratio of a family which did not last that long having belonged to this stratum was a hopeless 1 : 80. For families with ambivalent noble status or with strong ties to towns, such chances were virtually nonexistent.[64] These conclusions imply that continuity, too, can be used to evaluate the status of a noble family.

The continuity target set down for feuders' families in order to be counted here as high-status is the early seventeenth century.[65] By then the outbreak of the Thirty Years' War may have introduced a disastrously indiscriminate factor of selection. Of the seventy-two families in Sample-I, sixty-one (84.7 per cent) reached into the seventeenth and eighteenth centuries. Eleven families are certain to have become extinct by the year 1600. Of the twenty-eight families in Sample-II, twenty-six (92.9 per cent) survived the sixteenth century (see Table 4.3).[66]

The final family parameter to be weighed here is membership of the so-called tournament nobility (*Turnieradel*). Unlike the Bavarian,[67] Franconian nobles eligible for tournaments did not constitute a distinct social category, a kind of sub-estate. Yet, as various tournament ordinances decreed, participation was subject to exacting examinations of parentage.[68] The shrill insistence on exclu-

---

[64] Hans-Peter Baum, 'Soziale Schichtung im mainfränkischen Niederadel um 1400', *ZHF* 13 (1986), 129–48, at 147–8.

[65] Data for continuity are mainly from Erwin Riedenauer, 'Kontinuität und Fluktuation im Mitgliederstand der fränkischen Reichsritterschaft: Eine Grundlegung zum Problem der Adelsstruktur in Franken', in *Gesellschaft und Herrschaft: Forschungen zu sozial- und landesgeschichtlichen Problemen vornehmlich in Bayern. Eine Festgabe für Karl Bosl zum 60. Geburtstag* (Munich, 1969), 87–152; Eugen Schöler, *Historische Familienwappen in Franken: 1860 Wappenschilde und familiengeschichtliche Notizen von Geschlechtern des Adels und der Reichsstädte in Franken*, 2nd edn (Neustadt a.d. Aisch, 1982); Ernst Heinrich Kneschke, *Neues allgemeines deutsches Adels-Lexicon*, 9 vols. (Leipzig, 1859–70).

[66] The fate of one family, Marschall von Eiwang, is unclear because it could not be identified. It may well have been a cadet line of one of the families surnamed Marschall.

[67] Heinz Lieberich, *Landherren und Landleute: Zur politischen Führungsschicht Bayerns im Spätmittelalter* (Munich, 1964), 16–32.

[68] Heide Stamm (ed.), *Das Turnierbuch des Ludwig von Eyb (cgm 961). Edition und Untersuchung mit einem Anhang: Die Turnierchronik des Jörg Rugen (Textabdruck)* (Stuttgart, 1986), 168, 202, 220. See also William H. Jackson, 'Tournaments and the German Chivalric *renovatio*: Tournament Discipline and the Myth of Origins', in *Chivalry in the Renaissance*, ed. Sydney Anglo (Woodbridge, 1990), 77–91, at 86; Andreas Ranft, *Adelsgesellschaften: Gruppenbildung und Genossenschaft im spätmittelalterlichen Reich* (Sigmaringen, 1994), 166–7.

Table 4.3. *Distribution of feuders and their families across family parameters*

		Cathedral chapter	Continuity	Tournament nobility
Sample-I				
Families	72	47 (65.3%)	61 (84.7%)	62 (86.1%)
Persons	199	145 (72.9%)	177 (88.9%)	174 (87.4%)
Sample-II				
Families	28	25 (89.3%)	26 (92.9%)	27 (96.4%)
Persons	43	39 (90.7%)	41 (95.3%)	42 (97.7%)

Sources: Appendixes D and F.

sivity may initially have been directed against presumptuous city patricians. But some noble families found themselves hit by the 'collateral damage' caused by these measures. They faced eviction from this symbolic heartland of the nobility.[69] For instance, only thirty-five of the ninety-six Franconian noble families resident in the Gebürg region were permitted into the spectacles.[70] Tournaments thus became more than a criterion of membership in the nobility: at least in terms of social prestige, the tournament companions (*Turniergenossen*) were set above those nobles who were refused entry.

Of the seventy-two feuders' families in Sample-I, sixty-two (86 per cent) were of the tournament nobility; of the twenty-eight in Sample-II, twenty-seven families (96.4 per cent).[71] Thus, as Table 4.3 demonstrates, the analysis of the family parameters bears out that of the individual ones.[72] It is noteworthy that the aggregate number of high-status feuders (183) is almost equivalent to the number of feuders (184) coming from cathedral chapter families – the most 'demanding' family parameter. The number of feuders from families with continuity or with representation in tournaments is – not surprisingly – even higher. But this should probably not be taken as an indication that the samples conceal a larger number of noblemen of account: if one rates as high-status families only those which fall under at least two parameters, then 'only' 172 of

---

[69] For an example see Klaus Freiherr von Andrian-Werburg, 'Die niederadeligen Kemnater im Coburgischen: Zur politischen und wirtschaftlichen Existenz der mittelalterlichen adeligen Unterschicht', *Jahrbuch der Coburger Landesstiftung* 30 (1985), 97–136, at 98.

[70] Klaus Rupprecht, *Ritterschaftliche Herrschaftswahrung in Franken: Die Geschichte der von Guttenberg im Spätmittelalter und zu Beginn der Frühen Neuzeit* (Neustadt a.d. Aisch, 1994), 40.

[71] Data for tournament eligibility are from Wigulejus Hund, *Bayrisch Stammen Buch* (Ingolstadt, 1598); Stamm (ed.), *Turnierbuch des Ludwig von Eyb*; Ludwig Albert Freiherr von Gumppenberg (ed.), 'Nachrichten über die Turniere zu Würzburg und Bamberg in den Jahren 1479 und 1486', *AU* 19, no. 2 (1867), 164–210.

[72] The main reason for the figures in Sample-II being, in proportional terms, consistently higher than those in Sample-I is that twenty-three families appear in both.

the 183 high-status feuders came from such families. This is still a very firm statistical correlation (94 per cent), one which lends credence to the usefulness of the family parameters as a control test. By the same token, however, it means that the proportion of high-status feuders cannot have been as high as 76 per cent or 72 per cent (Sample-I and Sample-II, respectively). Yet even so, it would remain in the area of 70 per cent (172 among 242 identified feuders = 71 per cent).[73]

This figure, finally, still underrates the extent to which feuding was a preserve of the noble power élite. For no less important than the ratio of high-status nobles among the feuders is the ratio of feuds pursued by such nobles. The initial sample contained 255 feuds. On aggregate, 56 of them were conducted by unidentified nobles, and therefore have to be discounted here. Now of the remaining 199 feuds, 155 (77.9 per cent) were executed by high-status nobles – that is more than their actual proportion among all the (identified) feuders. The explanation for this discrepancy is not far to seek: they each prosecuted more feuds on average than low-status nobles. Thus, of the twenty-three nobles who were involved in three or more feuds,[74] nineteen held high offices.

The fact that some 70 per cent of the feuders were high-status nobles, and that between them these nobles carried out nearly four fifths of the feuds, has wide implications. The first concerns the social location of the feud within the nobility. The methodological weaknesses of the 'robber-knighthood thesis' have already been discussed.[75] By approaching the feud prosopographically one achieves results that contrast sharply with those of Werner Rösener, the chief proponent of this paradigm.[76] That there was an element of brigandage in the feud cannot be disproved. The feud was too multi-faceted a phenomenon to exclude this totally. All sorts of elements could graft themselves onto feuds because feuds could serve all sorts of aims: economic, legal and political. But the chief agents of feud violence were not noblemen on the fringes of their class. Quite the contrary, all too many of them were rich and powerful individuals and sons of prominent families.

---

[73] If one applies the probability ratio of 71 per cent to the seventy-one unidentified feuders, then, considering the status of their families, twenty-eight of them would have been high-status nobles. Adding these 28 to the 183 identified high-status feuders, the result is 68.5 per cent of the total of 308 feuders – identified and unidentified – in the two samples (these 308 feuders do not include five noblemen from the five families which could not be identified).

[74] Eukarius von Aufseß (4 feuds); Konrad (X) von Aufseß (3); Götz von Berlichingen (4); Erasmus von Eberstein (4); Christoph von Giech (3); Philipp von Guttenberg (3); Count Heinrich (XII) of Henneberg (5); Count Hermann (VIII) of Henneberg (3); Count Wilhelm (III) of Henneberg (3); Count Wilhelm (IV) of Henneberg (3); Count Otto (IV) of Henneberg (7); Lorenz von Hutten (4); Georg von Rain (3); Hermann (II) Riedesel (4); Hermann (III) Riedesel (4); Georg Riedesel (3); Georg von Rosenberg (6); Heinrich Rüdt von Collenberg (4); Baron Sigmund of Schwarzenberg (5); Reuß von Thüngen (3); Hildebrand von Steinrück (3); Veit von Vestenberg (8); Veit von Wallenrod (3). See Sources of Information for Appendixes C and E.

[75] See chap. 1.

[76] Werner Rösener, 'Zur Problematik des spätmittelalterlichen Raubrittertums', in *Festschrift für Berent Schwineköper zu seinem siebzigsten Geburtstag*, ed. Helmut Maurer and Hans Patze (Sigmaringen, 1982), 469–88.

The second implication concerns a political and constitutional approach to the feud. Otto Brunner's seminal model of the feud, associating it with a stateless society, cannot be accepted unmodified.[77] His explanation is incapable of accommodating the fact that the majority of feuders were actually servitors, not opponents, of the incipient state. This disturbing fact – that the men entrusted with maintaining order were apparently its very breakers – is the most consequential clue for a different interpretation of the feud.

[77] Otto Brunner, *'Land' and Lordship: Structures of Governance in Medieval Austria*, trans. Howard Kaminsky and James Van Horn Melton (Philadelphia, 1992), 1–94 and passim.

5

State, nobility, and lordship: the feud interpreted

In late 1462 Bishop Georg of Bamberg forbade Christoph Fuchs to graze his sheep in the marches of Niederhaide. Fuchs, who claimed he held the sheep-run in fee from the bishop of Würzburg, refused to comply with the directive. The incident led to a feud, the feud to a war between the bishops of Bamberg and Würzburg. Lorenz Fries, who chronicled these events, estimated the annual income from Fuchs's sheep-run at three gulden. He concluded that 'this was the beautiful Helen over which the two princes . . . went to a veritable Trojan War'.[1] Fries knew better, and his classical associations fail to come to grips with the realities of late medieval feud and war. Why would a nobleman risk a feud against a prince for a property yielding such a paltry revenue? Why would such a seemingly trivial episode develop into an internecine war between princes? The Iliad provides no adequate explanation.

The main difficulty involved in accounting for the causes of feuds is that, as Otto Brunner pointed out long ago, feuds were an integral part of the political process and inhered in the very fabric of German society.[2] As such, they bring into sight a form of interaction in which diverse motives and roles were acted out and on which divergent expectations converged. Accordingly, the variety of issues over which feuds broke out appears at first glance so wide as to defy systematisation: castles, forests, jurisdictions, fishponds, sheep-runs, hunting-grounds, subject peasants, rents and dues, tithes, outstanding debts, dowries, even cathedral chapter prebends.

To classify these instances as subgenera of a prevalent conflict over property rights is useful, but only up to a point. Such a classification overlooks the qualitative difference between, for example, feuds against princes and feuds

---

[1] Lorenz Fries, *Historie, Nahmen, Geschlecht, Wesen, Thaten, gantz Leben und Sterben des gewesenen Bischoffen zu Wirtzburg und Hertzogen zu Francken* [1544], in *Geschicht-Schreiber von dem Bischofftthum Wirtzbürg*, ed. Johann Peter Ludewig (Frankfurt am Main, 1713), 838–45.

[2] Otto Brunner, *'Land' and Lordship: Structures of Governance in Medieval Austria*, trans. Howard Kaminsky and James Van Horn Melton (Philadelphia, 1992), esp. 1–94. For programmatic reflections on the feud as a 'total social fact' see Joseph Morsel, '"Das sy sich mitt der besstenn gewarsamig schicken, das sy durch die widerwertigenn Franckenn nit nidergeworffen werdenn": Überlegungen zum sozialen Sinn der Fehdepraxis am Beispiel des spätmittelalterlichen Franken', in *Strukturen der Gesellschaft im Mittelalter: Interdisziplinäre Mediävistik in Würzburg*, ed. Dieter Rödel and Joachim Schneider (Wiesbaden, 1996), 140–67.

against cities. For the sets of property and other relations between noblemen on the one hand and princes or cities on the other were not identical in the first place. There were also quantitative differences. The 26,000-gulden debt of the bishop of Würzburg to the von Hirschhorn family must ostensibly have exerted a far greater pressure on them than the loss of his sheep-run did on Christoph Fuchs.[3] And yet both of these very dissimilar claims were considered equally worth feuding over, whereby the latter had by far the graver aftermath. 'Property' does not provide a sufficiently overarching concept to serve a study of the knightly feud.

Feuds, however, did have a number of salient traits in common: virtually all principal feuders were noblemen; most of these were of a high status;[4] and all of them – irrespective of their particular motives – drew on the same fixed repertoire of methods in carrying out their feuds. On that account feuds were executed by people from a similar background and according to conventionalised, well-understood rules of conduct. Thus, in terms of both practitioners and practice, the knightly feud enjoyed a good measure of coherence.

The sharp contrast between the routinised uniformity of the practice of feuding and the variability of its immediate causes prompts a change of perspective. It is by analysing the feud at the level of the sociopolitical order at large, with its compulsive strains, that the feud will acquire a comprehensive signification. Only then may the sundry goals pursued by feuders fall into place. This analysis will centre on 'lordship' both as the economic framework of noblemen's existence and as a set of relations of domination on which their social and political position rested. Briefly stated, the feud will be interpreted in terms of lordship as the point of intersection of two processes: princely state-building on the one hand and social stratification among the nobility on the other. From this vantage point, even the sensational feud of Christoph Fuchs and, more importantly, the consequent war are explicable and appear as anything but reckless.

FROM ARISTOCRACY TO NOBILITY

The years around 1400 marked a watershed in the social history of Franconia. It was about that time that the Franconian aristocracy – a loosely demarcated group of socially and politically dominant families – embarked on fashioning a novel and distinctive collective identity to set themselves apart from the rest of society. Henceforth this group – the nobility – was to become ever more integrated and exclusive, its boundaries ever less permeable.[5] It is noteworthy that the term

---

[3] Eberhard Lohmann, *Die Herrschaft Hirschhorn: Studien zur Herrschaftsbildung eines Rittergeschlechts* (Darmstadt, 1986), 45.

[4] See chap. 4.

[5] 'Aristocracy' is used in this particular context to emphasise political authority and leadership; 'nobility' to refer to a group whose distinctive identity is based on specific 'constitutional' rights – an *ordre juridique*.

'knighthood' (*Ritterschaft*) first came to designate a social group only as late as 1400, and that the word *Adel* had not applied to the nobility in a similar sense before that date.[6]

The year 1400 saw also the battle of Bergtheim. With most of the nobility fighting on the bishop of Würzburg's side, it dashed the episcopal territorial towns' aspiration for freedom.[7] A few months later Johann von Egloffstein, the commander of the victorious army and provost of the cathedral chapter, was elected bishop of Würzburg. His register of fiefs introduced a novel classification. Henceforth vassals were registered not primarily following the chronological order of their enfeoffment, as had been the rule hitherto, but according to their social estate (*Stand*). Noble feoffees were lumped together in one section. Each rank – princes, counts and barons, untitled nobles – was then recorded in a sub-section. Burghers and peasants, grouped together in another section, were entered into the *Lehenbücher* following their geographical origin.[8] Thus, the two groups – nobles and commoners – were subjected to two different taxonomic principles, the one feudal and personal, the other territorial and regnant.

Another momentous change followed: the appearance of the free knightly fief (*freies Rittermannlehen*). It engendered tangible inequality between noblemen and commoners with regard to successional procedures. Fiefs held by commoners were to devolve only upon direct descendants and to escheat to the bishop in their absence; free knightly fiefs, in contrast, could be bequeathed to collateral relations. The import of this legal discrimination can hardly be overstated: it also implied that no military service was required or expected from peasants and burghers holding from the bishop the so-called ignoble fiefs (*unedle Mannlehen*).[9] In a medieval martial society, this debarring of commoners from warfare amounted to degradation.[10] In view of these developments, it is reasonable to date

---

[6] Joseph Morsel, 'Une société politique en Franconie à la fin du Moyen Age: Les Thüngen, leurs princes, leurs pairs et leurs hommes (1275–1525)' (PhD thesis, University of Paris-IV Sorbonne, 1993), 607–13. For some of the ideological and discursive changes accompanying the formation of the nobility see Joseph Morsel, 'Changements anthroponymiques et sociogenèse de la noblesse en Franconie à la fin du Moyen Age', in *Genèse médiévale de l'anthroponymie moderne*, vol. III, *Enquêtes généalogiques et données prosopographiques*, ed. Monique Bourin and Pascal Chareille (Tours, 1995), 89–119; 'Die Erfindung des Adels: Zur Soziogenese des Adels am Ende des Mittelalters – Das Beispiel Frankens', in *Nobilitas: Funktion und Repräsentation des Adels in Alteuropa*, ed. Otto Gerhard Oexle and Werner Paravicini (Göttingen, 1996).

[7] J. B. Kestler, 'Archivalische Nachrichten über die Schlacht bei Bergtheim im Jahre 1400', *AU* 15, no. 1 (1860), 186–91; Alfred Wendehorst, *Das Bistum Würzburg*, 3 parts (Berlin, 1962–78), II, 118–23.

[8] Hans-Peter Baum, 'Der Lehenhof des Hochstifts Würzburg im Spätmittelalter (1303–1519): Eine rechts- und sozialgeschichtliche Studie', 3 vols. (*Habilitationsschrift*, University of Würzburg, 1990), I, 18–22.

[9] Ibid., 93–4, 103–5.

[10] The nobles themselves repeatedly stressed that their class privileges, such as tax exemption, were based on traditional military service. See Christian Meyer (ed.), 'Die Familienchronik des Ritters Michel von Ehenheim', *Hohenzollerische Forschungen* 5 (1897), 369–419, at 415–16; *RTA, mR*, v, 1249, no. 1708.

the closing of the ranks of the Franconian nobility as late as the first half of the fifteenth century.[11]

The induration of class boundaries set in motion, or at least intensified, a process of social change among the nobility as well. For fiefs became more than just a criterion for inclusion in, and exclusion from, the Franconian nobility. They also came to play a decisive role in ensuring continuity. This has been illuminated by Hans-Peter Baum's ground-breaking research into the *Lehenhof* of the bishops of Würzburg between 1303 and 1519. He has demonstrated that untitled noble families fared very differently depending on the quality, rather than quantity, of their fiefs and their appurtenant rights. Castles, for example, towered – not only literally – above any other form of property because they entailed the strongest claim to the exercise of lordship, the raison d'être of the nobility.[12] Families distinguished by their possession of such high-quality, lordship-conferring fiefs were over-represented among those which survived into the mid-sixteenth century.[13] A a close relation clearly obtained between this type of feudal wealth and continuity.[14]

The explanation for this correlation is, statistically speaking, simple: the families strongest on feudal property had also the largest average number of vassals in the *Lehenhof*. They alone were responsible for the growth in the average number of vassals per family from fewer than two in 1303 to more than five in 1519. Particularly startling is the case of the group of families which Baum rates as the top stratum in terms of feudal property. From 12 families and 37 persons (3.1 per family) in the beginning of the period, their number mounted to 51 families and 513 persons (10.1 per family) at its end. By 1519 this group constituted 28 per cent of the total of untitled noble lineages but 53 per cent of the individual vassals.[15] In other words, the Würzburg *Lehenhof* was absorbed, as it were, by some fifty large families endowed with superior fiefs. This makes plain why these families had better prospects of continuity than those with inferior fiefs.

Whether or not the actual number of male nobles rose at an equal pace is, albeit highly probable, impossible to ascertain. In any case, the crucial point is that the number of vassals representing a lineage in the *Lehenhof* was likely to

[11] Baum, 'Der Lehenhof des Hochstifts Würzburg', I, 198–9. For the older, now superseded view see Josef Fleckenstein, 'Die Entstehung des niederen Adels und das Rittertum', in *Herrschaft und Stand: Untersuchungen zur Sozialgeschichte im 13. Jahrhundert*, ed. Josef Fleckenstein (Göttingen, 1977), 17–39.

[12] Hans-Peter Baum, 'Burg', in *Lexikon des Mittelalters*, ed. Robert-Henri Bautier et al., vol. II (Munich, 1983), cols. 968–71; Michael Mitterauer, 'Probleme der Stratifikation in mittelalterlichen Gesellschaftssystemen', in *Theorien in der Praxis des Historikers*, ed. Jürgen Kocka (Göttingen, 1977), 13–43, at 28.

[13] Baum, 'Der Lehenhof des Hochstifts Würzburg', I, 177, 179–80.

[14] Ibid., 179–80. See also Gerhard Rechter, *Das Land zwischen Aisch und Rezat: Die Kommende Virnsberg Deutschen Ordens und die Rittergüter im oberen Zenngrund* (Neustadt a.d. Aisch, 1981), 218.

[15] Baum, 'Der Lehenhof des Hochstifts Würzburg', I, 171.

increase with the amplitude of superior fiefs this lineage held. This is all the more significant as a reverse order of causation is unwarranted. The number of authority-conferring fiefs could not be multiplied at pleasure. Although the number of castles granted in fee quintupled between 1303 and 1519, it was unable to keep abreast of the number of top-stratum vassals. And the increase in the amount of other kinds of valuable fiefs was slower still.[16]

There are two conclusions to be drawn from these findings which are particularly pertinent to the argument of this chapter. First, a considerable demographic pressure must have been building up with regard to lordship-conferring fiefs. As a result, these fiefs must have come to be looked upon by noble families, especially by leading ones, as vital to their fortune. It is easy to see how this situation was conducive to conflicts.[17] A fief was one of the main reasons for the feud between Hans von Egloffstein, a member of an elevated and very large family, and the bishop of Bamberg in 1545. The noble suggested he would forbear from feuding if the bishop invested him instead with a district governorship, 'so that he could provide for and maintain [his] wife and children'.[18] This points up the value of a governorship as well. It would have eased the pressure on the family of its occupier.[19] Hence both authority-conferring fiefs and district governorships were in strong demand – demand, however, which outstripped supply.

The second and related conclusion is that between 1300 and 1500 Franconia underwent a process of feudalisation. Fiefs both proliferated and grew in importance. Noblemen were increasingly tempted, sometimes forced, to transform allodial property into fiefs to be then received from princes.[20] By the early sixteenth century, it seems, the holdings of prominent families were composed of two main blocs, fiefs and pledges, with free assets few and far between.[21] At the same time, princes turned substantial portions of their cameral domains into fiefs to be distributed among noblemen.[22] In this last respect, pledge-lordships played

---

[16] Ibid., 172, 176–7.
[17] Cf. Klaus Rupprecht, *Ritterschaftliche Herrschaftswahrung in Franken: Die Geschichte der von Guttenberg im Spätmittelalter und zu Beginn der Frühen Neuzeit* (Neustadt a.d. Aisch, 1994), 160 n. 14.
[18] StAB, Hofrat Ansbach-Bayreuth, no. 579.
[19] Cf. Gerd Wunder, 'Die Ritter von Vellberg', in *Vellberg in Geschichte und Gegenwart*, ed. Hansmartin Decker-Hauff, vol. I, *Darstellungen* (Sigmaringen, 1984), 129–96, at 163–5; Rupprecht, *Ritterschaftliche Herrschaftswahrung in Franken*, 300.
[20] The various reasons for this will become clearer as the argument of this chapter unfolds. See Morsel, 'Une société politique en Franconie', 258–61, 263–5; Baum, 'Der Lehenhof des Hochstifts Würzburg', I, 72–4; Harold H. Kehrer, 'The von Sickingen and the German Princes 1262–1523' (PhD thesis, Boston University Graduate School, 1977), 49; Ferdinand Andraschko, *Schloß Schwarzenberg im Wandel der Zeiten: Ein Beitrag zu seiner Geschichte*, 2nd edn (Neustadt a.d. Aisch, 1967), 19.
[21] Baum, 'Der Lehenhof des Hochstifts Würzburg', I, 270–1; Rupprecht, *Ritterschaftliche Herrschaftswahrung in Franken*, 213, 221.
[22] Baum, 'Der Lehenhof des Hochstifts Würzburg', I, 173.

a part in the process somewhat similar to high-quality fiefs: both were appro-
priated by the princes exclusively for noblemen, and for overlapping purposes;
and both tended, albeit to an unequal extent, to be treated by noblemen as
patrimonial possessions, and for similar social and political needs. Indeed, on
occasion noblemen were prepared to convert their allodial property into fiefs only
in exchange for a district governorship – to be held, sometimes, for life.[23] The
cumulative effect was that by the year 1500 the allodial landscape of Franconia
had been eroded in favour of a feudal one.[24] But this feudalism was different
from the 'military feudalism' of an earlier period. For want of a better phrase, it
might be characterised as 'territorial' – perhaps even 'centralised' – feudalism.[25]
As the term implies, this was the paradoxical outcome of princes' attempts at
state-making.

TERRITORIALISING PRINCES AND FEUDING NOBLEMEN

In 1495 Emperor Maximilian tried to impose a new tax, the Common Penny.[26]
Nobles were not to be exempted. Maximilian enjoined on the three Franconian
princes to prepare lists of ratable knights in their territories. One of the many
problems the princes consequently faced must have been the prevalence of
multiple vassalage: the question was which of the three tax registers was to enrol
a vassal holding fiefs from more than one prince. The margrave of Brandenburg
named 62 noble lineages, the bishops of Würzburg and Bamberg 109 and 48,
respectively.[27] A cartography of the recorded lineages demonstrates that the
overriding criterion was territorial: lineages appeared on the list of the prince in

---

[23] *Unser Friderichen Freyherren von Schwartzenberg und zu Hohenlandsperg* . . . (1535), 24 (my
pagination). I have used the copy BL, cat. no. 708.h.25; Hermann Freiherr von Reitzenstein,
Geschichte der Familie von Reitzenstein (Munich, 1891), 166–7; Eberhard Graf von Fugger, *Die
Seinsheim und ihre Zeit: Eine Familien- und Kulturgeschichte von 1155–1890* (Munich, 1893),
Appendix 201; Hellmut Kunstmann, *Die Burgen der östlichen fränkischen Schweiz* (Würzburg, 1965),
254; Johannes Bischoff, *Genealogie der Ministerialen von Blassenberg und Freiherren von (und zu)
Guttenberg 1148–1970* (Würzburg, 1971), 81, 150. See also Friedrich Pröll, 'Geschichte des
ehemaligen markgräflich-bayreuthischen Schlosses und Amtes Osternohe und der dortigen
Kirche', *Jb.Mfr.* 50 (1903), 1–144, at 68; Rupprecht, *Ritterschaftliche Herrschaftswahrung in
Franken*, 135 n. 266. See also pp. 95, 113–14 below.
[24] Rolf Sprandel, 'Die territorialen Ämter des Fürstentums Würzburg im Spätmittelalter', *JffL* 37
(1977), 45–64, at 51; Baum, 'Der Lehenhof des Hochstifts Würzburg', I, 270–2. See also Erich
Freiherr von Guttenberg, *Das Bistum Bamberg*, part 1 (Berlin, 1937), 265–6, 269, 274, 278, 283–4;
Rupprecht, *Ritterschaftliche Herrschaftswahrung in Franken*, 145, 151, 221.
[25] For the instrumentalisation of feudal lordship see Ernst Schubert, *Fürstliche Herrschaft und
Territorium im späten Mittelalter* (Munich, 1996), 71–2.
[26] Peter Schmid, *Der Gemeine Pfennig von 1495: Vorgeschichte und Entstehung, verfassungsgeschichtliche,
politische und finanzielle Bedeutung* (Göttingen, 1989).
[27] StAW, Stb, no. 817, fols. 45^r–52^r. The list is reproduced alphabetically, disregarding the original
classification, in Constantin Höfler, *Franken, Schwaben und Bayern: Eine Rede gehalten zu Culmbach
am 8. Juli 1850. Nebst einer archivalischen Beilage: das älteste officielle Verzeichnis der fränkischen
Ritterschaft von 1495 enthaltend* (Bamberg, 1850), 13–16.

whose territory their main seats were, regardless of their feudal ties to other princes.[28]

The rolls expressed a statist vision from the princes' point of view. To a large extent they were also the product of a political fancy. For in 1495 noblemen, roused by the Common Penny, set about instituting the Imperial Knighthood. This organisation was to keep them, for the next three centuries, out of reach of the states envisioned by princes. The six cantons they constituted as administrative units cut across the three principalities. There was thus an inherent contradiction in the relations between princes and nobility: on the one hand individual noblemen controlled and ran district governorships, the building-blocks of princely territorial rule; on the other hand it was these very same noblemen who, as a group, hampered internal compacting of princely territories.[29] This contradiction had a counterpart which clarifies it: territorialisation of noblemen failed because they were essential to its success. It had to be carried out by the very noble lineages over which princes purported to hold sway. Their intermediary powers made noblemen the indispensable agents of princes' territorial designs.

The struggles between princes involved in territorialisation forced them to compete for the loyalty of noblemen capable of serving the business of state-building. The princes appreciated that the nobles were, in the words of Margrave Friedrich (1371–1440), their 'greatest treasure'.[30] They proved versatile hunters. Their techniques ranged from naming castles after chivalric virtues, founding orders of knighthood, putting on tournaments, to introducing legal reforms designed to draw noblemen to their sphere of influence.[31] Multiple vassalage came to play a decisive role in this competitive situation: by enfeoffing other lords' vassals princes sought not only to win over noblemen but also to gain a foothold in their rivals' territories. By the same token, they had to reckon with conceding enclaves to their adversaries. Thus, multiple vassalage both resulted

---

[28] Rolf Sprandel, 'Mittelalterliche Verfassungs- und Sozialgeschichte vom Blickpunkt einer Landschaft: Mainfranken', *ZHF* 7 (1980), 401–22, at 410–12.

[29] The leaders of the Franconian Knighthood were usually princes' most trusted office-holders and servitors. See chap. 6.

[30] Constantin Höfler (ed.), *Des Ritters Ludwig von Eyb zu Eybburg Denkwürdigkeiten brandenburgischer (hohenzollerischer) Fürsten* (Bayreuth, 1849), 119.

[31] Wilhelm Störmer, 'Die Rolle der höfischen Tugendbegriffe fröude, milte, êre im politischen Spannungsfeld zwischen dem Hochstift Würzburg und dem Erzstift Mainz', *Würzburger Diözesangeschichtsblätter* 42 (1980), 1–10; Hanns Hubert Hofmann, 'Der Adel in Franken', in *Deutscher Adel 1430–1555*, ed. Hellmuth Rößler (Darmstadt, 1965), 95–126, at 109; Andreas Ranft, *Adelsgesellschaften: Gruppenbildung und Genossenschaft im spätmittelalterlichen Reich* (Sigmaringen, 1994), 29; Hubertus von Wilmowsky, 'Die Geschichte der Ritterschaft Buchenau von ihren Anfängen bis zum Wiener Kongreß', *Fuldaer Geschichtsblätter* 40 (1964), 1–47, at 24; William H. Jackson, 'Tournaments and the German Chivalric *renovatio*: Tournament Discipline and the Myth of Origins', in *Chivalry in the Renaissance*, ed. Sydney Anglo (Woodbridge, 1990), 77–91, at 89; Wolfgang Leiser, 'Süddeutsche Land- und Kampfgerichte des Spätmittelalters', *WFr* 70 (1986), 5–17.

from, and reproduced, the political fragmentation of the Franconian principalities.[32] This made it imperative for princes to maintain in good repair their personal relations with noblemen, to cultivate the allegiance of as large a noble clientele as possible. Because of their seigneuries, with their control over land and people, noblemen could serve princes as a buffer against their enemies. Alternatively, they could be used by princes to stake out territorial claims.[33]

A case in point are the counts of Castell, whose lands lay mostly in the diocese of Würzburg. In 1452 the comital house was heavily indebted as well as threatened with extinction. Count Wilhelm's eldest son was killed boar-hunting. The younger son, Count Friedrich, was a canon in Strasbourg. The danger arose that Margrave Albrecht of Brandenburg would try to take control of the county. Indeed, he drew Count Friedrich, who had resigned from his benefice, to his court where he was married to a margravial maid of honour. Hence in 1453 Bishop Gottfried of Würzburg made a compact with Count Wilhelm. The latter covenanted not to sell or pledge property in the next twenty years. Würzburg was also granted preemption. In 1457 the county was made over to Bishop Gottfried's successor as a fief.[34] A territorial fragmentation of the bishopric was averted. Moreover, it stood to gain in territorial coherence, should the counts of Castell die out.

Similar territorial capacities were assumed by fiefs, district governorships and other pledge-lordships. In 1494 Engelhard von Buchenau sold extensive estates to the landgrave of Hesse for 2000 gulden. Engelhard held this property in fee from the prince-abbot of Fulda. The latter could not tolerate the landgrave's inroad into his territory – the second courtesy of the Buchenaus.[35] A feud broke out between the abbot and Engelhard.[36] In 1495 the latter's exertions were recom-

---

[32] Ernst Schubert, *Die Landstände des Hochstifts Würzburg* (Würzburg, 1967), 130–1. A typical example is a letter sent by one nobleman to the bishop of Würzburg: he cannot join the feudal host of the bishop, he says, for he has been called on to serve the margrave and the count of Württemberg (incidentally, the enemies of the bishop in the conflict which made the feudal muster necessary). See StAW, Stb, no. 717, fols. 605^{r-v}.

[33] Julius von Minutoli (ed.), *Das kaiserliche Buch des Markgrafen Albrecht Achilles: Kurfürstliche Periode von 1470–1486* (Berlin, 1850), 250, no. 223; Gustav Freiherr von Hasselholdt-Stockheim (ed.), *Urkunden und Beilagen zum Kampfe der wittelsbachischen und brandenburgischen Politik in den Jahren 1459 bis 1465*, vol. I, part 1 (Leipzig, 1865), 158–9, no. 31; Felix Priebatsch (ed.), *Politische Correspondenz des Kurfürsten Albrecht Achilles*, 3 vols. (Leipzig, 1894–1898), III, 351–5, no. 1046; Dietrich Deeg, *Die Herrschaft der Herren von Heideck: Eine Studie zu hochadliger Familien- und Besitzgeschichte* (Neustadt a.d. Aisch, 1968), 118–19; Reinhard Stauber, 'Herzog Georg der Reiche von Niederbayern und Schwaben: Voraussetzungen und Formen landesherrlicher Expansionspolitik an der Wende vom Mittelalter zur Neuzeit', *ZbLG* 49 (1986), 611–70, at 661–6, 668; Rupprecht, *Ritterschaftliche Herrschaftswahrung in Franken*, 128 n. 235.

[34] Pius Wittmann, (ed.), *Monumenta Castellana: Urkundenbuch zur Geschichte des fränkischen Dynastengeschlechtes der Grafen und Herren zu Castell, 1057–1546* (Munich, 1890), 265, 270–3, nos. 569, 583.

[35] For the first inroad facilitated by the Buchenaus see August Weber, 'Das Amt Haselstein', *Fuldaer Geschichtsblätter* 32 (1956), 8–11, at 8.

[36] Josef Leinweber, *Das Hochstift Fulda vor der Reformation* (Fulda, 1972), 22; Wilmowsky, 'Die Geschichte der Ritterschaft Buchenau', 40.

pensed for: he was invested with a landgravial district governorship for life.[37] The awareness of what was at stake in such dealings was acute among both princes and noblemen. In 1475 the margravial governor Hans von Redwitz told his prince that

it would be a great thing for Your Grace and the lordship (*herschaft*) if Your Grace drew Paul [von Streitberg] with his castle Streitberg into the lordship . . . Your Grace would win with Streitberg a bastion linking Your Grace's highlands and lowlands, which is [so] situated against the neighbouring princes . . . and Nuremberg, that if it came to pass that they set themselves against Your Grace, they all would stand in fear of it and rather spare Your Grace and your men the use of force.[38]

In return, Redwitz recommended, the margrave should nominate Paul von Streitberg to the governorship of Bayreuth or Zwernitz, both in the vicinity of the castle. In 1486 Eberhard von Streitberg, Paul's son, made the lineage's onomastic castle an open house for the margrave.[39] This put him in opposition to his cousins and co-lords. They were backed by the bishop of Bamberg, in whose territory the fortress lay and from whom it was held in fee. In 1497 the conflict came to a head. A domestic feud flared up which in turn brought the bishop and the margrave to the brink of war.[40] Meanwhile, Eberhard was appointed a margravial governor and councillor. In 1507 his son, Georg, sold the castle he did not own to his father in-law Ludwig von Leineck, who happened to be a margravial governor. It was a pro forma sale: in 1508 Leineck 'sold' the castle to the margrave. Georg von Streitberg was named district governor in Creusen.[41] In this way one line of the Streitbergs engineered its own social upgrading at the expense of another; and the margrave managed to seize a strategic stronghold at the expense of a rival prince. He later made Streitberg into a district governorship.[42]

Noblemen's lordships made them pivotal to the competition between Franconian territorial powers. Yet whether in the form of governorships or of superior fiefs, princely favours were in too limited supply to be able to satisfy demand. Inevitably, princes had to make choices, to prefer some 'applicants' to others.[43] Their efforts to create states affected in this way social stratification among the nobility. The

---

[37] Karl E. Demandt, *Der Personenstaat der Landgrafschaft Hessen im Mittelalter: Ein 'Staatshandbuch' Hessens vom Ende des 12. bis zum Anfang des 16. Jahrhunderts*, part 1 (Marburg, 1981), 115, no. 376.

[38] Priebatsch (ed.), *Politische Correspondenz des Kurfürsten Albrecht Achilles*, II, 191, no. 166.

[39] Paul Oesterreicher, *Die Burg Streitberg* (Bamberg, 1819), 15.

[40] *RTA, mR*, vi, *passim*; Reinhard Seyboth, *Die Markgraftümer Ansbach und Kulmbach unter der Regierung Markgraf Friedrichs des Älteren (1486–1515)* (Göttingen, 1985), 317–20.

[41] Oesterreicher, *Burg Streitberg*, 26–9, 40, 55–7.

[42] Hellmut Kunstmann, *Die Burgen der westlichen und nördlichen fränkischen Schweiz*, part 1, *Der Südwesten: unteres Wiesenttal und Trubachtal* (Würzburg, 1971), 62–7.

[43] The margrave explained to one angry nobleman that 'Wir haben vil diener in unnsern lannden hieaussen [*scil.* Franconia] und dynnen die nit hofgesind sind. Es trug unnser gut kawm all unnser hofgesind diener oder Landsessen stetigs zufuren die von dem adel geboren sind dann wir glauben das inn der Mark und hieaus treff auff [4000] geraisigs pferd': StAN, Ansbacher Historica, no. 210, prod. of Freitag vor Antonii [12 January] 1487.

competition between the princes compounded a competition between the nobles, even between lines of the same family. It revolved around proximity to princes to whom noblemen endeavoured to make themselves useful. Hence they advanced loans to rulers and transformed their private property into fiefs. The von Thüngen family, for example, converted five allodial castles into fiefs between 1430 and 1501. One was held from the prince-abbot of Fulda; one from the king of Bohemia; two from the margrave of Brandenburg; and one castle was held half-and-half from the cathedral chapter and the bishop of Würzburg. Remarkably, it was in the territory of the latter that this family's seats were concentrated. The Thüngens were clearly inclined to make their allods over to princes geographically remote from the property in question.[44] The Thüngens were no exception. It was customary, because essential, for noblemen to play on the rivalries between princes. By establishing multiple feudal ties noblemen tried to balance out the increasing pressure exerted on them by competing, territorialising rulers. The struggle among the nobility and the struggle between princes were intertwined. Those families which failed to gain access to multiple *Lehenhöfe* went down in the world, in large part because they were too dependent to count for much. Conversely, the more significant the fiefs held by a noble family from one feudal lord were, the likelier this family was to receive authority-conferring fiefs from several other feudal lords as well. Like offices, multiple vassalage was a passport to the élite.[45]

Ironically, it was mainly this élite that was responsible for thwarting the princely territorialisation which brought it into being. The power they arrogated to themselves enabled them to reinforce their feudal-personal ties with princes. They thereby secured their 'liberties' and foiled their transformation into subjects.[46] The logic was inexorable: the more strenuous the conflict between princes grew, the more these lineages gained in influence, and the less were princes able to compass territorialisation. In other words, class structure and the organisational form of the princely state determined each other. It was from this dialectic between state formation and social stratification that the feud emanated. Simultaneously, it took a hand in this interplay of factors. A first approximation of these suggestions can be gained by examining the wars which punctuated the ongoing contention between princes.

WARS AND FEUDS

Territorial conflicts in Franconia grew more momentous after 1440, when the belligerent Margrave Albrecht Achilles of Brandenburg arrived on the scene.[47]

---

[44] Morsel, 'Une société politique en Franconie', 250–2, 275.
[45] Baum, 'Der Lehenhof des Hochstifts Würzburg', I, 190–1.
[46] Schubert, *Die Landstände des Hochstifts Würzburg*, 63–76.
[47] For a biographical sketch see Ernst Schubert, 'Albrecht Achilles, Markgraf und Kurfürst von Brandenburg (1414–1486)', *Fränkische Lebensbilder* 4 (1971), 130–72.

With him the struggle for regional supremacy, especially against Würzburg, began in earnest.[48] The bishops, particularly under Gottfried (1443–55), reacted by reviving a programmatic claim to the presumptive title of duke of Franconia – a claim which later was to receive a grandiose pictorial representation by Giambattista Tiepolo.[49] Margrave Albrecht refused to recognise this pretension. Instead, with the pope's blessing, he took to sporting the title himself.[50] This was only the prelude. Using his Territorial Court as a vehicle, Albrecht went on to pursue an aggressively expansionist policy.[51] Soon enough, in 1460, he found himself beleaguered by an overpowering coalition of resentful princes.

The meddling of the margrave's Territorial Court in matters under other princes' jurisdiction figures large in the declarations of war of the Wittelsbach Duke Ludwig of Bavaria (30 March 1460) and of Bishop Johann of Würzburg (15 May).[52] A few days later they were joined by Bishop Georg of Bamberg. His cartel of defiance (22 May), too, gives pride of place to the encroachments of the margrave's Territorial Court, but then cites another reason: Hans von Rotenhan, who is in feud against him, the bishop, because of a pledge-lordship, is being aided and abetted by the margrave, 'housed, maintained and protected'.[53] This ruse, which was to become a staple tactic of the princes, did not help the margrave out. Massively outgunned, he had to give in. On 24 June 1460 he signed a peace treaty, the so-called *Rother Richtung*, which effectively put his Territorial Court out of action for the next thirty years.[54]

In 1461 the triumphant Bishop Johann of Würzburg disseised Georg von Gebsattel, an official and adherent of the margrave. Gebsattel responded by resorting to feuding against the bishop. The latter suspected the margrave of masterminding this feud and of thereby seeking pretexts for reprisals. Another all-out conflict was imminent. The margrave solicited the support of the Würzburg nobility, styling himself their 'champion'. But they were skilfully enticed from him by the so-called Gracious Pact (*Gnadenvertrag*) offered to them by Bishop Johann.[55] The concessions it made to the nobility seem to point out

---

[48] Heinz Quirin, 'Markgraf Albrecht Achilles von Brandenburg-Ansbach als Politiker: Ein Beitrag zur Vorgeschichte des süddeutschen Städtekriegs', *JffL* 31 (1971), 261–308. See also Jean-Marie Moeglin, '"Toi, Burgrave de Nuremberg, misérable gentilhomme dont la grandeur est si récente . . .": Essai sur la conscience dynastique des Hohenzollern de Franconie au xvᵉ siècle', *Journal des Savants* (1991), 91–131.

[49] Michael Levey, *Giambattista Tiepolo: His Life and Art* (New Haven, 1986), 182.

[50] For the struggle over the title of duke of Franconia see Lore Muehlon, 'Johann III. von Grumbach, Bischof von Würzburg und Herzog zu Franken (1455–1466)' (PhD thesis, University of Würzburg, 1935), 43–63; Wendehorst, *Das Bistum Würzburg*, II, 177; III, 5. Margrave Albrecht also ceased addressing Bishop Gottfried as a prince: StAW, Stb, no. 717, fol. 424ʳ.

[51] Seyboth, *Die Markgraftümer Ansbach und Kulmbach*, 108–11.

[52] Muehlon, 'Johann III. von Grumbach', 59.

[53] Gottfried Freiherr von Rotenhan, 'Streit und Fehde um die Burg Stuffenberg bei Baunach 1460/66', *Bericht des Historischen Vereins Bamberg* 129 (1993), 75–90, at 76.

[54] Muehlon, 'Johann III. von Grumbach', 60–1.

[55] Fries, *Historie*, 825–7, 834; Schubert, *Die Landstände des Hochstifts Würzburg*, 77, 95–8.

that it was mainly the élite whose support was sought: the first clause obligated the bishop to respect and to protect nobles' rights to peaceful enjoyment of whatever episcopal property they held in pledge.[56]

A second war indeed broke out and, for the margrave, it went better than the first.[57] It did not, however, alleviate Georg von Gebsattel's affliction. In 1462 he resumed his feud, preying on the bishop's subjects.[58] Bishop Johann entertained no doubts as to who was answerable for his troubles. He wrote to the margrave that

Despite the Roth peace treaty . . . you have been allowing your men to bring damage on my men. Indeed, Georg [von Gebsattel], who is your councillor and servitor . . . has taken to robbing and murdering my subjects . . . operating from your castles, towns, villages and territories. You have also failed to respect the second accord between us which was mediated by the king of Bohemia. It has not been adhered to by your district governors and your men . . . Furthermore, we have become enemy of Baron Sigmund of Schwarzenberg because of the misdeeds he has committed against us and our subjects; he is housed and sheltered and helped by you . . .[59]

And sure enough, Bishop Johann set out on a punitive expedition against both the margrave and his district governor Baron Sigmund of Schwarzenberg.[60] This round, the third, ended on 19 July 1462 with a resounding defeat of the margrave in the Battle of Giengen.

It was the feud of Christoph Fuchs against the bishop of Bamberg that gave Margrave Albrecht's schemes a new lease of life.[61] The anti-Brandenburg alliance between the bishops collapsed when Johann of Würzburg declined Georg of Bamberg's demand to turn Christoph Fuchs in: the latter was not just his vassal; he also held in pledge portions of the district governorship of Wallburg.[62] A war followed. Christoph Fuchs took an active part in it, assailing a castle of two relations-cum-councillors of the bishop of Bamberg. His helpers raided the village of Stettfeld, where they seized and extorted money from a villager who belonged to the Bamberg governorship of Stuffenberg. According to the governor there, Lamprecht von Seckendorff, the villagers were standing aside when this occurred. He punished them with a 'feud' of his own. Accompanied by 1000 men-at-arms, Lamprecht pillaged Stettfeld and burnt its houses down, inflicting damage estimated at 3000 gulden.[63]

[56] 'Nemlich das wir Bischove und Capitel obgenant alle unnser nachkomen stiffts und Capitels alle graven herren Ritter unnd knechte unnsers stifts . . . bey iren alten herkomen freyhaiten gerechtigkaiten unnd Erbschafften beleiben lassen ire auch irer pfandschafften und verschreibungen keinen bedranckh gewalt oder unrecht thun sollen noch wellen . . .': StAW, Stb, no. 947, fol. 66.
[57] Muehlon, 'Johann III. von Grumbach', 80–1.   [58] Fries, *Historie*, 834.
[59] Adolf Bachmann (ed.), *Briefe und Acten zur österreichisch-deutschen Geschichte im Zeitalter Kaiser Friedrich III.* (Vienna, 1885), 415–17, no. 323.
[60] Fries, *Historie*, 834–6. For Schwarzenberg's governorship see Karl Fürst zu Schwarzenberg, *Geschichte des reichsständischen Hauses Schwarzenberg* (Neustadt a.d. Aisch, 1963), 58.
[61] See p. 87 above.   [62] Fries, *Historie*, 838.
[63] StAW, Stb, no. 717, fols. 299^r, 300^v–301^v; Fries, *Historie*, 838–9. For the meaning of this and similar incidents see pp. 108–9 below.

The feud interpreted

In April 1464 the parties met in order to negotiate a peace settlement. The main points at issue were not Christoph Fuchs's sheep. They were the jurisdictions of the episcopal Territorial Courts, Safe Conduct, tolls and hunting-grounds[64] – all classic ingredients and insignia of 'sovereignty'. The terms of the treaty were more or less dictated to Bishop Georg of Bamberg by Bishop Johann of Würzburg. It was an offer he could not refuse. For Christoph Fuchs, assisted by Margrave Albrecht Achilles, had in the meantime recruited 1200 cavalrymen. They were ready for action in case the parley miscarried. Only two days later Bishop Georg publicly disowned the agreement, protesting that it had been forced on him and was therefore null and void. His plea of duress, even though supported with an imperial edict, was flatly rejected.[65]

Shortly afterward, in September 1464, a district governor of the bishop of Bamberg, Konrad von Aufseß, claimed that the bishop of Würzburg owed him 450 gulden, and declared a feud on him. Together with governor Lamprecht von Seckendorff and 200 horsemen he overran two villages.[66] A large contingent of Würzburg horsemen who were reconnoitring the area rushed in the direction of the billowing smoke and took the raiders unawares. A hundred and fifty of them, including forty noblemen, were captured. Konrad von Aufseß, who managed to escape, attributed this misadventure to the treachery of Heinz Fuchs, a servitor of the bishop of Würzburg. Attempts to reconcile the two nobles failed, and Aufseß recommenced his feud.[67]

In 1465 another effort to arbitrate between the two prince-bishops came to naught. The alleged reason was that Lamprecht von Seckendorff's sack of Stettfeld harmed not only Christoph Fuchs, but also his cousins Hans and Heinz, co-lords of the village. In order to be better able to pursue his claims against Seckendorff and his helpers, Heinz Fuchs made a compact with the bishop of Würzburg. It specified that neither the bishop (or his eventual successor) nor Heinz was to conclude any separate settlement with Bamberg without the other's consent.[68] Moreover, like Christoph Fuchs, Heinz had the backing of the margrave as well.[69] Under princely aegis, he was encouraged to turn on the subjects of Bishop Georg of Bamberg. The latter, suspecting Bishop Johann of connivance, unleashed his men on the monastery of Theres in the diocese of Würzburg. They looted horses, cows, some 1,200 sheep, and carried

---

[64] Fries, *Historie*, 839.

[65] Ibid., 840; Muehlon, 'Johann III. von Grumbach', 112; Joseph Chmel (ed.), *Regesta chronologico-diplomatica Friderici III. Romanorum Imperatoris (Regis IV.)* (Vienna, 1859), Appendix, 174–6, no. 130 K.

[66] Fries, *Historie*, 840; Otto Freiherr von Aufseß, *Geschichte des uradelichen Aufseß'schen Geschlechtes in Franken* (Berlin, 1889), 147.

[67] Fries, *Historie*, 840–1. For the escalation of this feud which also alienated from Bamberg Duke Wilhelm of Saxony see Aufseß, *Geschichte des uradelichen Aufseß'schen Geschlechtes*, 148.

[68] StAW, Stb, no. 717, fols. 243^{r-v}.

[69] Ibid., fol. 192^v; Bachmann (ed.), *Briefe und Acten zur österreichisch-deutschen Geschichte*, 559, no. 449.

off a number of peasants.[70] Bishop Georg also brandished his spiritual sword and had Heinz Fuchs placed under a ban. Heinz was not impressed. According to one report he forced the messenger who brought him the bull of excommunication to swallow the document.[71] The conflict soon threatened to get out of hand: troops of the bishop of Würzburg and allied princes laid waste the area of the Jagst. A few days later Bamberg's squadrons set alight nine villages in the Würzburg district governorship of Zabelstein. Even after Bishop Johann's death in 1466, which effectively terminated the hostilities, noblemen were still busy settling scores.[72]

The wars of the early 1460s illustrate a complex of interconnections between state-making, nobility, and feuding. Six years of intense conflict between princes over issues of 'sovereignty' set off a chain of rampant feuds involving at least seven noblemen as principal feuders and dozens of helpers.[73] In turn, these feuds fuelled wars. They could not be localised and contained, for they were closely linked to the larger political conflicts between princes – indeed, so closely that it is almost impossible to tell feud from war. What is crucial here is the nature of the link.

An important clue is the fact that all the seven principal feuders were princely high officials or pledge-holders. This suggests that their feuds were 'bespoke' by princes. Feuds of that sort were by no means a rarity. In 1493 margravial district governor Paul von Absberg thanked his prince for alerting him that Nuremberg's retainers were after him. Reminding the prince that he 'fell into this danger on behalf of Your Grace', Absberg added that 'if Your Grace wants me to bring more pain on [those of Nuremberg], Your Grace should let me know, and I would be happy to do that'.[74] An even more revealing account comes from the autobiography of that accomplished feud contractor, Götz von Berlichingen. In 1517 Georg Rüdt, a retainer of the Elector Palatine, was abducted. Rumours were abroad that the culprit was Konrad Schott. Götz was summoned by the Elector and entrusted with Rüdt's cause. However, himself a seasoned feuder, Konrad Schott proved too elusive even for Götz. In his place Götz ambushed Valentin

[70] Fries, *Historie*, 842–3.
[71] C. A. Schweitzer, 'Auszüge der Urkunden aus der Chronik des Michaelsberger Abtes Eberhard', *Bericht des Historischen Vereins Bamberg* 17 (1854), 1–175, at 101–2; Cyriacus Spangenberg, *Hennebergische Chronica: Der uralten löblichen Grafen und Fürsten zu Henneberg, Genealogia, Stamm-Baum und Historia, ihrer Ankunfft, Lob und denckwürdigen Tathen, Geschichten und Sachen wahre und gründliche Beschreibung*, ed. Christoph Albrecht Erck (Meiningen, 1755), 431.
[72] Joseph Würdinger, *Kriegsgeschichte von Bayern, Franken, Pfalz und Schwaben von 1347 bis 1506*, 2 vols. (Munich, 1868), II, 101–2; StAW, Stb, no. 865, fol. 331ᵛ.
[73] There were other noblemen involved in feuds which appear to have been related to the wars: StAB, Fehde-Akten, no. 125; Otto Freiherr von Waldenfels, *Die Freiherrn von Waldenfels: Stammfolgen mit urkundlichen Belegen*, vol. I (Munich, 1952), 142–3; Max Herrmann, *Albrecht von Eyb und die Frühzeit des deutschen Humanismus* (Berlin, 1893), 241–51. See also StAW, Stb, no. 717, passim.
[74] 'wa ich in aber fon eur genaden mer laids ton sol lassen mich eur genad wissen so wil ich es geren tun': StAN, Fstm.Ansb., Fehdeakten, no. 67b, prod. 1, 5.

Schott whom he suspected of sheltering Konrad's valets.[75] Such 'made-to-measure' feuds are probably what a Nuremberg chronicler had in mind when he commented that 'it was Duke Albrecht of Saxony who must have been the first to work out how to battle against big cities at low costs. When a lordless scoundrel who has nothing to lose proclaims a feud on a city, then everybody can seize the opportunity [and attack the city] under his name.'[76]

Practices like these account to some extent for the preponderance of top-ranking noblemen among feuders. It was only natural for princes to employ their most faithful noblemen as surrogates. Hence the sources seldom disclose princes' behind-the-scenes manipulation of feuds. Presumably, princes stage-managed more feuds than can be verified. Even so, it still does not explain most of the feuds involving high-status noblemen. For one thing, many noblemen became officials only during or after their feuds. For another, this assumption does not do justice to the complexity of the relations between princes and noblemen. Indeed, one reason for the ample space Götz von Berlichingen assigned in his memoirs to his dubious feud was that it was precisely that. The tale was an exercise in self-justification. For the feud tarnished his reputation among his Franconian fellows. He was defamed, especially by the ladies; and the gentlemen, for their part, planned retributive measures.[77]

Feuding noblemen, as this and other episodes indicate,[78] were not the myrmidons of princes.[79] One has to allow for a more diversified pattern of complicity, as well as of opposition, between princes and noblemen. Through their feuds noblemen were more often than not pursuing their own interests. But, and this was the crux of the feud, their agendas were inextricably entangled with those of princes. This did not rule out disagreement and conflict between princes and noblemen whose interests happened to be – at least temporarily – compatible.[80] But the partial overlap that did exist between the two sides' interests was sufficient to make them work together. In any case, whether opposition or co-operation, the central point of intersection was noblemen's control over land and people. It was this, lordship, which endowed the feud with its capacity to subserve *pari passu* the ends of both princes and noblemen against those of other princes and noblemen.

---

[75] Helgard Ulmschneider (ed.), *Götz von Berlichingen: Mein Fehd und Handlung* (Sigmaringen, 1981), 115–21.

[76] GNM, Hs. 22 547 (Fehdebuch der Reichsstadt Nürnberg 1381–1513), fol. 48ᵛ. The same is quoted by Minutoli (ed.), *Das kaiserliche Buch des Markgrafen Albrecht Achilles*, 404, no. 297.

[77] Helgard Ulmschneider, *Götz von Berlichingen: Ein adeliges Leben der deutschen Renaissance* (Sigmaringen, 1974), 100–1.

[78] For criticism of a governor-cum-master of the household for being a henchman of the prince see Morsel, 'Une société politique en Franconie', 346.

[79] This is the implication of some of the arguments of Regina Görner, *Raubritter: Untersuchungen zur Lage des spätmittelalterlichen Niederadels, besonders im südlichen Westfalen* (Münster in Westfalen, 1987), 189–92, 209–10, 220–3. She is contradicted by her own evidence: ibid., 122–54.

[80] The conflictive side of the relations between princes and nobles is discussed in chap. 6.

LORDSHIP, 'PROTECTION', AND THE FEUD

The term lordship or seigneury designates not only noblemen's ownership of land as the source of their livelihood, but also the social and political basis of their position as a ruling class. The purview of 'lordship' thus covers control over both land and people. Because lordship blended economic functions with social and political ones, it created the focal point of a network of relations of domination and dependency. Hence it provided the material basis for noblemen's existence *qua* noble lords.[81] Consequently, the ability to defend one's lordship against competitors and, alternatively, to expand it at their expense was imperative.

An important determinant of the competition between lords was the structure of appropriation of surplus value. Two features of this structure are particularly relevant here. The first is the individualised form of the rural labour process. The basic unit of production was the farmstead (*mansus*). Albeit integrated into communal organisation, it was from this unit that the production process proceeded self-dependently. This constrained the lords to make the farmstead or its members the index of their claims to surplus. It led to a quantitative and qualitative parcellation and hierarchisation of rights to appropriation. The result was an extraordinarily complex struggle over its distribution.[82] The second, related feature is that nobles' claims to surplus rested on their ownership of the land and on the binding of peasants to it and/or to the person of the noble. But whatever the legal basis of these controls, they were largely external, limited by the peasants' economic rights: unlike capitalists, late medieval feudal lords did not have effective power over the means of production. The effective possession of the subsistence-producing holding and of the tools was in the hands of the peasants. This certainly was the case in Franconia, where heritable lease was the prevalent form of tenure. From these circumstances could arise a concept of proprietorship based on rural labour which was antithetical to the concept of proprietorship based on lordship.[83] And from here there was only a short step to questioning the legitimacy of the lords' requisitions. It was in this context that

---

[81] Klaus Schreiner, '"Grundherrschaft": Entstehung und Bedeutungswandel eines geschichtswissenschaftlichen Ordnungs- und Erklärungsbegriffs', in *Die Grundherrschaft im späten Mittelalter*, ed. Hans Patze, 2 vols. (Sigmaringen, 1983), I, 11–74; Alain Guerreau, *Le féodalisme: Un horizon théorique* (Paris, 1980), 182; Robert Fossier, 'Seigneurs et seigneuries au Moyen Age', in *Seigneurs et seigneuries au Moyen Age* (Paris, 1993), 13–24. See also Rechter, *Das Land zwischen Aisch und Rezat*, 443, 446.

[82] Ludolf Kuchenbuch and Bernd Michael, 'Zur Struktur und Dynamik der "feudalen" Produktionsweise im vorindustriellen Europa', in *Feudalismus – Materialien zur Theorie und Geschichte*, ed. Ludolf Kuchenbuch and Bernd Michael (Frankfurt am Main, 1977), 694–761, at 709–12, 716–17.

[83] Peter Blickle, *Communal Reformation: The Quest for Salvation in Sixteenth-Century Germany*, trans. Thomas Dunlap (New Jersey, 1992), 174–6; Gadi Algazi, *Herrengewalt und Gewalt der Herren im späten Mittelalter: Herrschaft, Gegenseitigkeit und Sprachgebrauch* (Frankfurt am Main, 1996), 154–6. For a theoretical grounding of the distinction between economic and legal property rights see Yoram Barzel, *Economic Analysis of Property Rights* (Cambridge, 1989), esp. 1–12, 62–75, 110.

the feud acquired its function both as an invasion into the production process and as a strategy in the competition between lords. Both its form and its content were to a large extent patterned by these features of the structure of appropriation.

This view makes the means of feuding appear at first sight odd: whilst noblemen vied with each other, their feuds were in practice waged against those whose produce was at stake. Typically, a noble would raid the farmsteads of his opponent's subjects; he would pillage them and lay waste the land they tilled by plundering and burning. 'In short', one sixteenth-century commentator noticed, 'feud and war are conducted at the cost of the peasants on the land'. But he added that 'lords and cities profit therefrom'.[84] It is convenient to approach this problem of the relation of means to ends through Otto Brunner's paradigmatic discussion of it.

Brunner posited a correspondence between feud and land-lordship (*Grundherrschaft*). The substance of land-lordship was for him that its possession and utilisation presupposed in common law full arms-bearing rights. The lord had to be able to defend his domain against forced 'disseisin' and to protect the people of his house (which included tenants). Feud was one way of discharging these obligations. Hence it by definition constituted legitimate use of force. It was implied in the recognised rights of protection and safeguard (*Schutz und Schirm*) that a nobleman exercised in defence of his domain as its lord.[85]

Rights of protection and safeguard, according to Brunner, not only gave lords power over peasants; they also formed the basic nexus between them. To be a lord's subject (*Holde* or *Grundholde*) meant to enjoy his grace or favour (*Huld*), that is his protection. Falling out of favour had grave consequences, since protection was essential to a peasant's very existence, his ability to work. It was in recognition of this grim reality that peasants paid rents and dues and rendered labour services to their lords.[86] But if the lord failed to provide effective protection, his lordship itself was called into question.[87] His subjects were 'automatically' released from their obligations toward him. Brunner, however, was no neo-classical historian: protection and safeguard, he argued, was a great deal more than a contractual relationship. They entailed also mutual loyalty. An act of homage (*Huldigung*) through an oath of fealty created a personal bond of faith between lord and subject.[88]

It is in the context of this organic relationship that Brunner understood the

---

[84] 'Summa, Fheide unnd Krieg gehet uber die armen Leute auff dem Lande, Herren und Städte haben jhren nutz davon'. Quoted by Dieter Neitzert, *Die Stadt Göttingen führt eine Fehde 1485/86: Untersuchung zu einer Sozial- und Wirtschaftsgeschichte von Stadt und Umland* (Hildesheim, 1992), 31.

[85] Brunner, *'Land' and Lordship*, 209–10, 213, 219.

[86] Ibid., 214–15, 220–2, 240, 246, 258.

[87] Ibid., 219. Brunner cites in this connection the *Schwabenspiegel* of 1275: 'we should serve our lords for they protect us; if they do not protect us, justice does not oblige us to serve them': ibid., 218.

[88] Ibid., 217.

feud. Whereas 'the substance of the loyalty oath was the promise "to help (the lord) and prevent damage to him", the substance of the feud, correspondingly, was to do damage'.[89] The attacks on the subject peasants of a rival undermined the latter's protection and inevitably his authority as lord. Unable to defend his subjects, he was not entitled to the fruits of their labour; he lost his seigneurial legitimacy. The function of doing damage, of 'distressing' (*Schadentrachten*), was thus 'to compel an opponent either to accept the challenger's version of Right, or to seek arbitration, or to lodge a judicial complaint, or, in certain conditions, to offer battle. For both a formal complaint at law and offer of battle could bring an end to "plundering and burning"'.[90] By this account, the ability to pursue and withstand feuds was crucial to the nobles' status as lords; it was one of the foundations of their authority over their subject peasants, one of the things that distinguished them as noble lords from mere rentiers. Indeed, Brunner went so far as to claim that 'the condition of the peasantry would deteriorate during the early modern period, when the decline of the feud reduced the lord's dependence on the aid of his peasants'.[91]

There is a lot to commend this description of the place of feuding in society. It is perhaps Brunner's most original and lasting contribution to the study of the feud that he established the link between it and lordship.[92] And this connection is certainly what makes his explanation vastly superior to the 'robber-knighthood' thesis. Yet he got there in the wrong way, which in turn reflects on his reading of the feud. In particular, his analysis rests on two moot premises.[93] The first is that both the feud and lordship were givens. What made 'protection and safeguard' so important was simply the 'endemic violence of the time'. The feud in this formulation was self-existing and external to lordship. At the same time Brunner argued that protection from feuds could be granted only by those who had the legal right to wage feuds: those who *already* had 'a house of residence in the land that served as the organisational centre of the noble's estates, his lordship'.[94] Thus, both aspects of aristocratic power – lordship and the peasants' ineluctable need for protection – are taken for granted. Hence they also appear as only extrinsically coincident. Indeed, Brunner was careful not to set them too closely against each other.[95]

What enabled Brunner to keep the two issues separate in this way was his

---

[89] Ibid., 217 n. 68.   [90] Ibid., 69.   [91] Ibid., 285.

[92] For this link see also Hans Patze, 'Grundherrschaft und Fehde', in *Die Grundherrschaft im späten Mittelalter*, I, 263–94.

[93] For what follows concerning the connections between feud, protection and lordship, I acknowledge a large intellectual debt to Algazi, *Herrengewalt und Gewalt der Herren*. See also Gadi Algazi, '"Sie würden hinten nach so gail": Vom sozialen Gebrauch der Fehde im späten Mittelalter', in *Physische Gewalt: Studien zur Geschichte der Neuzeit*, ed. Thomas Lindenberger and Alf Lüdtke (Frankfurt am Main, 1995), 39–77.

[94] Brunner, *'Land' and Lordship*, 198–9, 213.

[95] Algazi, *Herrengewalt und Gewalt der Herren*, 135–40.

second problematic assumption, namely that the fundamental category of a study of lordship is the dyad lord-peasant: one lord protects his house and subjects against another, another lord does the same for his house and subjects, and so on. The result of this assumption is that both lords and peasants are disembedded from the social setting. For the sum total of lordships does not in and of itself constitute society.[96] But examined as a relation between lords and peasants not as individuals, but as social categories, 'protection' takes on an ominously different meaning.

Viewed as a group, noblemen were producers of both protection and violence. By producing violence nobles reproduced the peasants' need for protection. In other words, they offered protection from themselves. It is not 'protection and safeguard' as seen by Brunner, the benign, patriarchal function of lords, that explains the nobility's social hegemony.[97] Rather, they owed their hegemony, at least in large part, to their own potential and actual exercise of violence that made their 'protection and safeguard' indispensable in the first place. This is borne out by looking at a sociopolitical crisis which temporarily overturned peasant-lord relations: the Peasants' War of 1525. Through the threat and use of violence, peasants created in nobles the need for protection. Indeed, some nobles swore allegiance to peasants.[98] Expectedly, this situation was perceived by nobles as an inversion of the 'natural' order of things. The peasants' captain Feuerbacher, for instance, was accused of browbeating nobles into receiving protection from him and recognising him as a territorial lord.[99] It is noteworthy that after the revolt had been pacified, some noblemen reverted to feuding with a vengeance. In his feud against Rothenburg ob der Tauber, Adam von Thüngen refused to accept the customary payments for renunciation of burning (*Brandschatzung*). Carrying the red 'burn' banner, he set whole villages ablaze. When the peasants he captured were returned to Rothenburg, the city council found out that they had a legal problem in hand: the captives had been forced to swear an oath to become the serfs of a noble.[100]

Feuds were thus a great deal more than the lords' fulfilment of their duty as imposed by a feudal social contract. By carrying out their struggles through feuds, noblemen reproduced the peasants' status as consumers of protection and

---

[96] Ibid.

[97] Ibid., 136–7, 165. See also the remarks by G. E. M. de Ste. Croix, *The Class Struggle in the Ancient Greek World: From the Archaic Age to the Arab Conquests* (London, 1983), 83–4.

[98] StAN, Bauernkriegsakten, Tom. 8, prod. 54, fol. 117ʳ; Tom Scott and Bob Scribner (eds.), *The German Peasants' War: A History in Documents*, trans. Tom Scott and Bob Scribner (New Jersey, 1991), 197–201, 206–8, nos. 81–3, 87.

[99] André Holenstein, *Die Huldigung der Untertanen: Rechtskultur und Herrschaftsordnung (800–1800)* (Stuttgart, 1991), 367–9.

[100] Roy L. Vice, 'The German Peasants' War of 1525 and its Aftermath in Rothenburg ob der Tauber and Würzburg' (PhD thesis, University of Chicago, 1984), 417–18, 424, 482; Franz Ludwig Baumann (ed.), *Quellen zur Geschichte des Bauernkriegs aus Rotenburg an der Tauber* (Tübingen,1878), 570, 576–80, 610–15. See also Wunder, 'Die Ritter von Vellberg', 183.

consequently their own position as lords. In terms of business management, feud violence was the basis on which peasants, as 'customers' of protection, were internalised. This function of the feud and of comparable practices – *chevauchées, cavalcades* – has been noted by a number of historians working on various periods.[101] The effects, whether intended or not, were similar: they regimented the labourers, instilled fear in their hearts, rendered them vulnerable to seigneurial exploitation.

This property of feud violence was manipulated by noblemen in their contests over lordship. One not only undermined a rival's power by feuding, exposing the ineffectiveness of his protection; one simultaneously 'bid' one's own 'protection' as an alternative. The import of these tactics is illuminated by a printed pamphlet disseminated by Baron Friedrich of Schwarzenberg during his feud with Ludwig von Hutten. It is to all intents and purposes a disquisition about his honour and Hutten's improbity. All the same, its garrulity fails to prevent deeper motives from coming out: his subjects in Bullenheim were bullied by Hutten into abjuring their duties to him and into doing Hutten homage instead.[102] Schwarzenberg went so far as to offer a duel to decide who was the lord over the disputed peasants. He was right to perceive Hutten's advances as particularly menacing. Hutten was one of the wealthiest and most powerful nobles in Franconia. During that time he was engaged in putting together, at the expense of his neighbours, one of the most extensive lordships in the region. It was also not the first time he had encroached on the territory of the barons of Schwarzenberg.[103] The latter, however, resorted to precisely the same tactics when it suited them: in 1459 Baron Johann attempted to turn the village of Niedernscheinfeld into a mart. The subjects of another nobleman, whose rights in the village stood in the way of Johann's enterprise, were seized and harassed and dragooned into paying taxes. The purpose of these actions, that nobleman complained, was to oust him from

---

[101] Pierre Bonnassie, *La Catalogne du milieu du Xe à la fin du XIe siècle: Croissance et mutations d'une société*, vol. II (Toulouse, 1976), 599, 767; Georges Duby, *The Three Orders: Feudal Society Imagined*, trans. Arthur Goldhammer (Chicago, 1980), 151–5; Stephen D. White, 'Feuding and Peace-making in the Touraine around the Year 1100', *Traditio* 42 (1986), 195–263, at 260–1; Michael Mann, *The Sources of Social Power*, vol. I, *A History of Power from the Beginning to A.D. 1760* (Cambridge, 1986), 420; T. N. Bisson, 'The "Feudal Revolution"', *Past and Present* 142 (1994), 6–42; Algazi, *Herrengewalt und Gewalt der Herren*, esp. 149–53.

[102] 'Hutten . . . sich wievor gewalthetiger handlung unterstanden, einen der unsern gefangen, etliche zu Pülnheim geschlagen, von den pflichten damit sie uns zugethan und das sie ime angeloben müssen gedrungen': Geheimes Staatsarchiv, XX.HA: Hist. Staatsarchiv Königsberg, Herzogliches Briefarchiv, A 4, 1534 Januar 29 (K. 191). A copy of a pamphlet by Ludwig von Hutten is in BL, cat. no. c.38.k.16. For the Hutten-Schwarzenberg mixed lordship in Bullenheim see Elisabeth Fuchshuber, *Uffenheim* (Munich, 1982), 33.

[103] Richard Schmitt, 'Aus dem Zentrum des Hochstifts verdrängt: Die Herren von Hutten im Gebiet des Würzburger Bischofs', in *Ulrich von Hutten: Ritter, Humanist, Publizist 1488–1523. Katalog zur Ausstellung des Landes Hessen anläßlich des 500. Geburtstages*, ed. Peter Laub (Kassel, 1988), 103–12, at 109; *Unser Friderichen Freyherren von Schwartzenberg und zu Hohenlandsperg . . .*, 36 (my pagination).

the village. But this was not enough. In 1462, Baron Sigmund of Schwarzenberg captured seven burghers and seventeen peasants of Nuremberg. He forced an oath on them to the effect that they would not use any other trade-route but the one passing by Scheinfeld.[104]

Other feuds reveal the essence of such conflicts even more distinctly. In 1485 Veit von Vestenberg was accused by Kaspar von Vestenberg of seeking to make his [Kaspar's] subjects tributary and subservient to his advocacy (*gultpar und vogtpar*). Kaspar was in turn blamed for doing the same and for forcing Veit's subjects to perform 'complete homage (*gantzer huldigung*)'.[105] Similar language was employed by Baron Sigmund of Schwarzenberg. In 1479 he protested that Erkinger von Seinsheim had apprehended four men who were under his, Sigmund's, advocacy (*vogtbar menner*).[106] As these reproaches indicate, the bone of contention was rights of advocacy (*Vogtei*) which was, especially in Franconia, the pith of lordship. As such it frequently served noblemen as a stepping-stone to the expansion or usurpation of lordship.[107]

Conflicts between noblemen and cities were carried out in a similar manner. It is striking, however, that territorial towns were by and large spared noblemen's violence. One explanation is that they were under princely jurisdiction. Another, related explanation is that, being normally held in pledge by nobles, territorial towns were under their thumb anyway. Their resources were tapped peacefully. Real threat for the nobility was posed by the imperial cities alone.[108] Although aversion based on aristocratic class ideology could play an important role in feuds, differences were predominantly territorial and political. Noblemen's ties to the princes meant that they too were unfavourably disposed toward big, independent cities. A mid-fifteenth-century 'useful prescription . . . by Doctor [i.e. Margrave] Albrecht of Brandenburg, Franconia's dispensing chemist, for the malady of the poor margravial noblemen who are dispossessed by those of

---

104 StAW, Adel, no. 1114, prod. of Sexta post Corpus Christi [25 May] 1459; Johannes Müllner, *Die Annalen der Reichsstadt Nürnberg von 1623*, ed. Gerhard Hirschmann, 2 vols. (Nuremberg, 1972–84), II, 547.

105 StAN, Ansbacher Historica, no. 210, prod. of Viti [15 June]; prod. of Dienstag nach Johannis baptiste [28 June] 1485.

106 StAN, Fstm.Ansb., Fehdeakten, no. 52, prod. 1; Priebatsch (ed.), *Politische Correspondenz des Kurfürsten Albrecht Achilles*, II, 549, no. 593.

107 Hanns Hubert Hofmann, 'Freibauern, Freidörfer, Schutz und Schirm im Fürstentum Ansbach: Studien zur Genesis der Staatlichkeit in Franken vom 15. bis 18. Jahrhundert', *ZbLG* 23 (1960), 195–327, esp. 288–327; Lotte Köberlin, 'Die Einungsbewegung des fränkischen Adels bis zum Jahre 1494' (PhD thesis, University of Erlangen, 1924), 80; Kurt Andermann, 'Klösterliche Grundherrschaft und niederadelige Herrschaftsbildung: Das Beispiel Amorbach', in *Siedlungsentwicklung und Herrschaftsbildung im Hinteren Odenwald*, ed. Hermann Ehmer (Buchen, 1988), 29–50. See also Brunner, *'Land' and Lordship*, 258–9, 269.

108 Gerhard Rechter, 'Das Verhältnis der Reichsstädte Windsheim und Rothenburg ob der Tauber zum niederen Adel ihrer Umgebung im Spätmittelalter', *JffL* 41 (1981), 45–87; Gerhard Rechter, '"difficulteten und beschwerden": Beobachtungen zum Verhältnis der kleineren Reichsstädte Frankens zum niederen Adel am Beispiel Windsheim', in *Reichsstädte in Franken*, ed. Rainer A. Müller (Munich, 1987), 298–308.

Nuremberg' ran as follows: 'take 8 of the best merchants of Nuremberg, 7 of Augsburg, 6 of Ulm and 4 of Memmingen . . . put them in a dark vault . . . until each sweated out 20,000 gulden; give this sum to the unwell noblemen, for it would allay their melancholy'.[109] Imperial cities were also collective feudal lords. In the early sixteenth century, 39 patrician families of Nuremberg exercised land-lordship over some 3,000 peasants in the surrounding countryside.[110] This was an unfailing recipe for disputes with the landed nobility. Consequently, intimidation of, and violence against, cities' subjects took forms akin to feuds among the nobility:[111] 'there was a great discord between Count Wilhelm of Henneberg and the council because of the village Sendelfeld, of which the count wanted to take possession', reported a Schweinfurt chronicler. 'The council hampered this, hence followed that both parties captured each other's subjects.'[112]

'Protection', on that account, acquires a different signification from that attributed to it by Brunner. There is no denying the existence of that 'original' sense.[113] But precisely its reality (and ideology) meant that it could be mobilised by nobles in their struggles over lordship.[114] Noblemen repeatedly produced the danger and, at a price, shielded against it, thereby establishing themselves as lords. The feud, in a very real sense, was a protection racket. This is no mere figure of speech. In 1503 Paul von Absberg, a margravial district governor, was in feud with the bishop of Eichstätt. The humanist Kilian Leib went into the particulars of Absberg's performance:

Whoever contrived to harm the bishopric [of Eichstätt] fled to Paul, who would thereupon declare himself defender of the just cause of the postulant. Hence the inhabitants of the diocese were tormented with arson attacks, brigandage, pillage and abductions. Then, when the corn in the fields ripened, one would send to the peasants threatening messages, forbidding them from delivering to the clergy of Eichstätt the annual tithe which is their due and which is usually put up for sale. The clergy, pressed down by this guile and being either clerics or monks, would be compelled to redeem the tithe by paying high sums of

---

[109] Quoted by Ernst Schubert, 'Albrecht Achilles', 140.
[110] Michael Diefenbacher, 'Stadt und Adel – Das Beispiel Nürnberg', *ZGO* 141 (1993), 51–69, at 61.
[111] StAN, Bb, no. 42, fols. 18^{r-v}; no. 45, fols. 21^r, 61^v–62^r, 118^r, 151^r–153^r; no. 46, fols. 231^r, 231^v–232^v; no. 48, fols. 8^v, 37^{r-v}, 51^r, 73^r, 168^v–169^r; no. 54, fols. 302^v–303^r; no. 65, fol. 29^r; no. 69, fols. 131^r–132^r, 210^r; no. 74, fols. 140^v–141^v, 184^v–185^r; no. 81, fols. 100^{r-v}, 118^r; no. 90, fols. 97^v–98^r; no. 101, fols. 6^{r-v}, 71^r, 198^r, 206^{r-v}; no. 110, fol. 4^r; no. 112, fols. 77^v, 133^v–134^r; no. 113, fols. 181^r–182^r; no. 120, fols. 9^v–11^v, 27^{r-v}, 92^{r-v}; ibid., Fstm.Ansb., Fehdeakten, no. 29; ibid., Reichsstadt Nürnberg, 35 neue Laden der unteren Losungsstube, V 89/1 2065; Müllner, *Die Annalen der Reichsstadt Nürnberg*, II, 351, 363, 512, 547, 551, 557; Friedrich Pietsch (ed.), *Die Urkunden des Archivs der Reichsstadt Schwäbisch Hall*, vol. II (Stuttgart, 1972), 310, U 2503; 337, U 2636.
[112] Friedrich Stein (ed.), *Monumenta Suinfurtensia historica inde ab anno DCCXCI usque ad annum MDC: Denkmäler der Schweinfurter Geschichte bis zum Ende des sechzehnten Jahrhunderts* (Schweinfurt, 1875), 353.
[113] Holenstein, *Die Huldigung der Untertanen*, 399–401.
[114] Cf. Algazi, *Herrengewalt und Gewalt der Herren*, 147, 150, 166.

money. Paul would then mediate between them and the enemy, and he who mollified him with a consideration was granted a truce from the adversaries.[115]

Kilian Leib, himself a victim of a feud,[116] was of course concerned with representing Paul von Absberg in the worst possible light. But Absberg's feud can be interpreted otherwise. It was conducted apparently in support of a feud of a fellow nobleman. The latter's fief was confiscated by the cathedral chapter, and his own feud was an attempt to recover it.[117] This perhaps explains Absberg's actions against the peasants and local clergy. Depicted by Leib as rapine, Absberg may well have understood his deeds as (re-)constituting lordship. It is also in these terms that the attack described above of governor Lamprecht von Seckendorff on his own village of Stettfeld can be explained.[118] So should the scarcely disguised threats used by Heinz Fuchs and his clients against various villages during his feud against the bishop of Bamberg.[119] And the same holds good for the actions of Franconian princes during the wars of the 1460s. Fries related that Bishop Johann of Würzburg captured a number of villages and that these did not receive equal treatment: those which had been his before but yielded to the margrave and fell away from him were devastated completely.[120]

Being a lord was an ongoing process. Lordship had to be created, maintained, reproduced. But this was not enough. Mere reproduction of existing relations amounted to stagnation and inevitably led to decline. For one thing, given the persistent custom of partible inheritance, individual nobles were likely to see their estates shrink with each new generation.[121] For another, the unchecked expansion

---

[115] 'Quisquis etenim male voluisset episcopio Praesulive excogitata causa qualibet perfugiebat ad Paulum, qui mox iustitiae patronum sese fore asseruit postulanti. Hinc qui erant episcopii, incendiis, latrociniis, rapinis, carceribusque capti divexabantur; dumque iam adultae segetes maturescerent, scribebantur hostiles litterae rusticis iubebanturque, ut [ei] decimales fructus annue venumdari solitos a quovis Eychstetensi clerico emerent, quo clerici pressi dolo, canonici essent aut coenobitae, decimas suas multa auri argentive summa redimere et libarare cogebantur; Paulus enim inter hostes et clerum agebat se medium, et qui eum munere placavisset, indutias ab hostibus data pecunia carpebat': Joseph Schlecht (ed.), 'Die Kleinen Annalen des Kilian Leib, Priors zu Rebdorf. Nach dem Codex Münch im bischöfl. Ordinariats-Archiv zu Eichstätt', *Sammelblatt des Historischen Vereins Eichstätt* 2 (1887 [1888]), 39–68, at 43.

[116] Ibid., 65.

[117] StAN, Fstm.Ansb., Fehdeakten, no. 6 [alte Signatur], esp. prod. 15; H. Wilhelm, 'Die Edeln von und zum Absberg: Ein Beitrag zur fränkischen Geschichte', *Alt-Gunzenhausen* 8 (1931), 3–197, at 122; Theodor Neuhofer, *Gabriel von Eyb, Fürstbischof von Eichstätt 1455–1535: Ein Lebensbild aus der Wende vom Mittelalter zur Neuzeit* (Eichstätt, 1934), 54–5.

[118] See p. 98 above.

[119] Schweitzer, 'Chronik des Michaelsberger Abtes Eberhard', 85–6, 88, 93, 96. One community were told they must promptly respect their obligations if they wanted 'grossen schaden und unwillen zu vermeyden'.

[120] Fries, *Historie*, 834.

[121] An example is provided by the Truchseß von Wetzhausen, one of Franconia's leading families: in the mid-fifteenth century, Dietz Truchseß, master of the household of the bishop of Würzburg, held in fee half of the *Forstamt* 'uff dem haßberg'. Of five great-great-grandsons, two held a sixteenth of it, and three held a twenty-fourth each: StAW, Lehensachen, no. 2636 (Succession der Truchsessen zu Wetzhausen unnd Buntdorff im Forstmapt uff dem haßberg).

of one's neighbour's lordship meant sooner or later one's own diminution.[122] Each lordship was therefore under competitive pressure to expand. Hence the situation of all was precarious; all the more so as it was in the nature of lordship that the challenges from outside were coupled with those from within. In 1525 Georg von Rain accused Kilian von Seckendorff of setting fire to the property of the peasant Lienhard Hopf. He claimed Hopf was his bondman (*Leibeigener*), and demanded cessation of hostilities and reparation on Hopf's behalf.[123] Seckendorff did not deny the deeds imputed to him. But Hopf, he averred, was his subject peasant (*Hintersass*) and 'he had acted against his duties and oath, as well as against the Imperial Peace': Hopf had been with the band of insurgent peasants who besieged the episcopal castle of Würzburg in 1525.

As he returned from Würzburg, I ordered him to stay at home. He answered he would move around whenever he felt like it. In addition, as I took to the field to join [the forces of] my Gracious Lord the margrave, he accused me of forsaking my subject peasants (*armen leutten*). Thirdly, he had threatened me with an arson attack should I punish him. For this and other reasons mentioned above it followed that I could not allow such a disobedient, gallows-bird subject to abuse me . . . This is why he got his blaze. I have no doubt that you would have done [the same] in such a case.[124]

Here peeps out another – and the most sinister – face of the feud; a face that is searchingly gazing inward at one's own 'lordship' and that therefore seldom shows up.[125] At the same time it betrays the fragility of lordship, its lack of finality, its irresistible restlessness. It constantly had to assert itself against both rivals and subordinates.

The feud, then, was not a condition external to lordship, nor simply its corollary. It was one of its main agents. A small-scale 'violence-using enterprise',[126] it was an instrument noblemen employed in their conflicts over the distribution of returns from lordship. Lordship in Franconia was nothing more and nothing less than the sum total of diverse rights, a *summa iurium*. This in

---

[122] For the mechanism at work see Norbert Elias, *The Civilizing Process*, trans. Edmund Jephcott (Oxford, 1994), 345–439.

[123] StAN, Fstm.Ansb., Fehdeakten, no. 110, prod. 37.

[124] 'so hatt [der handel] die gestalt, das er wider seynn pflicht unnd ayd, unnd des hailigen reichs landtfridenn gehandelt, unnd mitt den baurnn fur wurtzburg zogenn ist, do er wider vonn wirtzburgk ist kummen, hab ich inne anheims bescheidenn, zepleibenn, hatt er gesagt, er woll zihenn wann es layd wer. Zum andernn so hatt er mich bezichtigt, do ich zw meinem gnedigenn hernn marggravenn inn das veldt zogen bynn, ich sey vonn meynn armen leuttenn fluchtig wordenn. Zum drittenn hatt er mir gedrott, wo ich inne straff wöll er mich verprennen, aus dem unnd andern obgemelten ursachen, hatt gevolgt, das ich mich eynn solchenn ungehorsamen, galgenmessigen hinttersessen . . . nitt puchen hab lassen wollen, doraus er dan seynn prant hatt empfangen, angezweyffelt, dw inn solchem vall, auch gehandelt hest': ibid., prod. 38.

[125] For another example see Gerhard Rechter, *Die Seckendorff: Quellen und Studien zur Genealogie und Besitzgeschichte*, vol. I (Neustadt a.d. Aisch, 1987), 156.

[126] The term is from Frederic Chapin Lane, 'Economic Consequences of Organized Violence', in *Venice and History: The Collected Papers of Frederic C. Lane* (Baltimore, 1966), 413–28, esp. 414.

turn meant that any one of its constituents could be alienated from one lord by another. And since lordship rested to such a large extent on 'protection and safeguard', 'racketeering' was equally effective both in wearing away one's rival lordships and in enlarging and cementing one's own. The long-term outcome could be the dissolution and absorption of one lordship by another (or more than one other). After all, it is in the nature of protection that, unlike other commodities, its quality is not distributed 'over a continuous scale with products at every level': one either has the ability to supply protection or one does not.[127] Hence the relations between lords were always volatile. Every dispute, even over ostensibly trifling articles, could ignite a feud. Christoph Fuchs was not an excessively petulant noble. Like other feuders he too was informed by the compulsive dynamism of seigneurial competition. The central implication of this interpretation is that feuds directly impinged on social stratification among the nobility. They helped to create winners and losers. In association with other strategies,[128] feuds could result in accumulation and concentration of lordship and protection in few hands.

STATE-MAKING AND THE FEUD

These properties of the feud placed it at the juncture of noblemen's and princes' interests. The capacity of feuds to bring about accumulation and concentration of one lordship at the cost of another bore directly on princely state-making. Due to Franconia's political gallimaufry, whereby noblemen had multiple and unfixed loyalties, knightly feuds could result also in an enhanced consolidation of one prince's territory and in a localised disintegration of his adversary's. Hence princes rarely failed to become embroiled in them, seeking either to take advantage of them or to take the edge off them. Their ability to control the political effects of feuds was, however, conditioned and constrained by the social and economic dimensions of their relations to the noblemen involved. As an earlier chapter has indicated, in Franconia it was noblemen who purveyed to princes two of the most important elements that went into state-making: coercion and capital.[129] Yet only wealthy noble families were in a position to cater effectively to these prerequisites of the developing state. German princes therefore had a direct stake in the economic viability and power of leading

---

[127] Diego Gambetta, *The Sicilian Mafia: The Business of Private Protection* (Cambridge, Mass., 1993), 40.

[128] Cf. Gerhard Fouquet, 'Reichskirche und Adel: Ursachen und Mechanismen des Aufstiegs der Kraichgauer Niederadelsfamilie v. Helmstatt im Speyerer Domkapitel zu Beginn des 15. Jahrhunderts', *ZGO* 129 (1981), 191–233.

[129] See chap. 3. Charles Tilly, *Coercion, Capital, and European States, AD 990–1992*, 2nd edn (Oxford, 1992), chaps. 1–6. For a discussion of Tilly's and other theories of state formation see Roland Axtmann, 'The Formation of the Modern State: the Debate in the Social Sciences', in *National Histories and European History*, ed. Mary Fulbrook (London, 1993), 21–45.

families. Like the French king, they were compelled to support such families and to carve out niches into which these families could be fitted so that their wealth and connections could 'function to strengthen the state'.[130]

Necessarily, this elicited a countenancing attitude toward feuds of members of this group.[131] Philippe de Commynes, who knew something about statecraft and duplicity, noted that '[t]hese people are hardly ever punished by the German princes, for the latter want to employ their services in time of need'.[132] The point was taken further by the Franconian humanist Ulrich von Hutten, scion of a feud-happy noble family. He observed that princes were not simply turning a blind eye to feuds, but rather actively colluding with their perpetrators, and for good reasons: 'the princes need them as the shield of their own power; indeed, the power of all princes rests on them. Hence, among [the princes], he who becomes enemy of another calls upon [the noblemen], using them as weapons of war'.[133] Feuds, by these accounts, were partly constitutive of the power of both princes and noblemen. Hence princely partiality could not but have serious consequences for all concerned: by making choices, by favouring some feuders over others, princes influenced the process of social stratification among the nobility. The process of territorial consolidation was otherwise hardly feasible. Yet precisely the social effects which their interested decisions could have on noblemen put princes in a political predicament. For most feuds occurred between noblemen belonging to the upper stratum.[134] These therefore were of a more or less equal usefulness to princes. They were also more or less of equal danger. Noblemen alienated by the real or imagined want of aid from one prince were likely to transfer their loyalty to another prince who would have been only too keen to embrace them. This placed each of the princes in a cleft stick: they had to intervene in feuds in order to secure territorial advantages or, at the least, to preserve the status quo; yet any such intervention risked proving counter-productive. Nowhere is the dynamic of this impasse more visible than in a series of conflicts around the turn of the fifteenth century – a time when imperial reforms lent urgency to the problem of 'sovereignty' in Franconia.

In 1498 a feud broke out between Veit von Vestenberg and the brothers Georg

---

[130] Robert R. Harding, *Anatomy of a Power Elite: The Provincial Governors of Early Modern France* (New Haven, 1978), 167. See also Sarah Hanley, 'Engendering the State: Family Formation and State Building in Early Modern France', *French Historical Studies* 16 (1989), 4–27.

[131] For a striking example see Joseph Baader (ed.) *Verhandlungen über Thomas von Absberg und seine Fehden gegen den Schwäbischen Bund 1519 bis 1530* (Tübingen, 1873), 3, 5–6, 9, 16–17.

[132] Samuel Kinser (ed.), *The Memoirs of Philippe de Commynes*, trans. Isabelle Cazeaux, vol. I (Columbia, South Carolina, 1969), 355.

[133] Ulrich von Hutten, 'Die Anschauenden', in *Ulrich von Hutten: Deutsche Schriften*, ed. Peter Ukena (Munich, 1970), 136–61, at 149–50. The charter of the 1517 union of the Franconian nobility declared that the princes could not maintain their rule 'an frumme getrewe Ritter und Knecht': Johann Christian Lünig, *Des Teutschen Reichs-Archiv partis sepecialis continuatio III*, part 2 (Leipzig, 1713), 7, no. 1.

[134] See chap. 4.

and Marx von Crailsheim.[135] In a missive he sent to the margrave in 1500, Veit professed that he 'was unwilling to practise robbery and to disturb the peace', but that if he failed to stand up against his enemies 'the feud would be his ruin'. He requested the prince to grant him clandestinely permission to take action against his adversaries. The margrave asked Veit to put off his plans until his return to Franconia so that they 'could discuss this and other matters not to be mentioned in a letter'.[136] What the prince had in mind may well have been Veit's allegations that the bishops of Bamberg and Würzburg were covertly helping Veit's enemies.[137] Veit seems to have succeeded in persuading the prince: disenchanted by his backing of Veit, the Crailsheim brothers proclaimed a feud on the margrave as well.[138] They found an ally in Moritz von Guttenberg, who was also at loggerheads with the margrave. His feud went back to 1482.[139]

Following a dispute with his relation Christoph, Philipp von Guttenberg (Moritz's cousin) began to build a new castle on the family's estates. The margrave, fearing a new, independent centre of power, responded by claiming he had the right to 'open house' in New-Guttenberg. Philipp rejected the claim out of hand. Shortly afterward, Christoph turned his allodial parts in Old-Guttenberg into fiefs to be held from the prince. This he did, Christoph said, for the sake of 'protection and safeguard' by the margrave. Already a margravial councillor, he was now appointed master of the household as well.[140] With these actions the margrave gained a foothold in the Guttenberg patrimony which would enable him to interpret Philipp's actions as prejudicial to his authority. This forced Philipp to look for protection as well. He found it in Duke Georg of Bavaria-Landshut, a territorial rival of the margrave. He made over to him his newly constructed castle and his portion in Old-Guttenberg, which he then received in fee. In return he was nominated to a ducal district governorship.[141] Margrave Friedrich perceived Philipp's steps as an immediate political threat: 'in view of the fact that [Philipp's] castle is built for the most part on Your Grace's [the margrave's] territory', opined the chancellor,

---

135 StAN, Fstm.Ansb., Fehdeakten, no. 10 [alte Signatur].
136 StAN, AA-Akten, no. 392, prod. of Sonntag nach Michaelis archang. [4 October] and prod. of Dienstag nach Francisci [6 October] 1500.
137 StAN, Fstm.Ansb., Fehdeakten, no. 10 [alte Signatur], esp. prod. 2; ibid., Akten des siebenfarbigen Alphabets, no. 35, prod. 49.
138 'Hochgeborner Furst und herr, herr Friderich, marggrave zw Brandeburg . . . Wisset, Nach dem ir wider uns jorgen und marxen von kreulsheim gebruder, veitten von vestenberg ritter unsern offen veintt, der unser gutlich und rechtlich erbietten zw merem mall veracht und nit annemen hatt wollen, hawset, herbergt, schutzt, und schirmt, das wir . . . ewr . . . offne abgesagtte veint sein wollen, in krafft ditz briffs': StAN, AA-Akten, no. 392 [n.d. = c. 1500]. See also ibid., AA-Akten, no. 1733.
139 Unless otherwise noted, the following is based on Rupprecht, *Ritterschaftliche Herrschaftswahrung in Franken*, 72–117.
140 Cf. Bischoff, *Freiherren von (und zu) Guttenberg 1148–1970*, 191.
141 StAN, AA-Akten, nos. 1753, 1788.

that it should deservedly be held in fee from you, that it lies in Your Grace's principality and abuts on your principal castle Plassenburg, His Grace [the duke of Bavaria] can judge whether it would please him if one whose seat is so close to Landshut or Burghausen [in Bavaria] went over to a Franconian or another prince.[142]

The margrave gave Philipp what turned out to be a last chance: Philipp should dissolve his feudal and contractual ties to the duke of Bavaria; in return for transferring his fiefs to the margrave, he would get 2000 gulden and a district governorship. Philipp declined the offer, and a feud ensued. At first the margrave persecuted Philipp by proxies, two of his governors in the area and personal enemies of Philipp.[143] Then he joined in. In 1498 Philipp was apprehended but obstinately refused to retract and to hand over his castle. In 1500 he died in prison in shadowy circumstances. Philipp paid dearly for his political miscalculation. He relied on a foreign ruler for whom castle Guttenberg was not worth a head-on collision with the margrave. And he was left in the lurch. Had he put his confidence in a Franconian prince he would probably have fared better.

The lesson was grasped by Moritz von Guttenberg. He carried on with the feud against the margrave, dexterously riding on the rising tide of territorial tension between the latter and the bishop of Bamberg. It was precisely then that, consequent upon the 'Streitberg affair', relations between the two princes were at their lowest ebb.[144] Furthermore, the bishop too was busy making his presence felt in the area around Guttenberg, arguing he had the right to try capital offences there. He also named Apel von Guttenberg (Philipp's brother) as his district governor – in return for the feudal lordship over Apel's hitherto allodial share in Old-Guttenberg. A sense of *déjà vu* must have descended on the margrave when he learnt this and that Moritz von Guttenberg was being assisted by the bishop.[145] One of the reports to this effect came from Darius von Heßberg.[146]

Darius was then in feud with the bishop as a result of a dispute between his land-lordship and the prince's territorial lordship: both asserted jurisdiction over the same peasants. Threatened with attack by the bishop's forces, Darius placed his trust in the margrave 'as the laudable prince of justice and noble virtues', and promised he 'will prove to be loyal with all [his] powers and [his] house'. Knowing that 'honeyed words', as he put it, were not enough, Darius made his castle Neuhaus available to the margrave. He boasted that he could accommodate there 2,000 to 3,000 men, and recruit 300 cavalrymen with which to serve the

---

[142] Ibid., no. 1753.

[143] Ibid.; Erich Freiherr von Guttenberg, 'Aus Fehdezeiten (1490–1506)', in *Lebens- und Kulturbilder aud der Geschichte des fränkischen Geschlechts von Guttenberg*, ed. Wilhelm Engel (Würzburg, 1958), 9–45, at 16; *RTA, mR*, vi, 256 n. 272.

[144] See p. 95 above.

[145] Rupprecht, *Ritterschaftliche Herrschaftswahrung in Franken*, 78, 91, 132. Moritz, too, negotiated with the bishop of Bamberg for a district governorship in return for making over his allodial part of Old-Guttenberg: ibid., 304.

[146] StAN, Fstm.Ansb., Fehdeakten, no. 26, prod. 39.

prince. He also hoped to broker for the margrave a loan of 3,000 gulden from another noble. To drive the message home, he explained that the margrave would not profit 'if I had to endure imprisonment in Bamberg . . . or if I was stabbed to death. With God's and Your Grace's help I want to avoid this as much as I can.'[147] In no time, men-at-arms and munitions made their way to Neuhaus. Darius now felt confident: 'the bishop and his lieutenants should try on a carnival play with someone else', he reassured the margrave.[148] That Darius had made a pact with his cousins stipulating the transmission of his castle after his death was no obstacle. He was prepared to part with the document and to arrange to disinherit his relations. Nor did the fact that he held this castle in fee from the bishop of Bamberg weigh much with him. By late 1499 castle Neuhaus was secure under the margrave's 'protection and safeguard'.[149] Soon afterward, acknowledging his valuable services, the margrave nominated Darius as councillor and offered him a district governorship as well.[150]

Heßberg's feud began as a dispute over seigneurial rights. So did the other feuds just described. And yet they all quickly developed into something much bigger, were drawn into the larger territorial conflicts between princes. This was almost inevitable: in view of the possible geopolitical outcomes of feuds, princes could not afford to remain passive; all the more so as each of them rationally feared a unilateral move by one of the others to exploit feuds. Conversely, there was also a positive incentive: short of costly, possibly ruinous wars, noblemen's feuds were one of the best means princes had of breaking the territorial stalemate prevalent in Franconia. During the final years of the fifteenth century the margrave proved himself master in actualising this potential of the feud. The feuds of Heßberg and of the Streitbergs provided him with an opportunity to take hold of two strategic castles to the detriment of the bishop of Bamberg; through the feud against the Guttenbergs he took over another. He then swiftly changed course and began to support the Guttenbergs, including Moritz, when they fell out with the bishop of Bamberg.[151] Around these years there were in progress four other knightly feuds against the bishop which can be traced back to the margrave.[152] The feuds of Konrad Schott and Christoph von Giech against

---

[147] Ibid., prod. 8, 49, 53. 'ich wil mein haus leib und gut trewlich zu e f genaden setzen da sollen e f g kein zweiffel einsetzen inn verhoffung e f g werden mich genediglich beduncken es wer e f g nichts damit beholffen das ich zu bamberg . . . im loch uffstand oder erstochen das wil ich verhuten mit hilf gots und e f g als vil ich mag': ibid., prod. 34.

[148] Ibid., prod. 40–2. 'der hochwirdig furst und sein regenten ein andern zu einem vaßtnachtspil mussen furnemen dann mich': ibid., prod. 27.

[149] Ibid., prod. 26, 27, 38. '. . . nachdem ewr furstlich gnade mein hawsfrauen mit irer verweysung und das Newhaws in schutz und schirm genomen'.

[150] Ibid., prod. 6, 16, 41.

[151] Rupprecht, *Ritterschaftliche Herrschaftswahrung in Franken*, 132–3.

[152] (1) Jobst von Lüchau was a margravial governor: StAB, Fehde-Akten, no. 152, prod. 3. (2) Ebold Stiebar was the son of a margravial governor: cf. ibid., prod. 25, ibid., no. 133, and Otto Graf Seefried, *Aus dem Stiebar-Archiv: Forschungen zur Familiengeschichte von Bauer, Bürger und*

Nuremberg enabled him to conjure up an occasion for war, to win over the nobility and to defeat the city.[153] His policy toward the nobility and their feuds paid off.

On the other hand, what this chain of feuds also shows is that princes constantly faced the danger of estranging powerful noblemen and of thereby compromising the territorial soundness of their own domains. Hence feuds between noblemen loyal primarily to one and the same prince were potentially as politically explosive as feuds between stalwarts of competing princes. Friend and foe were relative categories, alternating in quick succession.[154] If feuds were capable of promoting the territorial solidity of a principality, they were equally capable of destabilising the political fronts.[155] Consequently, the feud reproduced the princes' dependence on the noble élite. The use of noblemen's feuds by princes had its price. The frequent pacts made by princes against feuds are a monument to their dilemma.[156]

The nobles proved proficient in capitalising on the continual cut-throat contest between the princes. For one thing, they manipulated it so as to keep the princes at a certain arm's length, to retain a degree of independence and enough room for manoeuvre. For another, it is striking that many feuders were appointed to high

---

Edelmann in Ober- und Mittelfranken (Nuremberg, 1953), 8. (3) Hans von Reitzenstein was a margravial governor: cf. StAB, Fehde-Akten, no. 152, prod. 25 and Reitzenstein, *Familie von Reitzenstein*, 166–67. (4) Klaus von Bernheim was a member of the margravial Order of the Swan: cf. StAB, Fehde-Akten, no. 152, prod. 25 and Rudolf Graf Stillfried and Siegfried Haenle, *Das Buch vom Schwanenorden: Ein Beitrag zu den hohenzollerischen Forschungen* (Berlin, 1881), 195.

[153] See chap. 2.

[154] When in 1448 the margrave came into a territorial and economic conflict with the baron of Heideck, his tone changed from 'unsern oheim' to 'Nu wissen wir von keiner besundern fruntschaft': Deeg, *Die Herrschaft der Herren von Heideck*, 118.

[155] Apart from the examples given above see StAN, AA-Akten, no. 738, prod. 43–74; Priebatsch (ed.), *Politische Correspondenz des Kurfürsten Albrecht Achilles*, II, 324, no. 322; III, 172–5, 351–5, nos. 861, 1046; Fries, *Historie*, 815; Spangenberg, *Hennebergische Chronica*, 415–17; Adolph Friedrich Riedel (ed.), *Codex diplomaticus Brandenburgensis: Sammlung der Urkunden, Chroniken und sonstigen Quellenschriften für die Geschichte der Mark Brandenburg und ihrer Regenten*, part 2, *Urkunden-Sammlung zur Geschichte der auswärtigen Verhältnisse der Mark Brandenburg und ihrer Regenten*, 6 vols. (Berlin, 1843–58), V, 269–70, 272–3, 316–17, 351–2, 358–60, nos. 1984, 1986, 2023, 2057, 2065; cf. 'Hellers Chronic der Stadt Bayreuth', part 1, *AO* 1, no. 1 (1828), 102–47, at 130–1 and Carl August Hugo Burkhardt (ed.), *Das funfft merkisch Buech des Churfuersten Albrecht Achilles* (Jena, 1857), 225–6, 266–71, nos. 133, 153; Alban Freiherr von Dobeneck, 'Geschichte des ausgestorbenen Geschlechtes der von Sparneck', *AO* 22, no. 3 (1905), 1–65, at 41–4; Seyboth, *Die Markgraftümer Ansbach und Kulmbach*, 144–5; cf. ibid., 137 and Freiherr von Stetten, 'Ein Fehdebrief vom Jahre 1489', *Der deutsche Herold* 23 (1892), 114–15; Wilmowsky, 'Die Geschichte der Ritterschaft Buchenau', 39; Aufseß, *Geschichte des uradelichen Aufseß'schen Geschlechtes*, 150–4; Würdinger, *Kriegsgeschichte*, II, 107, 117–18.

[156] StAN, Fstm.Ansb., Fehdeakten, no. 26, prod. 66; Priebatsch (ed.), *Politische Correspondenz des Kurfürsten Albrecht Achilles*, III, 284, no. 986; Muehlon, 'Johann III. von Grumbach', 110; Riedel (ed.), *Codex diplomaticus*, part 2, V, 85–9, 450–1, nos. 1833, 2148; Johann Looshorn, *Die Geschichte des Bisthums Bamberg*, vol. IV, *Das Bisthum Bamberg von 1400–1556* (Munich, 1900), 448. See also Manfred Kaufmann, *Fehde und Rechtshilfe: Die Verträge brandenburgischer Landesfürsten zur Bekämpfung des Raubrittertums im 15. und 16. Jahrhundert* (Pfaffenweiler, 1993).

princely offices during or immediately following their feuds. Their feuds brought them to the fore and then closer to the prince by whom they chose to be supported. The consequent proximity to that prince was invigorating, empowering them to exercise lordship on an otherwise unattainable scale. Their status rose concordantly.

At the same time, however, these possible social consequences of the princes' intervention in knightly feuds indicate that the dependence was mutual. The competition among the nobility was far from free. It was regulated by the fact that its immediate objects – lordships – were in large part controlled or distributed by princes. That the demand was incomparably greater than the supply gave rulers a powerful leverage. They allocated lordships, particularly pledge-lordships, to those who could serve princely territorial designs most competently. In order to receive such lordships noblemen had to be able to extend loans, to command men-at-arms, to make castles and lands available to princes. These capabilities presupposed having considerable wherewithal at one's disposal. In other words, noblemen had to provide princes with capital and coercion in order to gain (or retain) access to capital and coercion.

It is in this context that the full import of the feud unfolds. Princely territorialisation put an immense strain on the nobility. Being able to mesh one's own interests with those of a prince promised economic and social success; failure to do so doomed a family to the ennui of the village at best,[157] to a complete eclipse at worst. The result was a fierce struggle for access to resources. Feuds functioned to effect the proximity to a prince which was the necessary condition for having this access. By expanding their lordships, partly through feuds, noblemen obtained the resources which could then be placed at a prince's disposal. Concurrently, they were able to spearhead the consolidation of the realm of the prince whose favour they either already enjoyed or sought. These services were often enough offered to the highest bidder among the princes. Reward came in the form of coercive powers, mainly district governorships. These were then turned to good account, put to use against both rival noblemen and subject commoners.

Expectedly, governorships and other pledge-lordships were not infrequently the unmediated motivation for feuds.[158] 'Hatred and envy' were aroused in the

---

[157] Officeless petty country gentlemen were apparently a social category. Margrave Albrecht explained that 'es sind hern, es sein rittermessig und sind gemein edelleut, die auf den hofen sitzen und nit beslost sind. das haissen bladecken': Priebatsch (ed.), *Politische Correspondenz des Kurfürsten Albrecht Achilles*, III, 107 n. 2, no. 804.

[158] StAB, Fehde-Akten, no. 133; StAW, Stb, no. 1012, fol. 445ᵛ; ibid., Ldf, no. 15, pp. 68–71; Müllner, *Die Annalen der Reichsstadt Nürnberg*, II, 557; Joseph Chmel (ed.), *Actenstücke und Briefe zur Geschichte des Hauses Habsburg im Zeitalter Maximilian's I.*, vol. I (Vienna, 1854), 488, no. 22; cf. Adolf Fischer, *Geschichte des Hauses Hohenlohe*, vol. I (Stuttgart, 1866; reprint, Schwäbisch Hall, 1991), 112–13 and Stetten, 'Ein Fehdebrief', 114–15; Klaus Peter Decker, 'Klientel und Konkurrenz: Die ritterschaftliche Familie von Hutten und die Grafen von Hanau und von Ysenburg', *Hessisches Jahrbuch für Landesgeschichte* 38 (1988), 23–48, at 41; Wilhelm Freiherr von

counts of Werdenberg when in 1486 Veringen, which they had until then held in pledge, was redeemed and re-pledged to the count of Zimmern, protégé of Duke Sigmund of Austria. They took their revenge by implicating the count of Zimmern in a domestic dispute of the Habsburgs. With the emperor's sponsorship they drove Zimmern out of his lands, and forced an oath of fealty (*phlicht und huldigung*) on his subjects.[159] Cases like this are similar to feuds noblemen made against their fellows or against cities in such a way as to further the cause of one prince against his enemies.[160] They are also homologous to feuds at the explicit behest of a prince.[161] In fact, these distinctions are tenuous. In practice the different causes and motives and pressures which were at work shaded into each other. Underlying them all was the concomitance of the competitions over accumulation and concentration of land-lordship and territorial lordship. These competitions converged on the capacity of the feud to subserve hand in hand the interests of some princes and some noblemen acting in tacit or overt unison against other princes, noblemen and cities. It was from this interface that the feud issued.

CONCLUSION

Feuds turned on lordship as a central constituent of noble status on the one hand, and of princely rule on the other. The process of state formation rendered lordships crucial to both princes and noblemen. This cannot be accounted for solely, probably not even primarily, in terms of their economic value. By the fifteenth century manorial lordship was not the main source of revenue of eminent noblemen, although it was still fundamental.[162] Seigneuries became so vital because they involved dominion over land and people and hence mattered politically to princes.[163] Franconia's geopolitical farrago, the legacy of the collapse

---

Bibra, *Beiträge zur Familien-Geschichte der Reichsfreiherrn von Bibra*, vol. II (Munich, 1882), 189–99; Wilhelm, 'Die Edeln von und zum Absberg', 50–1; Rotenhan, 'Streit und Fehde um die Burg Stuffenberg'; Rupprecht, *Ritterschaftliche Herrschaftswahrung in Franken*, 136, 297–8, 299 n. 635, 334 n. 814.

[159] Hansmartin Decker-Hauff (ed.), *Die Chronik der Grafen von Zimmern*, vol. I (Sigmaringen, 1964), 241–61.

[160] Apart from the examples given above see Gerhard Taddey, 'Macht und Recht im späten Mittelalter: Die Auseinandersetzungen zwischen Hohenlohe und Hessen um die Grafschaften Ziegenhain und Nidda', *WFr* 61 (1977), 79–110, at 96–7, 99. See also Kurt Andermann, 'Ritter – Edelknechte – Amtleute: Aspekte pfälzischer Adelsgeschichte im späten Mittelalter, skizziert am Beispiel der Familien von Mühlhofen und von Otterbach', *Pfälzer Heimat* 36 (1985), 1–8.

[161] StAN, Reichsstadt Nürnberg, 35 Neue Laden der unteren Losungsstube, V 90/2 2447; ibid., AA-Akten, nos. 1753, 1831; 'Hellers Chronic', part 1, 132–6.

[162] Kurt Andermann, *Studien zur Geschichte des pfälzischen Niederadels im Mittelalter: Eine vergleichende Untersuchung an ausgewählten Beispielen* (Speyer, 1982), 183; Wilhelm Störmer, 'Grundherrschaften des höheren und niederen Adels im Main-Tauber-Raum', in *Die Grundherrschaft im späten Mittelalter*, II, 25–45, at 36–7.

[163] Cf. Baum, 'Der Lehenhof des Hochstifts Würzburg', I, 235.

of the Staufen imperium, meant that territorial compacting could not proceed without the co-operation of noblemen. Only via the intermediary authority of powerful nobles with a stake in the state could princes govern the land. As Peter Moraw has emphasised, 'the nobility . . . which inclined toward a certain prince consolidated the territory's cohesion through their . . . familial networks and above all stabilised it toward the outside'.[164] The conflict between princes therefore entailed a competition over the enlistment of as large, as affluent, and as influential a noble clientele as possible. To fail to achieve this end was to court disaster. According to Lorenz Fries, Margrave Albrecht Achilles 'began to despise and to act aggressively toward the bishop of Würzburg because he considered him feeble for being unable to maintain the loyalty of his nobility'.[165] Loyalty, indeed, could not be taken for granted. Noblemen's support was obtained in exchange for lordships. This was one main reason why fiefs both propagated themselves and gained in political magnitude.

Those nobles who came into possession of important lordships were in a favourable position. They had higher chances than those who did not of installing themselves around the person of a prince; of being invested with offices; of striking advantageous marriage alliances. They made up the élite. State-building thus exerted massive social pressure on the nobility, so much so that it cut not only into the class as a whole, but into individual families as well. It touched off a violent contention over lordship.

This pattern is pointed up by an examination of the most notable exception to it, Franz von Sickingen. He was and is an intriguing figure because his career represented a dramatic break with the social and political traditions of the untitled nobility. The economic basis which enabled him to do so was established by his grandfather and father Swicker along familiar lines: in princely service.[166] Indeed, Swicker owed much of his prosperity to a feud he waged against Cologne in 1488. It arose out of a mixture of personal considerations and an attempt by the Elector Palatine to force the city to give up a newly acquired Rhine toll. He was, as Harold Kehrer has pointed out, 'at the cutting edge in a broad economic war of [the prince] against Cologne'. Swicker had already been an important princely official before the feud; but the feud drew him even closer to the prince. In 1501 he became master of the household.[167]

The wealth amassed by Swicker was drawn upon by Franz in his feud against the city of Worms in 1515. It was the starting-point of his stupendous ascent to national prominence. He emerged from it, as his father had from his feud with

---

[164] Peter Moraw, 'Landesgeschichte und Reichsgeschichte im 14. Jahrhundert', *Jahrbuch für westdeutsche Landesgeschichte* 3 (1977), 175–91, at 180.
[165] Fries, *Historie*, 801.
[166] Kehrer, 'The von Sickingen', 176–7; Harold H. Kehrer, 'Die Familie von Sickingen und die deutschen Fürsten 1262–1523', *ZGO* 129 (1981), 83–188, at 120–32.
[167] Kehrer, 'The von Sickingen', 200–4.

Cologne, as a feared and famed warlord. In 1518 he became a condotierre in Emperor Maximilian's employ.[168] But unlike other, meeker feuders-cum-military entrepreneurs,[169] Franz was not the man to be content with 'ploughing back' the prestige and the money he had acquired into conventional lordships and offices in princely administration. By now richer and mightier than some princes,[170] Franz was emboldened to undertake a revolutionary venture: a feud against the archbishopric of Trier. It was not – as it is commonly labelled – a Knights' Revolt. It was an effort to obtain the ultimate lordship, a principality.[171] This provoked an alliance of princes which brought him down. During the siege they laid to his castle in 1523 Franz met his death.

It was accepted as quite normal for noblemen to feud, even against princes, so long as only land-lordship was concerned; so long as social upward mobility was engineered within the limits circumscribed by princes. Franz would have none of this. His ambition to rise from the ranks of the untitled nobility to territorial lordship was unprecedented and intolerable. It threatened to play havoc with the sociopolitical order. Franz von Sickingen was unique. But it is his uniqueness that underscores the meaning of lordship as the centre of the symbiotic relationship between princes and noblemen.

Lordship was the cogwheel connecting two contests: one between princes over territorial lordship, the other between noblemen over land-lordship. The feud assumed here a decisive function. For it was very much the generator of lordship. It had the capacity, inherent in the uses of 'protection', to bring about an accumulation and concentration of lordship. It also had the capacity of gradually undoing lordship. Therefore feuds readily lent themselves to an application by princes to territorial consolidation. Princely state-making had – in Charles Tilly's formulation – the character of organised crime.[172]

This paradoxical nature of the gestation of the state, the violent establishment of a violence-controlling agency, explains the preponderance of eminent noblemen, especially high office-holders, among feuders. It was the result of a dialectic relationship between state formation and social stratification. The demands made on the nobility by the developing 'finance state' led to the creation of an élite of office-holding families. These owed their success to their ability to make themselves useful to princes. Instrumental in this achievement was their persistent prosecution of feuds. It facilitated the amalgamation of their interests

---

[168] Ibid., 223, 225, 229.
[169] Fritz Redlich, *The German Military Enterpriser and his Work Force: A Study in European Economic and Social History*, vol. I (Wiesbaden, 1964), 45–6, 71–94. See also Erhard Waldemar Kanter, *Hans von Rechberg von Hohenrechberg: Ein Zeit- und Lebensbild* (Zurich, 1903).
[170] As one chronicler put it, Franz 'war nicht geringer dann der fürnehmbsten fürsten einer geachtet': Christian Kolb (ed.), *Widmans Chronica* (Stuttgart, 1904), 47.
[171] Kehrer, 'The von Sickingen', 274–9.
[172] Charles Tilly, 'War Making and State Making as Organized Crime', in *Bringing the State Back In*, ed. Peter B. Evans, Dietrich Rueschemeyer, and Theda Skocpol (Cambridge, 1985), 169–91.

with those of princes. In the process they enhanced their control over commoners and marginalised other noblemen. It is perhaps revealing that the lot of many of the latter is scarcely known. If they had not sunk into the commonalty or become extinct altogether, they were extruded from active political life. By the late fifteenth century the competition among the nobility was largely restricted to a relatively small circle of participants struggling for a share in state power. Naturally enough, it was these very same men who, also in the late fifteenth century, assumed leadership of the aristocratic resistance against the growing power of the state.[173]

---

[173] See chap. 6.

6

The decline of the feud

In 1574 Emperor Maximilian II received from Lazarus von Schwendi, his councillor and military commander, a report on the political situation in Germany. It must have created mixed feelings in him to learn that

The emperors and even the popes and church councils had to look on and to permit the internal daily private wars and feuding (*die innerlichen täglichen Privat-Krieg und befehdung*) of the Germans; likewise the old law and custom of the judicial duel; likewise the disturbances of the peace and the robberies. And [they] could not restrain them because of their traditionally violent nature and disposition, until now, in the past hundred years, through . . . manners of living (*Manier zu leben*) and through the introduction of teaching and schools, but especially through the invention and usefulness of the printing press and of books, and then also through very wise assistance of former emperors, such harsh and all too impudent German nature has been softened, and everything brought to greater peace, better *Policey*, and more orderly life and circumstances.[1]

Schwendi provides a stunningly original account of the decline of the knightly feud in Germany, all the more so since what is considered as the last feud had ended only a few years earlier.[2] The account is also impressively precocious, its terms flashing up toward our own world: probably for the first time the feud is branded (and de-legitimised) as 'private war' – a distinctly modern perspective. And yet the praise for 'eradicating' the feud does not go to the intentional actions of public authorities. Rather, anticipating modern scholars,[3] the general identified the chief civilising agents as education, new mores and, above all, the printing press and the book.

Schwendi's explanation may serve as a corrective to widespread notions that the decline of the feud was the straightforward effect of the rise of the state.[4]

---

[1] Eugen von Frauenholz (ed.), *Des Lazarus von Schwendi Denkschrift über die politische Lage des deutschen Reiches von 1574* (Munich, 1939), 8.

[2] See pp. 143–5 below. For Schwendi's intervention to have this feud settled see Adolf Eiermann, *Lazarus von Schwendi, Freiherr von Hohenlandsberg: Ein deutscher Feldoberst und Staatsmann des XVI. Jahrhunderts* (Freiburg, 1904), 10–12.

[3] For an example see Kristen B. Neuschel, *Word of Honor: Interpreting Noble Culture in Sixteenth-Century France* (Ithaca, 1989).

[4] Otto Brunner, *'Land' and Lordship: Structures of Governance in Medieval Austria*, trans. Howard Kaminsky and James Van Horn Melton (Philadelphia, 1992), 323; Rudolf Endres, *Adel in der Frühen Neuzeit* (Munich, 1993), 60–1; Manfred Kaufmann, *Fehde und Rechtshilfe: Die Verträge brandenbur-*

Here lies its greater value, in the highly suggestive general tenor, not in the tall conclusions. It is surely true that the German nobility, like other European nobilities,[5] underwent a sweeping transformation of attitudes and comportment in the early modern period. A reformed *Weltanschauung* is manifest in all of the areas singled out by Schwendi.[6] Perhaps the most emblematic example in this regard is provided by Hans Pleickhard von Berlichingen (d. 1594). Whereas his grandfather, the famous feuder Götz, spent his days fighting people, Hans Pleickhard's main pastime was apparently collecting books: he had some 625 volumes in his library (his grandfather's autobiography not being one of them).[7] This example, however, is also problematic: even if it can be taken as representative, it still does not imply that the new mind-set it illustrates was what effected the decline of the feud. To put it bluntly, the emergence of a new mind-set may equally have been a result of the decline of the feud or, more plausibly, coterminous with it. This is, more or less perforce, the line of enquiry pursued in what follows. For there is no evidence, at most oblique indications, to establish that the decay of the feud originated in a meditative refashioning of the self by individual nobles. There is, on the other hand, a good deal of direct evidence to suggest that it was the outcome of a larger, collective, and essentially political undertaking by the nobility. This was the organisation of the Knighthood (*Ritterschaft*).

THE FORMATION OF THE KNIGHTHOOD

The Knighthood was built on a long tradition of confederations of nobles. The first aristocratic league had already appeared in Germany in 1331. Until the middle of the century, however, it had few successors. Then, after 1360, began a spate of new foundations. The majority of these associations were of politico-military orientation, stipulating for mutual protection of the members, especially in feuds, and for internal adjudication of disputes.[8] These were the attributes also of the four knightly societies established in Franconia in this period. The Society

---

gischer *Landesfürsten zur Bekämpfung des Raubrittertums im 15. und 16. Jahrhundert* (Pfaffenweiler, 1993), 102–3.

[5] J. H. Hexter, 'The Education of the Aristocracy in the Renaissance', in his *Reappraisals in History: New Views on History and Society in Early Modern Europe*, 2nd edn (Chicago, 1979), 45–70.

[6] Eva Pleticha, *Adel und Buch: Studien zur Geisteswelt des fränkischen Adels am Beispiel seiner Bibliotheken vom 15. bis zum 18. Jahrhundert* (Neustadt a.d. Aisch, 1983), esp. 1–55, 106–14, 138–40; Norbert Conrads, 'Tradition und Modernität im adligen Bildungsprogramm der Frühen Neuzeit', in *Ständische Gesellschaft und soziale Mobilität*, ed. Winfried Schulze (Munich, 1988), 389–403.

[7] Volker Honeman and Helgard Ulmschneider, 'Eine ritterschaftliche Bibliothek des 16. Jahrhunderts: Das Verzeichnis der Bücher des Hans Pleickhard von Berlichingen (†1594)', *Archiv für Geschichte des Buchwesens* 20, no. 4 (1979), 833–94.

[8] Holger Kruse, Werner Paravicini, and Andreas Ranft (eds.), *Ritterorden und Adelsgesellschaften im spätmittelalterlichen Deutschland: Ein systematisches Verzeichnis* (Frankfurt am Main, 1991), 1–191.

of the Griffin (1379) and the Society of St George (1381) were quintessentially feuding fellowships, created to answer immediate defensive needs of the participants at a time of political turbulence. The Society of Counts, Barons, Knights and Valets (1387) and the Society of the Clasp (1392) were of a different nature, devoted mainly to tournaments; but they too arranged for aid to members involved in feuds.[9]

These elements of collective military and judicial responsibility were taken over by the union formed by 113 Franconian noblemen in 1402.[10] Also like most of the preceding associations, it was ad hoc and relatively narrow in geographical reach, centring on the diocese of Würzburg. It represented none the less a new phase in the co-operative life of the Franconian nobility. For this league was not a reaction to a contingent, specific menace, princely or otherwise; nor was it concerned primarily with sociability and the festive reenactment of nobles' exclusive solidarity – even though the groundwork for the union was prepared during a tournament in 1401.[11] Rather, it was an attempt to get to grips with the general drift of the politics of the prince-bishop of Würzburg, and better to define the place of the nobility in the framework of the nascent episcopal state. It was no accident that the Würzburg nobles were the first in Franconia to make this effort; for it was the bishop of Würzburg who was the first among the Franconian princes to assert a new kind of authority: one based predominantly on territorial relations rather than predominantly on personal bonds.[12]

The process leading up to this attempted shift was, historically, in many ways archetypal: as a result of wars and other upheavals, as well as of the steadily soaring costs of consolidating a principality, the diocese of Würzburg entered the fifteenth century carrying along a gigantic debt of 2.5 million gulden.[13] Beside pledging episcopal property in return for loans, taxes and tolls were threatening to become a norm.[14] In 1400 the nobles consented to a levy on their and their tenants' property.[15] This still was well within the bounds of custom which, in times of crisis, sanctioned taxation as a material form of the 'aid and counsel' vassals owed their feudal lords. The next year, however, the bishop and the

---

[9] Ibid., 100, 115, 139, 156; Konrad Ruser, 'Zur Geschichte der Gesellschaften von Herren, Rittern und Knechten in Süddeutschland während des 14. Jahrhunderts', *Zeitschrift für Württembergische Landesgeschichte* 34/35 (1975/76), 1–100, esp. 30–1, 35. The most detailed study of the Society of the Clasp is by Andreas Ranft, *Adelsgesellschaften: Gruppenbildung und Genossenschaft im spätmittelalterlichen Reich* (Sigmaringen, 1994), 37–116.

[10] Lorenz Weinrich (ed.), *Quellen zur Verfassungsgeschichte des Römisch-Deutschen Reiches im Spätmittelalter (1250–1500)* (Darmstadt, 1893), 441–4, no. 109.

[11] Ernst Schubert, *Die Landstände des Hochstifts Würzburg* (Würzburg, 1967), 69.

[12] Ibid., 43–4, 65–6. The pair of concepts commonly used by German historians to describe this shift is *Personenverbandsstaat* and *institutioneller Flächenstaat*. See Ernst Schubert, *Fürstliche Herrschaft und Territorium im späten Mittelalter* (Munich, 1996), 57–8.

[13] Schubert, *Die Landstände des Hochstifts Würzburg*, 57.

[14] Angela Kulenkampff, 'Einungen und Reichsstandschaft fränkischer Grafen und Herren 1402–1641', *WFr* 45 (1971), 16–41, at 19–21.

[15] Schubert, *Die Landstände des Hochstifts Würzburg*, 55–6.

cathedral chapter imposed a levy once again but without consulting the nobility. This was what occasioned the union of 1402. Having proclaimed that it was not directed against the bishop, the charter of the union concluded with the proviso: 'unless, that is, our . . . Gracious Lord of Würzburg wanted to encumber us and our subjects with tolls, taxes, excise duties or other unjust impositions . . .'.[16]

This union laid the foundations for the future movement of the nobles, and not only on the negative point of inaugurating a fundamental opposition to princely policies. In its internal constitution, which in 1402 was still rudimentary, it also suggested an alternative view to the prince's of the position of the nobility in the principality. Militancy between members was forbidden, even in wartime. Instead, disputes had to be settled amicably by a committee of five (*die fünff*) who both presided over the union and made up its court of arbitration.[17] The Union formed in this way a self-regulated community of peace, thereby counteracting the jurisdictional authority of the prince.

This line became even more pronounced in the new nobiliary union of 1408, which was joined by the cathedral chapter of Würzburg. The immediate incentive to it was once again fiscal exactions: the episcopal Gulden Toll.[18] But in the compact with the union which the bishop hastened to sign there is no mention of it. Instead, it is the legal status of the nobility which looms large in the text. Two clauses in particular stand out. The first laid it down that untitled nobles summoned to the bishop's Territorial Court could choose between coming before it or before the Aulic Court, that is before the noble councillors of the prince. The second clause ruled that disputes between members of the union and the bishop would be decided by a board of arbitration with the leaguers having a majority of three to two votes.[19]

The terms of this agreement make abundantly clear what was at stake. Although the nobles stripped the bishop of one of his main instruments of territorial solidification, they did not repudiate his authority. In fact, they recognised that he had personal authority over each and every one of them. But precisely this was the central issue: they wanted him to remain their personal lord, and it was the prospect of him becoming something else that provoked them. This was a threat because their personal relations with the prince were the basis of their 'liberties', of their privileges in the original sense of *priva lex*. And the nobles took collective action to ensure that they continued to enjoy this position as individuals. Hence they repeatedly justified their leagues as aiming at

[16] Weinrich (ed.), *Quellen zur Verfassungsgeschichte des Römisch-Deutschen Reiches*, 443, no. 109.

[17] Ibid.

[18] Lotte Köberlin, 'Die Einungsbewegung des fränkischen Adels bis zum Jahre 1494' (PhD thesis, University of Erlangen, 1924), 20–1.

[19] Joseph Aschbach (ed.), *Wertheimisches Urkundenbuch*, part 2 of his *Geschichte der Grafen von Wertheim von den ältesten Zeiten bis zu ihrem Erlöschen in Mannsstamme im Jahre 1556* (Frankfurt am Main, 1843), 177–81, no. 133.

preserving 'old tradition' (*altes Herkommen*) from the unjust novelties introduced by the prince.

This 'old tradition' argument was itself becoming a tradition in the course of the fifteenth century. Almost every political crisis, every major power struggle, led to a new union of noblemen.[20] And in turn every union further impregnated the collective consciousness of the nobility.[21] In the proem to the charter of the union of 1483, for example, the nobles explained that they were following in the footsteps of their forefathers who

often united for the sake of securing their laudable tradition, as well as their liberties (*freyheiten*), which they gained from the former bishops of Würzburg by dint of spilling their own blood . . .[22]

The nobles had thus come to believe in the efficacy of concerted action. The personal bonds – feudal, jurisdictional and otherwise – which tied them to the prince endured. But superimposed on them was now a corporative will. This made the unions a political factor to be reckoned with. Already in 1424 the Franconian princes made an alliance with a union of Würzburg nobles. A few years later, in 1441, union nobles dominated the council of five regents which was constituted to supervise the bishop.[23] And even as steadfast a prince as Bishop Rudolf von Scherenberg of Würzburg found it necessary in 1467 to join forces with the nobility in order to restore stability to the diocese.[24]

The very fact, however, that the nobles had to renew their unions time and again shows that the bishops of Würzburg had never really come to terms with the restrictions on their authority.[25] And yet, throughout most of the fifteenth century, they were unable to keep the nobility down. Franconia's geopolitical medley, and the fierce competition between the princes over, among other things, noblemen's loyalty, enabled the latter to elude territorialisation.[26] Perhaps this is what Bishop Rudolf of Würzburg had in mind when he put it to Margrave Albrecht Achilles that if they formed a coalition they would between them be 'the

[20] For the various unions, dates of foundation and aims, see Köberlin, 'Die Einungsbewegung des fränkischen Adels'; Constance Proksch, 'Die Auseinandersetzung um den Austrag des Rechts zwischen Fürsten und Ritterschaft in Franken vom Ende des 14. bis in die Mitte des 16. Jahrhunderts', in *Strukturen der Gesellschaft im Mittelalter: Interdisziplinäre Mediävistik in Würzburg*, ed. Dieter Rödel and Joachim Schneider (Wiesbaden, 1996), 168–95.

[21] Cf. Joachim Schneider, 'Überregionale Integrationstendenzen im deutschen Niederadel: Zwei Briefzeitungen von 1427 und die Adelseinungen der Hussitenzeit', in *Strukturen der Gesellschaft im Mittelalter*, 115–39. Exemplars of the crucially important Gracious Pact of 1461 are to be found in noble family archives: StAW, Adelsarchiv Fuchs von Bimbach, no. 2, fols. 77–80; Michael Renner (ed.), *Archiv der Grafen Wolffskeel von Reichenberg* (Munich, 1961), 56, no. 341 (misdated).

[22] Aschbach (ed.), *Wertheimisches Urkundenbuch*, 298–300, no. 194.

[23] Schubert, *Die Landstände des Hochstifts Würzburg*, 86–8.

[24] StAW, Ldf, no. 77, pp. 45–50.

[25] Cf. Robert Fellner, *Die fränkische Ritterschaft von 1495–1524* (Berlin, 1905), 101; Proksch, 'Die Auseinandersetzung um den Austrag des Rechts', 182.

[26] See chaps. 3 and 5, passim.

lords of the lords'.[27] The margrave, however, had different priorities, and his policy for the nobility was accordingly much more obliging.[28] His proclivity to present himself as 'sympathiser with the nobility', especially when they were involved in conflicts with other princes, was more than propaganda.[29] It is therefore not surprising that there was very little in a way of a movement of the nobility in his domains until late in the century. The same was the case with the diocese of Bamberg, in large part because it was territorially too interlaced with the margaviate to allow the same degree of 'caging' that was taking shape in Würzburg.[30]

All the same, the balance of power between the nobles and the princes was gradually tipping in favour of the latter. The same process of territorialisation which, since around 1400, had roused tension within the diocese of Würzburg began, from around 1440, to create tension between the Franconian principalities. The main bone of contention was intersecting, competing jurisdictions, and in the 1460s the struggle erupted into wars. The nobles, it has been shown, were caught up between the princes and could not avoid becoming embroiled in their rivalries. They did of course try to make the most of them. Indeed, in 1461, as a price for their fidelity, the nobles managed to wring out of the bishop of Würzburg the vitally important Gracious Pact which solemnly affirmed their 'ancient tradition'.[31] Already by then, however, the process of territorialisation was cutting both ways. It not only gave the nobles the benefit of making choices between the princes, but was also forcing them to make choices. And the more the process of territorialisation evolved its own dynamics, the more exclusive grew the demands made of nobles by the princes, and the more lasting and difficult to reverse these choices threatened to become. In the new situation, whereby the political interstices between the principalities were narrowing,[32] to play one prince off against another was increasingly tantamount to binding oneself permanently to one of them.

In the long run, the cumulative effect on the nobles of the numerous conflicts between the princes was not unlike that which the conflicts between the nobles had on the peasants. They made them seek princely protection and consequently dependent on one prince or another. Moreover, the princes consciously exploited the vulnerability of the nobles to offer them what the nobles offered to their own

---

[27] Felix Priebatsch (ed.), *Politische Correspondenz des Kurfürsten Albrecht Achilles*, vol. II (Leipzig, 1897), 532, no. 571.

[28] See chaps. 3 and 5, passim.   [29] Schubert, *Die Landstände des Hochstifts Würzburg*, 98.

[30] Klaus Rupprecht, *Ritterschaftliche Herrschaftswahrung in Franken: Die Geschichte der von Guttenberg im Spätmittelalter und zu Beginn der Frühen Neuzeit* (Neustadt a.d. Aisch, 1994), 366–9. The term 'caging' is from Michael Mann, *The Sources of Social Power*, vol. I, *A History of Power from the Beginning to A.D. 1760* (Cambridge, 1986), passim, where it is used in a different yet related sense.

[31] StAW, Stb, no. 947, fols. 63–71.

[32] Gerhard Pfeiffer, 'Fürst und Land: Betrachtungen zur Bayreuther Geschichte', *AO* 57/58 (1977/78), 7–20, at 11; Rupprecht, *Ritterschaftliche Herrschaftswahrung in Franken*, 121–2, 144–5.

tenants: the two-pronged 'protection and safeguard', that is from themselves as well as from a third party. This analogy, if not exactly in these terms, was made by a prince who knew this method inside out: Margrave Albrecht of Brandenburg. He was accused by Duke Ludwig of Bavaria of trying to take jurisdictional control of the nobles living in the border area between the principalities. The margrave rejoined that it was actually Duke Ludwig who was hectoring the nobles into 'performing an act of perpetual homage (*erbhuldigung*) to the land of Bavaria, as our peasants are used to do to us and to our nobility'.[33]

'Protection and safeguard' was offered by the princes, often actively requested from them, also in circumstances of disputes and feuds between nobles.[34] Which was, perhaps, a more fateful means – because more regularly and speciously employed – of bringing princely authority to bear on nobles. An extreme example, yet not untypical for that, is provided by the conflict among the von Guttenberg family in the late fifteenth century.[35] The ensuing involvement in it of three rival princes – the margrave, the bishop of Bamberg, and the duke of Bavaria – enabled the Guttenbergs to prevent the castle from falling under the exclusive power of one of them. But to achieve this effect different members of the family had to ask for the 'protection and safeguard' of different princes.[36] To do this was to give hostages to fortune, yet there was no other course of action the Guttenbergs could take. The outcome was disastrous: in the span of a few years the lineage allodial castle was reduced to the status of a fief held from three domineering territorial lords.

As the feud of the Guttenbergs suggests, by the end of the fifteenth century Franconian noblemen faced an acute dilemma: the process of territorialisation, in which they played such a vital role and on which their strong position largely rested, had gone too far for their own good.[37] The competition between the

---

[33] Gustav Freiherr von Hasselholdt-Stockheim (ed.), *Urkunden und Beilagen zum Kampfe der wittelsbachischen und brandenburgischen Politik in den Jahren 1459 bis 1465*, vol. I, part 1 (Leipzig, 1865), 158, no. 31. Duke Ludwig's answer is worth quoting: 'Als er [*scil.* Margrave Albrecht] dann furter schreibet Er lass Ritter und knecht bey und neben im sizzen etc. Mag sein so er Ir bedürff Er sprech in gütlich zu'. Ibid., 163, no. 32.

[34] StAN, Ansbacher Historica, no. 210, prod. of Dienstag nach dem Sonntag Jubilate [11 May] 1484; ibid., Fstm.Ansb., Verträge mit dem Adel, Velberg 1; ibid., Fstm.Ansb., Fehde-Akten, no. 26, prod. 26, 27, 38; ibid., Fstm.Ansb., Fehdeakten, no. 110, prod. 10; ibid., AA-Akten, no. 392 [n.d. = *c.* 1500]; ibid., AA-Akten, no. 738, prod. 40, 44, 61; ibid., AA-Akten, no. 1788, prod. of Sonntag Misericordia domini [29 April] 1498; ibid., Akten des siebenfarbigen Alphabets, no. 35, prod. 40, 41; StAW, Adel, no. 1114, prod. of Montag nach Lucie [18 December] 1508; FA, Schrank 5, prod. of 18 March 1549.

[35] See pp. 113–14 above.

[36] In the case of Philipp von Guttenberg it was explained that he 'durch bedrangung mercklicher beswerde, nam und unrechttuns, so ym obgemeltter [Margrave Friedrich] und die seinen getan unserm gnedigen herrn hertzog [Georg of Bavaria] umb schutzes willen unterworffen': StAN, AA-Akten, no. 1788, prod. of Sonntag Misericordia domini [29 April] 1498.

[37] For the arsenal of rights, apart from 'protection and safeguard', of which the princes were making increasing use also against nobles see Rupprecht, *Ritterschaftliche Herrschaftswahrung in Franken*, 314, 332; Köberlin, 'Die Einungsbewegung des fränkischen Adels', passim; Reinhard Stauber,

princes reached a point where it began to limit severely the very room for manoeuvre it had provided the nobles with in the first place. In other words, the princely state, the mainstay of nobles' power, was also curtailing that power. It was growing increasingly difficult to reconcile the two fundamental political maxims of the nobility: proximity to and distance from princes. The implications and urgency of this problem were brought into focus by the events of 1495, which marked a turning-point in the way nobles tried to grapple with it.

THE COMMON PENNY OF 1495

In his biography of Willibald von Schaumberg, intended to edify fellow nobles, Ludwig von Eyb related that during 'an Imperial Diet in Worms . . . it was weighed and resolved, especially by the Franconians, that they would not let themselves be put on a level with the French [nobility], who once were also free'.[38] Eyb was referring to the Imperial Diet of 1495 whose resolutions, two in particular, delivered a heavy blow to the nobility: the total abrogation of the right to feud and the levy on them and their subjects of the Common Penny tax. The Common Penny was supposed to finance, among other things, the Imperial Chamber Court (*Reichskammergericht*), the main instrument of the Perpetual General Peace. The two programmes were linked in another – and as far as the nobility was concerned – more ominous way: both assigned a leading executory role to the princes and hence were bound to enhance their claims to 'sovereignty'.[39] The Imperial Diet of Worms was therefore a milestone of paramount significance on the road leading from the medieval state to the early modern absolutist state. The noblemen's campaign to 'remain free Franconians' in the face of this development now began in earnest.[40]

On 14 December 1495, at the invitation of the bishops of Bamberg and Würzburg and the margrave of Brandenburg as delegates of the emperor, the nobles assembled in Schweinfurt, where the bills passed at the Diet of Worms were to be announced to them. Present also were two emissaries of the emperor. The latter lectured to the nobles about the grave situation of the Holy Roman Empire, the costs of the imminent wars with France, the Swiss Confederacy, and

'Herzog Georg der Reiche von Niederbayern und Schwaben: Voraussetzungen und Formen landesherrlicher Expansionspolitik an der Wende vom Mittelalter zur Neuzeit', *ZbLG* 49 (1986), 611–70, at 633–53.

[38] Adalbert von Keller (ed.), *Die Geschichten und Taten Wilwolts von Schaumburg* (Stuttgart, 1859), 156.

[39] Schubert, *Die Landstände des Hochstifts Würzburg*, 103–4, 124; Peter Schmid, *Der Gemeine Pfennig von 1495: Vorgeschichte und Entstehung, verfassungsgeschichtliche, politische und finanzielle Bedeutung* (Göttingen, 1989), 235–6, 242–3, 450, 452–3; Heinz Durchhardt, 'Reichsritterschaft und Reichs-kammergericht', *ZHF* 5 (1978), 315–37, at 317; Proksch, 'Die Auseinandersetzung um den Austrag des Rechts', 185.

[40] Citation from Wilhelm Engel (ed.), *Die Rats-Chronik der Stadt Würzburg (XV. und XVI. Jahrhundert)* (Würzburg, 1950), 55, no. 165.

the Sublime Porte, and demanded that they consented to taxation. The nobles' answer was negative. The princes and the imperial commissaries must be aware, they said, that the Franconian nobles had always served the emperors, kings and princes loyally and shed their own blood for them, and that therefore they had been exempted from taxes. They made it perfectly clear that this was a basic principle and that no amount of negotiation would make them budge. They concluded by asking the princes to intercede with the emperor that he leave them unmolested as free Christian knights.[41]

The nobles' resistance to the Common Penny was only superficially similar to their previous confrontations with the princes over taxation. Their main, usual argument against it had smaller persuasive force than ever before. In their contestations with the princes, in whose feudal armies they enlisted as vassals, there was some ground to their claim to freedom from tax. In the case of the Common Penny, which was to fund, among other things, imperial troops, this justification was unfounded. Too few nobles were imperial vassals for it to have any substance. As Maximilian's envoys to Schweinfurt contended, these were 'mere words . . . just a pretext'.[42] This essential difference between imperial and princely taxation had a number of disturbing implications for the nobles. Whereas until 1495 they faced one prince at a time, they now had to oppose not only the emperor but also the three princes as his proxies at once. Moreover, the latter, thanks to the 1495 reforms, were mightier than formerly: entrusted with collecting the Common Penny, their assertions of territorial supremacy were greatly bolstered. All these changes conspired to raise the fundamental question of what the 'constitutional' and legal status of the Franconian nobility was – in the Holy Roman Empire in general and in the principalities in particular.[43]

It was in this way that the Common Penny, since it affected each and every noble, gave the decisive impetus to the organisation of the Franconian Knighthood. A proclamation dated 9 February 1496 stated that the nobles who had gathered in Schweinfurt (in December 1495) undertook 'to arrange the Knighthood of the Land of Franconia in six parts', each headed by two nobles.[44] It was also planned for simultaneous assemblies of the nobles of each of these six divisions to meet on 24 February, where they were to take an oath not to pay the tax. In addition, military preparations were made in case of an attempt to coerce them into paying it.[45] The import of this new form of association was far-reaching: unlike the unions of the previous hundred years or so, it was no longer local in scope; it covered the entirety of Franconia, transcending the boundaries of the principalities. It thus erected a political edifice whose underlying concept

---

[41] *RTA, mR*, v, 1241–51, no. 1708.   [42] Ibid., 1247, no. 1708.
[43] Schmid, *Der Gemeine Pfennig von 1495*, 235–6, 242–3, 403, 450, 452–3.
[44] Ibid., 403–4; Fellner, *Die fränkische Ritterschaft*, 115–16. The six 'parts', later cantons, were Altmühl, Baunach, Gebirg-Voigtland, Odenwald, Röhn-Werra, Steigerwald.
[45] Fellner, *Die fränkische Ritterschaft*, 117–19, 125–6.

contrasted with that of the three princes. The nobles, as a collective, were on the verge of abandoning the principalities as their frame of reference, of placing themselves beside and outside them. That this would provoke a crisis in their relationship with the princes was merely a matter of time. The time came in 1507, two years after the Common Penny project had been given up.

Early that year, in a meeting in Schweinfurt, the nobles drew up a list of twenty-five economic, jurisdictional, and political grievances they had against the princes.[46] They then reached the conclusion that the only remedy for them was that 'we found and make a suitable, equable, finite, effective, speedy and useful [procedure for the] legal settlement [of disputes] between us and Bamberg, Würzburg and Brandenburg, as well as between ourselves. From this will flow all other good order . . .'[47] Shortly afterward, their delegates were to convey to the three princes the following message: the nobles knew full well that they were being suspected and accused by the emperor, princes, and others of being responsible for robberies and other 'surreptitious and malicious deeds'. Although this was an unfair generalisation, it none the less prompted them to deliberate in their assembly over ways to prevent disorder and misdemeanour. They concluded, however, that 'we lack in Franconia in equable, speedy, finite and useful justice, and that without equable, speedy and useful justice there can be no lasting peace, and without peace no good order'. Hence they were moved to search for ancient treaties which their forefathers and the princes had once made for the sake of peace and justice. They found one, introduced some amendments into it so as to bring it up to date, and would soon hand a copy of it to the princes. Lastly, the princes were to be told that if they were to turn down the proposed treaty, the nobles could not be held accountable for renewed 'military and evil conflicts in Franconia'.[48]

The 'outline of a legal settlement' between the three princes and the nobility, composed by two nobles, was submitted to the princes in late February or early March 1507.[49] It embodied the medieval legal sensibility of 'restitutive justice' or 'communal law', while making a gesture to 'punitive justice' or 'state law'.[50] The main point it suggested was that disputes between nobles and princes would be processed by a board of arbitration made up of nine persons. Each of the three

[46] StAW, Stb, no. 892, fols. 97ᵛ–99ᵛ. See also ibid., Stb, no. 948, fols. 85–6.

[47] '. . . und solch unser gemein beschwerd, auch wie die abzuwenden sin mochten guter getruwer meynung betrachtet und bewegen daz uns allen nichts Notigers und nutzlichers sin kont, dan daz wir mit Bamberg wirtzburg und brandenburg . . . auch wir selbst undereinander eynen zimlichen glichmessigen entlichen schleunigen hilfflichen Rechtlichen außtrag funden und machten auß dem volget alle ander gute ordenung . . .': StAW, Stb, no. 892, fol. 106ʳ.

[48] Ibid., fols. 107ʳ–108ʳ.

[49] Ibid., fols. 109ʳ–113ᵛ; Fellner, *Die fränkische Ritterschaft*, 156–8.

[50] For these concepts see Bruce Lenman and Geoffrey Parker, 'The State, the Community and the Criminal Law in Early Modern Europe', in *Crime and the Law: The Social History of Crime in Western Europe since 1500*, ed. V. A. C. Gatrell, Bruce Lenman, and Geoffrey Parker (London, 1980), 11–48, at 23.

princes was to have two representatives on the board (of whom at least one was to be a nobleman), the counts and barons one, and the knights two. The Nine also had the duty of reforming the princely courts of law. The treaty was to serve as the groundwork for a ten-year union between the nobility and the princes. During this period, feuds and violence between the members were strictly banned. In case one of them was attacked, whether by another member or by an outsider, it was incumbent upon the Nine to marshal the forces of the union to help him.

The princes responded swiftly. On 16 March the bishops of Bamberg and Würzburg met in Gerolzhofen. They decided that each of them should demand from his nobles that they relinquish their programme and abide by the recesses promulgated by the Imperial Diet of Worms. In case this was of no avail, then each of them should warn his councillors, courtiers and district governors of the utmost disfavour they would incur if they joined the planned union of the nobles or travelled to the assembly.[51] On 21 March, the bishop of Bamberg met with the margrave of Brandenburg in the monastery of Langheim. They condemned the venture of the nobility as injurious to the authority of the princes and the emperor, and declared it intolerable.[52] They then concluded an agreement similar to the one made between the two bishops, whereby the bishop of Bamberg signed also on behalf of the bishop of Würzburg.[53] Here, in the events of 1507 and of subsequent years, in the series of failed endeavours by the nobles to sort out their relations with the princely state,[54] was the beginning of the end of the feud.

THE END OF THE FEUD

As the consistently antagonistic reactions of the princes make plain, the two sides had drifted too far apart for them to be able to find a common ground. The convenient unclarities and ambiguities that prevailed in the fifteenth century were being straightened out by the process of state formation. For the nobility it must have become increasingly clear that, as things stood, the choice was between complete subjection to and complete emancipation from the princes. Lesser noblemen may well have been prepared to accept subservience to the princes, if that was what it should take to maintain close ties to them. This would have secured them some basic privileges but not modified their condition radically. For their eminent fellows, on the other hand, either option

---

[51] StAW, Stb, no. 892, fols. 114^r–115^r.   [52] Ibid., fols. 115^v–116^r.

[53] Ibid., fols. 115^v–116^v. See also ibid., fols. 117^r–119^v; ibid., Stb, no. 948, fols. 17–20, 29–36; Constantin Höfler (ed.), 'Fränkische Studien IV.', parts 1–3, *Archiv für Kunde österreichischer Geschichts-Quellen* 7 (1851), 1–146; 8 (1852), 235–322; 11 (1853), 1–56: part 2, 241–3, no. 133.

[54] For this succession of failures see Rupprecht, *Ritterschaftliche Herrschaftswahrung in Franken*, 393–8; Fellner, *Die fränkische Ritterschaft*, 154–216.

meant a setback. Their special relations with the state, which had been the source of their power, threatened to turn them into mere creatures of the princes. Indeed, as the terms of the agreements between Bamberg, Würzburg and Brandenburg demonstrate, it was on them that the princes concentrated their pressure.[55] But the alternative these nobles had, which was to give the princes a wide berth, would have had the equally nasty consequence of undermining their own power. The experience of Baron Johann of Schwarzenberg sums up their dilemma: master of the household of the bishop of Bamberg and author of the Penal Code of the diocese, he was one of the two nobles who drafted the 1507 'outline of a legal settlement' between the three princes and the nobility.[56] He was therefore accused by the bishop of Bamberg of being a nobility-rouser.[57] In a letter to the bishop, Schwarzenberg tried to explain away his activities. He is also reported to have said that if 'he further helped to reform the land, then one should give him a tonsure as to a monk . . . the princes mattered to him more than the league [of the nobility]'.[58]

Like Schwarzenberg, most leaders of the Knighthood movement were prominent nobles. They were of two distinct groups. One consisted of the Franconian magnates, especially the counts of Castell, Henneberg, and Wertheim. They were the driving force in the first three decades of the sixteenth century.[59] The second group was made up mostly of untitled nobles holding high posts in princely administrations.[60] Already in 1495, nine of the twelve captains of the six 'parts' were high office-holders. Some of these acted also as creditors and guarantors of

---

[55] For the agreement between the bishops of Bamberg and Würzburg see n. 51 above. The agreement between the bishop of Bamberg and the margrave of Brandenburg stated that each of them should summon 'die *treffenlichsten* auß den sinen der Ritterschafft' and communicate to them his displeasure at their undertaking: StAW, Stb, no. 892, fol. 115ᵛ (italics added). Another document highly revealing in this regard is in Höfler (ed.), 'Fränkische Studien IV.', part 2, 238, no. 130.

[56] See n. 49 above. For biographical sketches of Baron Johann of Schwarzenberg see Karl Fürst zu Schwarzenberg, *Geschichte des reichsständischen Hauses Schwarzenberg* (Neustadt a.d. Aisch, 1963), 60–8; Friedrich Merzbacher, 'Johann Freiherr zu Schwarzenberg', *Fränkische Lebensbilder* 4 (1971), 173–85.

[57] 'anfaher oder ursacher . . . solichs der Ritterschaft unnotturfftiges furnemens': StAW, Stb, no. 892, fol. 100ᵛ.

[58] Ibid., fols. 100ᵛ–102ᵛ. The other author of the 'outline of a legal settlement', Dr Sebastian von Rotenhan, was to find himself in a similar contradiction in 1523, when he was master of the household of the bishop of Würzburg. See *RTA, jR*, iii, 914–17, nos. 244–45.

[59] StAW, Stb, no. 892, fols. 96ᵛ–97ʳ, 183ʳ–185ʳ; Fellner, *Die fränkische Ritterschaft*, 254.

[60] Marlene LeGates, 'The Knights and the State in Sixteenth-Century Germany' (PhD thesis, Yale University, 1970), 66, 150, 178; Uwe Müller, *Die ständische Vertretung in den fränkischen Markgraftümern in der ersten Hälfte des 16. Jahrhunderts* (Neustadt a.d. Aisch, 1984), 95–108; Berthold Jäger, *Das geistliche Fürstentum Fulda in der Frühen Neuzeit: Landesherrschaft, Landstände und fürstliche Verwaltung. Ein Beitrag zur Verfassungs- und Verwaltungsgeschichte kleiner Territorien des Alten Reiches* (Marburg, 1986), 167; Rupprecht, *Ritterschaftliche Herrschaftswahrung in Franken*, 315. High office-holders were the leaders of the Knighthood also in other parts of south Germany. See Eugen Hillenbrand, 'Die Ortenauer Ritterschaft auf dem Weg zur Reichsritterschaft', *ZGO* 137 (1989), 241–57; Harold H. Kehrer, 'The von Sickingen and the German Princes 1262–1523' (PhD thesis, Boston University Graduate School, 1977), 405–6.

princes.[61] That this would be the sociopolitical profile of the Knighthood's leadership was quite natural. For these nobles had a vested interest in the fifteenth-century status quo, in retaining the dual stance of proximity to and distance from the princes. But as their attempts were rebuffed by the princes one after another, they were forced to become more and more self-reliant. They set about, almost in spite of themselves, streamlining the organisational structure of the Knighthood and reinforcing its cohesion so as to make it an effective vehicle of political self-determination.

These developments manifested themselves already in 1511, when a new union of the nobility was planned.[62] The proposed covenant stipulated that each of the six administrative districts (*Orte*) was to have one captain instead of two, and that these would be under the control of a principal captain (*obersten hauptman*) of the Knighthood. A chain of command was thus forged, whereby the officers were charged with mobilising the union whenever one of its members was persecuted by a prince.[63] They were also responsible – and this was the core of the compact – for keeping order in the six districts. Feuds were absolutely proscribed and the principal captain was authorised to confiscate the property of offenders. Moreover, anyone found guilty of even assisting a feuder was to be thrown out of the union.[64]

The union failed to materialise. There was too much disagreement among the nobility itself, too much distrust of a rigid hierarchy which would compromise personal freedom. Also, some noblemen dithered, fearing to fall foul of their feudal lords, others worried about their careers in princely service.[65] All the

---

[61] For the list of names see Fellner, *Die fränkische Ritterschaft*, 115–16 n. 24. The nine office-holders were Konrad von Berlichingen (Friedrich Graf von Berlichingen-Rossach, 'Ritter Conrad von Berlichingen und seine Ahnen', *WFr* 5, no. 2 [1860], 173–202); Georg von Rosenberg (StAN, AA-Akten, no. 1402, fols. 54^{r-v}); Konrad von Hutten (Hans Körner, 'Die Familie von Hutten: Genealogie und Besitz bis zum Ende des alten Reiches', in *Ulrich von Hutten: Ritter, Humanist, Publizist 1488–1523. Katalog zur Ausstellung des Landes Hessen anläßlich des 500. Geburtstages*, ed. Peter Laub [Kassel, 1988], 57–78, at 64); Anton von Bibra (Wilhelm Freiherr von Bibra, *Beiträge zur Familien-Geschichte der Reichsfreiherrn von Bibra*, vol. II [Munich, 1882], 273; Karl E. Demandt, *Der Personenstaat der Landgrafschaft Hessen im Mittelalter: Ein 'Staatshandbuch' Hessens vom Ende des 12. bis zum Anfang des 16. Jahrhunderts*, vol. I [Marburg, 1981], 53, no. 188); Konrad von Schaumberg (Fellner, *Die fränkische Ritterschaft*, 116 n. 24); Apel von Seckendorff (StAN, Ansbacher Historica, no. 340, fol. 71^v; ibid., AA-Akten, no. 1402, fols. 46^v, 56^v, 73^r, 198^r); Paul von Absberg (StAN, Fstm.Ansb., Fehdeakten, no. 67b, prod. 1); Eberhard von Streitberg (Paul Oesterreicher, *Die Burg Streitberg* [Bamberg, 1819], 29, 40); Kaspar von Waldenfels (Otto Freiherr von Waldenfels, *Die Freiherrn von Waldenfels: Stammfolgen mit urkundlichen Belegen*, vol. II [Munich, 1956], 37).

[62] For the opposition of the three princes to this union see Höfler (ed.), 'Fränkische Studien IV.', part 2, 243–4, no. 134.

[63] This gave the Franconian princes some cause for concern. The bishops of Bamberg and Würzburg announced that 'the union, *the captaincy* and other things . . . are against and to the detriment of their both Princely Graces' authority': StAW, Stb, no. 892, fol. 134^{r-v} (italics added). See also ibid., fols. 124^v–126^r.

[64] Ibid, fols. 127^v–133^r; Fellner, *Die fränkische Ritterschaft*, 164–5.

[65] Fellner, *Die fränkische Ritterschaft*, 167–8; Schubert, *Die Landstände des Hochstifts Würzburg*, 133.

same, the motion marked out the path for the future. Significant sections of the élite, at least, had began to move away from attempts to regulate relations with the princes toward attempts at self-regulation. Collectively imposed self-control, especially with regard to feuds, was well in the tradition of the nobility. Internal pacification was an integral part of the platforms of most fifteenth-century knightly societies and leagues, and the tournament ordinances of the 1480s set down punishments for those judged to have carried out illicit feuds.[66] But between these limited, ad hoc and often quite elastic rules and those enacted by the political unions of the early sixteenth century there was a world of difference.

First, the rules became more detailed, comprehensive and unconditional. Feuds were periodically outlawed not only between members of the union but generally.[67] Moreover, other disagreeable features of noblemen's behaviour were simultaneously brought under scrutiny. 'Boozing', apparently a prevalent vice in Germany's ruling classes, was being inveighed against as 'handicapping the Franconians in war and thought and other honourable things' and as damaging to the 'soul, body, honour and property. . . .'.[68] And that man of parts, Baron Johann of Schwarzenberg, wrote in 1512 a satirical work on drunkenness as well as a poem on the 'murderous depravity of robbing'.[69] Sumptuary restrictions on dress and family celebrations were also put into force.[70] All these concerns then took pride of place in the 'amicable, fraternal and neighbourly union' of 1517, whose charter reads more like a manual of practical social ethics than a political document.[71]

Secondly and more importantly, the Knighthood was becoming institutionalised. This is not to say that it was capable of enforcing its statutes. In 1512, shortly after resolving that anyone culpable of dishonourable conduct such as robbery should be apprehended and penalised, the leaders complained that they had 'no coercive power at all'.[72] Nor did they have the will to take the available

For the internal problems besetting the Knighthood see Marlene Jahss LeGates, 'The Knights and the Problem of Political Organizing in Sixteenth-Century Germany', *Central European History* 7 (1974), 99–136.

[66] Kruse, Paravicini, Ranft (eds.), *Ritterorden und Adelsgesellschaften*, passim; Heide Stamm (ed.), *Das Turnierbuch des Ludwig von Eyb (cgm 961). Edition und Untersuchung mit einem Anhang: Die Turnierchronik des Jörg Rugen (Textabdruck)* (Stuttgart, 1986), 170, 207.

[67] StAW, Stb, no. 892, fols. 127^v–133^r; Fellner, *Die fränkische Ritterschaft*, 164–5, 187–8.

[68] Fellner, *Die fränkische Ritterschaft*, 166 n. 1, 187 n. 59. See also StAW, Stb, no. 892, fol. 100^r; Constantin Höfler, 'Betrachtungen über das deutsche Städtewesen im XV. und XVI. Jahrhunderte', *Archiv für Kunde österreichischer Geschichts-Quellen* 11 (1853), 177–229, at 186 (no. 13).

[69] Baron Johann of Schwarzenberg, *Das Büchlein vom Zutrinken*, ed. Willy Scheel (Halle, 1900); *Ain Lied mit vorgehender anzaygung / wider das mordlaster des raubens*. I have used the copy BL, cat. no. 1347.i.7. In 1513 Schwarzenberg himself was the subject of an abusive poem which attacked his anti-feud activities. See Friedrich Merzbacher, 'Ein Schmählied auf Johann Freiherrn zu Schwarzenberg', *MJfGK* 3 (1951), 288–98.

[70] StAW, Stb, no. 892, fols. 154$^{r–v}$; Fellner, *Die fränkische Ritterschaft*, 187.

[71] Johann Christian Lünig, *Des Teutschen Reichs-Archiv partis sepecialis continuatio III*, part 2 (Leipzig, 1713), 3–9, no. 1.

[72] StAW, Stb, no. 892, fols. 150^r–151^r, 159^r.

measures, such as social boycotting, against those who did not toe the line.[73] Given the widespread vacillation and the pressure of the princes,[74] there was deep anxiety that harshness might only put off rather than draw in the uncommitted and apathetic, and these were very many. As LeGates has shown, there was a running battle not only between the Knighthood and the princes but also between the leaders of the Knighthood and the rank and file. The bulk of the knights were only reluctant participants in the movement and their poor attendance at the assemblies of the cantons gave clear expression to their misgivings.[75]

But precisely this difference in determination and dedication to the cause was perhaps the most crucial factor in bringing about the decline of the feud. For one thing, the leaders, enmeshed in the structure of command, were not left a free hand. As one of them put it, he 'was pushed into [the union] verily as a horse into a stable'.[76] They must have felt particularly bound to their own decisions. For another, it was not only that they ruled decidedly against feuds; drawn almost without exception from the power élite, they were by definition also the nobles most susceptible to becoming involved in them.[77] They did not need to read Ulrich von Hutten to know that this was to a large extent due to their especially close relations with the princes.[78] They seem also to have realised that in turn these feuds exposed them to conflicting claims by the princes and consequently made their position dangerously precarious, and that steps had to be taken to solve this problem.

As early as 1494, a union of margravial noblemen decreed that 'on behalf of no prince or lord should anyone do damage to life and limb and property of another'.[79] This new *esprit de corps* was acted out in various ways. Beginning in the last decade of the fifteenth century, one finds noblemen who, offered contracts as princes' indentured servitors (*Diener von Haus aus*), inserted a clause exempting them from taking action against members of the Franconian Knighthood.[80] In 1508 and 1510 attempts were also made to persuade noble high office-holders to withdraw from princely service.[81] As these examples show, the

---

[73] Cf. Jahss LeGates, 'The Knights and the Problem of Political Organizing', 127.

[74] For a telling example of both see StAW, Stb, no. 892, fols. 174ᵛ–176ʳ.

[75] LeGates, 'The Knights and the State in Sixteenth-Century Germany', 36, 52, 101; Jahss LeGates, 'The Knights and the Problem of Political Organizing', 119.

[76] *RTA, jR*, iii, 916, no. 245.   [77] See chaps. 4 and 5.

[78] Ulrich von Hutten, 'Die Anschauenden', in *Ulrich von Hutten: Deutsche Schriften*, ed. Peter Ukena (Munich, 1970), 136–61, at 149–50.

[79] Höfler, 'Betrachtungen über das deutsche Städtewesen', 186 (no. 14).

[80] StAN, Fstm.Ansb., Fehdeakten, no. 83a; ibid., AA-Akten, no. 1402, fol. 227ʳ; Eberhard Graf von Fugger, *Die Seinsheim und ihre Zeit: Eine Familien- und Kulturgeschichte von 1155 bis 1890* (Munich, 1893), Appendix 212; Joseph Morsel, 'Une société politique en Franconie à la fin du Moyen Age: Les Thüngen, leurs princes, leurs pairs et leurs hommes (1275–1525)' (PhD thesis, University of Paris-IV Sorbonne, 1993), 345.

[81] Fellner, *Die fränkische Ritterschaft*, 163.

corporative organisation of the nobles was increasingly outweighing personal obligations to the princes in order to circumscribe their unpleasant effects. They also show, however, that the organisation was overriding the individual's discretion and interest. This emerges most forcefully from the protocols of the co-heirship (*Ganerbschaft*) of the Rothenberg.

The Rothenberg castle with its extensive territory and lordship was purchased in 1478 by forty-six leading noblemen from Duke Otto of the Upper Palatinate. There are a number of indications that this transaction was part of the communal movement of the Franconian nobility. First, the nobles chose a castle that was located just outside the sphere of influence of the margrave and placed under the protection of a rival, Wittelsbach prince.[82] Secondly, as with the leadership of the Knighthood, many of the forty-six buyers and most of the burgraves of the Rothenberg were high office-holders in princely administrations.[83] This overlap became manifest in 1507, when the burgrave and his deputies took the initiative and convoked a general assembly of the 'Knighthood of the land of Franconia'.[84] And thirdly, the impregnable castle seems to have essentially been intended to serve as a safe haven and military base in the event of feuds against territorial powers.[85] Indeed, no other issue preoccupied the co-heirs in their meetings more than whether or not to let this or that colleague use the castle during his feud.

What is striking about these deliberations is the discrepancy they disclose between the behaviour of these nobles as individuals and their behaviour as an organised group. Although so many of them had a feud against a prince or a city and wished to operate from the castle, it proved each time very difficult to gain permission to do that from the other co-heirs. In 1507, for example, Wolf Gottsmann applied to Burgrave Albrecht Gottsmann for leave to use the castle in his feud against the bishop of Bamberg. The burgrave, having polled the opinion of the members (*gemein umbfragen*), refused his relation's request, arguing that the latter should try harder to reach a peaceful settlement.[86] Also that year, the co-heirs turned down Christoph von Stein's bid to buy a share in the castle and be admitted as a co-heir, for he was already 'engaged in open feuds'.[87] In 1521 the petition of the former burgrave, Albrecht Gottsmann, to be allowed to operate from the castle against Nuremberg was declined. The co-heirs, explaining that this feud had to do with his duties as a Bamberg district

---

[82] Rupprecht, *Ritterschaftliche Herrschaftswahrung in Franken*, 378–80.
[83] For the names of the buyers see Martin Schütz, 'Die Ganerbschaft vom Rothenberg in ihrer politischen, juristischen und wirtschaftlichen Bedeutung' (PhD thesis, University of Erlangen, 1924), 121. For a list of the burgraves see ibid., 100–1.
[84] StAA, Ganerbschaft Rothenberg, no. 2538a, anno 1507.
[85] Schütz, 'Die Ganerbschaft vom Rothenberg', 7, 126–7.
[86] StAA, Ganerbschaft Rothenberg, no. 2538a, anno 1507.
[87] Ibid. For Stein's feud against the bishop of Würzburg see also StAW, Stb, no. 788, part 3, under 'S'.

governor, offered instead to discuss the matter on his behalf with the bishop or the city.[88]

These examples suggest that as a collective the noble co-heirs, like the knights, had a stake in controlling feuds. Unlike the knights, however, they enjoyed a fair ability to attain this goal.[89] A compact company, the practical problems with which the Rothenberg co-heirs had to cope were much less daunting. The difference was thus in degree, not in kind. This implies that if – and to the extent to which – the Knighthood were to become definitively institutionalised, formal and binding, it would make feuds less likely to break out. This process was under way, but by spurts and haphazardly: the unions of the early sixteenth century, too, were terminable and merely instrumental; a full-blown, permanent organisation was neither envisaged nor deemed necessary. It was the dangers and humiliations that the nobles endured in the 1520s which, by shaking them violently out of old habits and established attachments, changed their approach.

In 1520 The Franconian noble Hans Thomas von Absberg killed Count Joachim of Oettingen. With this outrage he and his many accomplices made an implacable, mighty enemy: the Swabian League, of which the count was a member. A punitive expedition of the League was a foregone conclusion. It was postponed time and again, but finally triggered by the events of 1522.[90] That was the year in which Franz von Sickingen tried to take electoral Trier. Few Franconian nobles took part in his enterprise.[91] But after he failed and with the princes of Trier, Hesse, and the Palatinate closing in on him, Sickingen sought to stir the Franconians to come to his rescue. His agents were charged with communicating to them that the princes were aiming at nothing less 'than to violently force all of us of the Knighthood into obedience on their own terms'.[92] Sickingen, for all his enormous prestige with the Franconian nobles, did not obtain any meaningful support. But the whole affair inflamed the already agitated nobles. In late November about a hundred of them convened in Schweinfurt, where they received a dispatch from the Imperial Diet then in session in Nuremberg. It warned them against assisting Sickingen in no uncertain terms. In response the nobles sent a list of seventy-four grievances articulated in an

---

[88] 'dieweil es ampt halben geschehen': StAA, Ganerbschaft Rothenberg, no. 2538a, anno 1521. For Gottsmann's governorship see Wilhelm Schwemmer, *Burg und Amt Veldenstein-Neuhaus* (Nuremberg, 1961), 114.

[89] For other examples see StAA, Ganerbschaft Rothenberg, no. 2538a, anno 1503–6, 1508, 1513–14, 1516–17, 1519–20, 1522, 1525.

[90] Peter Ritzmann, '"Plackerey in teutschen Landen": Untersuchungen zur Fehdetätigkeit des fränkischen Adels im frühen 16. Jahrhundert und ihrer Bekämpfung durch den Schwäbischen Bund und die Reichsstadt Nürnberg, insbesondere am Beispiel des Hans Thomas von Absberg und seiner Auseinandersetzung mit den Grafen von Oettingen (1520–31)' (PhD thesis, University of Munich, 1993), 292–9.

[91] Kehrer, 'The von Sickingen', 275–6.

[92] Quoted by Fellner, *Die fränkische Ritterschaft*, 235. See also Helgard Ulmschneider, *Götz von Berlichingen: Ein adeliges Leben der deutschen Renaissance* (Sigmaringen, 1974), 131.

uncharacteristically strident tone.[93] They censured the Imperial Chamber Court, the General Peace (*Landfrieden*), The Imperial Regiment, the Swabian League, and the commercial monopolies. The greater part of the criticism, however, was levelled at the princes and their jurisdictions. The list shows how polarised the princes and nobles had grown. It is most telling that, first, the grievances were presented to the governmental organs of the empire and not to the princes themselves; and that, secondly, the very first article complained about the violence and threats princes use in order to thwart unions of the nobility.

The nobles in Schweinfurt also issued a call for a general assembly of the Franconian nobility. It opened on 26 January 1523. Some 400 nobles arrived, an unusually large number. On the agenda were the transgressions of the Swabian League; the wrongful offensive of the Rhenish princes against Sickingen; feuding as a necessary means of self-defense given the impaired state of the judicial system in Franconia; and suggestions for improvements in the processing of disputes between nobles and princes.[94] A new union was also set up for three years. It was conceived as mainly a military association: the text of the pact dealt thoroughly with the funding and logistics of warfare. Two programmatic points are of particular interest. First, all members were to suspend their feudal obligations toward a prince who unlawfully attacked one of their number, so that they would not be inhibited from standing by the latter in a feud. This drastic measure was designed to enable the union to muster all its resources and present the princes with a united front. Indeed, shortly afterward some Würzburg district governors tendered their resignation.[95] It is not surprising that a rumour spread that the Franconian nobility plotted to overthrow the bishop of Würzburg and to have Count Wilhelm of Henneberg, the principal captain of the union, installed as a new duke of Franconia.[96]

The second major point qualified the first: members whose feuds were indefensible were not to enjoy the succour of the union. Moreover, anyone suspected of misdeeds had to clear himself before a magistrate or else be ejected from the union.[97] The nobles thus drew a formal, rather than rhetorical, distinction between just and unjust feuds and between the innocent and the guilty – a theme they had already broached in 1512 and 1515 but then left it at that.[98] It came to a head early in 1523 because of the impending expedition of the Swabian League and its preceding ultimatum to Absberg and his accessories to appear before its judges and acquit themselves of all charges under oath.

Few of them complied, and in June the League set out on its Franconian

---

[93] *RTA, jR*, iii, 693–726, nos. 112–13.   [94] Ibid., 727–34, no. 116.
[95] Fellner, *Die fränkische Ritterschaft*, 263, 278.   [96] *RTA, jR*, iii, 931, no. 259.
[97] Ibid., 914 n. 1, no. 244; Fellner, *Die fränkische Ritterschaft*, 240–55.
[98] StAW, Stb, no. 892, fols. 159ʳ, 171ʳ⁻ᵛ; ibid., Stb, no. 948, fol. 396. A weaker, conditional form of this distinction was already included in the treaty of the 1517 union: Lünig, *Des Teutschen Reichs-Archiv partis sepecialis continuatio III*, part 2, 7, no. 1.

campaign. In a terrifying show of force, its 12,000-strong army demolished 23 castles in a matter of a month.[99] The union of the nobility did not lift a finger, nor did the Franconian princes do much for their vassals, despite the pleas of some nobles. The princes, themselves members of the Swabian League, probably saw no reason why they should extend protection to nobles who defied their authority.[100] For the nobles, and not only for those who suffered punishment, all this was a scathing lesson in vulnerability. The union of 1523 collapsed to all intents and purposes.[101] And if this was not enough, then the Peasants' War of 1525 dispelled any uncertainty about how untenable their position had become. The peasants carried out in full their threat to 'tear down castles and robber-nests [*Raubheuser*], the source of diverse violence, disadvantage and damage to the labourers and common men'.[102] Within ten days, approximately 200 fortresses were ravaged or burnt down in the diocese of Bamberg alone.[103] The revolt was put down by the Swabian League and the princes, and the latter were quick to arrogate to themselves the right to control almost all aspects of the assessment of damages and payment of reparations.[104] The result was that the nobles were once again proved dependent on the princes. As one noble wrote with hindsight in 1539, some counts, barons and Knights had recently become 'too much beholden and subordinated to the princes'.[105] The sense of confusion and disorientation that engulfed the nobility is reflected in a 1525 debate among the co-heirs of the Rothenberg on whether or not to permit Ernst von Redwitz to use the castle against the bishop of Eichstätt. 'One has to consider', they reasoned, 'the present dangerous situation of the nobility; if Ernst was granted licence to use the castle, this might rebound on all the nobility, not only in the Rothenberg, but also in their other castles and property, to [their] considerable and insuperable detriment'.[106]

Feuding, then, emerged from the turmoil and tribulations of the 1520s largely discredited in the eyes of many nobles.[107] Indeed, their 'official' interpretation of

---

[99] Ritzmann, '"Plackerey in teutschen Landen"', 300–41; Thomas Steinmetz, '"Conterfei etlicher Kriegshandlungen von 1523 bis in das 1527 Jar": Zu Burgendarstellungen über die "Absberger Fehde" oder den "Fränkischen Krieg"', in *Beiträge zur Erforschung des Odenwaldes und seiner Randlandschaften, IV*, ed. Winfried Wackerfuß (Breuberg-Neustadt, 1986), 365–86.

[100] Fellner, *Die fränkische Ritterschaft*, 280, 282–3; Rupprecht, *Ritterschaftliche Herrschaftswahrung in Franken*, 309–11.

[101] Ritzmann, '"Plackerey in teutschen Landen"', 375.

[102] *Ermanung an Churfursten, Fursten, Hern und Stende teutzscher nation; der brüderlichen versamlung im land zu Francken, begangen ubels zü straffen, und gmeynen frieden hinfürter zü füdern und handthaben* (Würzburg?, 1525). I have used the copy BL, cat. no. 3900.b.28.

[103] Rudolf Endres, 'Der Bauernkrieg in Franken', *Blätter für deutsche Landesgeschichte* 109 (1973), 31–68, at 61.

[104] Ibid., 64–5; StAN, Bauernkriegsakten, Tom. 8, fols. 27ʳ–28ᵛ, 33ʳ–34ʳ, 146ʳ⁻ᵛ, 185ʳ.

[105] Quoted by Gerhard Pfeiffer, 'Studien zur Geschichte der fränkischen Reichsritterschaft', *JffL* 22 (1962), 173–280, at 199.

[106] StAA, Ganerbschaft Rothenberg, no. 2538a, anno 1525.

[107] Cf. Ritzmann, '"Plackerey in teutschen Landen"', 379.

it was now almost exclusively in terms of a regrettable but unavoidable recourse to self-defense against the infractions of the princes.[108] Hence feuding could be totally disowned once alternative security arrangements, as it were, had been made. The crucial step in this direction was taken in 1528. On 2 September, a letter was sent by Balthasar Merklin, provost of Waldkirch and vice-chancellor of Emperor Charles V, to Count Michael of Wertheim. Merklin asked Wertheim to work together with other Franconian counts and barons to summon an assembly of the six districts of the Knighthood, where he was to confer with them about a business of great importance to the emperor. As the magnates predicted, this was to be a request by Charles V that the nobles render him military service.[109] The nobles saw the opportunity and they seized it. Whereas in 1511 they had refused a similar request by Emperor Maximilian,[110] now they approved it. Ironically, four years later they also began to pay tax – initially the *Türkensteuer* – directly to the emperor, albeit taking care to name it *subsidium charitativum* so as to underscore its optional character.[111]

From this date, 1528, one can speak of the Imperial Knighthood. For what the nobles demanded in return was imperial protection and safeguard from the Swabian League and the princes, and a recognition of their free status, subordinate to the emperor alone. This ambition was not fulfilled as soon as they would have liked; there was much objection to it from the Imperial Estates. The nobles, however, were adamant. They understood that this was perhaps their last chance to escape the tightening grip of the princely states. And tightening it was: the bishops of Würzburg and Bamberg pressed the nobles for payment of various taxes, and in 1539 the margrave insisted that the nobles of his territories consent to a levy.[112] As a result, the Provincial Diet that the margrave called for this purpose was the last one to be attended by the local nobles. The remonstrances they formulated later that year, when they gathered in Schweinfurt, explain why. In Franconia, they argue, it is traditional to differentiate between high, middle, and low authority. This notwithstanding, the princes now disregard this distinction and, wherever they have the high, capital jurisdiction, seek to turn it into a prerogative overriding all others. They thus violate the lordship rights of the nobles in the manner of the Meissen, Bavarian and Saxonian princes. Yet the Franconian nobility, like the Swabian, is 'subject only to the empire and not to the princes' (*immediate dem reich und nicht den fursten underworfen*).[113]

This new self-perception of the nobility was vindicated in 1542. A Common Penny tax was imposed anew by the Imperial Diet of Speyer to help finance King

108 *RTA, jR*, iii, 730, no. 116.
109 Aschbach (ed.), *Wertheimisches Urkundenbuch*, 335–8, nos. 215–16.
110 StAW, Stb, no. 948, fols. 149–53.
111 Schubert, *Die Landstände des Hochstifts Würzburg*, 127–8.
112 Ibid., 135–6; Müller, *Die ständische Vertretung*, 111, 197–216.
113 Pfeiffer, 'Studien zur Geschichte der fränkischen Reichsritterschaft', 201–2.

Ferdinand's war against the Ottomans in Hungary. Unlike in 1495, however, the knights were approached directly by the king, not through the princes. Furthermore, Ferdinand assigned nobles – usually those princely office-holders who doubled as leaders of the cantons – to the collection of the tax from their fellows. He also mandated that whoever did not pay his assessment through the Knighthood could not belong to it and would be regarded as a princely subject (*Landsass*). The Knighthood ceased to be a voluntary body, participation was no longer based on peer pressure alone.[114] On 24 August 1542 Ferdinand confirmed the Franconian Knighthood in their position as 'those who are subordinate to a Roman Emperor and King without any intermediary', and promised them protection and safeguard.[115]

For the nobility, the year 1542 was at once the culmination of a long evolution and a sharp break with the past. For it finally proved conclusively impossible to square the primary principles of the territorial state with the aristocratic tenet of personal allegiance to the princes as the sole basis for submission. The unions of the nobility had been striving for nothing more than preserving this old political form by adjusting it to the new one and by embedding it in the framework of the expanding princely state. The 'outline of a legal settlement' suggested by the nobles epitomised this quest. The responses of the princes, on the other hand, demonstrated how incompatible the nobles' outlook was with their own. The bishops, in particular the bishop of Würzburg, always insisted on dealing only with the nobles of their respective territories.[116] No credible compromise was workable, and the two sides had to part ways. The nobles remained of course vassals of the princes, and they also continued to serve them as officials. But on the crucial question of 'sovereignty' they did not acknowledge the princes as their overlords. Instead, they placed themselves and their seigneuries under the empire, later (1547) under the person of the emperor as their 'God-ordained authority and lord'.[117] With this new legal status the knights departed from the territorial entities forged by the princes. They created their own territorial associations, the six cantons, each endowed with a central administration and the power of taxation.

This transformation finally removed the deep causes of feuds. The dissolution of the territorial ties to the princes meant that the nobles and their lordships lost their former value as elements of state-building. They no longer were the objects of conflicting claims by the princes. Having become Imperial Knights, the nobles by definition extricated themselves from the competition between the princes to

---

[114] Volker Press, *Kaiser Karl V., König Ferdinand und die Entstehung der Reichsritterschaft*, 2nd edn (Wiesbaden, 1980), 40–51.

[115] Lünig, *Des Teutschen Reichs-Archiv partis sepecialis continuatio III*, part 2, 310–11, no. 142.

[116] StAW, Stb, no. 892, fols. 114ʳ, 115ʳ, 183ʳ–184ʳ; Fellner, *Die fränkische Ritterschaft*, 160, 169–70, 186, 279, 280 n. 100.

[117] Quoted by Rupprecht, *Ritterschaftliche Herrschaftswahrung in Franken*, 413.

which their feuds were so intimately linked. With this official distancing, frictions among the nobility, too, were bound to lose their political significance and hence were less likely to develop into feuds. The Gordian knot which had tied up proximity to princes with social eminence was loosened, if not cut altogether. Moreover, the establishment of the Imperial Knighthood secured the noble status of all the members, delineating it in legal terms. The dialectic relationship between state formation and social stratification, from which the feud stemmed, broke off.

The difference which these new circumstances made was brought to light by the 1552–4 Franconian war and its aftermath.[118] As usual, both Margrave Albrecht Alcibiades of Brandenburg on the one side and Würzburg, Bamberg and Nuremberg on the other called on the nobles for support.[119] Yet whereas previous wars between princes had touched off chains of knightly feuds, this one did not. Only one nobleman, the breathtakingly audacious Wilhelm von Grumbach, became seriously implicated in it. Unfortunately for him, his margravial patron was routed on the battlefield. Grumbach paid dearly for having thrown in his lot with the margrave. He estimated the damage inflicted on him by the forces of the avenging bishops and the 'Nuremberg rabble' at 56,000 gulden and saw no hope of recouping it.[120] Construing the spoliation of his property as just another instance of the princes' systematic abuse of power, Grumbach became an unappeasable malcontent and started a feud against his mortal enemy, Bishop Melchior Zobel of Würzburg. In 1558, in an attempt to abduct the prince, one of Grumbach's retainers unintentionally killed him.[121]

In October 1563, Grumbach overran the city of Würzburg with 800 cavalry and 500 infantry. Threatening to turn the soldiery loose on the city, he extorted from the cathedral chapter a treaty providing for the restitution of his property. In the tense atmosphere of Germany just after the 1555 Peace of Augsburg, this raid was liable to create a political storm as calamitous to Grumbach as to anyone else. Würzburg was a member of the Union of Landsberg, a league generally intended to sustain the beleaguered Catholic Estates and, specifically, to offer a system of regional defense against incursions of marauding troops.[122] The captain of the Union was Duke Albrecht V of Bavaria. For him, too, 1563 was a time of

---

[118] Alfred Wendehorst, *Das Bistum Würzburg*, 3 parts (Berlin, 1962–78), III, 115–19; Bernhard Sicken, 'Albrecht Alcibiades von Brandenburg-Kulmbach', *Fränkische Lebensbilder* 6 (1975), 130–60.

[119] Johannes Voigt, *Markgraf Albrecht Alcibiades von Brandenburg-Kulmbach*, 2 vols. (Berlin, 1852), I, 285–6; II, 171–2.

[120] Bayerisches Hauptstaatsarchiv München, Kurbayern, Äußeres Archiv, no. 2004. See also M. Koch, *Quellen zur Geschichte des Kaisers Maximilian II.*, 2 vols. (Leipzig, 1857–61), I, 45.

[121] Wendehorst, *Das Bistum Würzburg*, III, 128–30; Koch, *Quellen zur Geschichte des Kaisers Maximilian II.*, I, 57.

[122] Maximilian Lanzinner, 'Der Landsberger Bund und seine Vorläufer', in *Alternativen zur Reichsverfassung in der Frühen Neuzeit?*, ed. Volker Press and Dieter Stievermann (Munich, 1995), 65–79.

peril: the moment of truth in the power struggle against the duchy's Protestant high nobility. In the impounded papers of their ringleader, Duke Albrecht discovered a letter from another nobleman saying that the capture of Würzburg by Grumbach 'is an extraordinary mirror for the bishop and the princes to look at'.[123] The spectre of a 'new Franz von Sickingen' came back to haunt the princes – a revolt of the nobility?[124]

Grumbach was in fact hatching an extravagant scheme to liberate the entire German nobility, that is in the north as well as in the south, from the yoke of the princes. It was a radical aristocratic utopia that reversed the terms of the alliance as struck between the emperor and the Franconian and Swabian Knighthoods: the nobles were not only to be protected by the emperor from the princes, but to help him subdue them once and for all and to establish an hereditary monarchy in Germany.[125] But despite Grumbach's best efforts to incite the Franconian nobility, they did not line up behind him. Guided by the captain of the Franconian Circle (*Kreis*), Georg Ludwig von Seinsheim, who denounced Grumbach's undertaking as 'against God, law and the emperor', they formally turned away from him in 1564. In the view of the majority of them, the Knighthood was to maintain its autonomy by respecting the equilibrium between emperor and princes, not by irresponsibly challenging the latter. And it was this view, reassuringly transmitted to the princes, which carried the day.[126]

Grumbach's last hope was Emperor Maximilian II, who before acceding to the throne in 1564, and for some time after, was conciliatory toward him.[127] But Maximilian, too, soon found good reasons for intransigence: Grumbach's new patron, Duke Johann Friedrich of Saxony-Gotha, was bent on regaining the electoral dignity of which his Ernestine line was divested after the catastrophe at Mühlberg, and with which the Albertine line was invested. A malcontent himself, he appreciated the good use to which Grumbach's searing bitterness could be

---

[123] Stefan Weinfurter, 'Herzog, Adel und Reformation: Bayern im Übergang vom Mittelalter zur Neuzeit', *ZHF* 10 (1983), 1–39. Citation from Walter Goetz and Leonhard Theobald (eds.), *Beiträge zur Geschichte Herzog Albrechts V. und der sog. Adelsverschwörung von 1563* (Leipzig, 1913), 127, no. 42. See also ibid., 346, no. 132.

[124] Walter Goetz (ed.), *Beiträge zur Geschichte Herzog Albrechts V. und des Landsberger Bundes 1556–1598* (Munich, 1898), 272–3, no. 213. See also ibid., 278–9, no. 217; Goetz and Theobald (eds.), *Geschichte Herzog Albrechts V. und der sog. Adelsverschwörung*, 244–5, no. 104; Volker Press, 'Wilhelm von Grumbach und die deutsche Adelskrise der 1560er Jahre', *Blätter für deutsche Landesgeschichte* 113 (1977), 396–431.

[125] Koch, *Quellen zur Geschichte des Kaisers Maximilian II.*, II, 39; Goetz (ed.), *Geschichte Herzog Albrechts V. und des Landsberger Bundes*, 306, no. 243; Press, 'Wilhelm von Grumbach', 415–22.

[126] Georg Ludwig von Seinsheim, *Kurtze Ablainung und Verantwortung / etlicher unbeständiger unerfindlicher schmählicher Zulagen / Die Wilhelm von Grumbach / und seine Zugewandte / Ihme von Seinßheim / inn den im Truck außgangen Büchern / So inn der Einnam der Vestung Grimmenstein / Anno 1567 gefunden / zugemessen worden* ([1568] 1590), fol. 6; Press, 'Wilhelm von Grumbach', 419, 423–6.

[127] Press, 'Wilhelm von Grumbach', 416; Viktor Bibl (ed.), *Die Korrespondenz Maximilians II.*, 2 vols. (Vienna, 1916–21), I, 61–2, no. 50.

put. Indeed, Maximilian accused Duke Johann Friedrich of agitating the nobility against the princes and of actually becoming the head of the prospective rebels.[128] The duke obviously was much less interested than the emperor in the delicate status quo of 1555. Thus, the emperor, the other members of the Union of Landsberg, the Elector August of Saxony and some other important princes – all these wanted to see Grumbach destroyed. Despite the supplications of other princes, his doom was spelled. With the execution of the imperial ban delegated to Elector August, a death-warrant was effectively issued.[129]

Grumbach knew that. But before anything dramatic could come out of his plan to link up with Dutch insurgents,[130] on 13 April 1567 Gotha fell. And although he presumably was well equipped, mentally and otherwise, to take his own life,[131] Grumbach was captured alive. On 18 April he was quartered in the market-square of Gotha. In Würzburg a Te Deum was sung.[132] Grumbach's was the last 'feud' in Franconia.

Grumbach's fate notwithstanding, it was not the power of the princely state that put an end to the feud. Yet Lazarus von Schwendi was wrong to omit it from his theory of the decline of the feud. The state did play a role, but an indirect one. By expanding its purview and putting into practice its pretension to territorial domination over all the inhabitants, it compelled the nobility to redefine their relations with the princes and by extension their attitude to feuding. The main avenue the nobles explored led to a dead end. They hit on the way out elsewhere, in an alliance with the emperor. The conditions of liberty which the nobles once maintained by playing off one prince against another were created anew in the dualism of emperor and princes – itself a recent phenomenon.[133] To accomplish this, however, took a great deal more than – in Schwendi's words – the 'very wise assistance of . . . emperors'. The actions of Emperor Charles V and of King Ferdinand presupposed an operative, viable organisation of the nobility. This was at hand and was the work of the nobles, or rather their leaders. Theirs was a considerable achievement, and not only because

---

[128] Koch, *Quellen zur Geschichte des Kaisers Maximilian II.*, I, 53–4. Cf. also Bibl (ed.), *Die Korrespondenz Maximilians II.*, II, 135 n. 3, no. 122.

[129] Wendehorst, *Das Bistum Würzburg*, III, 139–42; Press, 'Wilhelm von Grumbach', 416–17. For Elector August's fears of an attempt on his life by Grumbach see Goetz (ed.), *Geschichte Herzog Albrechts V. und des Landsberger Bundes*, 362, no. 304.

[130] For the links with the Dutch see Koch, *Quellen zur Geschichte des Kaisers Maximilian II.*, II, 36–48; *Venetianische Depeschen vom Kaiserhof (Dispacci di Germania)*, vol. III, ed. Gustav Turba (Vienna, 1895), 333 n. 2, no. 162; Bibl (ed.), *Die Korrespondenz Maximilians II.*, II, 133–4, 204–5, nos. 122, 193.

[131] The Venetian ambassador to Vienna reported that Grumbach 'non solo portava il veneno adosso, per servisene, quando si vedesse in manifesto pericolo de perdersi, ma si faceva de continuo accompagnar et venir dietro un paggio con un archibuso carrico [!] per farsi amazzar da quello, à causa di non venir vivo nelle mani de nemici': *Venetianische Depeschen*, 386, no. 176.

[132] Wendehorst, *Das Bistum Würzburg*, III, 143.

[133] Peter Moraw, 'Fürstentum, Königtum und "Reichsreform" im deutschen Spätmittelalter', *Blätter für deutsche Landesgeschichte* 122 (1986), 117–36.

no other social group was able to evade the grasp of the state. More important is the fact that to fulfil this objective the nobles had to go out of their way to collaborate in a project of conscious self-disciplining. It was not a moral crusade that impelled this campaign, but political expedience and will. It aimed at and succeeded in, among other things, suppressing the feud – hitherto a central component of aristocratic identity. The leaders, drawing upon their personal experience, realised that this was a price worth paying: individual freedom could be saved only by institutionalised political solidarity which necessarily constrained it. In the end they overcame both the obstructionism of the princes and the indecision of their fellow knights.

The 1590 Knights' Ordinance, which greatly fortified the corporation and its institutions, virtually sealed the victory of the leaders and their vision.[134] A few months after it was ratified by the emperor, someone appended a crude yet expressive ditty to the protocol of a meeting of the officers of the Knighthood:

> Freedom is the highest good
> Unity brings enlargement
> And raises to greatness
> That which is held cheap and disdained
> Great power and grandeur
> By discord is ruined
> Therefore you should love unity
> So that you remain free in perpetuity.[135]

---

[134] Lünig, *Des Teutschen Reichs-Archiv partis sepecialis continuatio III*, part 2, 15–30, 177–8, nos. 6, 89. See also Rupprecht, *Ritterschaftliche Herrschaftswahrung in Franken*, 427–30.

[135] Höfler (ed.), 'Fränkische Studien IV.', part 2, 273, no. 167.

A note on Appendixes

(a) Asterisk means that the nobleman or family in question falls under the respective category.

(b) In the Sources of Information, the references to Appendixes A, C, D, E, and F are ordered according to the numbers marking the respective columns in the Appendixes.

(c) References to columns (6), (7) and (8) are not given. The sources for them are referred to in chapter 4.

Appendix A

Creditors and guarantors of the margraves of Brandenburg

Name	(1) Creditor	(2) Guarantor	(3) Office
Hans Christoph v. Absberg	*	*	*
Hans Georg v. Absberg		*	*
Karl v. Absberg	*		*
Hans Sigmund v. Absberg	*	*	*
Hieronimus Adelmann v. Adelmannsfelden		*	
Melchior Adelmann v. Adelmannsfelden	*		*
Konrad v. Berlichingen		*	
Marx v. Berlichingen		*	*
Philipp v. Biberern	*	*	*
Christoph v. Bibra	*		*
Wilhelm v. Bibra		*	*
Melchior v. Birkenfels	*	*	
Stefan v. Birkenfels	*	*	
Peter v. Castell	*		
Kaspar v. Castell	*		*
Count Johann of Castell	*	*	*
Kaspar v. Crailsheim		*	
Wolf v. Crailsheim	*	*	*
Hans Georg v. Cronheim		*	
Wilhelm v. Ehenheim	*		
Wolfhard v. Ehenheim		*	*
Engelhard v. Ehenheim		*	*
Konrad v. Ehenheim		*	

	1	2	3
Konrad v. Ellrichshausen		*	
Ludwig v. Ellrichshausen	*		
Martin v. Eyb		*	
Sebastian v. Eyb		*	*
Hans Christoph v. Eyb		*	
Ludwig v. Eyb		*	*
Georg Ludwig v. Eyb		*	
Eberhard Förtsch		*	*
Christoph Fuchs (v. Bimbach)		*	*
Hans Fuchs (v. Dornheim)		*	*
Dietrich Fuchs v. Bimbach	*	*	*
Albrecht Gailing		*	*
Eberhard Geyer	*	*	*
Florian Geyer	*		
Mathes v. Giech		*	*
Georg v. Gnottstadt	*	*	*
Sigmund v. Haberkorn		*	
Florian v. Haberkorn	*		
Friedrich v. Haldermannstetten gen. Stettner	*		*
Hans v. Haldermannstetten gen. Stettner	*		*
Heinz v. Haldermannstetten gen. Stettner		*	
Wolf v. Hausen	*		
Endres v. Hausen	*	*	*
Baron Georg of Heideck	*		*
Alweg v. Heimenhofen	*		*
Philipp v. Helb	*		
Wilhelm v. Heßberg		*	
Karl v. Heßberg		*	*
Philipp v. Heßberg		*	*
Greif v. Heßberg		*	
Wolf v. Heßberg	*	*	*
Sigmund v. Heßberg		*	*
Bernhard v. Heßberg		*	*

Name	(1) Creditor	(2) Guarantor	(3) Office
Count Albrecht of Hohenlohe		*	
Ernst v. Horckheim	*		
Ulrich v. Hutten	*		*
Erasmus v. Hutten	*		*
Bernhard v. Hutten		*	*
Ludwig v. Hutten	*	*	*
Martin v. Jahrsdorf	*		
Jakob v.d. Kere	*	*	*
Hans v. Knöringen	*	*	*
Ulrich v. Knöringen	*	*	*
Wolf v. Künsberg		*	
Hans v. Leineck		*	*
Veit v. Lentersheim	*	*	*
Kraft v. Lentersheim		*	
Alexander v. Lentersheim		*	*
Christoph v. Lentersheim	*	*	*
Friedrich v. Lentersheim	*		*
Sigmund v. Lentersheim		*	*
Wilhelm v. Leonrod		*	
Hans v. Leonrod		*	*
Albrecht v. Leonrod		*	*
Konrad v. Leonrod		*	*
Hieronimus v. Lichtenstein	*		*
Wolf Linck	*		*
Hans Dietrich Lochinger	*		
Götz Lochinger	*	*	*
Count Ludwig (I) of Löwenstein	*		
Count Ludwig (II) of Löwenstein	*		
Count Friedrich (I) of Löwenstein	*		
Bernhard v. Lüchau	*	*	*
Christoph v. Lüchau		*	*
Hans Günter v. Lüchau		*	

Moritz Marschall v. Ostheim	*		*
Reinhard Marschall v. Ostheim	*		*
Hartung Marschall v. Ostheim	*		*
Christoph Marschall v. Pappenheim	*	*	*
Stefan v. Menzingen	*		*
Hermann Hans v. Ochsenbach	*		*
Wolf v. Rechberg	*	*	*
Balthasar v. Rechenberg	*	*	*
Ernst v. Rechenberg		*	*
Peter v. Redwitz		*	*
Christoph v. Rosenau		*	
Anton v. Rosenau	*		
Lienhard v. Rosenberg		*	*
Georg v. Rosenberg		*	*
Konrad v. Rosenberg		*	*
Martin v. Schaumberg		*	*
Wilhelm v. Scheinberg		*	
Hans v. Scheinberg		*	
Pankraz Schenk v. Arberg	*		*
Christoph (I) Schenk v. Geyern		*	*
Christoph (II) Schenk v. Geyern		*	
Baron Gottfried Schenk v. Limpurg		*	
Baron Friedrich Schenk v. Limpurg		*	*
Hans Schenk v. Schenkenstein	*		*
Kaspar Schenk v. Schenkenstein	*	*	*
Heinrich v. Schirnding		*	*
Count Stefan Schlick	*		
Konrad Schott	*		*
Konrad Schrimpf	*		
Hans v.d. Schulenburg	*		*
Mathes v.d. Schulenburg	*		
Baron Friedrich of Schwarzenberg		*	*
Baron Wolfgang of Schwarzenberg	*	*	*

Name	(1) Creditor	(2) Guarantor	(3) Office
Baron Johann of Schwarzenberg		*	*
Apel v. Seckendorff	*	*	*
Moritz v. Seckendorff–Aberdar		*	*
Philipp v. Seckendorff	*	*	*
Arnold v. Seckendorff		*	*
Hans v. Seckendorff		*	*
Kilian v. Seckendorff	*	*	
Melchior v. Seckendorff		*	*
Christoph v. Seckendorff		*	*
Jordan v. Seckendorff	*	*	
Burkhard v. Seckendorff		*	*
Erkinger v. Seckendorff		*	*
Sixt v. Seckendorff		*	*
Friedrich Joachim v. Seckendorff		*	*
Hans v. Seckendorff–Aberdar	*	*	*
Hans v. Seckendorff–Bechhofen	*		*
Hans v. Seckendorff–Obernzenn		*	*
Georg v. Seckendorff		*	
Hans Georg v. Seckendorff	*		
Hans Melchior v. Seckendorff	*		
Hans Sebastian v. Seckendorff	*		
Hans Wilhelm v. Seckendorff	*		
Anstand v. Seckendorff		*	
Götz v. Seinsheim	*		*
Albrecht v. Seldeneck	*		
Wolf v. Steinau gen. Steinrück	*		*
Dr Georg v. Streitberg		*	*
Lienhard v.d. Tann	*		*
Hans Thanhäuser	*		
Bernhard v. Thüngen		*	*
Kaspar v. Thüngen	*		
Georg v. Thüngen		*	*

Adam v. Thüngen	*		*
Daniel v. Thüngen	*		
Wilhelm Truchseß v. Henneberg	*		
Jakob Truchseß v. Henneberg	*		
Wolf Truchseß v. Pommersfelden		*	*
Philipp Truchseß v. Pommersfelden	*	*	*
Paul Truchseß (zu Unsleben)		*	
Hans Truchseß v. Wetzhausen		*	*
Sigmund v. Ussigheim	*		
Georg v. Vellberg	*		*
Wilhelm v. Vellberg	*	*	*
Wolf v. Vellberg	*		*
Ehrenfried v. Vellberg	*		*
Anton v. Vestenberg		*	
Albrecht v. Vestenberg	*	*	*
Florian v. Vestenberg		*	
Kaspar v. Vestenberg		*	
Weiprecht v. Vinsterlohe		*	
Hans v. Waldenfels	*	*	*
Sebastian v. Waldenfels	*		*
Wilhelm v. Wiesenthau	*	*	*
Wolf Christoph v. Wiesenthau	*	*	*
Wolf v. Wilhermsdorf		*	
Albrecht v. Wilhermsdorf		*	
Baron Balthasar of Wolfstein	*		*
Maximilian Wolf v. Wolfsthal		*	
Hans Wolf v. Wolmarshausen		*	
Burkhard v. Wolmarshausen	*		*
Christoph v. Wolmarshausen		*	*
Ernst v. Wolmarshausen		*	*
Sigmund v. Zedwitz	*	*	*
Peter v. Zedwitz		*	
Eukarius Zobel	*	*	

153

Appendix A

Name	(1) Creditor	(2) Guarantor	(3) Office
Fritz Zobel	*		
Stefan Zobel		*	*

Appendix B

Sample of intermarriages among the noble élite

Dr Georg von Absberg: cf. StAN, Ansbacher Historica, no. 340, fol. 29ʳ and Gerhard Rechter, *Die Seckendorff: Quellen und Studien zur Genealogie und Besitzgeschichte*, 2 vols. (Neustadt a.d. Aisch, 1987–90), I, 151, 157.

Hans Christoph von Absberg: cf. Appendix A and Gerd Wunder, 'Die Ritter von Vellberg', in *Vellberg in Geschichte und Gegenwart*, ed. Hansmartin Decker-Hauff, vol. I, *Darstellungen* (Sigmaringen, 1984), 129–96, at 135, 167.

Paul von Absberg: cf. StAN, Ansbacher Historica, no. 340, fol. 32ᵛ and H. Wilhelm, 'Die Edeln von und zum Absberg: Ein Beitrag zur fränkischen Geschichte', *Alt-Gunzenhausen* 8 (1931), 3–197, at 117.

Wolf von Crailsheim: cf. Appendix A, Johann Gottfried Biedermann, *Geschlechtsregister der Reichsfrey unmittelbaren Ritterschaft Landes zu Franken löblichen Orts Steigerwald* (Nuremberg, 1748), table 44, Hellmut Kunstmann, *Die Burgen der östlichen fränkischen Schweiz* (Würzburg, 1965), 383 and Eberhard Freiherr von Eyb, *Das reichsritterliche Geschlecht der Freiherren von Eyb* (Neustadt a.d. Aisch, 1984), 167.

Hans von Eyb: Eyb, *Freiherren von Eyb*, 114.

Kaspar d.J. von Feilitzsch: Hans Hofner, 'Zur Geschichte des vogtländischen Adels: Die Herren von Feilitzsch auf Feilitzsch', *AO* 54 (1974), 257–317, at 284.

Dietrich Fuchs von Bimbach: cf. Appendix A and Otto Freiherr von Waldenfels, *Die Freiherrn von Waldenfels: Stammfolgen mit urkundlichen Belegen*, 5 vols. (Munich, 1952–70), II, 23.

Georg Fuchs von Schweinshaupten: cf. StAW, Adelsarchiv Fuchs von Bimbach, no. 2, fols. 23–5 and Rudolf Karl Reinhard Freiherr von Thüngen, 'Zur Genealogie der Familie derer von Thüngen', *AU* 54 (1912), 1–180, at 96.

Hans Fuchs von Bimbach: cf. StAW, Würzburger Lehenbücher, no. 27, fol. 249ᵛ and Harold H. Kehrer, 'Die Familie von Sickingen und die deutschen Fürsten 1262–1523', *ZGO* 127 (1979), 73–158, at 96, 101–2.

Christoph von Guttenberg: Johannes Bischoff, *Genealogie der Ministerialen von Blassenberg und Freiherren von (und zu) Guttenberg 1148–1970* (Würzburg, 1971), 191.

Endres von Hausen: cf. Appendix A and Karl Hannakam and Ludwig Veit (eds.), *Archiv der Freiherrn Schenk von Geyern auf Schloß Syburg* (Munich, 1958), 16 and 46, U 59b.

Sigmund von Heßberg: cf. StAN, AA-Akten, no. 728, prod. of Montag nach Quasimodogeniti [28 April] 1511 and Georg Sigmund Graf Adelmann von Adelmannsfelden, *Das Geschlecht der Adelmann von Adelmannsfelden* (Ellwangen, 1948), 11–12.

Wolf von Heßberg: cf. Appendix A, Sigmund Freiherr von Crailsheim, *Die Reichsfreiherrn von Crailsheim*, 2 vols. (Munich, 1905), II, 144–6 and Gerhard Rechter (ed.), *Die Archive der Grafen und Freiherren von Seckendorff: Die Unrkundenbestände der*

Appendix B

Schloßarchive Obernzenn, Sugenheim, Trautskirchen und Unternzenn, vol. I (Munich, 1993), 226, no. 610.

Jakob von der Kere: cf. Appendix A and Frank Baron Freytag von Loringhoven, *Europäische Stammtafeln: Stammtafeln zur Geschichte der europäischen Staaten*, n.s., ed. Detlev Schwennicke (Marburg, 1980-   ), XVI, table 13.

Christoph von Lentersheim: cf. Appendix A, Otto Rohn, 'Die Herren von Lentersheim. Zweiter Teil: Vom Erwerb des Schlosses Altenmuhr im Jahre 1430 bis zum Erlöschen des Stammes im Jahre 1799', *Alt-Gunzenhasen* 38 (1979), 108–45, at 112 and Gustav Voit, *Die Wildensteiner* (Nuremberg, 1964), 22–3.

Veit von Lentersheim: cf. Appendix A, Rohn, 'Die Herren von Lentersheim. Zweiter Teil', 115 and StAN, Ansbacher Historica, no. 340, fol. 29^r.

Gottfried Lochinger von Archshofen: cf. Appendix A and Rechter, *Die Seckendorff*, II, 77, 106.

Balthasar von Rechenberg: cf. Appendix A, Hugo A. Braun, *Das Domkapitel zu Eichstätt: Von der Reformationszeit bis zur Säkularisation (1535–1806). Verfassung und Presonalgeschichte* (Stuttgart, 1991), 406 and Rechter, *Die Seckendorff*, II, 85–6.

Baron Johann of Schwarzenberg: cf. Friedrich Merzbacher, 'Johann Freiherr zu Schwarzenberg', *Fränkische Lebensbilder* 4 (1971), 173–85 and Theodor Ruf, *Die Grafen von Rieneck: Genealogie und Territorienbildung*, vol. I (Würzburg, 1984), 108.

Baron Wolfgang of Schwarzenberg: cf. Appendix A and Bischoff, *Freiherren von (und zu) Guttenberg*, 150–2.

Hans von Seckendorff-Aberdar: cf. Appendix A and Eyb, *Freiherren von Eyb*, 114, 160.

Hans von Seckendorff-Aberdar: cf. Gerhard Rechter, *Das Land zwischen Aisch und Rezat: Die Kommende Virnsberg Deutschen Ordens und die Rittergüter im oberen Zenngrund* (Neustadt a.d. Aisch, 1981), 174* and Eyb, *Freiherren von Eyb*, 114, 160.

Erkinger von Seinsheim: cf. StAN, Ansbacher Historica, no. 340, fol. 29^r and Eberhard Graf von Fugger, *Die Seinsheim und ihre Zeit: Eine Familien- und Kulturgeschichte von 1155 bis 1890* (Munich, 1893), 160–1 and Eyb, *Freiherren von Eyb*, 78, 120.

Bernhard von Thüngen: cf. Heinzjürgen N. Reuschling, *Die Regierung des Hochstifts Würzburg 1495–1642: Zentralbehörden und führende Gruppen eines geistlichen Staates* (Würzburg, 1984), 184–5, Thüngen, 'Zur Genealogie der Familie derer von Thüngen', 27 and C. Binder, 'Das ehemalige Amt Lichtenberg vor der Rhön', *Zeitschrift des Vereins für thüringische Geschichte und Altertumskunde*, n.s., 10 (1897), 61–245, at 234.

Dietz Truchseß von Wetzhausen: cf. Sebastian Zeißner, 'Zwei Mitarbeiter des Fürstbischofs Rudolf von Scherenberg', *MJfGK* 3 (1951), 127–38, at 132 and Richard von Steinau-Steinrück, 'Abriß aus der Geschichte des fränkischen Geschlechtes von Steinau genannt Steinrück in bezug auf seine Zugehörigkeit zu dem Hochstifte Würzburg und im besonderen auf seine Besitzungen daselbst', *AU* 49 (1907), 1–134, at 43, 65.

Wilhelm von Vellberg: cf. Appendix A, Wunder, 'Die Ritter von Vellberg', 174 and Crailsheim, *Die Reichsfreiherrn von Crailsheim*, II, 39.

Hans von Waldenfels: cf. Appendix A, Waldenfels, *Freiherrn von Waldenfels*, II, 89 and Rudolf Graf Stillfried and Sigmund Haenle, *Das Buch vom Schwanenorden: Ein Beitrag zu den hohenzollerischen Forschungen* (Berlin, 1881), 168.

Hans Zobel von Giebelstadt: Reuschling, *Die Regierung des Hochstifts Würzburg*, 227–8 and Wilhelm Freiherr von Bibra, *Beiträge zur Familien-Geschichte der Reichsfreiherrn von Bibra*, vol. II (Munich, 1882), 433–5.

Appendix C

Individual parameters of feuders (Sample-I)

Name	(1) Marriage	(2) Office	(3) Creditor/ Guarantor
Hans v. Abenberg			
Engelhard v. Absberg		*	
Hans Georg v. Absberg		*	
Hans Thomas v. Absberg	*		
Hans Christoph v. Absberg	*	*	*
Paul v. Absberg	*	*	
Eukarius v. Aufseß		*	*
Konrad (X) v. Aufseß		*	
Wilhelm v. Bebenburg		*	
Engelhard v. Berlichingen	*	*	
Götz v. Berlichingen		*	*
Klaus v. Bernheim			
Lorenz v. Bibra		*	
Heinrich v. Bibra	*	*	*
Bartholomäus v. Bibra		*	*
Konrad v. Bibra		*	
Georg v. Bibra			
Adam v. Bibra		*	
Anton v. Bibra		*	*
Eustachius v. Birkenfels			
Albrecht v. Brandenstein		*	
Eberhard v. Brandenstein	*		*
Ernst v. Brandenstein			

Name	(1) Marriage	(2) Office	(3) Creditor/ Guarantor
Engelhard v. Buchenau		*	
Kaspar d.J. v. Buchenau		*	
Marx v. Crailsheim		*	
Sebastian v. Crailsheim		*	
Wilhelm v. Crailsheim		*	*
Kaspar v. Crailsheim	*		*
Georg v. Crailsheim			
Kunemund v. Dobeneck			
Erasmus v. Eberstein		*	
Gerlach v. Eberstein		*	*
Philipp v. Eberstein			*
Georg v. Ellrichshausen		*	
Hans Christoph v. Eyb			*
Albrecht v. Eyb		*	
Friedrich v. Feilitzsch			
Hans v. Feilitzsch		*	
Christoph Fuchs v. Bimbach		*	*
Heinz Fuchs v. Bimbach		*	*
Hans d.J. Fuchs v. Preppach			
Georg v. Gebsattel		*	
Christoph v. Giech			
Wolf Gottsmann		*	
Wilhelm v. Grumbach		*	
Hans d.Ä. v.d. Grün			
Hans d.J. v.d. Grün			
Philipp v. Guttenberg	*	*	*
Moritz v. Guttenberg	*	*	
Heinz v. Guttenberg	*	*	
Achaz v. Guttenberg			
Hektor v. Guttenberg		*	

Individual parameters of feuders (Sample-I)

Baron Konrad of Heideck		*	*
Count Wilhelm (II) of Henneberg			
Count Wilhelm (III) of Henneberg	*		*
Count Wilhelm (IV) of Henneberg	*	*	*
Count Otto (IV) of Henneberg		*	*
Count Hermann (VIII) of Henneberg	*	*	
Count Heinrich (XII) of Henneberg		*	
Count Friedrich (II) of Henneberg		*	*
Wolf v. Herbilstadt		*	
Darius v. Heßberg	*	*	
Count Albrecht (II) of Hohenlohe			
Count Kraft (V) of Hohenlohe		*	
Count Kraft (VI) of Hohenlohe		*	
Ulrich v. Hutten		*	*
Lorenz v. Hutten	*	*	*
Konrad v. Hutten	*	*	
Konrad v. Hutten	*	*	*
Frowin v. Hutten		*	
Lorenz v. Hutten			
Hans v. Hutten		*	
Ludwig v. Hutten		*	*
Ludwig v. Hutten			
Frowin v. Hutten			
Friedrich v. Hutten			
Apel v. Lichtenstein		*	
Jobst v. Lüchau		*	
Konrad v. Lüchau		*	*
Heinz v. Lüchau	*		
Sigmund v. Machwitz		*	
Werner Marschall v. Ostheim	*		
Karl Marschall v. Ostheim			
Alexander Marschall v. Pappenheim		*	
Wolf Marschall v. Pappenheim		*	

159

Name	(1) Marriage	(2) Office	(3) Creditor/ Guarantor
Heinrich Marschall v. Pappenheim		*	
Konrad Marschall v. Pappenheim		*	
Heimeran v. Muggenthal			*
Count Joachim of Oettingen	*		
Count Wolfgang of Oettingen		*	
Count Johann of Oettingen	*		*
Götz v. Plassenberg		*	
Götz v. Rain			
Georg v. Rain		*	
Ernst v. Rechenberg		*	*
Ernst v. Redwitz			
Hans v. Reitzenstein		*	
Balthasar v. Reitzenstein			
Christoph v. Reitzenstein			
Hans Sixt v. Reitzenstein			
Georg Ernst v. Reitzenstein			
Thomas v. Reitzenstein		*	
Thomas v. Reitzenstein	*	*	
Hermann (II) Riedesel		*	*
Hermann (III) Riedesel	*	*	
Georg Riedesel		*	
Georg v. Rosenberg			
Friedrich v. Rosenberg			
Friedrich v. Rosenberg			
Arnold v. Rosenberg			
Eberhard v. Rotenhan			
Hans v. Rotenhan		*	*
Lutz v. Rotenhan	*	*	*
Erasmus v. Rotenhan			
Heinrich Rüdt v. Collenberg			

Individual parameters of feuders (Sample-I)

Silvester v. Schaumberg	*	*	*
Adam v. Schaumberg		*	
Karl v. Schaumberg		*	
Konrad v. Schaumberg		*	
Karl Schenk v. Arberg			
Baron Gottfried Schenk v. Limpurg			*
Simon (VI) v. Schlitz gen. v. Görtz		*	*
Ludwig (I) v. Schlitz gen. v. Görtz			
Heinrich (II) v. Schlitz gen. v. Görtz		*	
Otto v. Schlitz gen. v. Görtz			
Konrad Schott	*	*	*
Heinz Schott		*	
Lutz Schott		*	
Baron Sigmund of Schwarzenberg		*	
Baron Johann of Schwarzenberg	*	*	
Baron Hermann of Schwarzenberg		*	*
Baron Friedrich of Schwarzenberg		*	*
Kilian v. Seckendorff			*
Hans v. Seckendorff	*	*	*
Lamprecht v. Seckendorff		*	
Hans Arnold v. Seckendorff	*		*
Balthasar v. Seckendorff		*	
Hans v. Seckendorff		*	
Hans v. Seckendorff		*	
Hans v. Seinsheim			
Erkinger v. Seinsheim	*	*	
Philipp v. Seinsheim		*	
Ludwig v. Seinsheim		*	
Neidhard v. Seinsheim			
Baron Michael v. Seinsheim-Schwarzenberg	*	*	*
Hans v. Selbitz			
Sebastian v. Sparneck			*
Fritz v. Sparneck		*	

Name	(1) Marriage	(2) Office	(3) Creditor/ Guarantor
Wolf v. Sparneck			
Hertnidt v. Stein		*	
Siegfried v. Stein	*	*	*
Hans v. Steinau		*	*
Jakob v. Steinau		*	*
Heinrich v. Steinrück	*	*	*
Heinrich v. Steinrück		*	*
Hildebrand v. Steinrück		*	
Otto v. Steinrück			*
Konrad v. Steinrück	*		*
Wilhelm d.J. v. Stetten			
Kaspar v. Stetten	*		
Hans v. Stetten			
Kilian v. Stetten			
Sebastian Stiebar		*	
Albrecht d.J. Stiebar	*	*	
Ebold Stiebar			
Rochus v. Streitberg		*	
Balthasar v. Streitberg			
Gabriel v. Streitberg		*	
Paul v. Streitberg		*	*
Eberhard v. Streitberg		*	
Melchior Süzel	*		
Reuß v. Thüngen		*	
Sigmund v. Thüngen		*	
Philipp v. Thüngen		*	
Eustachius v. Thüngen		*	
Werner v. Thüngen	*	*	
Heinz v. Thüngfeld			
Wilhelm v. Vellberg		*	*

Individual parameters of feuders (Sample-I)

Wolf v. Vellberg	*	*	*
Stefan v. Vestenberg		*	
Veit v. Vestenberg	*	*	
Matern v. Vestenberg		*	
Kaspar v. Vestenberg		*	
Eukarius v. Vestenberg		*	
Konrad v. Vestenberg			
Veit v. Wallenrod		*	*
Reinwold v. Wemding		*	
Count Wilhelm of Wertheim		*	
Count Albrecht of Wertheim		*	
Count Erasmus of Wertheim	*	*	
Count Johann of Wertheim		*	*
Moritz v. Wildenstein		*	
Albrecht v. Wirsberg		*	
Konrad v. Wirsberg		*	
Soldan v. Wirsberg		*	
Albrecht (IV) v. Wolfstein		*	
Hans (II) v. Wolfstein		*	
Martin Zollner v. Rothenstein	*	*	

Appendix D

Family parameters of feuders (Sample-I)

Name	(4) Father	(5) Cathedral Chapter	(6) Tourmanent Nobility	(7) Continuity
Hans v. Abenberg		*	*	*
Engelhard v. Absberg	*	*	*	*
Hans Georg v. Absberg	*	*	*	*
Hans Thomas v. Absberg	*	*	*	*
Hans Christoph v. Absberg	*	*	*	*
Paul v. Absberg	*	*	*	*
Eukarius v. Aufseß	*	*	*	*
Konrad (X) v. Aufseß	*	*	*	*
Wilhelm v. Bebenburg			*	
Engelhard v. Berlichingen	*	*	*	*
Götz v. Berlichingen	*	*	*	*
Klaus v. Bernheim				*
Lorenz v. Bibra	*	*	*	*
Heinrich v. Bibra	*	*	*	*
Bartholomäus v. Bibra		*	*	*
Konrad v. Bibra	*	*	*	*
Georg v. Bibra		*	*	*
Adam v. Bibra		*	*	*
Anton v. Bibra	*	*	*	*
Eustachius v. Birkenfels				
Albrecht v. Brandenstein			*	*
Eberhard v. Brandenstein	*		*	*
Ernst v. Brandenstein			*	*

Family parameters of feuders (Sample-I)

Engelhard v. Buchenau		*		*
Kaspar d.J. v. Buchenau		*		*
Marx v. Crailsheim			*	*
Sebastian v. Crailsheim	*		*	*
Wilhelm v. Crailsheim	*		*	*
Kaspar v. Crailsheim	*		*	*
Georg v. Crailsheim			*	*
Kunemund v. Dobeneck				*
Erasmus v. Eberstein	*	*	*	*
Gerlach v. Eberstein	*	*	*	*
Philipp v. Eberstein		*	*	*
Georg v. Ellrichshausen		*	*	*
Hans Christoph v. Eyb		*	*	*
Albrecht v. Eyb	*	*	*	*
Friedrich v. Feilitzsch			*	*
Hans v. Feilitzsch			*	*
Christoph Fuchs v. Bimbach	*	*	*	*
Heinz Fuchs v. Bimbach	*	*	*	*
Hans d.J. Fuchs v. Preppach		*	*	*
Georg v. Gebsattel			*	*
Christoph v. Giech	*	*	*	*
Wolf Gottsmann		*	*	*
Wilhelm v. Grumbach	*	*	*	*
Hans d.Ä. v.d. Grün				*
Hans d.J. v.d. Grün				*
Philipp v. Guttenberg	*	*	*	*
Moritz v. Guttenberg	*	*	*	*
Heinz v. Guttenberg	*	*	*	*
Achaz v. Guttenberg	*	*	*	*
Hektor v. Guttenberg	*	*	*	*
Baron Konrad of Heideck	*	*	*	*
Count Wilhelm (II) of Henneberg	*	*	*	
Count Wilhelm (III) of Henneberg		*	*	

Appendix D

Name	(4) Father	(5) Cathedral Chapter	(6) Tournament Nobility	(7) Continuity
Count Wilhelm (IV) of Henneberg	*	*	*	
Count Otto (IV) of Henneberg	*	*	*	
Count Hermann (VIII) of Henneberg	*	*	*	
Count Heinrich (XII) of Henneberg	*	*	*	
Count Friedrich (II) of Henneberg	*	*	*	
Wolf v. Herbilstadt		*	*	*
Darius v. Heßberg		*	*	*
Count Albrecht (II) of Hohenlohe		*	*	*
Count Kraft (V) of Hohenlohe		*	*	*
Count Kraft (VI) of Hohenlohe	*	*	*	*
Ulrich v. Hutten	*	*	*	*
Lorenz v. Hutten		*	*	*
Konrad v. Hutten		*	*	*
Konrad v. Hutten	*	*	*	*
Frowin v. Hutten	*	*	*	*
Lorenz v. Hutten	*	*	*	*
Hans v. Hutten	*	*	*	*
Ludwig v. Hutten	*	*	*	*
Ludwig v. Hutten	*	*	*	*
Frowin v. Hutten	*	*	*	*
Friedrich v. Hutten	*	*	*	*
Apel v. Lichtenstein		*	*	*
Jobst v. Lüchau	*		*	*
Konrad v. Lüchau			*	*
Heinz v. Lüchau			*	*
Sigmund v. Machwitz				*
Werner Marschall v. Ostheim	*	*	*	*
Karl Marschall v. Ostheim		*	*	*
Alexander Marschall v. Pappenheim	*	*	*	*

Wolf Marschall v. Pappenheim	*	*	*	*
Heinrich Marschall v. Pappenheim	*	*	*	*
Konrad Marschall v. Pappenheim	*	*	*	*
Heimeran v. Muggenthal	*			*
Count Joachim of Oettingen	*	*	*	*
Count Wolfgang of Oettingen	*	*	*	*
Count Johann of Oettingen	*	*	*	*
Götz v. Plassenberg	*			*
Götz v. Rain	*			
Georg v. Rain	*			
Ernst v. Rechenberg	*	*	*	
Ernst v. Redwitz		*	*	*
Hans v. Reitzenstein			*	*
Balthasar v. Reitzenstein			*	*
Christoph Reitzenstein			*	*
Hans Sixt v. Reitzenstein			*	*
Georg Ernst v. Reitzenstein			*	*
Thomas v. Reitzenstein			*	*
Thomas v. Reitzenstein	*		*	*
Hermann (II) Riedesel				*
Hermann (III) Riedesel	*			*
Georg Riedesel	*			*
Georg v. Rosenberg		*	*	*
Friedrich v. Rosenberg	*	*	*	*
Friedrich v. Rosenberg	*	*	*	*
Arnold v. Rosenberg	*	*	*	*
Eberhard v. Rotenhan		*	*	*
Hans v. Rotenhan	*	*	*	*
Lutz v. Rotenhan	*	*	*	*
Erasmus v. Rotenhan		*	*	*
Heinrich Rüdt v. Collenberg	*	*	*	*
Silvester v. Schaumberg		*	*	*
Adam v. Schaumberg	*	*	*	*

Name	(4) Father	(5) Cathedral Chapter	(6) Tourmanent Nobility	(7) Continuity
Karl v. Schaumberg		*	*	*
Konrad v. Schaumberg		*	*	*
Karl Schenk v. Arberg				
Baron Gottfried Schenk v. Limpurg		*	*	*
Simon (VI) v. Schlitz gen. v. Görtz	*			*
Ludwig (I) v. Schlitz gen. v. Görtz	*			*
Heinrich (II) v. Schlitz gen. v. Görtz				*
Otto v. Schlitz gen. v. Görtz				*
Konrad Schott	*	*		*
Heinz Schott	*	*		*
Lutz Schott		*		*
Baron Sigmund of Schwarzenberg	*	*	*	*
Baron Johann of Schwarzenberg	*	*	*	*
Baron Hermann of Schwarzenberg	*	*	*	*
Baron Friedrich of Schwarzenberg	*	*	*	*
Kilian v. Seckendorff	*	*	*	*
Hans v. Seckendorff		*	*	*
Lamprecht v. Seckendorff	*	*	*	*
Hans Arnold v. Seckendorff	*	*	*	*
Balthasar v. Seckendorff		*	*	*
Hans v. Seckendorff		*	*	*
Hans v. Seckendorff		*	*	*
Hans v. Seinsheim	*	*	*	*
Erkinger v. Seinsheim	*	*	*	*
Philipp v. Seinsheim		*	*	*
Ludwig v. Seinsheim	*	*	*	*
Neidhard v. Seinsheim		*	*	*
Baron Michael of Seinsheim-Schwarzenberg	*	*	*	*
Hans v. Selbitz				*
Sebastian v. Sparneck	*		*	*

Family parameters of feuders (Sample-I)

	1	2	3	4
Fritz v. Sparneck			*	*
Wolf v. Sparneck	*		*	*
Hertnidt v. Stein		*	*	*
Siegfried v. Stein		*	*	*
Hans v. Steinau	*	*	*	*
Jakob v. Steinau	*	*	*	*
Heinrich v. Steinrück	*	*	*	*
Heinrich v. Steinrück	*	*	*	*
Hildebrand v. Steinrück	*	*	*	*
Otto v. Steinrück	*	*	*	*
Konrad v. Steinrück	*	*	*	*
Wilhelm d.J. v. Stetten			*	*
Kaspar v. Stetten			*	*
Hans v. Stetten			*	*
Kilian v. Stetten			*	*
Sebastian Stiebar	*	*	*	*
Albrecht d.J. Stiebar		*	*	*
Ebold Stiebar	*	*	*	*
Rochus v. Streitberg		*	*	*
Balthasar v. Streitberg		*	*	*
Gabriel v. Streitberg		*	*	*
Paul v. Streitberg		*	*	*
Eberhard v. Streitberg		*	*	*
Melchior Süzel		*	*	
Reuß v. Thüngen		*	*	*
Sigmund v. Thüngen	*	*	*	*
Philipp v. Thüngen	*	*	*	*
Eustachius v. Thüngen	*	*	*	*
Werner v. Thüngen	*	*	*	*
Heinz v. Thüngfeld		*	*	*
Wilhelm v. Vellberg	*		*	
Wolf v. Vellberg	*		*	
Stefan v. Vestenberg		*	*	*

169

Appendix D

Name	(4) Father	(5) Cathedral Chapter	(6) Tourmanent Nobility	(7) Continuity
Veit v. Vestenberg	*	*	*	*
Matern v. Vestenberg		*	*	*
Kaspar v. Vestenberg	*	*	*	*
Eukarius v. Vestenberg	*	*	*	*
Konrad v. Vestenberg		*	*	*
Veit v. Wallenrod			*	*
Reinwold v. Wemding		*		
Count Wilhelm of Wertheim	*	*	*	
Count Albrecht of Wertheim		*	*	
Count Erasmus of Wertheim	*	*	*	
Count Johann of Wertheim	*	*	*	
Moritz v. Wildenstein	*		*	*
Albrecht v. Wirsberg		*	*	*
Konrad v. Wisberg		*	*	*
Soldan v. Wirsberg		*	*	*
Albrecht (IV) v. Wolfstein		*	*	*
Hans (II) v. Wolfstein		*	*	*
Martin Zollner v. Rothenstein		*	*	

Appendix E

Individual parameters of feuders (Sample-II)

Name	(1) Marriage	(2) Office	(3) Creditor/ Guarantor
Paul v. Absberg	*	*	
Konrad (X) v. Aufseß		*	
Götz v. Berlichingen		*	*
Erasmus v. Eberstein		*	
Mangold v. Eberstein		*	
Kaspar v. Eyb		*	
Christoph v. Giech			
Albrecht Gottsmann		*	
Count Wilhelm (III) of Henneberg	*		*
Darius v. Heßberg	*	*	
Karl v. Heßberg		*	*
Ludwig v. Hutten			
Hans v. Kotzau			
Hans d.J. v. Kotzau			
Jobst v. Lüchau		*	
Erhard Marschall v. Eiwang		*	
Georg Marschall v. Pappenheim	*	*	
Count Ulrich of Oettingen	*	*	
Georg v. Rosenberg			
Albrecht v. Rosenberg	*		
Thomas v. Rosenberg			
Lutz v. Rotenhan	*	*	*
Heinrich Rüdt v. Collenberg			

Name	(1) Marriage	(2) Office	(3) Creditor/ Guarantor
Eberhard Rüdt v. Collenberg			
Veit v. Schaumberg		*	
Konrad Schott	*	*	*
Baron Georg of Schwarzenberg		*	*
Sebastian v. Seckendorff			
Sigmund v. Seckendorff		*	
Burkhard v. Seckendorff		*	
Friedrich v. Seckendorff			
Engelhard v. Seinsheim			
Wilhelm v. Seinsheim			
Erkinger v. Seinsheim	*	*	
Baron Michael of Seinsheim-Schwarzenberg		*	*
Adam v. Thüngen	*	*	*
Sigmund v. Thüngen		*	
Reuß v. Thüngen		*	
Hans v. Vestenberg			*
Eitel Voit v. Rieneck		*	
Friedrich v. Waldenfels		*	*
Hans v. Waldenfels	*	*	*
Wendel v. Wolfskeel		*	

Appendix F

Family parameters of feuders (Sample-II)

Name	(4)	(5) Cathedral Chapter	(6) Tournament Nobility	(7) Continuity
Paul v. Absberg	*	*	*	*
Konrad (X) v. Aufseß	*	*	*	*
Götz v. Berlichingen	*	*	*	*
Erasmus v. Eberstein	*	*	*	*
Mangold v. Eberstein		*	*	*
Kaspar v. Eyb	*	*	*	*
Christoph v. Giech	*	*	*	*
Albrecht Gottsmann	*	*	*	*
Count Wilhelm (III) of Henneberg		*	*	
Darius v. Heßberg		*	*	*
Karl v. Heßberg		*	*	*
Ludwig v. Hutten		*	*	*
Hans v. Kotzau			*	*
Hans d.J. v. Kotzau	*		*	*
Jobst v. Lüchau	*		*	*
Erhard Marschall v. Eiwang				
Georg Marschall v. Pappenheim	*	*	*	*
Count Ulrich of Oettingen	*	*	*	*
Georg v. Rosenberg		*	*	*
Albrecht v. Rosenberg		*	*	*
Thomas v. Rosenberg		*	*	*
Lutz v. Rotenhan	*	*	*	*
Heinrich Rüdt v. Collenberg	*	*	*	*

Name	(4)	(5) Cathedral Chapter	(6) Tournament Nobility	(7) Continuity
Eberhard d.J. Rüdt v. Collenberg		*	*	*
Veit v. Schaumberg		*	*	*
Konrad Schott	*	*		*
Baron Georg of Schwarzenberg	*	*	*	*
Sebastian v. Seckendorff		*	*	*
Sigmund v. Seckendorff		*	*	*
Burkhard v. Seckendorff		*	*	*
Friedrich v. Seckendorff	*	*	*	*
Engelhard v. Seinsheim		*	*	*
Wilhelm v. Seinsheim	*	*	*	*
Erkinger v. Seinsheim	*	*	*	*
Baron Michael of Seinsheim-Schwarzenberg	*	*	*	*
Adam v. Thüngen	*	*	*	*
Sigmund v. Thüngen	*	*	*	*
Reuß v. Thüngen		*	*	*
Hans v. Vestenberg		*	*	*
Eitel Voit v. Rieneck		*	*	*
Friedrich v. Waldenfels	*	*	*	*
Hans v. Waldenfels	*	*	*	*
Wendel v. Wolfskeel	*	*	*	*

Sources of information for Appendix A

Hans Christoph von Absberg: (1) Uwe Müller, *Die ständische Vertretung in den fränkischen Markgraftümern in der ersten Hälfte des 16. Jahrhunderts* (Neustadt a.d. Aisch, 1984), 347. (2)(3) StAN, AA-Akten, no. 1402, fols. 51^v, 184^r–185^v.

Hans Georg von Absberg: (2)(3) Ibid., fol. 51^v.

Karl von Absberg: (1) Ibid., fol. 129^v. (3) Peter Ritzmann, ' "Plackerey in teutschen Landen": Untersuchungen zur Fehdetätigkeit des fränkischen Adels im frühen 16. Jahrhundert und ihrer Bekämpfung durch den Schwäbischen Bund und die Reichsstadt Nürnberg, insbesondere am Beispiel des Hans Thomas von Absberg und seiner Auseinandersetzung mit den Grafen von Oettingen (1520–31)' (PhD thesis, University of Munich, 1993), 53.

Hans Sigmund von Absberg. (1) Müller, *Die ständische Vertretung*, 347. (2)(3) StAB, Hofrat Ansbach-Bayreuth, no. 95, fols. 49^v–51^r.

Hieronimus Adelmann von Adelmannsfelden: (1) Ibid., fol. 43^r.

Melchior Adelmann von Adelmannsfelden: (1) StAN, AA-Akten, no. 1402, fols. 83^v–85^r, 140^r–141^v. (3) Georg Sigmund Graf Adelmann von Adelmannsfelden, *Das Geschlecht der Adelmann von Adelmannsfelden* (Ellwangen, 1948), 11, no. 52.

Konrad von Berlichingen: (2) StAN, AA-Akten, no. 1402, fol. 39^r.

Marx von Berlichingen: (2) Ibid., fols. 134^r–136^v. (3) StAW, Stb, no. 788, fol. 5^v.

Philipp von Biberern: (1) Müller, *Die ständische Vertretung*, 334. (2)(3) StAN, AA-Akten, no. 1402, fols. 184^r–185^v.

Christoph von Bibra: (1) Ibid., fols. 226^r–227^r. (3) Wilhelm Freiherr von Bibra, *Beiträge zur Familien-Geschichte der Reichsfreiherrn von Bibra*, 3 vols. (Munich, 1880–88), II, 36.

Wilhelm von Bibra: (2) StAN, AA-Akten, no. 1402, fols. 226^r–227^r. (3) Bibra, *Reichsfreiherrn von Bibra*, II, 360.

Melchior von Birkenfels: (1)(2) StAN, AA-Akten, no. 1402, fols. 87^r, 134^r–136^v.

Stefan von Birkenfels: (1) Müller, *Die ständische Vertretung*, 341. (2) StAN, AA-Akten, no. 1402, fol. 83^r.

Peter von Castell: (1) Ibid., fol. 121^r.

Kaspar von Castell: (1)(3) Ibid.

Count Johann of Castell: (1)(2)(3) Ibid., fols. 29^r, 62^v.

Kaspar von Crailsheim: (2) Ibid., fol. 50^r.

Wolf von Crailsheim: (1)(2)(3) Ibid., fols. 48^r, 62^v.

Hans Georg von Cronheim: (2) StAB, Hofrat Ansbach-Bayreuth, no. 95, fols. 44^v–45^v.

Wilhelm von Ehenheim: (1) StAN, AA-Akten, no. 1402, fols. 26^r–27^v.

Wolfhard von Ehenheim: (2)(3) StAB, Hofrat Ansbach-Bayreuth, no. 95, fol. 6^v.

Engelhard von Ehenheim: (2) Ibid., fol. 59^r. (3) Karl Hannakam and Ludwig Veit (eds.), *Archiv der Freiherrn Schenk von Geyern auf Schloß Syburg* (Munich, 1958), 48, U 65.

Konrad von Ehenheim: (2) StAB, Hofrat Ansbach-Bayreuth, no. 95, fols. 69^v–71^r.

Konrad von Ellrichshausen: (2) StAN, AA-Akten, no. 1402, fols. 134^r–136^v.

Ludwig von Ellrichshausen: (1) Ibid., fols. 224^v–225^v.

Martin von Eyb: (2) Ibid., fol. 142^r.

Sebastian von Eyb: (2) Ibid., fols. 134^r–136^v. (3) Eberhard Freiherr von Eyb, *Das reichsritterliche Geschlecht der Freiherren von Eyb* (Neustadt a.d. Aisch, 1984), 153.

Hans Christoph von Eyb: (2) StAN, AA-Akten, no. 1402, fol. 264^r.

Ludwig von Eyb: (2) Günther Schuhmann (ed.), *Stadtarchiv Ansbach* (Munich, 1956), 15, U 50. (3) Eyb, *Freiherren von Eyb*, 171.

Georg Ludwig von Eyb: (2) Schuhmann (ed.), *Stadtarchiv Ansbach*, 14, U 48.

Eberhard Förtsch: (2) StAN, AA-Akten, no. 1402, fol. 63^r. (3) StAN, Ansbacher Historica, no. 340, fol. 71^v; ibid., AA-Akten, no. 1753; ibid., Bb, no. 65, fol. 83^v.

Christoph Fuchs (von Bimbach): (2)(3) StAN, AA-Akten, no. 1402, fol. 50^r.

Hans Fuchs ([von Dornheim] zu Neidenfels): (2) Ibid., fol. 125^r. (3) FA, Urkunden, no. 31; Manfred Krebs, 'Die kurpfälzischen Dienerbücher 1476–1685', *ZGO* 94 (1942), m7–m64, at m53.

Dietrich Fuchs von Bimbach: (1)(2) StAN, AA-Akten, no. 1402, fols. 48^r, 56^v. (3) StAW, Stb, no. 790, fols. 66^v–68^r; ibid., Würzburger Lehenbücher, no. 36, fol. 33^r.

Albrecht Gailing: (2)(3) StAN, AA-Akten, no. 1402, fol. 46^v.

Eberhard Geyer: (1)(2)(3) Ibid., fols. 48^r, 59.

Florian Geyer: (1) Ibid., fols. 90^v–92^v.

Mathes von Giech: (2) Ibid., fols. 164^{r-v}. (3) Frank Baron Freytag von Loringhoven, *Europäische Stammtafeln: Stammtafeln zur Geschichte der europäischen Staaten*, n.s., ed. Detlev Schwennicke (Marburg, 1980–), V, table 25.

Georg von Gnottstadt: (1)(2) StAN, AA-Akten, no. 1402, fols. 50^r, 185^v–187^r. (3) Cf. Eyb, *Freiherren von Eyb*, 171 and Heinzjürgen N. Reuschling, *Die Regierung des Hochstifts Würzburg: Zentralbehörden und führende Gruppen eines geistlichen Staates* (Würzburg, 1984), 188.

Sigmund von Haberkorn: (2) StAN, AA-Akten, no. 1402, fol. 125^r.

Florian von Haberkorn: (1) Ibid., fol. 193^v.

Friedrich von Haldermannstetten genannt Stettner: (1) StAB, Hofrat Ansbach-Bayreuth, no. 95, fols. 60^r–62^r. (3) Cf. ibid., Sigmund Haenle, 'Urkunden und Nachweise zur Geschichte des Schwanen-Ordens', *Jb.Mfr.* 39 (1873/74), 1–178, at 164 and StAN, Ansbacher Historica, no. 340, fols. 32^v, 71^v.

Hans von Haldermannstetten genannt Stettner: (1) StAB, Hofrat Ansbach-Bayreuth, no. 95, fols. 60^r–62^r. (3) Cf. ibid., Haenle, 'Urkunden und Nachweise', 164, StAN, Ansbacher Historica, no. 340, fols. 24^r, 71^v and ibid., Fstm.Ansb., Fehdeakten, no. 77a, prod. 21.

Heinz von Haldermannstetten genannt Stettner: (2) Schuhmann (ed.), *Stadtarchiv Ansbach*, 11, U 36.

Wolf von Hausen: (1) StAN, AA-Akten, no. 1402, fol. 194^r.

Endres von Hausen: (1) Müller, *Die ständische Vertretung*, 350. (2)(3) StAN, AA-Akten, no. 1402, fols. 103^r, 190^r–191^r.

Sources of information for Appendixes

Baron Georg of Heideck: (1) Ibid., fol. 113^v. (3) Dietrich Deeg, *Die Herrschaft der Herren von Heideck* (Neustadt a.d. Aisch, 1968), 49.

Alweg von Heimenhofen: (1) StAN, AA-Akten, no. 1402, fols. 52^{r-v}. (3) Wilhelm Schwemmer, *Burg und Amt Veldenstein-Neuhaus* (Nuremberg, 1961), 114.

Philipp von Helb: (1) StAN, AA-Akten, no. 1402, fols. 78^r–79^v.

Wilhelm von Heßberg: (2) Ibid., fol. 113^v.

Karl von Heßberg: (2)(3) Ibid., fols. 23^v–24^r.

Philipp von Heßberg: (2) Ibid., fols. 226^r–227^r. (3) Bibra, *Reichsfreiherrn von Bibra*, II, 369.

Greif von Heßberg: (2) StAN, AA-Akten, no. 1402, fols. 226^r–227^r.

Wolf von Heßberg: (1) Müller, *Die ständische Vertretung*, 335. (2)(3) Schuhmann (ed.), *Stadtarchiv Ansbach*, 13, U 44.

Sigmund von Heßberg: (2)(3) StAN, AA-Akten, no. 1402, fols. 23^v–24^r.

Bernhard von Heßberg: (2)(3) Ibid., fol. 48^r.

Count Albrecht of Hohenlohe: (2) Ibid., fol. 46^v.

Ernst von Horckheim: (1) StAB, Hofrat Ansbach-Bayreuth, no. 95, fols. 37^v–43^r.

Ulrich von Hutten: (1) StAN, AA-Akten, no. 1402, fols. 241^v–243^v. (3) Hans Körner, 'Die Familie von Hutten: Genealogie und Besitz bis zum Ende des Alten Reiches', in *Ulrich von Hutten: Ritter, Humanist, Publizist 1488–1523. Katalog zur Ausstellung des Landes Hessen anläßlich des 500. Geburtstages*, ed. Peter Laub (Kassel, 1988), 57–78, at 69.

Erasmus von Hutten: (1) StAN, AA-Akten, no. 1402, fols. 118^v–121^r. (3) Körner, 'Die Familie von Hutten', 64.

Bernhard von Hutten: (2) StAN, AA-Akten, no. 1402, fol. 72^v. (3) Körner, 'Die Familie von Hutten', 69.

Ludwig von Hutten: (1)(2) StAN, AA-Akten, no. 1402, fols. 48^r, 56^v, 241^v–243^v. (3) Körner, 'Die Familie von Hutten', 69.

Martin von Jahrsdorf: (1) StAB, Hofrat Ansbach-Bayreuth, no. 95, fols. 49^v–51^r.

Jakob von der Kere: (1) Müller, *Die ständische Vertretung*, 340. (2) StAN, AA-Akten, no. 1402, fols. 226^r–227^r. (3) StAW, Stb, no. 792, fols. 7^v–8^v.

Hans von Knöringen: (1)(3) Müller, *Die ständische Vertretung*, 339. (2) StAN, AA-Akten, no. 1402, fol. 125^r.

Ulrich von Knöringen: (1)(2)(3) Ibid., fol. 46^v; StAB, Hofrat Ansbach-Bayreuth, no. 95, fols. 44^v–45^v.

Wolf von Künsberg: (2) StAN, AA-Akten, no. 1402, fol. 87^r.

Hans von Leineck: (2)(3) Ibid., fols. 161^v–164^v.

Veit von Lentersheim: (1) Müller, *Die ständische Vertretung*, 338. (2)(3) StAN, AA-Akten, no. 1402, fol. 43^r.

Kraft von Lentersheim: (2) Ibid., fol. 46^v.

Alexander von Lentersheim: (2) Ibid., fol. 264^r. (3) Otto Rohn, 'Die Herren von Lentersheim. Zweiter Teil: Vom Erwerb des Schlosses Altenmuhr im Jahr 1430 bis zum Erlöschen des Stammes im Jahr 1799', *Alt-Gunzenhausen* 38 (1979), 108–45, at 113.

Christoph von Lentersheim: (1) Müller, *Die ständische Vertretung*, 348. (2) StAN, AA-Akten, no. 1402, fols. 134^r–136^v. (3) Rohn, 'Die Herren von Lentersheim. Zweiter Teil', 112.

Friedrich von Lentersheim: (1) StAB, Hofrat Ansbach-Bayreuth, no. 95, fols. 32^v–35^r. (3) StAN, Ansbacher Historica, no. 340, fol. 36^r.

Sigmund von Lentersheim: (2)(3) StAN, AA-Akten, no. 1402, fol. 43^r.

Wilhelm von Leonrod: (2) Ibid., fol. 46^v.

Hans von Leonrod: (2)(3) StAB, Hofrat Ansbach-Bayreuth, no. 95, fols. 69^v–71^r.

Albrecht von Leonrod: (2) StAN, AA-Akten, no. 1402, fol. 98r. (3) Cf. StAN, Ansbacher Historica, no. 340, fol. 29^r and Müller, *Die ständische Vertretung*, 99, 100 (no. 59).

Konrad von Leonrod: (2)(3) StAB, Hofrat Ansbach-Bayreuth, no. 95, fols. 49^v–51^r.

Hieronimus von Lichtenstein: (1) StAN, AA-Akten, no. 1402, fols. 125^{r-v}. (3) StAN, Bb, no. 81, fol. 222^v.

Wolf Linck: (1)(3) StAN, AA-Akten, no. 1402, fols. 25^r–26^v.

Hans Dietrich Lochinger: (1) Schuhmann (ed.), *Stadtarchiv Ansbach*, 16, U 54.

Götz Lochinger: (1) Müller, *Die ständische Vertretung*, 350. (2) Schuhmann (ed.), *Stadtarchiv Ansbach*, 15, U 50. (3) Eyb, *Freiherren von Eyb*, 182.

Count Ludwig (I) of Löwenstein: (1) StAN, AA-Akten, no. 1402, fols. 87^r–90^r.

Count Ludwig (II) of Löwenstein: (1) Ibid., fols. 246^r–249^r.

Count Friedrich (I) of Löwenstein: (1) Ibid.

Bernhard von Lüchau: (1)(2) Ibid., fols. 44^v, 85^r. (3) Alban Freiherr von Dobeneck, 'Geschichte des ausgestorbenen Geschlechtes von Lüchau', *AO* 24, no. 3 (1911), 22–194, at 129.

Christoph von Lüchau: (2)(3) StAN, AA-Akten, no. 1402, fol. 98^r.

Hans Günter von Lüchau: (2) Schuhmann (ed.), *Stadtarchiv Ansbach*, 14, U 47.

Moritz Marschall von Ostheim: (1)(3) StAN, AA-Akten, no. 1402, fols. 106^r–110^r.

Reinhard Marschall von Ostheim: (1) Ibid., fol. 110^r. (3) Rudolf M. Kloos (ed.), *Nachlass Marschalk von Ostheim: Urkunden* (Neustadt a.d. Aisch, 1974), 10, U 34.

Hartung Marschall von Ostheim: (1) StAN, AA-Akten, no. 1402, fol. 110^r. (3) StAN, Ansbacher Lehensurkunden, no. 506.

Christoph Marschall von Pappenheim: (1) Müller, *Die ständische Vertretung*, 350. (2)(3) Schuhmann (ed.), *Stadtarchiv Ansbach*, 16, U 54.

Stefan von Menzingen: (1) StAN, AA-Akten, no. 1402, fol. 76^r. (3) Matthias Thiel (ed.), *Archiv der Freiherren Stromer von Reichenbach auf Burg Grünsberg*, vol. I, *Urkunden* (Neustadt a.d. Aisch, 1972), 160, U 328; StAN, Fstm.Ansb., Fehdeakten, no. 11, prod. 15.

Hermann Hans von Ochsenbach: (1)(3) StAN, AA-Akten, no. 1402, fols. 54^{r-v}.

Wolf von Rechberg: (1) Müller, *Die ständische Vertretung*, 334. (2)(3) StAB, Hofrat Ansbach-Bayreuth, no. 95, fols. 32^v–35^r.

Balthasar von Rechenberg: (1) Müller, *Die ständische Vertretung*, 338. (2)(3) StAN, AA-Akten, no. 1402, fol. 51^v.

Ernst von Rechenberg: (2)(3) Ibid., fols. 54^{r-v}.

Peter von Redwitz: (2)(3) Ibid., fols. 161^v–164^v.

Christoph von Rosenau: (2) Ibid., fols. 226^r–227^r.

Anton von Rosenau: (1) Ibid., fols. 56^r–58^r.

Lienhard von Rosenberg: (2) Schuhmann (ed.), *Stadtarchiv Ansbach*, 11, U 36. (3) StAN, Ansbacher Historica, no. 340, fol. 62^r.

Georg von Rosenberg: (2)(3) StAN, AA-Akten, no. 1402, fols. 54^{r-v}.

Konrad von Rosenberg: (2) Ibid., fol. 29^v. (3) Cf. ibid., StAW, Stb, no. 792, fols. 21^r–22^v

and Walther Möller, *Stamm-Tafeln westdeutscher Adels-Geschlechter im Mittelalter*, vol. II (Darmstadt, 1933), table 75.

Martin von Schaumberg: (2) StAN, AA-Akten, no. 1402, fol. 40^r. (3) Schuhmann (ed.), *Stadtarchiv Ansbach*, 11, U 36.

Wilhelm von Scheinberg: (2) StAN, AA-Akten, no. 1402, fols. 226^r–227^r.

Hans von Scheinberg: (2) Ibid.

Pankraz Schenk von Arberg: (1) Ibid., fol. 40^v. (3) Schuhmann (ed.), *Stadtarchiv Ansbach*, 11, U 36.

Christoph (I) Schenk von Geyern: (2) StAN, AA-Akten, no. 1402, fol. 51^v. (3) Hannakam and Veit (eds.), *Archiv der Freiherrn Schenk von Geyern*, 33–4, 36, U 34, U 37, U 39.

Christoph (II) Schenk von Geyern: (2) StAB, Hofrat Ansbach-Bayreuth, no. 95, fols. 49^v–51^r.

Baron Gottfried Schenk von Limpurg: (2) StAN, AA-Akten, no. 1402, fol. 29^r.

Baron Friedrich Schenk von Limpurg: (2) Ibid., (3) StAN, Ansbacher Historica, no. 340, fol. 62^v.

Hans Schenk von Schenkenstein: (1)(3) StAN, AA-Akten, no. 1402, fols. 261^{r-v}.

Kaspar Schenk von Schenkenstein: (1) Ibid., fols. 261^v–262^r. (2)(3) Ibid., fol. 46^v.

Heinrich von Schirnding: (2) Ibid., fol. 125^r. (3) Cf. Alban Freiherr von Dobeneck, 'Zur Geschichte des erloschenen Geschlechtes der Rabensteiner von Doehlau', *AO* 25, no. 3 (1914), 37–115, at 111 and Johann Gottfried Biedermann, *Geschlechts Register der löblichen Ritterschaft im Voigtland* (Kulmbach, 1752), table 189.

Count Stefan Schlick: (1) StAN, AA-Akten, no. 1402, fol. 28^v.

Konrad Schott: (1)(3) Ibid., fols. 69^v, 79^r, 161^v–164^v, 169^v–171^v.

Konrad Schrimpf: (1) Ibid., 72^v.

Hans von der Schulenburg: (1)(3) Ibid., fols. 94^r–95^r.

Mathes von der Schulenburg: (1) Ibid.

Baron Friedrich of Schwarzenberg: (2) Ibid., fol. 50^r. (3) Ibid., fol. 62^v.

Baron Wolfgang of Schwarzenberg: (1)(2)(3) Ibid., fols. 51^v, 56^v.

Baron Johann of Schwarzenberg: (2) StAN, AA-Akten, no. 1402, fols. 87^r–90^r. (3) Karl Fürst zu Schwarzenberg, *Geschichte des reichsständischen Hauses Schwarzenberg* (Neustadt a.d. Aisch, 1963), 61.

Apel von Seckendorff: (1) StAN, AA-Akten, no. 1402, fols. 73^r, 198^r. (2)(3) Ibid., fols. 46^v, 56^v; StAN, Ansbacher Historica, no. 340, fol. 71^v.

Moritz von Seckendorff-Aberdar: (2) StAN, AA-Akten, no. 1402, fol. 44^v. (3) Gerhard Rechter, *Das Land zwischen Aisch und Rezat: Die Kommende Virnsberg Deutschen Ordens und die Rittergüter im oberen Zenngrund* (Neustadt a.d. Aisch, 1981), 174*.

Philipp von Seckendorff: (1)(3) StAB, Hofrat Ansbach-Bayreuth, no. 95, fols. 32^v–35^r. (2) StAN, AA-Akten, no. 1402, fols. 52^{r-v}.

Arnold von Seckendorff: (2)(3) StAB, Hofrat Ansbach-Bayreuth, no. 95, fols. 32^v–35^r.

Hans von Seckendorff: (2)(3) StAN, AA-Akten, no. 1402, fols. 23^v–24^r.

Kilian von Seckendorff: (1) Müller, *Die ständische Vertretung*, 341. (2) StAN, AA-Akten, no. 1402, fol. 40^v.

Melchior von Seckendorff: (2) Ibid., fol. 43^r. (3) Gerhard Rechter, *Die Seckendorff: Quellen und Studien zur Genealogie und Besitzgeschichte*, 2 vols. (Neustadt a.d. Aisch, 1987–90), II, 56.

Christoph von Seckendorff: (2) StAN, AA-Akten, no. 1402, fol. 98^r. (3) Rechter, *Die Seckendorff*, II, 84–5.

Jordan von Seckendorff: (1) Müller, *Die ständische Vertretung*, 349. (2) StAN, AA-Akten, no. 1402, fol. 264^r.

Burkhard von Seckendorff: (2) Ibid., fol. 56^v. (3) Rechter, *Die Seckendorff*, II, 164.

Erkinger von Seckendorff: (2) StAN, AA-Akten, no. 1402, fol. 98^r. (3) StAN, Ansbacher Historica, no. 340, fol. 48^r.

Sixt von Seckendorff: (2) StAN, AA-Akten, no. 1402, fols. 172^r–173^r. (3) StAN, Ansbacher Historica, no. 340, fol. 40^r.

Friedrich Joachim von Seckendorff: (2)(3) Schuhmann (ed.), *Stadtarchiv Ansbach*, 16, U 54.

Hans von Seckendorff-Aberdar: (1)(2)(3) StAN, AA-Akten, no. 1402, fols. 29^v, 46^v.

Hans von Seckendorff-Bechhofen: (1) Ibid., fol. 67^r. (3) Rechter, *Die Seckendorff*, II, 204.

Hans von Seckendorff-Obernzenn: (2) StAN, AA-Akten, no. 1402, fols. 134^r–136^v. (3) Gerhard Rechter (ed.), *Die Archive der Grafen und Freiherren von Seckendorff: Die Urkundenbestände der Schloßarchive Obernzenn, Sugenheim, Trautskirchen und Unternzenn*, vol. II (Munich, 1993), 526–7, nos. 1292, 1294.

Georg von Seckendorff: (2) Schuhmann (ed.), *Stadtarchiv Ansbach*, 15, U 52.

Hans Georg von Seckendorff: (1) StAN, AA-Akten, no. 1402, fols. 159^{r-v}.

Hans Melchior von Seckendorff: (1) Ibid.

Hans Sebastian von Seckendorff: (1) Ibid.

Hans Wilhelm von Seckendorff: (1) Ibid.

Anstand von Seckendorff: (2) StAB, Hofrat Ansbach-Bayreuth, no. 95, fol. 59^r.

Götz von Seinsheim: (1) StAN, AA-Akten, no. 1402, fol. 52^r. (3) Eberhard Graf von Fugger, *Die Seinsheim und ihre Zeit: Eine Familien- und Kulturgeschichte von 1155 bis 1890* (Munich, 1893), 154.

Albrecht von Seldeneck: (1) StAB, Hofrat Ansbach-Bayreuth, no. 95, fols. 69^v–71^r.

Wolf von Steinau genannt Steinrück: (1) StAN, AA-Akten, no. 1402, fol. 63^r. (3) StAW, Stb, no. 792, fols. 4^r–5^v; Richard von Steinau-Steinrück, 'Abriß aus der Geschichte des fränkischen Geschlechtes von Steinau genannt Steinrück', *AU* 49 (1907), 1–134, at 101.

Dr Georg von Streitberg: (2) Schuhmann (ed.), *Stadtarchiv Ansbach*, 15, U 52. (3) Paul Oesterreicher, *Die Burg Streitberg* (Bamberg, 1819), 68.

Lienhard von der Tann: (1) StAN, AA-Akten, no. 1402, fol. 40. (3) StAN, BK, D, 20.

Hans Thanhäuser: (1) StAN, AA-Akten, no. 1402, fol. 142^r.

Bernhard von Thüngen: (2)(3) Ibid., fol. 72^v.

Kaspar von Thüngen: (1) Ibid., fol. 43^r.

Georg von Thüngen: (2) Ibid., fols. 223^v–224^v. (3) Cf. ibid., Rudolf Karl Reinhard Freiherr von Thüngen, 'Zur Genealogie der Familie derer von Thüngen', *AU* 54 (1912), 1–181, at 106 and Joseph Morsel, 'Une société politique en Franconie à la fin du Moyen Age: Les Thüngen, leurs princes, leurs pairs et leurs hommes (1275–1525)' (PhD thesis, University of Paris-IV Sorbonne, 1993), 341.

Adam von Thüngen: (1)(3) StAN, AA-Akten, no. 1402, fols. 81^r–82^v.

Daniel von Thüngen: (1) Ibid., fol. 43^r.

Wilhelm Truchseß von Henneberg: (1) Ibid., fol. 50^r.

Jakob Truchseß von Henneberg: (1) Ibid.

Wolf Truchseß von Pommersfelden: (2)(3) Ibid., fols. 257^r–258^v.

Philipp Truchseß von Pommersfelden: (1) Schuhmann (ed.), *Stadtarchiv Ansbach*, 15–16, U 51–2. (2)(3) Cf. StAN, AA-Akten, no. 1402, fol. 72^v and Georg Spath, *Die letzten Truchsesse von Pommersfelden* (Höchstadt a.d. Aisch, 1936), 7.

Paul Truchseß (zu Unsleben): (2) StAN, AA-Akten, no. 1402, fols. 226^r–227^r.

Hans Truchseß von Wetzhausen: (2)(3) Ibid., fols. 23^v–24^r.

Sigmund von Ussigheim: (1) Ibid., fol. 259^r.

Georg von Vellberg: (1) Ibid., fol. 206^r. (3) Cf. ibid. and Gerd Wunder, 'Die Ritter von Vellberg', in *Vellberg in Geschichte und Gegenwart*, ed. Hansmartin Decker-Hauff, vol. I, *Darstellungen* (Sigmaringen, 1984), 129–96, at 168, 182.

Wilhelm von Vellberg: (1)(2) StAN, AA-Akten, no. 1402, fols. 113^v, 202^r–203^r. (3) Cf. ibid., 202^r–203^r and Wunder, 'Die Ritter von Vellberg', 175–7.

Wolf von Vellberg: (1) StAN, AA-Akten, no. 1402, fol. 206^r. (3) StAN, Ansbacher Historica, no. 340, fol. 51^r.

Ehrenfried von Vellberg: (1)(3) StAN, AA-Akten, no. 1402, fols. 5^v–6^r.

Anton von Vestenberg: (2) Ibid., fol. 56^v.

Albrecht von Vestenberg: (1) Müller, *Die ständische Vertretung*, 344. (2)(3) StAN, AA-Akten, no. 1402, fols. 54^{r-v}.

Florian von Vestenberg: (2) Schuhmann (ed.), *Stadtarchiv Ansbach*, 14, U 47.

Kaspar von Vestenberg: (2) StAN, AA-Akten, no. 1402, fol. 18^r.

Weiprecht von Vinsterlohe: (2) Ibid., fol. 39^r.

Hans von Waldenfels: (1) Müller, *Die ständische Vertretung*, 350. (2) StAN, AA-Akten, no. 1402, fol. 113^v. (3) Otto Freiherr von Waldenfels, *Die Freiherrn von Waldenfels: Stammfolgen mit urkundlichen Belegen*, 5 vols. (Munich, 1952–70), II, 89, 91.

Sebastian von Waldenfels: (1) StAB, Hofrat Ansbach-Bayreuth, no. 166^i, fol. 48^v. (3) Waldenfels, *Freiherrn von Waldenfels*, I, 258.

Wilhelm von Wiesenthau: (1) StAN, AA-Akten, no. 1402, fols. 104^r–105^v. (2) StAB, Hofrat Ansbach-Bayreuth, no. 95, fol. 59^r. (3) Müller, *Die ständische Vertretung*, 99, 100 (no. 18).

Wolf Christoph von Wiesenthau: (1) Ibid., 350. (2)(3) StAN, AA-Akten, no. 1402, fols. 134^r–136^v.

Wolf von Wilhermsdorf: (2) StAB, Hofrat Ansbach-Bayreuth, no. 95, fols. 60^r–62^r.

Albrecht von Wilhermsdorf: (2) StAN, AA-Akten, no. 1402, fols. 23^v–24^r.

Baron Balthasar of Wolfstein: (1) Ibid., fol. 61^r. (3) Cf. ibid., fols. 133^r–134^r, StAN, Ansbacher Gemeinbücher, Tom. 7, fol. 5^v and Hannakam and Veit (eds.), *Archiv der Freiherrn Schenk von Geyern*, 38, U 43.

Maximilian Wolf von Wolfsthal: (2) StAN, AA-Akten, no. 1402, fol. 264^r.

Hans Wolf von Wolmarshausen: (2) Ibid., fol. 125^r.

Burkhard von Wolmarshausen: (1) Ibid., (3) Ibid., fols. 134^r–136^v.

Christoph von Wolmarshausen: (2)(3) Ibid., fol. 46^v.

Ernst von Wolmarshausen: (2)(3) Ibid., fol. 43^r.

Sigmund von Zedwitz: (1) Müller, *Die ständische Vertretung*, 338. (2)(3) StAN, AA-Akten, no. 1402, fols. 54^{r-v}.

Peter von Zedwitz: (2) Ibid., fol. 102^r.

Sources of information for Appendixes

Eukarius Zobel: (1) Müller, *Die ständische Vertretung*, 342. (2) StAN, AA-Akten, no. 1402, fol. 40.
Fritz Zobel: (1) Ibid., fol. 29^v.
Stefan Zobel: (2)(3) Ibid., fols. 141^v–142^r.

Sources of information for Appendixes C and D

Hans von Abenberg (1497–8): StAN, Fstm.Ansb., Fehdeakten, no. 77a.

Engelhard von Absberg (1462): StAN, AA-Akten, no. 392, prod. of Pfintztag nach Petri et Pauli [1 July] 1462. (2) H. Wilhelm, 'Die Edeln von und zum Absberg: Ein Beitrag zur fränkischen Geschichte', *Alt-Gunzenhausen* 8 (1931), 3–197, at 57. (4) Ibid., 46.

Hans Georg von Absberg (1484–1519): StAN, Fstm.Ansb., Fehdeakten, no. 69, prod. 10, 11. (2) Wilhelm, 'Die Edeln von und zum Absberg', 59. (4) Ibid., 50.

Hans Thomas von Absberg (1520): Joseph Baader (ed.), *Verhandlungen über Thomas von Absberg und seine Fehden gegen den Schwäbischen Bund 1519 bis 1530* (Tübingen, 1873), 1–2; Peter Ritzmann, '"Plackerey in teutschen Landen": Untersuchungen zur Fehdetätigkeit des fränkischen Adels im frühen 16. Jahrhundert und ihrer Bekämpfung durch den Schwäbischen Bund und die Reichsstadt Nürnberg, insbesondere am Beispiel des Hans Thomas von Absberg und seiner Auseinandersetzung mit den Grafen von Oettingen (1520–31)' (PhD thesis, University of Munich, 1993), 131–2. (1) Cf. Gerd Wunder, 'Die Ritter von Vellberg', in *Vellberg in Geschichte und Gegenwart*, ed. Hansmartin Decker-Hauff, vol. I, *Darstellungen* (Sigmaringen, 1984), 129–96, at 139, 178, 180 and Walther Pfeilsticker (ed.), *Neues Württembergisches Dienerbuch*, 2 vols. (Stuttgart, 1957–63), I, no. 1127. (4) Wilhelm, 'Die Edeln von und zum Absberg', 59.

Hans Christoph von Absberg (1544): Christian Kolb (ed.), *Widmans Chronica* (Stuttgart, 1904), 290. (1) Wunder, 'Die Ritter von Vellberg', 135, 167–8. (2) StAN, Ansbacher Historica, no. 340, fol. 50^v. (3) Uwe Müller, *Die ständische Vertretung in den fränkischen Markgraftümern in der ersten Hälfte des 16. Jahrhunderts* (Neustadt a.d. Aisch, 1984), 347. (4) Wilhelm, 'Die Edeln von und zum Absberg', 59.

Paul von Absberg (1503): Joseph Schlecht (ed.), 'Die Kleinen Annalen des Kilian Leib, Priors zu Rebdorf. Nach dem Codex Münch im bischöfl. Ordinariats-Archiv zu Eichstätt', *Sammelblatt des Historischen Vereins Eichstätt* 2 (1887 [1888]), 39–68, at 43; Wilhelm, 'Die Edeln von und zum Absberg', 122. (1) Louis Ferdinand Freiherr von Eberstein, *Entwurf einer zusammenhängenden Stammreihe des freifränkischen Geschlechts Eberstein* (Berlin, 1887), 51. (2) StAN, Ansbacher Historica, no. 340, fol. 32^v. (4) Wilhelm, 'Die Edeln von und zum Absberg', 57.

Eukarius von Aufseß (1488–1518): StAA, Ganerbschaft Rothenberg, no. 2538a, anno 1509; Otto Freiherr von Aufseß, *Geschichte des uradelichen Aufseß'schen Geschlechtes in Franken* (Berlin, 1888), 183–93. (2) Ibid., 189. (3) Ibid., 187; Johann Looshorn, *Die Geschichte des Bisthums Bamberg*, 5 vols. (Munich and Bamberg, 1886–1903), IV, 400. (4) Aufseß, *Geschichte des uradelichen Aufseß'schen Geschlechtes*, 147.

Konrad (X) von Aufseß (1464–88): StAW, Stb, no. 717, fol. 266^r; ibid., Stb, no. 892, fols.

266ᵛ–267ʳ; Lorenz Fries, *Historie, Nahmen, Geschlecht, Wesen, Thaten, gantz Leben und Sterben der gewesenen Bischoffen zu Wirtzburg und Hertzogen zu Francken* [1544], in *Geschicht-Schreiber von dem Bischoffthum Wirtzbürg*, ed. Johann Peter Ludewig (Frankfurt am Main, 1713), 840–1; Joseph Chmel (ed.), *Actenstücke und Briefe zur Geschichte des Hauses Habsburg im Zeitalter Maximilian's I.*, vol. I (Vienna, 1854), 473–92; Felix Priebatsch (ed.), *Politische Correspondenz des Kurfürsten Albrecht Achilles*, 3 vols. (Leipzig, 1894–98), I, 597–8, 601, nos. 734, 739; Aufseß, *Geschichte des uradelichen Aufseß'schen Geschlechtes*, 146–63. (2) Aufseß, *Geschichte des uradelichen Aufseß'schen Geschlechtes*, 147, 149. (4) Ibid., 117.

Wilhelm von Bebenburg (1502): Johann Herolt, *Chronica zeit- unnd Jarbuch von der Statt Hall ursprung und was sich darinnen verloffen unnd wasz fur Schlösser umb Hall gestanden*, ed. Christian Kolb (Stuttgart, 1894), 122–3. (2) Cf. StAN, AA-Akten, no. 838, fol. 3ʳ, ibid., AA-Akten, no. 132/1, prod. of Mittwoch vor Corpus Christi [1 June] 1496 and Eugen Schöler, *Historische Familienwappen in Franken* (Neustadt a.d. Aisch, 1982), 30.

Engelhard von Berlichingen (1470): Friedrich Pietsch (ed.), *Die Urkunden des Archivs der Reichsstadt Schwäbisch Hall*, vol. II (Stuttgart, 1972), 337, U 2633. (1) Cf. Friedrich Wolfgang Götz Graf von Berlichingen-Rossach, *Geschichte des Ritters Götz von Berlichingen mit der eisernen Hand und seiner Familie* (Leipzig, 1861), 185 and Wilhelm Freiherr von Bibra, *Beiträge zur Familien-Geschichte der Reichsfreiherrn von Bibra*, 3 vols. (Munich, 1880–88), II, 414, 417. (2) H. Bauer, 'Die Herrn von Berlichingen in Bayern', *AU* 16, no. 1 (1863), 129–78, at 134. (4) Ibid.

Götz von Berlichingen (1515–18): Helgard Ulmschneider (ed.), *Götz von Berlichingen: Mein Fehd und Handlung* (Sigmaringen, 1981), 81–121. (2) Helgard Ulmschneider, *Götz von Berlichingen: Ein adeliges Leben der deutschen Renaissance* (Sigmaringen, 1974), 97. (3) Ibid., 204. (4) Rudolf Karl Reinhard Freiherr von Thüngen, 'Zur Genealogie der Familie derer von Thüngen', *AU* 54 (1912), 1–181, at 21–5.

Klaus von Bernheim (1501): StAN, Fstm.Ansb., Fehdeakten, no. 83a; StAB, Fehde-Akten, no. 152, prod. 25.

Lorenz von Bibra (1498): StAB, Hofrat Ansbach-Bayreuth, no. 557; StAN, Kaiserliches Landgericht Nürnberg, Akten, no. 211, fol. 109ʳ. (2) Bibra, *Reichsfreiherrn von Bibra*, II, 429. (4) Ibid., 414.

Heinrich von Bibra (1473): StAN, AA-Akten, no. 728, prod. of Dienstag nach Assumptio Marie [17 August] and Donnerstag nach Assumptio Marie [19 August] 1473. (1) Bibra, *Reichsfreiherrn von Bibra*, II, 105. (2) Ibid., 101. (3) Ibid., 104–5. (4) Ibid., 76–86.

Bartholomäus von Bibra (1451–5): ibid., 189–99. (2) Ibid., 189. (3) Ibid., 198.

Konrad von Bibra (1492): Leopold Auer (ed.), 'Die undatierten Fredriciana des Haus-, Hof- und Staatsarchivs', *Mitteilungen des österreichischen Staatsarchivs* 27 (1974), 405–30, at 425, no. 105. (2) Bibra, *Reichsfreiherrn von Bibra*, II, 113. (4) Cf. ibid., 100 and Richard von Steinau-Steinrück, 'Abriß aus der Geschichte des fränkischen Geschlechtes von Steinau genannt Steinrück in bezug auf seine Zugehörigkeit zu dem Hochstifte Würzburg und im besonderen auf seine Besitzungen daselbst', *AU* 49 (1907), 1–134, at 38, 49.

Georg von Bibra (1461): Eduard Edwin Becker, *Die Riedesel zu Eisenbach: Geschichte des*

Geschlechts der Riedesel, Freiherrn zu Eisenbach, Erbmarschälle zu Hessen, 3 vols. (Offenbach, 1923–27), I, 208.

Adam von Bibra (1459): ibid. (2) Bibra, *Reichsfreiherrn von Bibra*, II, 20–1.

Anton von Bibra (1486–7): ibid., 270. (2) Ibid., 273. (3) Karl E. Demandt, *Der Personenstaat der Landgrafschaft Hessen im Mittelalter: Ein 'Staatshandbuch' Hessens vom Ende des 12. bis zum Anfang des 16. Jahrhunderts*, 2 vols. (Marburg, 1981), I, 53, no. 188. (4) Bibra, *Reichsfreiherrn von Bibra*, II, 243.

Eustachius von Birkenfels (1496): StAN, Fstm.Ansb., Fehdeakten. no. 6 [alte Signatur].

Albrecht von Brandenstein (1493): StAB, Hofrat Ansbach-Bayreuth, no. 545. (2) Ibid., prod. 4.

Eberhard von Brandenstein (1503–6): StAA, Ganerbschaft Rothenberg, no. 2538a, anno 1503, 1505, 1506. (1) Cf. *Genealogisches Handbuch des Adels* (Limburg a.d. Lahn, 1951-), XXVII, 15 and Frank Baron Freytag von Loringhoven, *Europäische Stammtafeln: Stammtafeln zur Geschichte der europäischen Staaten*, n.s., ed. Detlev Schwennicke (Marburg, 1980-), V, tables 104, 105. (3) Looshorn, *Bamberg*, IV, 399. (4) *Genealogisches Handbuch des Adles*, XXVII, 15.

Ernst von Brandenstein (1510): Cyriacus Spangenberg, *Hennebergische Chronica: Der uralten löblichen Grafen und Fürsten zu Henneberg, Genealogia, Stamm-Baum und Historia, ihrer Ankunfft, Lob und denckwürdigen Tathen, Geschichten und Sachen wahre und gründliche Beschreibung*, ed. Christoph Albrecht Erck (Meiningen, 1755), 462–5.

Engelhard von Buchenau (1494): Josef Leinweber, *Das Hochstift Fulda vor der Reformation* (Fulda, 1972), 22; Spangenberg, *Hennebergische Chronica*, 403–4. (2) Cf. Hubertus von Wilmowsky, 'Die Geschichte der Ritterschaft Buchenau von ihren Anfängen bis zum Wiener Kongreß', *Fuldaer Geschichtsblätter* 40 (1964), 1–47, at 42 and Demandt, *Der Personenstaat*, I, 115, no. 376.

Kaspar d.J. von Buchenau (1479): Fries, *Historie*, 855. (2) Cf. Wilmowsky, 'Ritterschaft Buchenau', 42 and Demandt, *Der Personenstaat*, I, 117, no. 378.

Marx von Crailsheim (1498–1500): StAN, Fstm.Ansb., Fehdeakten. no. 10; StAN, AA-Akten, no. 1733. (2) StAW, Stb, no. 790, fols. 71^v–73^r.

Sebastian von Crailsheim (1519): StAN, Fstm.Ansb., Fehdeakten, no. 105a. (2) Sigmund Freiherr von Crailsheim, *Die Reichsfreiherrn von Crailsheim*, 2 vols. (Munich, 1905), II, 65. (4) Ibid., 61.

Wilhelm von Crailsheim (1519): StAN, Fstm.Ansb., Fehdeakten, no. 105a. (2) Crailsheim, *Reichsfreiherrn von Crailsheim*, II, 98. (3) Müller, *Die ständische Vertretung*, 349. (4) Crailsheim, *Reichsfreiherrn von Crailsheim*, II, 61.

Kaspar von Crailsheim (1519): StAN, Fstm.Ansb., Fehdeakten, no. 105a. (1) Cf. Crailsheim, *Reichsfreiherrn von Crailsheim*, II, 39, 40, 93 and StAN, Kaiserliches Landgericht Nürnberg, Akten, no. 211, fol. 64^v. (3) StAN, AA-Akten, no. 1402, fols. 50^r, 62^v, 136^v. (4) Crailsheim, *Reichsfreiherrn von Crailsheim*, II, 61.

Georg von Crailsheim (1498–1500): StAN, Fstm.Ansb., Fehdeakten, no. 10; ibid., AA-Akten, no. 1733.

Kunemund von Dobeneck (1474–5): StAN, Fstm.Ansb., Urfehden, Fehdesachen, Urkunden, no. 33; Priebatsch (ed.), *Politische Correspondenz des Kurfürsten Albrecht Achilles*, II, 192–3, no. 167.

Erasmus von Eberstein (1450–66): Fries, *Historie*, 806, 815; StAB, Hofrat Ansbach-Bayreuth, no. 507, prod. 1–2; Steinau-Steinrück, 'Geschichte des fränkischen

Geschlechtes von Steinau genannt Steinrück', 62. (2) Eberstein, *Stammreihe des freifränkischen Geschlechts Eberstein*, 44–6. (4) Ibid., 42.

Gerlach von Eberstein (1450): StAW, Stb, no. 1012, fol. 498^r. (2) Eberstein, *Stammreihe des freifränkischen Geschlechts Eberstein*, 42. (3) Ibid., (4) Ibid., 11, 42.

Philipp von Eberstein (1520s): Klaus Peter Decker, 'Klientel und Konkurrenz: Die ritterschaftliche Familie von Hutten und die Grafen von Hanau und von Ysenburg', *Hessisches Jahrbuch für Landesgeschichte* 38 (1988), 23–48, at 43. (3) Eberstein, *Stammreihe des freifränkischen Geschlechts Eberstein*, 40.

Georg von Ellrichshausen (1462): Max Herrmann, *Albrecht von Eyb und die Frühzeit des deutschen Humanismus* (Berlin, 1893), 241–53. (2) Adolf Bachmann (ed.), *Briefe und Acten zur österreichisch-deutschen Geschichte im Zeitalter Kaiser Friedrich III.* (Vienna, 1885), 622, no. 508; Lore Muehlon, 'Johann III. von Grumbach, Bischof von Würzburg und Herzog zu Franken (1455–1466)' (PhD thesis, University of Würzburg, 1935), 153.

Hans Christoph von Eyb (1542): Gerhard Rechter, *Die Seckendorff: Quellen und Studien zur Genealogie und Besitzgeschichte*, 2 vols. (Neustadt a.d. Aisch, 1987–90), II, 215. (3) StAN, AA-Akten, no. 1402, fol. 264^r.

Albrecht von Eyb (1462): Herrmann, *Albrecht von Eyb*, 241–53. (2) Ibid., 246. (4) Eberhard Freiherr von Eyb, *Das reichsritterliche Geschlecht der Freiherren von Eyb* (Neustadt a.d. Aisch, 1984), 68, 108.

Friedrich von Feilitzsch (*c.* 1478–82): Priebatsch (ed.), *Politische Correspondenz des Kurfürsten Albrecht Achilles*, II, 600–8, no. 659; III, 172–4, no. 861; Alban Freiherr von Dobeneck, *Geschichte der Familie von Dobeneck* (Schöneberg-Berlin, 1906), 368–72; Hans Hofner, 'Zur Geschichte des vogtländischen Adels: Die Herren von Feilitzsch auf Feilitzsch', *AO* 54 (1974), 257–317, at 282.

Hans von Feilitzsch (1530–1): StAB, Hofrat Ansbach-Bayreuth, no. 574. (2) Ibid., prod. of Sonntag Reminiscere [5 March] 1531.

Christoph Fuchs von Bimbach (1462–6): StAW, Stb, no. 717, fols. 257^{r-v}; Fries, *Historie*, 838–45. (2)(3) Cf. Fries, *Historie*, 838–45 and chap. 4, n. 26 above. (4) Cf. StAW, Ldf, no. 13, pp. 81–2, 177–9, ibid., Stb, no. 717, fols. 297^{r-v} and chap. 4, Figure 4.3 above.

Heinz Fuchs von Bimbach (1462–7): StAW, Stb, no. 717, fols. 142^v, 192^v, 243^{r-v}; ibid., Stb, no. 865, fol. 331^v; Bachmann (ed.), *Briefe und Acten zur österreichisch-deutschen Geschichte*, 559, no. 449; Spangenberg, *Hennebergische Chronica*, 430–2; Fries, *Historie*, 838–45. (2)(3) Cf. Fries, *Historie*, 838–45 and chap. 4, n. 8 above. (4) Cf. StAW, Ldf, no. 13, pp. 81–2, 177–9, ibid., Stb, no. 717, fols. 297^{r-v} and chap. 4, Figure 4.3 above.

Hans d.J. Fuchs von Preppach (*c.* 1460): StAW, Ldf, no. 12, p. 733.

Georg von Gebsattel (1461–2): Fries, *Historie*, 825–6, 833; Bachmann (ed.), *Briefe und Acten zur österreichisch-deutschen Geschichte*, 415–17, no. 323. (2) Bachmann (ed.), *Briefe und Acten zur österreichisch-deutschen Geschichte*, 415, no. 323.

Christoph von Giech (1492–4): StAB, Hofrat Ansbach-Bayreuth, no. 545. (4) Freytag von Loringhoven, *Europäische Stammtafeln*, n.s., V, table 25.

Wolf Gottsmann (1493–1507): StAN, AA-Akten, no. 392, prod. of 30 June 1493; StAA, Ganerbschaft Rothenberg, no. 2538a, anno 1507; Klaus Rupprecht, *Ritterschaftliche Herrschaftswahrung in Franken: Die Geschichte der von Guttenberg im Spätmittelalter und zu Beginn der Frühen Neuzeit* (Neustadt a.d. Aisch, 1994), 136 n. 271. (2) StAN, Ansbacher Historica, no. 340, fol. 29^v; ibid., Fstm.Ansb., Fehdeakten, no. 77a, prod. 8.

Wilhelm von Grumbach: (1552–67): Bayerisches Hauptstaatsarchiv München, Kurbayern, Äußeres Archiv, no. 2004, fols. 3–6; Volker Press, 'Wilhelm von Grumbach und die deutsche Adelskrise der 1560er Jahre', *Blätter für deutsche Landesgeschichte* 113 (1977), 396–431. (2) Heinzjürgen N. Reuschling, *Die Regierung des Hochstifts Würzburg: Zentralbehörden und führende Gruppen eines geistlichen Staates* (Würzburg, 1984), 221–3. (4) Thomas Beyer, 'Zu Familienstruktur und Konnubium des niederadeligen Geschlechtes von Grumbach im Spätmittelalter' (*Zulassungsarbeit*, University of Würzburg, 1977), lxxxv.

Hans d.Ä. von der Grün (1540): StAB, Hofrat Ansbach-Bayreuth, no. 578.

Hans d.J. von der Grün (1540): ibid.

Philipp von Guttenberg (1488–1500): StAN, AA-Akten, nos. 1753, 1788, 1831; Erich Freiherr von Guttenberg, 'Aus Fehdezeiten (1490–1501)', in *Lebens- und Kultur-Bilder aus der Geschichte des fränkischen Geschlechts von Guttenberg*, ed. Wilhelm Engel (Würzburg, 1958), 9–45; Rupprecht, *Ritterschaftliche Herrschaftswahrung in Franken*, 72–99, 297–8, 334 n. 814. (1) Johannes Bischoff, *Genealogie der Ministerialen von Blassenberg und Freiherren von (und zu) Guttenberg 1148–1970* (Würzburg, 1971), 154. (2) Ibid., 153 (3) Ibid., (4) Ibid., 150.

Moritz von Guttenberg (1497–1502): StAN, AA-Akten, no. 1788; Guttenberg, 'Aus Fehdezeiten'; Rupprecht, *Ritterschaftliche Herrschaftswahrung in Franken*, 72–99. (1) Bischoff, *Freiherren von (und zu) Guttenberg*, 77, 154. (2) Ibid., 77. (4) Ibid., 75.

Heinz von Guttenberg (1477): StAB, Fehde Akten, no. 76; Priebatsch, (ed.), *Politische Correspondenz des Kurfürsten Albrecht Achilles*, II, 311, no. 305. (1) Bischoff, *Freiherren von (und zu) Guttenberg*, 78. (2) Ibid., (4) Ibid., 75.

Achaz von Guttenberg (1520–36): ibid., 151; Rupprecht, *Ritterschaftliche Herrschaftswahrung in Franken*, 186. (4) Bischoff, *Freiherren von (und zu) Guttenberg*, 150–1.

Hektor von Guttenberg (1536): Rupprecht, *Ritterschaftliche Herrschaftswahrung in Franken*, 186. (2) Ibid., 307 n. 675. (4) Bischoff, *Freiherren von (und zu) Guttenberg*, 153–4.

Baron Konrad of Heideck (1462): StAN, AA-Akten, no. 392, prod. of Pfintztag nach Petri et Pauli [1 July] 1462. (2) Dietrich Deeg, *Die Herrschaft der Herren von Heideck: Eine Studie zu hochadeliger Familien- und Besitzgeschichte* (Neustadt a.d. Aisch, 1968), 42. (3) Ibid., (4) Ibid., 38.

Count Wilhelm (II) of Henneberg (1441): Spangenberg, *Hennebergische Chronica*, 407–8; Johann Adolph Schultes, *Diplomatische Geschichte des Gräflichen Hauses Henneberg*, 2 vols. (Hildburghausen, 1788–91), II, 107. (4) Cf. Freytag von Loringhoven, *Europäische Stammtafeln*, n.s., XVI, table 147 and Alfred Wendehorst, *Das Bistum Würzburg*, 3 parts (Berlin, 1962–78), II, 159.

Count Wilhelm (III) of Henneberg (1462–73): Becker, *Die Riedesel*, I, 253; StAN, AA-Akten, no. 728, prod. of Dienstag nach Assumptio Marie [17 August] and of Donnerstag nach Assumptio Marie [19 August] 1473. (1) Freytag von Loringhoven, *Europäische Stammtafeln*, n.s., XVI, table 147. (3) Sebastian Zeißner, *Rudolf II. von Scherenberg: Fürstbischof von Würzburg 1466–1495*, 2nd edn (Würzburg, 1952), 42.

Count Wilhelm (IV) of Henneberg (1501–12): StAN, AA-Akten, no. 728, prod. of Freitag nach Francisci [8 October] 1501; Spangenberg, *Hennebergische Chronica*, 462–5. (1) Freytag von Loringhoven, *Europäische Stammtafeln*, n.s., XVI, table 147. (2) Schultes, *Geschichte des Gräflichen Hauses Henneberg*, I, 387 n. i. (3) Ibid., (4) Cf. Freytag von

Sources of information for Appendixes

Loringhoven, *Europäische Stammtafeln*, n.s., XVI, table 147 and Zeißner, *Rudolf II. von Scherenberg*, 42.

Count Otto (IV) of Henneberg (1469–89): StAN, AA-Akten, no. 392, prod. of Freitag nach Assumptio [21 August] 1478 and of Dienstag nach Matthei [22 Spetember] 1478; ibid., AA-Akten, no. 737, prod. of Peterstag ad cathedram [22 February] 1469; ibid., AA-Akten, no. 738, prod. 6, 26–8, 31, 35, 37–9, 43–74; StAB, Fehde-Akten, no. 79; StAW, Stb, no. 1012, fol. 350ᵛ; Priebatsch (ed.), *Politische Correspondenz des Kurfürsten Albrecht Achilles*, II, 408, no. 420; Spangenberg, *Hennebergische Chronica*, 277; Friedrich Stein (ed.), *Monumenta Suinfurtensia historica inde ab anno DCCXCI usque ad annum MDC: Denkmäler der Schweinfurter Geschichte bis zum Ende des sechzehnten Jahrhunderts* (Schweinfurt, 1875), 364. (2) Demandt, *Der Personenstaat*, I, 331, no. 1158; Priebatsch (ed.), *Politische Correspondenz des Kurfürsten Albrecht Achilles*, II, 518, no 557; Wendehorst, *Das Bistum Würzburg*, III, 33; Schultes, *Geschichte des Gräflichen Hauses Henneberg*, I, 388. (3) Schultes, *Geschichte des Gräflichen Hauses Henneberg*, I, 388. (4) Ibid., 361.

Count Hermann (VIII) of Henneberg (*c*. 1490–1501): Christoph Albrecht Erck (ed.), *Rapsodiae sive Chronicon Hennebergicum Weyland M. Sebastian Glasers, Hennebergischen Cantzlers vom Jahr 1078. bis 1559. Welches noch niemahlen im Druck erschienen, sondern nur in einigen Bibliothecis priuatis latitiret, zur Erläuterung der spangenberg-hennebergischen Chronic* (Meiningen, 1755), 84; StAN, AA-Akten, no. 728, prod. of Freitag nach Francisci [8 October] 1501; ibid., AA-Akten, no. 515 (unpaginated, n.d.). (1) Freytag von Loringhoven, *Europäische Stammtafeln*, n.s., XVI, table 148. (2) Schultes, *Geschichte des Gräflichen Hauses Henneberg*, I, 651–5, no. 118. (4) Cf. Freytag von Loringhoven, *Europäische Stammtafeln*, n.s., XVI, table 148 and StAW, Stb, no. 1012, fol. 523ᵛ.

Count Heinrich (XII) of Henneberg (1444–70): StAN, AA-Akten, no. 515, prod. of Johannis baptiste [25 June] 1448; ibid. [n.d. = *c*. 1450]; StAB, Hofrat Ansbach-Bayreuth, no. 504; Spangenberg, *Hennebergische Chronica*, 388–401, 403–4; Wilhelm Engel (ed.), *Die Rats-Chronik der Stadt Würzburg (XV. und XVI. Jahrhundert)* (Würzburg, 1950), 31–2, nos. 96–7. (2) StAN, AA-Akten, no. 515 [n.d. = 1448]; Demandt, *Der Personenstaat*, I, 331, no. 1158; Erck (ed.), *Rapsodiae sive Chronicon*, 201; Eckart Henning, *Die gefürstete Grafschaft Henneberg-Schleusingen im Zeitalter der Reformation* (Cologne, 1981), 19. (4) Cf. Freytag von Loringhoven, *Europäische Stammtafeln*, n.s., XVI, 147 and Wendehorst, *Das Bistum Würzburg*, II, 159.

Count Friedrich (II) of Henneberg (1488): Fritz Luckhard (ed.), *Die Regesten der Herren von Ebersberg genannt Weyhers in der Röhn (1170–1518)* (Fulda, 1963), 190, no. 728. (2) StAW, Stb, no. 1012, fol. 523ᵛ. (3) Ibid., (4) Cf. Freytag von Loringhoven, *Europäische Stammtafeln*, n.s., XVI, table 148 and Muehlon, 'Johann III. von Grumbach', 154.

Wolf von Herbilstadt (1512): Spangenberg, *Hennebergische Chronica*, 465. (2) Cf. Demandt, *Der Personenstaat*, I, 334–5, no. 1176, Johann Gottfried Biedermann, *Geschlechtsregister der Reichsfrey unmittelbaren Ritterschaft Landes zu Franken löblichen Orts Rhön und Werra* (Bayreuth, 1749), tables 401 and C. Binder, 'Das ehemalige Amt Lichtenberg vor der Rhön', parts 1–3, *Zeitschrift des Vereins für thüringische Geschichte und Altertumskunde*, n.s., 8 (1893), 233–309; 9 (1895), 75–294; 10 (1897), 61–245: part 3, 233.

Darius von Heßberg (1470–1500): StAN, Fstm.Ansb., Fehdeakten, no. 26. (1) Cf. ibid., prod. 55, Rudolf M. Kloos (ed.), *Die Inschriften des Landkreises Bamberg bis 1650* (Munich, 1980), 32, no. 75 and Otto Graf Seefried, *Aus dem Stiebar-Archiv: Forschungen zur Familiengeschichte von Bauer, Bürger und Edelmann in Ober- und Mittelfranken* (Nuremberg, 1953), 7. (2) StAN, Fstm.Ansb., Fehdeakten, no. 26, prod. 6, 16, 41.

Count Albrecht (II) of Hohenlohe (1451–89): Gerhard Taddey, 'Macht und Recht im späten Mittelalter: Die Auseinandersetzungen zwischen Hohenlohe und Hessen um die Grafschaft Ziegenhain und Nidda', *WFr* 61 (1977), 79–110, at 96; Freiherr von Stetten, 'Ein Fehdebrief vom Jahre 1489', *Der deutsche Herold* 23 (1892), 114–15.

Count Kraft (V) of Hohenlohe (1451): Taddey, 'Macht und Recht', 96. (2) Eberhard Emil von Georgii-Georgenau (ed.), *Fürstlich Württembergisch Dienerbuch: IX. bis zum XIX. Jahrhundert* (Stuttgart, 1877), 5.

Count Kraft (VI) of Hohenlohe (1488–9): Stetten, 'Ein Fehdebrief vom Jahre 1489'. (2) Pfeilsticker (ed.), *Neues Württembergisches Dienerbuch*, I, no. 1129. (4) Cf. Wilhelm Karl Prinz von Isenburg and Frank Baron Freytag von Loringhoven, *Europäische Stammtafeln: Stammtafeln zur Geschichte der europäischen Staaten*, 5 vols. (Marburg, 1956–78), V, table 3 and Georgii-Georgenau (ed.), *Fürstlich Württembergisch Dienerbuch*, 5.

Ulrich von Hutten (1492–3): Friedrich Battenberg (ed.), *Isenburger Urkunden: Regesten zu Urkundenbeständen und Kopiaren der fürstlichen Archive in Birstein und Büdingen 947–1500*, 3 vols. (Darmstadt, 1976), II, 818, no. 3406. (2) Demandt, *Der Personenstaat*, I, 409–10, no. 1404; Berthold Jäger, 'Die Beziehungen zwischen dem geistlichen Fürstentum Fulda und der Familie von Hutten', in *Ulrich von Hutten: Ritter, Humanist, Publizist 1488–1523. Katalog zur Ausstellung des Landes Hessen anläßlich des 500. Geburtstages*, ed. Peter Laub (Kassel, 1988), 87–101, at 92, 95. (3) Jäger, 'Die Beziehungen', 95. (4) Cf. ibid., 92, Hans Körner, 'Die Familie von Hutten: Genealogie und Besitz bis zum Ende des alten Reiches', in *Ulrich von Hutten*, 57–78, at 59 and Battenberg (ed.), *Isenburger Urkunden*, II, 523, no. 1981.

Lorenz von Hutten (1462–93): StAN, AA-Akten, no. 738, prod. 43–74; Battenberg (ed.), *Isenburger Urkunden*, II, 600, 649, 818, nos. 2343, 2587, 3406; Joseph Morsel, 'Une société politique en Franconie à la fin du Moyen Age: Les Thüngen, leurs princes, leurs pairs et leurs hommes (1275–1525)' (PhD thesis, University of Paris-IV Sorbonne, 1993), 784. (1) Morsel, 'Une société politique en Franconie', 302, 1501. (2) Jäger, 'Die Beziehungen', 92. (3) Ibid.; Battenberg (ed.), *Isenburger Urkunden*, II, 523, no. 1981.

Konrad von Hutten (1448): StAN, AA-Akten, no. 515, prod. of Dienstag nach Johannis baptiste [25 June] 1448. (1) Cf. Körner, 'Die Familie von Hutten', 64 and Morsel, 'Une société politique en Franconie', 302, 1504. (2) Körner, 'Die Familie von Hutten', 64.

Konrad von Hutten (1470–2): StAN, AA-Akten, no. 738, prod. 6. (1) Cf. Körner, 'Die Familie von Hutten', 64 and Freytag von Loringhoven, *Europäische Stammtafeln*, n.s., XI, table 63. (2) Körner, 'Die Familie von Hutten', 64. (3) Karl August Eckhardt (ed.), *Quellen zur Rechtsgeschichte der Stadt Eschwege*, vol. I, *Urkunden und Stadtbücher* (Marburg, 1959), 214–15, no. 222. (4) Körner, 'Die Familie von Hutten', 64.

Frowin von Hutten (1520s): Decker, 'Klientel und Konkurrenz', 43. (2) Körner, 'Die

189

Familie von Hutten', 62; Jäger, 'Die Beziehungen', 96. (4) Cf. Jäger, 'Die Beziehungen', 95 and Körner, 'Die Familie von Hutten', 59.

Lorenz von Hutten (1520s): Decker, 'Klientel und Konkurrenz', 43. (4) Cf. Jäger, 'Die Beziehungen', 95 and Körner, 'Die Familie von Hutten', 59.

Hans von Hutten (1520s): Decker, 'Klientel und Konkurrenz', 43. (2) Körner, 'Die Familie von Hutten', 62; Jäger, 'Die Beziehungen', 93, 96. (4) Cf. Jäger, 'Die Beziehungen', 95 and Körner, 'Die Familie von Hutten', 59.

Ludwig von Hutten (1531–5): Geheimes Staatsarchiv, XX.HA: Hist. Staatsarchiv Königsberg, Herzogliches Briefarchiv, A 4, 1534 January 29 (K. 191); *Unser Friderichen Freyherren von Schwartzenberg und zu Hohenlandsperg . . .* (1535). (2) Richard Schmitt, 'Aus dem Zentrum des Hochstifts verdrängt: Die Herren von Hutten im Gebiet des Würzburger Bischofs', in *Ulrich von Hutten*, 103–12, at 107. (3) Ibid., 110–11. (4) Körner, 'Die Familie von Hutten', 65.

Ludwig von Hutten (1492–3): Battenberg (ed.), *Isenburger Urkunden*, II, 818, no. 3406. (4) Cf. Körner, 'Die Familie von Hutten', 59, Jäger, 'Die Beziehungen', 92 and Battenberg (ed.), *Isenburger Urkunden*, II, 523, no. 1981.

Frowin von Hutten (1472): Spangenberg, *Hennebergische Chronica*, 277; Stein (ed.), *Monumenta Suinfurtensia*, 364. (4) Cf. Walther Möller, *Stamm-Tafeln westdeutscher Adels-Geschlechter im Mittelalter*, n.s., part 2 (Darmstadt, 1951), table 79, Körner, 'Die Familie von Hutten', 71 and Morsel, 'Une société politique en Franconie', 302, 1504.

Friedrich von Hutten (1492–3): *Isenburger Urkunden*, II, 818, no. 3406. (4) Cf. Körner, 'Die Familie von Hutten', 59, Jäger, 'Die Beziehungen', 92 and Battenberg (ed.), *Isenburger Urkunden*, II, 523, no. 1981.

Apel von Lichtenstein (1474): 'Hellers Chronic der Stadt Bayreuth', part 1, *AO* 1, no. 1 (1828), 102–47, at 132–6. (2) Ibid.

Jobst von Lüchau (1500): StAB, Fehde-Akten, no. 152, prod. 3, 23. (2) Ibid., prod. 3. (4) Alban Freiherr von Dobeneck, 'Geschichte des ausgestorbenen Geschlechtes von Lüchau', *AO* 24, no. 3 (1911), 22–194, at 117.

Konrad von Lüchau (1478–80): Priebatsch (ed.), *Politische Correspondenz des Kurfürsten Albrecht Achilles*, II, 600–8, no. 659; Dobeneck, *Geschichte der Familie von Dobeneck*, 368–72. (2) Dobeneck, 'Lüchau', 60, 64. (3) Ibid., 66–7.

Heinz von Lüchau (1523): Baader (ed.), *Verhandlungen über Thomas von Absberg*, 60. (1) Cf. Alban Freiherr von Dobeneck, 'Geschichte des ausgestorbenen Geschlechtes der von Sparneck', parts 1 and 2, *AO* 22, no. 3 (1905), 1–65; 23, no. 1 (1906), 1–56: part 2, 63–4 and Dobeneck, 'Lüchau', 79.

Sigmund von Machwitz (1531): StAB, Hofrat Ansbach-Bayreuth, no. 574. (2) Cf. Heinrich Bauer, *Geschichte der Stadt Pegnitz und des Pegnitzer Bezirkes* (Pegnitz, 1909), 533 and Dobeneck, *Familie von Dobeneck*, 377–9.

Werner Marschall von Ostheim (1480–1): StAN, AA-Akten, no. 738, prod. 37–9. (1) Cf. Morsel, 'Une société politique en Franconie', 339, 1502 and Thüngen, 'Familie derer von Thüngen', 101. (4) Cf. Binder, 'Amt Lichtenberg vor der Rhön', part 1, 267–8, part 3, 235 and August Amrhein, 'Gotfrid Schenk von Limpurg: Bischof von Würzburg und Herzog zu Franken 1442–1455', part 3, *AU* 53 (1911), 1–153, at 104.

Karl Marschall von Ostheim (1486): Bibra, *Reichsfreiherrn von Bibra*, II, 270.

Alexander Marschall von Pappenheim (1553): StAN, Herrschaft Pappenheim, Akten, no. 2797. (2) Haupt Graf zu Pappenheim, *Die Frühen Pappenheimer Marschälle: Zweiter*

Teil der Hausgeschichte vom XV. bis zum XVIII. Jahrhundert (Munich, 1951), 61. (4) Ibid., 55.

Wolf Marschall von Pappenheim (1553): StAN, Herrschaft Pappenheim, Akten, no. 2797. (2) Pappenheim, *Pappenheimer Marschälle*, 40. (4) Ibid., 36.

Heinrich Marschall von Pappenheim (1440–4): J. A. Giefel (ed.), 'Die Ellwanger und Neresheimer Geschichtsquellen', *Württembergische Vierteljahrshefte für Landesgeschichte* 11 (1888 [1889]), 1–78, at 48; Ritzmann, '"Plackerey in teutschen Landen"', 117–19; Pappenheim, *Pappenheimer Marschälle*, 31. (2) Pappenheim, *Pappenheimer Marschälle*, 32. (4) Ibid., 17.

Konrad Marschall von Pappenheim (1440–4): Giefel (ed.), 'Die Ellwanger und Neresheimer Geschichtsquellen', 48; Ritzmann, '"Plackerey in teutschen Landen"', 117–19; Pappenheim, *Pappenheimer Marschälle*, 31. (2) Pappenheim, *Pappenheimer Marschälle*, 26–7. (4) Ibid., 17.

Heimeran von Muggenthal (1456): StAN, Fstm.Ansb., Fehdeakten, no. 27. (3) Cf. ibid., prod. 2, Wilhelm Volkert (ed.), *Schloßarchiv Sandersdorf* (Munich, 1962), 4, U 12, Johann Gottfried Biedermann, *Geschlechtsregister der Reichsfrey unmittelbaren Ritterschaft Landes zu Franken löblichen Orts Ottenwald* (Kulmbach, 1751), table 220 and J. Anselm Pangkofer, 'Chronik des Schlosses und der Herrschaft Hexenagger an der Schambach', *Verhandlungen der historischen Vereins für den Regenkreis* 2 (1833), 322–40, at 328. (4) Biedermann, *Orts Ottenwald*, table 220.

Count Joachim of Oettingen (1488–1520): Reinhard Stauber, *Herzog Georg von Bayern-Landshut und seine Reichspolitik: Möglichkeiten und Grenzen reichsfürstlicher Politik im wittelsbachisch-habsburgischen Spannungsfeld zwischen 1470 und 1505* (Kallmünz, 1993), 478–83; Baader (ed.), *Verhandlungen über Thomas von Absberg*, 1–2; Ritzmann, '"Plackerey in teutschen Landen"', 131–2. (1) Freytag von Loringhoven, *Europäische Stammtafeln*, n.s., XVI, table 99. (4) Cf. ibid. and Pfeilsticker (ed.), *Neues Württembergisches Dienerbuch*, I, no. 1130.

Count Wolfgang of Oettingen (1488–1520): Stauber, *Herzog Georg von Bayern-Landshut*, 478–83; Ritzmann, '"Plackerey in teutschen Landen"', 131–2. (2) StAW, Stb, no. 892, fol. 156ᵛ; Stauber, *Herzog Georg von Bayern-Landshut*, 475; Georgii-Georgenau (ed.), *Fürstlich Württembergisch Dienerbuch*, 5. (4) Cf. Freytag von Loringhoven, *Europäische Stammtafeln*, n.s., XVI, table 99 and Georgii-Georgenau (ed.), *Fürstlich Württembergisch Dienerbuch*, 5.

Count Johann of Oettingen (1440–4): Giefel (ed.), 'Die Ellwanger und Neresheimer Geschichtsquellen', 48; Ritzmann, '"Plackerey in teutschen Landen"', 117 19; Pappenheim, *Pappenheimer Marschälle*, 31. (1)(3) Cf. Isenburg and Freytag von Loringhoven, *Europäische Stammtafeln*, III, table 44 and Freytag von Loringhoven, *Europäische Stammtafeln*, n.s., XVI, table 99.

Götz von Plassenberg (1465–73): StAB, Hofrat Ansbach-Bayreuth, no. 519; Franz Karl Freiherr von Guttenberg, 'Regesten des "Geschlechtes von Blassenberg" und dessen Nachkommen', *AO* 22, no. 3 (1907), 112–232, at 225, no. 226. (2) Guttenberg, 'Regesten des "Geschlechtes von Blassenberg" und dessen Nachkommen', 225, no. 224. (4) Cf. ibid., 219–20, no. 52a and 224, no. 220

Götz von Rain (1524–9): StAN, Fstm.Ansb., Fehdeakten, no. 110. (4) Cf. StAN, Lehensurkunden, no. 1713 and ibid., BK, R, 21.

Georg von Rain (1524–9): StAN, Fstm.Ansb., Fehdeakten, no. 110. (2) StAW, Stb, no.

791, fols. 161^v–163^r; Kolb (ed.), *Widmans Chronica*, 290. (4) Cf. StAN, Lehensurkunden, no. 1713 and ibid., BK, R, 21.

Ernst von Rechenberg (1498–9): StAB, Hofrat Ansbach-Bayreuth, no. 557; StAN, Kaiserliches Landgericht Nürnberg, Akten, no. 211, fol. 109^r. (2) StAN, Ansbacher Gemeinbücher, Tom. 7, fols. 4^r–5^r; ibid., BK, R, 12. (3) StAN, AA-Akten, no. 1402, fol. 43^r. (4) Cf. StAN, Ansbacher Gemeinbücher, Tom. 7, fols. 4^r–5^r, Johann Gottfried Biedermann, *Geschlechtsregister der Reichsfrey unmittelbaren Ritterschaft Landes zu Franken löblichen Orts Altmühl* (Bamberg, 1748), table 234 and Hugo A. Braun, *Das Domkapitel zu Eichstätt: Von der Reformationszeit bis zur Säkularisation (1535–1806). Verfassung und Personalgeschichte* (Stuttgart, 1991), 405–6.

Ernst von Redwitz (1519–25): StAA, Ganerbschaft Rothenberg, no. 2538a, anno 1519, 1520, 1525.

Hans von Reitzenstein (1500–8): StAB, Fehde-Akten, no. 152, prod. 25; ibid., Fehde-Akten, no. 166; Joseph Würdinger, *Kriegsgeschichte von Bayern, Franken, Pfalz und Schwaben von 1347 bis 1506*, 2 vols. (Munich, 1868), II, 118. (2) Hermann Freiherr von Reitzenstein, *Geschichte der Familie von Reitzenstein* (Munich, 1891), 166–7.

Balthasar von Reitzenstein (1549): StAB, Fehde-Akten, no. 221.

Christoph von Reitzenstein (1549): ibid.

Hans Sixt von Reitzenstein (1549): ibid.

Georg Ernst von Reitzenstein (1549): ibid.

Thomas von Reitzenstein (1472): Carl August Hugo Burkhardt (ed.), *Das funfft merckisch Buech des Churfuersten Albrecht Achilles* (Jena, 1857), 211; Würdinger, *Kriegsgeschichte*, II, 110. (2) Georg Heinz, 'Selbitz, ein alter fränkischer Rittersitz', *AO* 28, no. 2 (1922), 1–75, at 17–18.

Thomas von Reitzenstein (1480–1507): Adolph Friedrich Riedel (ed.), *Codex diplomaticus Brandenburgensis: Sammlung der Urkunden, Chroniken und sonstigen Quellenschriften für die Geschichte der Mark Brandenburg und ihrer Regenten*, part 2, *Urkunden-Sammlung zur Geschichte der auswärtigen Verhältnisse der Mark Brandenburg und ihrer Regenten*, vol. V (Berlin, 1848), 351, no. 2057; Priebatsch (ed.), *Politische Correspondenz des Kurfürsten Albrecht Achilles*, III, 173, no. 861; Heinz, 'Selbitz', 19. (1) Bischoff, *Freiherren von (und zu) Guttenberg*, 155. (2) Ibid.; StAB, Hofrat Ansbach-Bayreuth, no. 552, prod. 1; Heinz, 'Selbitz', 19. (4) Heinz, 'Selbitz', 17–18.

Hermann (II) Riedesel (1459–62): Becker, *Die Riedesel*, I, 208, 253. (2) Demandt, *Der Personenstaat*, I, 680–1, no. 2422. (3) Ibid., 680, no. 2422.

Hermann (III) Riedesel (1465–89): StAW, Stb, no. 1012, fol. 350^v; Becker, *Die Riedesel*, I, 254–62. (1) Freytag von Loringhoven, *Europäische Stammtafeln*, n.s., VIII, table 110. (2) Demandt, *Der Personenstaat*, I, 682, no. 2423. (4) Cf. ibid., 680–1, no. 2422 and Becker, *Die Riedesel*, I, 253–4.

Georg Riedesel (1465–76): Becker, *Die Riedesel*, I, 254–62. (2) Demandt, *Der Personenstaat*, I, 679, no. 2421. (4) Cf. ibid., 680–1, no. 2422 and Becker, *Die Riedesel*, I, 253–4.

Georg von Rosenberg (1476–87): StAW, Stb, no. 1012, fol. 445^v; StAN, AA-Akten, no. 738, prod. 14; StAN, Reichsstadt Nürnberg, 35 Neue Laden der unteren Losungsstube, V 90/2 2447; Fries, *Historie*, 857; Engel (ed.), *Die Rats-Chronik*, 45–6, no. 141.

Friedrich von Rosenberg (1470): StAN, Fstm.Ansb., Fehdeakten, no. 39a. (4) H. Bauer, 'Die Herrn von Rosenberg', *WFr* 9, no. 2 (1872), 177–221, at 200–2.

Friedrich von Rosenberg (1486–7): StAW, Stb, no. 1012, fol. 445ᵛ; Fries, *Historie*, 857; Engel (ed.), *Die Rats-Chronik*, 45–6, no. 141. (4) Walther Möller, *Stamm-Tafeln westdeutscher Adels-Geschlechter im Mittelalter*, 3 vols. (Darmstadt, 1922–36), II, table 74.

Arnold von Rosenberg (1486–7): Fries, *Historie*, 857; Engel (ed.), *Die Rats-Chronik*, 45–6, no. 141. (4) Möller, *Stamm-Tafeln*, II, table 74.

Eberhard von Rotenhan (?–1495): StAW, Stb, no. 1012, fol. 454ʳ.

Hans von Rotenhan (1460): Gottfried Freiherr von Rotenhan, 'Streit und Fehde um die Burg Stuffenberg bei Baunach 1460/66', *Bericht des Historischen Vereins Bamberg* 129 (1993), 75–90, at 76–7. (2) Gottfried Frieherr von Rotenhan, *Die Rotenhan: Genealogie einer fränkischen Familie von 1229 bis zum Dreißigjährigen Krieg* (Neustadt a.d. Aisch, 1985), 127. (3) Rotenhan, 'Streit und Fehde', 75. (4) Rotenhan, *Die Rotenhan*, 68.

Lutz von Rotenhan (1460–6): Rotenhan, 'Streit und Fehde'; Bachmann (ed.), *Briefe und Acten zur österreichisch-deutschen Geschichte*, 72, no. 57. (1) Cf. Rotenhan, *Die Rotenhan*, 195 and Pappenheim, *Pappenheimer Marschälle*, 32, 34. (2)(3) Rotenhan, *Die Rotenhan*, 195–8. (4) Ibid., 120–1.

Erasmus von Rotenhan (1489): StAW, Ldf, no. 15, pp. 219–21.

Heinrich Rüdt von Collenberg (1465–73): StAB, Hofrat Ansbach-Bayreuth, no. 528; Priebatsch (ed.), *Politische Correspondenz des Kurfürsten Albrecht Achilles*, I, 521, 523, 540, nos. 597, 602, 641. (4) Gabriele Enders, 'Genealogie der Familie Rüdt von Collenberg und Bödigheim im Spätmittelalter', (*Zulassungsarbeit*, University of Würzburg, 1979), 69.

Silvester von Schaumberg (1501–3): StAB, Fehde-Akten, no. 133. (1) Alban Freiherr von Dobeneck, 'Geschichte des ausgestorbenen Geschlechtes der von Sparneck', part 1, 50; Oskar Freiherr von Schaumberg, *Neuaufstellungen der Stammtafeln des uradelig fränkischen Geschlechts von Schaumberg* (Bamberg, 1953), table 5. (2) StAW, Stb, no. 791, fols. 96ʳ–97ᵛ. (3) Müller, *Die ständische Vertretung*, 344.

Adam von Schaumberg (1507): Heinz, 'Selbitz', 19. (2) Cf. Eyb, *Freiherren von Eyb*, 160 and Schaumberg, *Stammtafeln*, table 6. (4) Cf. Schaumberg, *Stammtafeln*, table 6 and Albert Werminghoff, *Ludwig von Eyb der Ältere (1417–1502): Ein Beitrag zur fränkischen und deutschen Geschichte im 15. Jahrhundert* (Halle, 1919), 151.

Karl von Schaumberg (1483–91): StAB, Fehde-Akten, no. 133; Priebatsch (ed.), *Politische Correspondenz des Kurfürsten Albrecht Achilles*, III, 284, 300, nos. 986, 1001; Adalbert von Keller (ed.), *Die Geschichten und Taten Wilwolts von Schaumburg* (Stuttgart, 1859), 58. (2) Keller (ed.), *Wilwolts von Schaumburg*, 58; Hellmut Kunstmann, *Die Burgen der östlichen fränkischen Schweiz* (Würzburg, 1965), 58.

Konrad von Schaumberg (1479): Priebatsch (ed.), *Politische Correspondenz des Kurfürsten Albrecht Achilles*, II, 545–6, no. 586. (2) Schaumberg, *Stammtafeln*, table 7.

Karl Schenk von Arberg (*c.* 1520): Schlecht (ed.), 'Die Kleinen Annalen des Kilian Leib', 65.

Baron Gottfried Schenk von Limpurg (1511): Herolt, *Chronica zeit- unnd Jarbuch von der Statt Hall*, 121–2. (3) StAN, AA-Akten, no. 1402, fol. 29ʳ.

Simon (VI) von Schlitz genannt von Görtz (1484): Friedrich Battenberg (ed.), *Schlitzer Urkunden: Regesten zum Urkundenarchiv der Grafen von Schlitz gen. von Görtz (Abt. B 8) 1285–1939*, 2 vols. (Darmstadt, 1979), I, 35–6, no. 143. (2) Ibid., II, table 1. (3)

Ibid., I, 44, no. 149. (4) Cf. ibid., II, table 1 and Demandt, *Der Personenstaat*, II, 763, no. 2686.

Ludwig (I) von Schlitz genannt von Görtz (1484): Battenberg (ed.), *Schlitzer Urkunden*, I, 35–6, no. 143. (4) Cf. ibid., II, table 1 and Demandt, *Der Personenstaat*, II, 763, no. 2686.

Heinrich (II) von Schlitz genannt von Görtz (1445): Luckhard (ed.), *Regesten der Herren von Ebersberg*, 135, no. 489. (2) Demandt, *Der Personenstaat*, II, 763, no. 2685.

Otto von Schlitz genannt von Görtz (1445): Luckhard (ed.), *Regesten der Herren von Ebersberg*, 135, no. 489.

Konrad Schott (*c.* 1490): Keller (ed.), *Wilwolts von Schaumburg*, 70–1. (1) Cf. Wilhelm, 'Die Edeln von und zum Absberg', 59, 84 and StAN, AA-Akten, no. 1402, fols. 164^v–168^v. (2) StAN, AA-Akten, no. 1402, fols. 169^v–171^v. (3) StAN, Brandenburger Literalien, no. 582. (4) Cf. Karl Hofmann, 'Das pfälzische Amt Boxberg zur Zeit des Bauernaufstands 1525', *ZGO* 97 (1949), 467–97, at 467, Rochus Freiherr von Liliencron (ed.), *Die historischen Volkslieder der Deutschen vom 13. bis 16. Jahrhundert*, vol. II (Leipzig, 1866), 351–3, no. 193 and Keller (ed.), *Wilwolts von Schaumburg*, 7, 70.

Heinz Schott (1470): StAN, AA-Akten, no. 737, prod. of Samstag nach Oculi [31 March] 1470. (2) Cf. ibid., prod. of Sonntag Judica [8 April] 1470 and Johann Gottfried Biedermann, *Geschlechtsregister der Reichsfrey unmittelbaren Ritterschaft Landes zu Franken löblichen Orts Baunach* (Bayreuth, 1747), table 157. (4) Cf. StAW, Würzburger Lehenbücher, no. 24, fol. 127^v and Biedermann, *Orts Baunach*, table 157.

Lutz Schott (1473): StAN, Reichsstadt Nürnberg, 35 Neue Laden der unteren Losungs-stube, V 90/2 2447. (2) Hofmann, 'Das pfälzische Amt Boxberg', 467.

Baron Sigmund of Schwarzenberg (1460–92): StAN, Fstm.Ansb., Fehdeakten, nos. 32a, 52; StAB, Hofrat Ansbach-Bayreuth, no. 535; ibid., Fehde-Akten, no. 102; Bachmann (ed.), *Briefe und Acten zur österreichisch-deutschen Geschichte*, 415–17, no. 323; Fries, *Historie*, 834, 836; Constantin Höfler (ed.), 'Fränkische Studien IV.', parts 1–3, *Archiv für Kunde österreichischer Geschichtsquellen* 7 (1851), 1–146; 8 (1852), 235–322; 11 (1853), 1–56: part 1, 127, no. 113. (2) Karl Fürst zu Schwarzenberg, *Geschichte des reichsständischen Hauses Schwarzenberg* (Neustadt a.d. Aisch, 1963), 58. (4) Ibid., 43.

Baron Johann of Schwarzenberg (1519): StAN, Fstm.Ansb., Fehdeakten, no. 69, prod. 10–11. (1) Theodor Ruf, *Die Grafen von Rieneck: Genealogie und Territorienbildung*, 2 vols. (Würzburg, 1984), I, 108. (2) Schwarzenberg, *Schwarzenberg*, 61. (4) Ibid., 58.

Baron Hermann of Schwarzenberg (1448): StAN, AA-Akten, no. 515, prod. of Dienstag nach Johannis baptiste [25 June] 1448; StAB, Hofrat Ansbach-Bayreuth, no. 504. (2) StAB, Hofrat Ansbach-Bayreuth, no. 504. (3) Amrhein, 'Gotfrid Schenk von Limpurg', part 3, 102; Zeißner, *Rudolf II. von Scherenberg*, 39. (4) Schwarzenberg, *Schwarzenberg*, 43.

Baron Friedrich of Schwarzenberg (1531–44): Geheimes Staatsarchiv, XX.HA: Hist. Staatsarchiv Königsberg, Herzogliches Briefarchiv, A 4, 1534 January 29 (K. 191); *Unser Friderichen Freyherren von Schwartzenberg und zu Hohenlandsperg . . .*; Kolb (ed.), *Widmans Chronica*, 290. (2) StAN, AA-Akten, no. 1402, fol. 62^v; Schwarzenberg, *Schwarzenberg*, 69; Reuschling, *Die Regierung des Hochstifts Würzburg*, 191–2. (3) StAN, AA-Akten, no. 1402, fol. 50^r. (4) Schwarzenberg, *Schwarzenberg*, 61.

Kilian von Seckendorff (1524–9): StAN, Fstm.Ansb., Fehdeakten, no. 110. (3) StAN,

Fstm.Ansb., Landtagsakten, Tom. 8, no. 36, fol. 145^r. (4) Rechter, *Die Seckendorff*, I, 137, 142.

Hans von Seckendorf (1524–9): StAN, Fstm.Ansb., Fehdeakten, no. 110. (1) Cf. Rechter, *Die Seckendorff*, II, 204 and StAN, BK, R, 21. (2) Rechter, *Die Seckendorff*, II, 204. (3) Ibid., 205.

Lamprecht von Seckendorff (1463–5): StAW, Stb, no. 717, fols. 299^r–301^v; ibid., Stb, no. 892, fols. 266^v–267^r; Fries, *Historie*, 838–40. (2) StAW, Stb, no. 717, fol. 299^r. (4) Rechter, *Die Seckendorff*, I, 120.

Hans Arnold von Seckendorff (1542): Rechter, *Die Seckendorff*, II, 215. (1) Cf. ibid., 214 and Eyb, *Freiherren von Eyb*, 153, 189. (3) Rechter, *Die Seckendorff*, II, 215. (4) Ibid., 204.

Balthasar von Seckendorff (1510): Rechter, *Die Seckendorff*, II, 55. (2) Ibid., 54.

Hans von Seckendorff (1445): Würdinger, *Kriegsgeschichte*, I, 287; Rechter, *Die Seckendorff*, I, 150. (2) Ibid., 148.

Hans von Seckendorff (1472): 'Hellers Chronic', part 1, 130–1; Burkhardt (ed.), *Das funfft merckisch Buech*, 225–6, 266–71, nos. 133, 153. (2) Gerhard Rechter, *Die Seckendorff: Quellen und Studien zur Genealogie und Besitzgeschichte*, vol. III (forthcoming), 32–5.

Hans von Seinsheim (1501–12): StAW, Stb, no. 788, part 3, under 'S'; ibid., Stb, no. 1012, fol. 479^v; StAN, Fstm.Ansb., Fehdeakten, no. 11; StAB, Hofrat Ansbach-Bayreuth, no. 561; Engel (ed.), *Die Rats-Chronik*, 70, no. 213. (4) Cf. StAN, Fstm.Ansb., Fehdeakten, no. 11, prod. 10 and Amrhein, 'Gottfrid Schenk von Limpurg', part 3, 104.

Erkinger von Seinsheim (1479–81): StAN, Fstm.Ansb., Fehdeakten, no. 52. (1) Eyb, *Freiherren von Eyb*, 78, 120. (2) Eberhard Graf von Fugger, *Die Seinsheim und ihre Zeit: Eine Familien- und Kulturgeschichte von 1155 bis 1890* (Munich, 1893), 160–1. (4) Cf. ibid., 159–61 and StAN, Fstm.Ansb., Fehdeakten, no. 25b, prod. 3.

Philipp von Seinsheim (1460): StAN, Fstm.Ansb., Fehdeakten, no. 32a. (2) Fugger, *Die Seinsheim*, 183–4.

Ludwig von Seinsheim (1455–6): StAN, Fstm.Ansb., Fehdeakten, no. 25b. (2) Ibid., prod. 3. (4) Fugger, *Die Seinsheim*, 144, 159.

Neidhard von Seinsheim (*c.* 1460): StAW, Ldf, no. 12, p. 733.

Baron Michael of Seinsheim-Schwarzenberg (1469): Engel (ed.), *Die Rats-Chronik*, 31–2, nos. 96–7. (1) Cf. Schwarzenberg, *Schwarzenberg*, 47, Dieter Michael Feineis, 'Überblick über die Geschichte der Herrschaft Klingenberg bis zum Beginn des 16. Jahrhunderts', *Würzburger Diözesangeschichtsblätter* 54 (1992), 153–76, at 176 and Körner, 'Die Familie von Hutten', 64. (2) Engel (ed.), *Die Rats-Chronik*, 31, no. 96. (3) Priebatsch (ed.), *Politische Correspondenz des Kurfürsten Albrecht Achilles*, II, 567, no. 621; Steinau-Steinrück, 'Geschichte des fränkischen Geschlechtes von Steinau genannt Steinrück', 64; Zeißner, *Rudolf II. von Scherenberg*, 39. (4) Schwarzenberg, *Schwarzenberg*, 48.

Hans von Selbitz (*c.* 1500): StAN, AA-Akten, no. 515 [unpaginated, n.d.].

Sebastian von Sparneck (1512–23): StAB, Hofrat Ansbach-Bayreuth, no. 563; Baader (ed.), *Verhandlungen über Thomas von Absberg*, 60. (3) Cf. StAN, AA-Akten, 1402, fol. 169^r, Dobeneck, 'Geschichte des ausgestorbenen Geschlechtes der von Sparneck', part 1, 63–4 and Müller, *Die ständische Vertretung*, 350. (4) Dobeneck 'Geschichte des ausgestorbenen Geschlechtes der von Sparneck', part 1, 63–4.

Sources of information for Appendixes

Fritz von Sparneck (1472): Burkhardt (ed.), *Das funfft merckisch Buech*, 211. (2) Priebatsch (ed.), *Politische Correspondenz des Kurfürsten Albrecht Achilles*, III, 363, no. 1050.

Wolf von Sparneck (1523): Baader (ed.), *Verhandlungen über Thomas von Absberg*, 60. (4) Dobeneck 'Geschichte des ausgestorbenen Geschlechtes der von Sparneck', part 1, 35.

Hertnidt von Stein (zu Ostheim) (1465–71): Becker, *Die Riedesel*, I, 254–62. (2) Matthias Thumser, *Hertnidt vom Stein (ca. 1427–1491): Bamberger Domdekan und markgrä-flich-brandenburger Rat. Karriere zwischen Kirche und Fürstendienst* (Neustadt a.d. Aisch, 1989), 73.

Siegfried von Stein (zu Ostheim) (1465–71): Becker, *Die Riedesel*, I, 254–62. (1) *Genealogisches Handbuch des in Bayern immatrikulierten Adels*, vol. VI (Neustadt a.d. Aisch, 1957), 316. (2) Ibid., (3) StAW, Ldf, no. 15, pp. 142–6.

Hans von Steinau (1459): Johann Friedrich Schannat (ed.), *Fuldischer Lehn-Hof sive de clientela fuldensi beneficiaria nobili et equestri tractatus* (Frankfurt am Main, 1726), 335, no. 477. (2)(3) Steinau-Steinrück, 'Geschichte des fränkischen Geschlechtes von Steinau genannt Steinrück', 29, 38, 49, 56. (4) Ibid., 28–9.

Jakob von Steinau (1459): Schannat (ed.), *Fuldischer Lehn-Hof*, 335, no. 477. (2)(3) Steinau-Steinrück, 'Geschichte des fränkischen Geschlechtes von Steinau genannt Steinrück', 29, 38, 49–50, 55. (4) Ibid., 28–9.

Heinrich von Steinrück (1457): Steinau-Steinrück, 'Geschichte des fränkischen Ge-schlechtes von Steinau genannt Steinrück', 62. (1) Cf. Ibid., 36 and Morsel, 'Une société politique en Franconie', 339. (2) Steinau-Steinrück, 'Geschichte des frän-kischen Geschlechtes von Steinau genannt Steinrück', 38. (3) Ibid., 38–9. (4) Ibid., 33–4.

Heinrich von Steinrück (1459): Schannat (ed.), *Fuldischer Lehn-Hof*, 335, no. 477. (2)(3) Steinau-Steinrück, 'Geschichte des fränkischen Geschlechtes von Steinau genannt Steinrück', 71–2. (4) Ibid., 38–9, 43.

Hildebrand von Steinrück (1459–73): Schannat (ed.), *Fuldischer Lehn-Hof*, 335, no. 477; Spangenberg, *Hennebergische Chronica*, 404; StAW, Adel, no. 1114, prod. of Donners-tag nach Francisci [7 October] 1473. (2) Steinau-Steinrück, 'Geschichte des fränkischen Geschlechtes von Steinau genannt Steinrück', 72. (4) Ibid., 38–9, 43.

Otto von Steinrück (1459): Schannat (ed.), *Fuldischer Lehn-Hof*, 335, no. 477; Spangen-berg, *Hennebergische Chronica*, 404. (3) Steinau-Steinrück, 'Geschichte des frän-kischen Geschlechtes von Steinau genannt Steinrück', 43, 65. (4) Ibid., 38–9, 43.

Konrad von Steinrück (1459): Schannat (ed.), *Fuldischer Lehn-Hof*, 335, no. 477. (1) Cf. Steinau-Steinrück, 'Geschichte des fränkischen Geschlechtes von Steinau genannt Steinrück', 63 and Bibra, *Reichsfreiherrn von Bibra*, II, 101, 106. (3) Steinau-Steinrück, 'Geschichte des fränkischen Geschlechtes von Steinau genannt Steinrück', 43. (4) Ibid., 38–9, 43.

Wilhelm d.J. von Stetten (1460–1): StAB, Hofrat Ansbach-Bayreuth, no. 513.

Kaspar von Stetten (1460–1): ibid. (1) Cf. Möller, *Stamm-Tafeln*, II, table 74 and Jürgen Rauser, 'Die Ahnen der Herren von Stetten 1166–1966', *Hohenloher Historische Hefte* 17 (1967), 1–66, at 39.

Hans von Stetten (1460–1): StAB, Hofrat Ansbach-Bayreuth, no. 513.

Kilian von Stetten (1488–9): Stetten, 'Ein Fehdebrief vom Jahre 1489'.

Sebastian Stiebar (1508–9): StAA, Ganerbschaft Rothenberg, no. 2538a, anno 1508, 1509.

(2) Seefried, *Stiebar-Archiv*, 47–8. (4) Cf. ibid., 47 and Johann Gottfried Biedermann, *Geschlechtsregister der Reichsfrey unmittelbaren Ritterschaft Landes zu Franken löblichen Orts Gebürg* (Bamberg, 1747), table 235.

Albrecht d.J. Stiebar (1492–1501): StAA, Ganerbschaft Rothenberg, no. 2538a, anno 1501; StAB, Fehde-Akten, no. 133; Seefried, *Stiebar-Archiv*, 8–9; Würdinger, *Kriegsgeschichte*, II, 117. (1) Cf. Biedermann, *Orts Gebürg*, table 235, Otto Schnell, 'Geschichte der Salzburg an der fränkischen Saale: Mit besonderer Rücksicht auf die Zeit von der Uebergabe der Burg an Bischof Heinrich von Würzburg bis auf den heutigen Tag', *AU* 29 (1886), 1–128, at 37 and Seefried, *Stiebar-Archiv*, 8. (2) Seefried, *Stiebar-Archiv*, 8. (4) Biedermann, *Orts Gebürg*, table 235.

Ebold Stiebar (1500): StAB, Fehde-Akten, no. 152, prod. 25; ibid., Fehde-Akten, no. 133. (4) Cf. StAB, Fehde-Akten, no. 133 and Seefried, *Stiebar-Archiv*, 8.

Rochus von Streitberg (1530): Looshorn, *Bamberg*, IV, 789–91; A. Grötsch, 'Eine blutige Ritterfehde aus dem 16. Jahrhundert (Familie Streitberg)', *Die Oberpfalz* 16 (1922), 119–20. (2) StAN, AA-Akten, no. 838, fol. 4ʳ.

Balthasar von Streitberg (1530): Looshorn, *Bamberg*, IV, 789–91; A. Grötsch, 'Eine blutige Ritterfehde'.

Gabriel von Streitberg (1530): Looshorn, *Bamberg*, IV, 789–91; Grötsch, 'Eine blutige Ritterfehde'. (2) Cf. Hellmut Kunstmann, *Die Burgen der westlichen und nördlichen fränkischen Schweiz*, vol. II, *Der Nordwesten und Norden: Leinleitertal, Aufsesstal und oberes Wiesenttal und Randgebiete* (Würzburg, 1972), 9, 16, 278 and StAB, Bauernkriegsakten, no. 7, Streitberg, prod. 5.

Paul von Streitberg (*c.* 1479): Priebatsch (ed.), *Politische Correspondenz des Kurfürsten Albrecht Achilles*, II, 606 n. 1, no. 659; Paul Oesterreicher, *Die Burg Streitberg* (Bamberg, 1819), 14. (2) Oesterreicher, *Burg Streitberg*, 14. (3) Ibid., 15; StAB, Fehde-Akten, no. 111.

Eberhard von Streitberg (1498): Oesterreicher, *Burg Streitberg*, 46. (2) Ibid., 29, 40.

Melchior Süzel (1503): StAW, Stb, no. 788, part 3, under 'S'; StAA, Ganerbschaft Rothenberg, no. 2538a, anno 1503. (1) Cf. StAW, Stb, no. 1012, fol. 560ᵛ, Biedermann, *Orts Ottenwald*, table 418 and Seefried, *Stiebar-Archiv*, 7.

Reuß von Thüngen (1448): Amrhein, 'Gotfrid Schenk von Limpurg', part 3, 90–1; Morsel, 'Une société politique en Franconie', 784. (2) Morsel, 'Une société politique en Franconie', 339–40.

Sigmund von Thüngen (1486–92): StAB, Fehde-Akten, no. 102; Höfler (ed.), 'Fränkische Studien IV.', part 1, 127, no. 113. (2) Morsel, 'Une société politique en Franconie', 341. (4) Thüngen, 'Familie derer von Thüngen', 99.

Philipp von Thüngen (1472): Spangenberg, *Hennebergische Chronica*, 277; Stein (ed.), *Monumenta Suinfurtensia*, 364. (2) Morsel, 'Une société politique en Franconie', 305. (4) Ibid., 304, 1504.

Eustachius von Thüngen (1511): Herolt, *Chronica zeit- unnd Jarbuch von der Statt Hall*, 121–2; Ulmschneider (ed.), *Mein Fehd und Handlung*, 88–90. (2) Morsel, 'Une société politique en Franconie', 305–6. (4) Ibid., 304, 1509.

Werner von Thüngen (1473–82): Morsel, 'Une société politique en Franconie', 784. (1) Cf. ibid., 1508 and Steinau-Steinrück, 'Geschichte des fränkischen Geschlechtes von Steinau genannt Steinrück', 38, 49. (2) Thüngen, 'Familie derer von Thüngen', 21. (4) Morsel, 'Une société politique en Franconie', 339, 1508.

Sources of information for Appendixes

Heinz von Thüngfeld (1463): StAN, Fstm.Ansb., Urfehden, Fehdesachen, Urkunden, no. 25.

Wilhelm von Vellberg (1519): StAN, Fstm.Ansb., Fehdeakten, no. 105a. (2) Wunder, 'Die Ritter von Vellberg', 135, 167, 177. (3) StAN, Verträge mit dem Adel, Velberg 1. (4) Wunder, 'Die Ritter von Vellberg', 135, 167.

Wolf von Vellberg (1519): StAN, Fstm.Ansb., Fehdeakten, no. 105a. (1) Walter Bernhardt, *Die Zentralbehörden des Herzogtums Württemberg und ihre Beamten 1520–1629*, vol. II (Stuttgart, 1972), 681. (2) StAN, BK, F, 15; Wunder, 'Die Ritter von Vellberg', 184–5. (3) Müller, *Die ständische Vertretung*, 348. (4) Wunder, 'Die Ritter von Vellberg', 135, 168.

Stefan von Vestenberg (1466–73): StAN, AA-Akten, no. 580, prod. 2; ibid., Fstm.Ansb., Fehdeakten, no. 42, prod. 6, 12. (2) Ibid., Fstm.Ansb., Fehdeakten, no. 42, prod. 3.

Veit von Vestenberg (1466–1501): StAN, Fstm.Ansb., Fehdeakten, nos. 10, 42; ibid., Urfehden, Fehdesachen, Urkunden, nos. 25, 30, 32; ibid., AA-Akten, no. 580, prod. 2; ibid., AA-Akten, no. 392, prod. of Sonntag nach Michaelis archang. [4 October] and of Dienstag nach Francisci [6 October] 1500; ibid., Ansbacher Historica, no. 210; ibid., Akten des siebenfarbigen Alphabets, no. 35, prod. 49; StAB, Hofrat Ansbach-Bayreuth, nos. 522, 535; StAW, Adel, no. 1114, prod. of Donnerstag nach Francisci [7 October] 1473. (1) Cf. Otto Rohn, 'Die Herren von Lentersheim im Mittelalter', *Alt-Gunzenhausen* 37 (1977), 31–47 at 35 and Otto Rohn, 'Die Herren von Lentersheim. Zweiter Teil: Vom Erwerb des Schlosses Altenmuhr im Jahr 1430 bis zum Erlöschen des Stammes im Jahr 1799', *Alt-Gunzenhausen* 38 (1979), 108–45, at 142. (2) StAN, AA-Akten, no. 392, prod. of Dienstag nach Assumptio Marie [18 August] 1500. (4) StAW, Ldf, no. 13, pp. 343–5.

Matern von Vestenberg (1512–14): StAA, Ganerbschaft Rothenberg, no. 2538a, anno 1512–anno 1515. (2) StAN, AA-Akten, no. 808, fol. 63; StAW, Stb, no. 791, fols. 54ʳ–56ʳ.

Kaspar von Vestenberg (1466–89): StAN, AA-Akten, no. 580, prod. 2; ibid., Ansbacher Historica, no. 210; StAB, Hofrat Ansbach-Bayreuth, no. 522. (2) StAN, Ansbacher Historica, no. 210, prod. of Veitstag [15 June] 1485. (4) Cf. ibid., prod. of Dienstag nach Matthei ap. [22 September] 1489 and StAW, Stb, no. 1012, fol. 545ʳ.

Eukarius von Vestenberg (1484–9): StAN, Ansbacher Historica, no. 210. (2) StAW, Stb, no. 790, fols. 4ᵛ–5ʳ; Theodor Neuhofer, *Gabriel von Eyb, Fürstbischof von Eichstätt 1455–1535: Ein Lebensbild aus der Wende vom Mittelalter zur Neuzeit* (Eichstätt, 1934), 35, 41. (4) Cf. StAN, Ansbacher Historica, no. 210, prod. of Dienstag nach Matthei ap. [22 September] 1489 and StAW, Stb, no. 1012, fol. 545ʳ.

Konrad von Vestenberg (1466–89): StAN, AA-Akten, no. 580, prod. 2; ibid., Fstm.Ansb., Fehdeakten, no. 42, prod. 12; ibid., Ansbacher Historica, no. 210.

Veit von Wallenrod (1477–96): StAB, Fehde-Akten, no. 76; StAN, AA-Akten, no. 1753; Priebatsch (ed.), *Politische Correspondenz des Kurfürsten Albrecht Achilles*, II, 311, no. 305; Würdinger, *Kriegsgeschichte*, II, 107; Rupprecht, *Ritterschaftliche Herrschaftswahrung in Franken*, 297–8, 299 n. 635, 334 n. 814. (2)(3) Rupprecht, *Ritterschaftliche Herrschaftswahrung in Franken*, 299 n. 635, 334.

Reinwold von Wemding (1502): StAN, Fstm.Ansb., Fehdeakten, no. 85a. (2) Cf. ibid., Wigulejus Hund, *Bayrisch Stammen Buch*, part 2 (Ingolstadt, 1598), 362, StAN, Ansbacher Historica, 340, fol. 71ᵛ and ibid., BK, W, 46.

Count Wilhelm of Wertheim (1469): StAN, AA-Akten, no. 737, prod. of Peterstag ad cathedram [22 February] 1469. (2) Wilhelm Störmer, *Miltenberg: Die Ämter Amorbach und Miltenberg des Mainzer Oberstifts als Modelle geistlicher Territorialität und Herrschaftsintensivierung* (Munich, 1979), 178. (4) Freytag von Loringhoven, *Europäische Stammtafeln*, n.s., XVI, table 153.

Count Albrecht of Wertheim (1460–1): StAB, Hofrat Ansbach-Bayreuth, no. 513. (2) Ibid., prod. 2; Joseph Aschbach, *Geschichte der Grafen von Wertheim von den ältesten Zeiten bis zu ihrem Erlöschen im Mannsstamme im Jahre 1556* (Frankfurt am Main, 1843), 227.

Count Erasmus of Wertheim (1505): Aschbach, *Grafen von Wertheim*, 285; Joseph Aschbach (ed.), *Wertheimisches Urkundenbuch*, part 2 of his *Grafen von Wertheim*, 311–13, no. 205. (1) Ruf, *Die Grafen von Rieneck*, I, 98, 102. (2) StAN, Ansbacher Historica, no. 340, fol. 50^v. (4) Cf. Freytag von Loringhoven, *Europäische Stammtafeln*, n.s., XVI, table 153 and Störmer, *Miltenberg*, 178.

Count Johann of Wertheim (1494): Joseph Chmel (ed.), *Urkunden, Briefe und Actenstücke zur Geschichte Maximilian's I. und seiner Zeit* (Stuttgart, 1845), 27–8, 33, nos. 35, 39. (2)(3) Zeißner, *Rudolf II. von Scherenberg*, 38. (4) Freytag von Loringhoven, *Europäische Stammtafeln*, n.s., XVI, table 153.

Moritz von Wildenstein (1549): StAB, Fehde-Akten, no. 221. (2) Reitzenstein, *Familie von Reitzenstein*, 280. (4) Cf. ibid., 278 and Dobeneck, 'Lüchau', 60.

Albrecht von Wirsberg (1491): StAB, Hofrat Ansbach Bayreuth, no. 543, prod 1. (2) Eduard Margerie (ed.), *Die Herren von Wirsberg: Urkundenauszüge von 1138–1719* (n.d., n.p.), 5.

Konrad von Wirsberg (1496): StAN, AA-Akten, no. 1753, 1831. (2) Ibid., AA-Akten, no. 1753, prod. of Mittwoch nach Jubilate [27 April] 1496; Margerie (ed.), *Herren von Wirsberg*, 63–4.

Soldan von Wirsberg (1474): 'Hellers Chronic', part 1, 132–6. (2) Eduard Margerie (ed.), *Die Wirsberger Blätter* (n.p., 1953–6), 4.

Albrecht (IV) von Wolfstein (1451): Amrhein, 'Gotfrid Schenk von Limpurg', part 3, 135–6. (2) Freytag von Loringhoven, *Europäische Stammtafeln*, n.s., XVI, table 91.

Hans (II) von Wolfstein (1451): Amrhein, 'Gotfrid Schenk von Limpurg', part 3, 135–6. (2) Freytag von Loringhoven, *Europäische Stammtafeln*, n.s., XVI, table 91.

Martin Zollner von Rothenstein (1479): Werner Spielberg, 'Martin Zollner von Rothenstein und seine Sippe', parts 1 and 2, *Familiengeschichtliche Blätter* 15 (1917), 129–36; 167–80, at 169. (1) Ibid., 133. (2) Ibid., 171; StAW, Ldf, no. 15, pp. 82–3.

Sources of information for Appendixes E and F

Paul von Absberg (1493): StAN, Fstm.Ansb., Fehdeakten, no. 67b. (1) Louis Ferdinand Freiherr von Eberstein, *Entwurf einer zusammenhängenden Stammreihe des freifränkischen Geschlechts Eberstein* (Berlin, 1887), 51. (2) StAN, Ansbacher Historica, no. 340, fol. 32ᵛ. (4) H. Wilhelm, 'Die Edeln von und zum Absberg: Ein Beitrag zur fränkischen Geschichte', *Alt-Gunzenhausen* 8 (1931), 57.

Konrad (X) von Aufseß (1463): Otto Freiherr von Aufseß, *Geschichte des uradelichen Aufseß'schen Geschlechtes in Franken* (Berlin, 1888), 147. (2) Ibid., 147, 149. (4) Ibid., 117.

Götz von Berlichingen (1505–14): Helgard Ulmschneider (ed.), *Götz von Berlichingen: Mein Fehd und Handlung* (Sigmaringen, 1981), 81–8, 91–8. (2) Helgard Ulmschneider, *Götz von Berlichingen: Ein adeliges Leben der deutschen Renaissance* (Sigmaringen, 1974), 97. (3) Ibid., 204. (4) Rudolf Karl Reinhard Freiherr von Thüngen, 'Zur Genealogie der Familie derer von Thüngen', *AU* 54 (1912), 1–181, at 21–5.

Erasmus von Eberstein (1456): Johannes Müllner, *Die Annalen der Reichsstadt Nürnberg von 1623*, ed. Gerhard Hirschmann, 2 vols. (Nuremberg, 1972–84), II, 512. (2) Eberstein, *Stammreihe des freifränkischen Geschlechts Eberstein*, 44–6. (4) Ibid., 42.

Mangold von Eberstein (1516–22): Louis Ferdinand Freiherr von Eberstein (ed.), *'Dem Landfrieden ist nicht zu trauen': Fehde Mangold's von Eberstein zum Brandenstein gegen die Reichsstadt Nürnberg 1516–1522. Charakterbild der rechtlichen und wirtschaftlichen Zustände im deutschen Reiche unmittelbar vor dem grossen Bauernkriege* (Nordhausen, 1868). (2) Eberstein, *Stammreihe des freifränkischen Geschlechts Eberstein*, 37.

Kaspar von Eyb (1510): StAN, Fstm.Ansb., Fehdeakten, no. 13. (2) Ibid., prod. 4. (4) Eberhard Freiherr von Eyb, *Das reichsritterliche Geschlecht der Freiherren von Eyb* (Neustadt a.d. Aisch, 1984), 90.

Christoph von Giech (1499–1500): StAN, Bb, no. 45, passim; *Verhandlungen zwischen der Stadt Nürnberg und der fränkischen Ritterschaft wegen Christoph von Giech und Contz Schott* (Nuremberg, 1500). (4) Frank Baron Freytag von Loringhoven, *Europäische Stammtafeln: Stammtafeln zur Geschichte der europäischen Staaten*, n.s., ed. Detlev Schwennicke (Marburg, 1980–   ), V, table 25.

Albrecht Gottsmann (1521): StAA, Ganerbschaft Rothenberg, no. 2538a, anno 1521. (2) Cf. ibid. and Wilhelm Schwemmer, *Burg und Amt Veldenstein-Neuhaus* (Nuremberg, 1961), 114. (4) Hugo A. Braun, *Das Domkapitel zu Eichstätt: Von der Reformationszeit bis zur Säkularisation (1535–1806). Verfassung und Personalgeschichte* (Stuttgart, 1991), 241–2.

Count Wilhelm (III) of Henneberg (1455): Friedrich Stein (ed.), *Monumenta Suinfurtensia historica inde ab anno DCCXCI usque ad annum MDC: Denkmäler der Schweinfurter*

Geschichte bis zum Ende des sechzehnten Jahrhunderts (Schweinfurt, 1875), 353. (1) Freytag von Loringhoven, *Europäische Stammtafeln*, n.s., XVI, table 147. (3) Sebastian Zeißner, *Rudolf II. von Scherenberg: Fürstbischof von Würzburg 1466–1495*, 2nd edn (Würzburg, 1952), 42.

Darius von Heßberg (1489): *Die Chroniken der fränkischen Städte, Nürnberg*, 5 vols. (Leipzig, 1862–74), V, 551. (1) Cf. StAN, Fstm.Ansb., no. 26, prod. 55, Rudolf M. Kloos (ed.), *Die Inschriften des Landkreises Bamberg bis 1650* (Munich, 1980), 32, no. 75 and Otto Graf Seefried, *Aus dem Stiebar-Archiv: Forschungen zur Familiengeschichte von Bauer, Bürger und Edelmann in Ober- und Mittelfranken* (Nuremberg, 1953), 7. (2) StAN, Fstm.Ansb., Fehdeakten, no. 26, prod. 6, 16, 41.

Karl von Heßberg (1524): StAN, AA-Akten, no. 392, prod. of Mittwoch nach Esto mihi [9 February] 1524. (2) Ibid., (3) StAN, AA-Akten, no. 1402, fols. 23ᵛ–24ʳ.

Ludwig von Hutten (1441): GNM, Hs. 22 547, fol. 44ᵛ; Müllner, *Die Annalen der Reichsstadt Nürnberg*, II, 349.

Hans von Kotzau (1463): Alban Freiherr von Dobeneck, 'Die Geschichte des ausgestorbenen Geschlechts von Kotzau', *AO* 24, no. 1 (1909), 1–111, at 63.

Hans d.J. von Kotzau (1459–63): ibid., 56–7. (4) Ibid., 49.

Jobst von Lüchau (1502): StAN, Bb, no. 48, fol. 179ʳ–180ʳ. (2) Alban Freiherr von Dobeneck, 'Geschichte des ausgestorbenen Geschlechtes von Lüchau', *AO* 24, no. 3 (1911), 22–194, at 117. (4) Ibid.

Erhard Marschall von Ebwang (1472): *Chroniken der fränkischen Städte, Nürnberg*, IV, 332–3. (2) Felix Priebatsch (ed.), *Politische Correspondenz des Kurfürsten Albrecht Achilles*, 3 vols. (Leipzig, 1894–98), I, 459, no. 493.

Georg Marschall von Pappenheim (1514–15): StAN, Fstm. Ansb., Fehdeakten, no. 97a. (1) Cf. Haupt Graf zu Pappenheim, *Die Frühen Pappenheimer Marschälle: Zweiter Teil der Hausgeschichte vom XV. bis zum XVIII. Jahrhundert* (Munich, 1951), 63 and Wigulejus Hund, *Bayrisch Stammen Buch*, part 2 (Ingolstadt, 1598), 189. (2) Pappenheim, *Pappenheimer Marschälle*, 63. (4) Ibid., 62–3.

Count Ulrich of Oettingen (1448): StAN, Fstm.Ansb., Fehdeakten, no. 16 [alte Signatur]. (1) Frank Baron Freytag von Loringhoven, *Europäische Stammtafeln: Stammtafeln zur Geschichte der europäischen Staaten*, n.s., ed. Detlev Schwennicke, (Marburg, 1980–), XVI, table 99. (2) Walther Pfeilsticker (ed.), *Neues Württembergisches Dienerbuch*, 2 vols. (Stuttgart, 1957–63), I, no. 1130. (4) Wilhelm Karl Prinz von Isenburg and Frank Baron Freytag von Loringhoven, *Europäische Stammtafeln: Stammtafeln zur Geschichte der europäischen Staaten*, 5 vols. (Marburg, 1956–78), V, table 150.

Georg von Rosenberg (1467–1500): StAN, Reichsstadt Windsheim, Akten, no. 15; Friedrich Pietsch (ed.), *Die Urkunden des Archivs der Reichsstadt Schwäbisch Hall*, 2 vols. (Stuttgart, 1972), II, 337, U 2636; Müllner, *Die Annalen der Reichsstadt Nürnberg*, II, 574–5; Karl Klüpfel (ed.), *Urkunden zur Geschichte des Schwäbischen Bundes (1488–1533)*, 2 vols. (Stuttgart, 1846–53), I, 429.

Albrecht von Rosenberg (1539–55): Joseph Frey, 'Die Fehde der Herren von Rosenberg auf Boxberg mit dem Schwäbischen Bund und ihre Nachwirkungen (1523–1555)' (PhD thesis, University of Tübingen, 1924); StAN, Bb, no. 134, fols. 3ᵛ–5ʳ; 39ᵛ–42ᵛ. (1) (I) Cf. Walther Möller, *Stamm-Tafeln westdeutscher Adels-Geschlechter im Mittelalter*, 3 vols. (Darmstadt, 1922–36), II, table 74 and Eberhard Graf von Fugger, *Die Seinsheim und ihre Zeit: Eine Familien- und Kulturgeschichte von 1155 bis 1890*

(Munich, 1893), 187; (II) cf. Johann Gottfried Biedermann, *Geschlechtsregister der Reichsfrey unmittelbaren Ritterschaft Landes zu Franken löblichen Orts Ottenwald* (Kulmbach, 1751), table 404a, Möller, *Stamm-Tafeln,* II, table 74 and Seefried, *Stiebar-Archiv,* 48.

Thomas von Rosenberg (1441): Müllner, *Die Annalen der Reichsstadt Nürnberg,* II, 349.

Lutz von Rotenhan (1455): Stein (ed.), *Monumenta Suinfurtensia,* 353. (1) Cf. Gottfried Freiherr von Rotenhan, *Die Rotenhan: Genealogie einer fränkischen Familie von 1229 bis zum Dreißigjährigen Krieg* (Neustadt a.d. Aisch, 1985), 195 and Pappenheim, *Pappenheimer Marschälle,* 32, 34. (2)(3) Rotenhan, *Die Rotenhan,* 195–8. (4) Ibid., 120–1.

Heinrich Rüdt von Collenberg (1455–65): StAN, Fstm.Ansb., Fehdeakten, no. 29; Pietsch (ed.), *Urkunden des Archivs der Reichsstadt Schwäbisch Hall,* II, 310, U 2503; Müllner, *Die Annalen der Reichsstadt Nürnberg,* II, 507–8. (4) Gabriele Enders, 'Genealogie der Familie Rüdt von Collenberg und Bödigheim im Spätmittelalter', (*Zulassungsarbeit,* University of Würzburg, 1979), 69, 71.

Eberhard d.J. Rüdt von Collenberg (1452–5): StAN, Reichsstadt Windsheim, Akten, no. 14; StAN, Fstm.Ansb., Fehdeakten, no. 29; Müllner, *Die Annalen der Reichsstadt Nürnberg,* II, 507–8.

Veit von Schaumberg (1449): Müllner, *Die Annalen der Reichsstadt Nürnberg,* II, 407. (2) Cf. Oskar Freiherr von Schaumberg, *Neuaufstellungen der Stammtafeln des uradelig fränkischen Geschlechts von Schaumberg* (Bamberg, 1953), table 6 and Priebatsch, *Politische Correspondenz des Kurfürsten Albrecht Achilles,* III, 284, no. 986.

Konrad Schott (1499): StAN, Bb, no. 45, passim; *Verhandlungen zwischen der Stadt Nürnberg und der fränkischen Ritterschaft.* (1) Cf. Wilhelm, 'Die Edeln von und zum Absberg', 59, 84 and StAN, AA-Akten, no. 1402, fols. 164ᵛ–168ᵛ. (2) StAN, AA-Akten, no. 1402, fols. 169ᵛ–171ᵛ. (3) StAN, Brandenburger Literalien, no. 582. (4) Cf. Karl Hofmann, 'Das pfälzische Amt Boxberg zur Zeit des Bauernaufstands 1525', *ZGO* 97 (1949), 467–97, at 467, Rochus Freiherr von Liliencron (ed.), *Die historischen Volkslieder der Deutschen vom 13. bis 16. Jahrhundert,* vol. II (Leipzig, 1866), 351–3, no. 193 and Adalbert von Keller (ed.), *Die Geschichten und Taten Wilwolts von Schaumburg* (Stuttgart, 1859), 7, 70.

Baron Georg of Schwarzenberg (1454): Lorenz Fries, *Historie, Nahmen, Geschlecht, Wesen, Thaten, gantz Leben und Sterben des gewesenen Bischoffen zu Wirtzburg und Hertzogen zu Francken,* in *Geschicht-Schreiber von dem Bischofftum Wirtzbürg* ed. Johann Peter Ludewig (Frankfurt am Main, 1713), 807–8; Fugger, *Die Seinsheim,* 145. (2)(3) Lore Muehlon, 'Johann III. von Grumbach, Bischof von Würzburg und Herzog zu Franken (1455–1466)' (PhD thesis, University of Würzburg, 1935), 171. (4) Cf. Freytag von Loringhoven, *Europäische Stammtafeln,* n.s., V, table 104 and StAB, Hofrat Ansbach-Bayreuth, no. 504.

Sebastian von Seckendorff (1508–12): StAN, Bb, no. 68, fol. 21ʳ; Gerhard Rechter, *Die Seckendorff: Quellen und Studien zur Genealogie und Besitzgeschichte,* 2 vols. (Neustadt a.d. Aisch, 1987–90), II, 71.

Sigmund von Seckendorff (1443): StAN, Reichsstadt Nürnberg, 35 neue Laden der unteren Losungsstube, V 89/1 2065. (2) Rechter, *Die Seckendorff,* II, 155.

Burkhard von Seckendorff (*c.* 1450): ibid., 153. (2) Ibid., 141.

Friedrich von Seckendorff (1462): ibid., 153. (4) Ibid., 141.

Sources of information for Appendixes

Engelhard von Seinsheim (1454): StAN, Reichsstadt Windsheim, Akten, no. 13, prod. 41.
Wilhelm von Seinsheim (1463): Müllner, *Die Annalen der Reichsstadt Nürnberg*, II, 551. (4) Cf. Fugger, *Die Seinsheim*, 159–61 and StAN, Fstm.Ansb., Fehdeakten, no. 25b, prod. 3.
Erkinger von Seinsheim (1463): Müllner, *Die Annalen der Reichsstadt Nürnberg*, II, 551. (1) Eyb, *Freiherren von Eyb*, 78, 120. (2) Fugger, *Die Seinsheim*, 160–1. (4) Cf. ibid., 159–61 and StAN, Fstm.Ansb., Fehdeakten, no. 25b, prod. 3.
Baron Michael of Seinsheim-Schwarzenberg (1442): Stein (ed.), *Monumenta Suinfurtensia*, 352. (2)(3) August Amrhein, 'Gotfrid Schenk von Limpurg: Bischof von Würzburg und Herzog zu Franken 1442–1455', part 3, *AU* 53 (1911), 1–153, at 102. (4) Freytag von Loringhoven, *Europäische Stammtafeln*, n.s., V, table 104.
Adam von Thüngen (1525–6): Franz Ludwig Baumann (ed.), *Quellen zur Geschichte des Bauernkriegs aus Rotenburg an der Tauber* (Tübingen,1878), 570, 576–80, 610–15. (1)(2)(3) StAN, AA-Akten, no. 1402, fols. 81^r–82^v. (4) Joseph Morsel, 'Une société politique en Franconie à la fin du Moyen Age: Les Thüngen, leurs princes, leurs pairs et leurs hommes (1275–1525)' (PhD thesis, University of Paris-IV Sorbonne, 1993), 341, 1505.
Sigmund von Thüngen (1500): Klüpfel (ed.), *Urkunden zur Geschichte des Schwäbischen Bundes*, I, 429. (2) Morsel, 'Une société politique en Franconie', 341. (4) Thüngen, 'Familie derer von Thüngen', 99.
Reuß von Thüngen (1462): Stein (ed.), *Monumenta Suinfurtensia*, 360. (2) Morsel, 'Une société politique en Franconie', 339.
Hans von Vestenberg (1450): StAN, Fstm.Ansb., Fehdeakten, no. 21 [alte Signatur]. (3) StAW, Ldf, no. 13, pp. 343–5.
Eitel Voit von Rieneck (1447): Müllner, *Die Annalen der Reichsstadt Nürnberg*, II, 392. (2) Amrhein, 'Gotfrid Schenk von Limpurg', part 3, 82–4, 104.
Friedrich von Waldenfels (1441–6): GNM, Hs. 22 547, fol. 46^r; Müllner, *Die Annalen der Reichsstadt Nürnberg*, II, 365–70; *Chroniken der fränkischen Städte, Nürnberg*, IV, 161. (2) Otto Freiherr von Waldenfels, *Die Freiherrn von Waldenfels: Stammfolgen mit urkundlichen Belegen*, 5 vols. (Munich, 1952–70), I, 159. (3) Ibid., 138. (4) ibid., 71.
Hans von Waldenfels (1441–6): GNM, Hs. 22 547, fol. 46^r; Müllner, *Die Annalen der Reichsstadt Nürnberg*, II, 365–70; *Chroniken der fränkischen Städte, Nürnberg*, IV, 161. (1) Cf. Waldenfels, *Freiherrn von Waldenfels*, I, 135 and StAB, Hofrat Ansbach-Bayreuth, no. 504. (2) Waldenfels, *Freiherrn von Waldenfels*, I, 141–2. (3) Ibid., 138, 141. (4) Ibid., 71.
Wendel von Wolfskeel (1517): StAN, Fstm.Ansb., Fehdeakten, no. 104, prod. 1. (2) Cf. StAW, Stb, no. 788, fols. 72^{r-v}, 74^{r-v}, Biedermann, *Orts Ottenwald*, table 6, Michael Renner (ed.), *Archiv der Grafen Wolffskeel von Reichenberg* (Munich, 1961), 3, 51, 52 and Freytag von Loringhoven, *Europäische Stammtafeln*, n.s., V, table 25.

Selected bibliography

MANUSCRIPT SOURCES

Staatsarchiv Amberg

Ganerbschaft Rothenberg (Rep. A I 20): 2538a.

Staatsarchiv Bamberg

Bauernkriegsakten (Rep. B 48): 7.
Fehde-Akten (Rep. J 8^I): 76; 79; 93; 101; 102; 111, 125; 133; 152; 166; 204; 211; 221.
Hofrat Ansbach-Bayreuth (Rep. C 3): 95; 166^i; 501; 504; 507; 508; 513; 519; 521; 522; 524; 527; 528; 529; 532; 535; 540; 543; 545; 546; 552; 553; 557; 559; 561; 563; 565; 574; 578; 579.

Geheimes Staatsarchiv, Preußischer Kulturbesitz, Berlin

XX.HA: Hist. Staatsarchiv Königsberg, Herzogliches Briefarchiv, A 4, 1534 Januar 29 (K. 191).

Freiherrlich Fuchs'sches Archiv, Schloß Burgpreppach

Schrank 1, 3, 4, 5; Urkunden.

Bayerisches Hauptstaatsarchiv München

Kurbayern, Äußeres Archiv: 2004.

Bibliothek des Germanischen Nationalmuseums Nürnberg

Hs 22 547.

Staatsarchiv Nürnberg

AA-Akten (Rep. 139a): 132/1; 392; 515; 580; 728; 737; 738; 808; 838; 891; 1402; 1733; 1753; 1788; 1821; 1831.

204

Akten des siebenfarbigen Alphabets (Rep. 2c): 35.

Amts- und Standbücher (Rep. 526): 146; 150; 340.

Ansbacher Gemeinbücher (Rep. 134 II): Tom. 5, 7.

Ansbacher Historica (Rep. 110): 210, 340.

Ansbacher Lehensurkunden (Rep. 135): 102; 106; 107; 249; 506; 513; 514; 516; 517; 518; 519; 520; 522; 552; 588; 590; 609; 1202; 1203; 1205; 1206; 1207; 1210; 1212; 1215; 1216; 1217; 1218; 1274; 1275; 1276; 1277; 1280; 1282; 1283; 1284; 1285; 1350; 1356; 1358; 1359; 1394; 1448; 1662; 1713; 1714; 2216; 2222; 4287; 4531; 4683; 4685; 4686; 5620; 5621; 5734; 5738; 5750; 5802.

Bauernkriegsakten (Rep. 107 I): Tom. 7, 8.

Beamtenkartei

Brandenburg-Ansbachische Lehenbücher (Rep. 135a I): 8, 9, 10, 11, 12.

Brandenburger Literalien (Rep. 103a II): 582.

Fehdeakten (Rep. 106a): 4 [alte Signatur]; 5 [alte Signatur]; 6 [alte Signatur]; 7 [alte Signatur]; 8 [alte Signatur]; 9 [alte Signatur]; 10 [alte Signatur]; 11 [alte Signatur]; 13 [alte Signatur]; 16 [alte Signatur]; 21 [alte Signatur]; 25b; 26 [alte Signatur]; 26; 27; 27a; 29; 32a; 33b; 39a; 42; 44; 52; 67b; 69; 77a; 81; 83a; 85a; 92; 96; 97a; 98; 104; 105a; 110.

Herrschaft Pappenheim (Rep. 211 d / 2): 2797.

Landtagsakten (Rep. 139): Tom. 7, 8.

Kaiserliches Landgericht Burggraftums Nürnberg, Akten (Rep. 119a): 211; 212; 232.

Reichsgrafschaft Geyer, Akten (Rep. 167a): 49.

Reichsstadt Nürnberg, Briefbücher des Inneren Rates (Rep. 61a): 42; 45; 46; 48; 51; 54; 65; 68; 69; 74; 81; 90; 101; 110, 112; 113; 120; 134; 142; 158.

Reichsstadt Nürnberg, 35 neue Laden der unteren Losungsstube (Rep. 2a): V 89/1 2065; V 90/2 2447; V 93/1 3026.

Reichsstadt Windsheim, Akten (Rep. 204): 13, 14; 15.

Seckendorff-Gutend, Veit Leo Freiherr von. *Quellenbände [zur seckendorffischen Familiengeschichte]*.

Urfehden, Fehdesachen, Urkunden (Rep. 106): 25; 30; 32; 33; 55.

Verträge mit dem Adel (Rep. 103b): Heßberg 1a; Velberg 1; Truchsesse von Baldersheim 1.

Staatsarchiv Würzburg

Adel: 1114.

Adelsarchiv Fuchs von Bimbach: 2, 5.

Lehensachen: 1948, 2636.

Libri diversarum formarum: 12, 13, 15, 77.

Literaliensammlung des Historischen Vereins von Unterfranken und Aschaffenburg: Ms f. 1044; Ms f. 1671.

Standbücher: 46, 717, 788, 790, 791, 792, 817, 865, 892, 947, 948, 1012.

Würzburger Lehenbücher: 18, 21, 24, 27, 29, 36.

Selected bibliography

PRINTED SOURCES

Albrecht, Joseph (ed.). *Conrads von Weinsberg, des Reichs-Erbkämmerers, Einnahmen- und Ausgaben-Register von 1437 und 1438.* Stuttgart, 1850.

Aschbach, Joseph (ed.). *Wertheimisches Urkundenbuch.* Part 2 of his *Geschichte der Grafen von Wertheim von den ältesten Zeiten bis zu ihrem Erlöschen in Mannsstamme im Jahre 1556.* Frankfurt am Main, 1843.

Auer, Leopold (ed.). 'Die undatierten Fredriciana des Haus-, Hof- und Staatsarchivs.' *Mitteilungen des österreichischen Staatsarchivs* 27 (1974), 405–30.

Baader, Joseph (ed.). *Verhandlungen über Thomas von Absberg und seine Fehden gegen den Schwäbischen Bund 1519 bis 1530.* Tübingen, 1873.

Bachmann, Adolf (ed.). *Briefe und Acten zur österreichisch-deutschen Geschichte im Zeitalter Kaiser Friedrich III.* Vienna, 1885.

Battenberg, Friedrich (ed.). *Isenburger Urkunden: Regesten zu Urkundenbeständen und Kopiaren der fürstlichen Archive in Birstein und Büdingen 947–1500.* Vol. II. Darmstadt, 1976.

Battenberg, Friedrich (ed.). *Schlitzer Urkunden: Regesten zum Urkundenarchiv der Grafen von Schlitz gen. von Görtz (Abt. B 8) 1285–1939.* 2 vols. Darmstadt, 1979.

Baumann, Franz Ludwig (ed.). *Quellen zur Geschichte des Bauernkrieges aus Rotenburg an der Tauber.* Tübingen, 1878.

Bibl, Viktor (ed.). *Die Korrespondenz Maximilians II.* 2 vols. Vienna, 1916–21.

Borchardt, Karl (ed.). *Die Würzburger Inschriften bis 1525.* Wiesbaden, 1988.

Burkhardt, Carl August Hugo (ed.). *Das funfft merkisch Buech des Churfuersten Albrecht Achilles.* Jena, 1857.

Chmel, Joseph (ed.). *Urkunden, Briefe und Actenstücke zur Geschichte Maximilian's I. und seiner Zeit.* Stuttgart, 1845.

Chmel, Joseph (ed.). *Actenstücke und Briefe zur Geschichte des Hauses Habsburg im Zeitalter Maximilian's I.* Vol. I. Vienna, 1854.

Chmel, Joseph (ed.). *Regesta chronologico-diplomatica Friderici III. Romanorum Imperatoris (Regis IV.).* Vienna, 1859.

Decker-Hauff, Hansmartin (ed.). *Die Chronik der Grafen von Zimmern.* 3 vols. Sigmaringen, 1964–72.

Deutsche Reichstagsakten, jüngere Reihe. Vol. III. Edited by Adolf Wrede. Gotha, 1901.

Deutsche Reichstagsakten, mittlere Reihe. Vol. V, *Reichstag von Worms 1495.* Edited by Heinz Angermeier. Göttingen, 1981. Vol. VI, *Reichstage von Lindau, Worms und Freiburg 1496–1498.* Edited by Heinz Gollwitzer. Göttingen, 1979.

Die Chroniken der fränkischen Städte, Nürnberg. Vols. IV, V. Die Chroniken der deutschen Städte vom 14. bis ins 16. Jarhundert, vols. X, XI. Leipzig, 1872–4.

Eberstein, Louis Ferdinand Freiherr von (ed.). *'Dem Landfrieden ist nicht zu trauen': Fehde Mangold's von Eberstein zum Brandenstein gegen die Reichsstadt Nürnberg 1516–1522. Charakterbild der rechtlichen und wirtschaftlichen Zustände im deutschen Reiche unmittelbar vor dem grossen Bauernkriege.* Nordhausen, 1868.

Eckhardt, Karl August (ed.). *Quellen zur Rechtsgeschichte der Stadt Eschwege.* Vol. I, *Urkunden und Stadtbücher.* Marburg, 1959.

Ehrensberger. 'Freiherrlich von Zobel'sches Archiv zu Messelhausen.' *ZGO* 52 (1898), m121–m150.

Engel, W. (ed.). *Die Rats-Chronik der Stadt Würzburg (XV. und XVI. Jahrhundert)*. Würzburg, 1950.

Engel, Wilhelm (ed.). *Die Würzburger Bischofschronik des Grafen Wilhelm Werner von Zimmern und die Würzburger Geschichtsschreibung des 16. Jahrunderts*. Würzburg, 1952.

Erck, Christoph Albrecht (ed.). *Rapsodiae sive Chronicon Hennebergicum Weyland M. Sebastian Glasers, Hennebergischen Cantzlers vom Jahr 1078. bis 1559. Welches noch niemahlen im Druck erschienen, sondern nur in einigen Bibliothecis priuatis latitiret, zur Erläuterung der spangenberg-hennebergischen Chronic*. Meiningen, 1755.

Ermanung an Churfursten, Fursten, Hern und Stende teutzscher nation; der brüderlichen versamlung im land zu Francken, begangen ubels zü straffen, und gmeynen frieden hinfürter zü füdern und handthaben. Würzburg?, 1525.

Falckenstein, Johann Heinrich von (ed.). *Urkunden und Zeugnisse vom achten Seculo bis auf gegenwärtige Zeiten worinnen die wichtigsten das hochfürstl. Burggrafthum Nürnberg und die von demselben absprossende beide in diesem Landesbezirk situirte hochfürstliche Häuser, Brandenburg-Anspach und Baireuth betreffende hohe Vorrechte, Freiheiten, Begnadungen, Concessiones und desgleichen mehr enthalten, die an Orten, wo es nötig, mit historisch-genealogisch-chronologisch-geographisch- und critischen Anmerkungen erkläret*. 2 vols. Neustadt a.d. Aisch, 1789.

Frauenholz, Eugen von (ed.). *Des Lazarus von Schwendi Denkschrift über die politische Lage des deutschen Reiches von 1574*. Munich, 1939.

Fries, Lorenz. *Historie, Nahmen, Geschlecht, Wesen, Thaten, gantz Leben und Sterben des gewesenen Bischoffen zu Wirtzburg und Hertzogen zu Francken*. In *Geschicht-Schreiber von dem Bischoffthum Wirtzbürg*, ed. Johann Peter Ludewig, 373–930. Frankfurt am Main, 1713.

Fries, Lorenz. *Die Geschichte des Bauernkrieges in Ostfranken*. Vol. II. Edited by August Schäffler and Theodor Henner. Aalen, 1978.

Giefel, J. A. (ed.). 'Die Ellwanger und Neresheimer Geschichtsquellen.' *Württembergische Vierteljahrshefte für Landesgeschichte* 11 (1888 [1889]), 1–78.

Gilman, Sander L. (ed). *Johannes Agricola: Die Sprichwörtersammlungen*. Vol. I. Berlin, 1971.

Goetz, Walter (ed.). *Beiträge zur Geschichte Herzog Albrechts V. und des Landsberger Bundes 1556–1598*. Munich, 1898.

Goetz, Walter and Leonhard Theobald (eds.). *Beiträge zur Geschichte Herzog Albrechts V. und der sog. Adelsverschwörung von 1563*. Leipzig, 1913.

Gumppenberg, Ludwig Albert Freiherr von (ed.). 'Nachrichten über die Turniere zu Würzburg und Bamberg in den Jahren 1479 und 1486.' *AU* 19, no. 2 (1867), 164–210.

Guttenberg, Franz Karl Freiherr von. 'Regesten des "Geschlechtes von Blassenberg" und dessen Nachkommen.' *AO* 22, no. 3 (1907), 112–232.

Hagmaier, Otto. 'Gräflich von Berlichingen'sches Archiv in Neunstetten.' *ZGO* 60 (1906), m47–m110.

Hannakam, Karl, and Ludwig Veit (eds.). *Archiv der Freiherrn Schenk von Geyern auf Schloß Syburg*. Munich, 1958.

Hasselholdt-Stockheim, Gustav Freiherr von (ed.). *Urkunden und Beilagen zum Kampfe der wittelsbachischen und brandenburgischen Politik in den Jahren 1459 bis 1465*. Vol. I, part i. Leipzig, 1865.

Selected bibliography

'Hellers Chronic der Stadt Bayreuth.' Part 1. *AO* 1, no. 1 (1828), 102–47.

Herolt, Johann. *Chronica zeit- unnd Jarbuch von der Statt Hall ursprung und was sich darinnen verloffen unnd wasz fur Schlösser umb Hall gestanden*. Edited by Christian Kolb. Stuttgart, 1894.

Höfler, Constantin (ed.). *Des Ritters Ludwig von Eyb zu Eybburg Denkwürdigkeiten brandenburgischer (hohenzollerischer) Fürsten*. Bayreuth, 1849.

Höfler, Constantin. *Franken, Schwaben und Bayern: Eine Rede gehalten zu Culmbach am 8. Juli 1850. Nebst einer archivalischen Beilage: das älteste officielle Verzeichnis der fränkischen Ritterschaft von 1495 enthaltend*. Bamberg, 1850.

Höfler, Constantin (ed.). 'Fränkische Studien IV.' Parts 1–3. *Archiv für Kunde österreichischer Geschichts-Quellen* 7 (1851), 1–146; 8 (1852), 235–322; 11 (1853), 1–56.

Hofmann, Conrad (ed.). *Des Matthias von Kemnat Chronik Friedrich I. des Siegreichen*. Munich, 1862.

Hund, Wigulejus. *Bayrisch Stammen Buch*. Ingolstadt, 1598.

Hutten, Ulrich von. 'Die Räuber.' In *Gespräche von Ulrich von Hutten*, ed. and trans. David Friedrich Strauß, 315–89. Leipzig, 1860.

Keller, Adalbert von (ed.). *Die Geschichten und Taten Wilwolts von Schaumburg*. Stuttgart, 1859.

Kinser, Samuel (ed.). *The Memoirs of Philipp de Commynes*. Translated by Isabelle Cazeaux. Vol. I. Columbia, South Carolina, 1969.

Kloos, Rudolf M. (ed.). *Nachlass Marschalk von Ostheim: Urkunden*. Neustadt a.d. Aisch, 1974.

Kloos, Rudolf M. (ed.). *Die Inschriften des Landkreises Bamberg bis 1650*. Munich, 1980.

Klüpfel, Karl (ed.). *Urkunden zur Geschichte des Schwäbischen Bundes (1488–1533)*. Vol. I. Stuttgart, 1846.

Koch, M. *Quellen zur Geschichte des Kaisers Maximilian II*. 2 vols. Leipzig, 1857–61.

Kolb, Christian (ed.). *Widmans Chronica*. Stuttgart, 1904.

Letts, Malcolm (ed.). *The Diary of Jörg von Ehingen*. Translated by Malcolm Letts. London, 1929.

Liliencron, Rochus Freiherr von (ed.). *Die historischen Volkslieder der Deutschen vom 13. bis 16. Jahrhundert*. Vol. II. Leipzig, 1866.

Lochner, Georg Wolfgang Karl (ed.). *Das deutsche Mittelalter in den wesentlichsten Zeugnissen seiner geschichtlichen Urkunden, Chroniken und Rechtsdenkmäler*. Part 2. Nuremberg, 1851.

Luckhard, Fritz (ed.). *Die Regesten der Herren von Ebersberg genannt Weyhers in der Röhn (1170–1518)*. Fulda, 1963.

Luckhard, Fritz. 'Das Archiv der Ritter von Mörlau zu Steinau an der Haun.' Parts 1–3. *Fuldaer Geschichtsblätter* 40 (1964), 107–26; 151–70; 187–96.

Lünig, Johann Christian. *Des Teutschen Reichs-Archiv partis sepecialis continuatio III*. Part 2. Leipzig, 1713.

Maierhofer, Isolde (ed.). *Die Inschriften des Landkreises Hassberge*. Munich, 1979.

Meyer, Christian. (ed.). *Aus dem Gedenkbuch des Ritters Ludwig des Älteren von Eyb, Hofmeister und Rath des Markgrafen Albrecht Achilles von Ansbach*. Ansbach, 1890.

Meyer, Christian (ed.). 'Die Familienchronik des Ritters Michel von Ehenheim.' *Hohenzollerische Forschungen* 5 (1897), 369–419.

Selected bibliography

Minutoli, Julius von (ed.). *Das kaiserliche Buch des Markgrafen Albrecht Achilles: Kurfürstliche Periode von 1470–1486*. Berlin, 1850.

Müller, Johann Joachim. *Des Heil. Römischen Reichs Teutscher Nation ReichsTags Theatrum, wie selbiges unter Keyser Maximilians I. allerhöchsten Regierung gestanden, und was auf selbigem in Geist- und Weltlichen Reichs-Händeln berahtschlaget, tractiret und geschlossen worden*. Part 2. Jena, 1719.

Müllner, Johannes. *Die Annalen der Reichsstadt Nürnberg von 1623*. Edited by Gerhard Hirschmann. Vol. II. Nuremberg, 1984.

Pietsch, Friedrich (ed.). *Die Urkunden des Archivs der Reichsstadt Schwäbisch Hall*. Vol. II. Stuttgart, 1972.

Priebatsch, Felix (ed.). *Politische Correspondenz des Kurfürsten Albrecht Achilles*. 3 vols. Leipzig, 1894–8.

Rauch, Moritz von (ed.). *Urkundenbuch der Stadt Heilbronn*. Vol. III. Stuttgart, 1916.

Rechter, Gerhard (ed). *Die Archive der Grafen und Freiherren von Seckendorff: Die Unrkundenbestände der Schloßarchive Obernzenn, Sugenheim, Trautskirchen und Unternzenn*. 3 vols. Munich, 1993.

Reicke, Emil (ed.). *Willibald Pirckheimers Briefwechsel*. Vol. I. Munich, 1940.

Renner, Michael (ed.). *Archiv der Grafen Wolffskeel von Reichenberg*. Munich, 1961.

Riedel, Adolph Friedrich. (ed.). *Codex diplomaticus Brandenburgensis: Sammlung der Urkunden, Chroniken und sonstigen Quellenschriften für die Geschichte der Mark Brandenburg und ihrer Regenten. Part 2, Urkunden-Sammlung zur Geschichte der auswärtigen Verhältnisse der Mark Brandenburg und ihrer Regenten*. 6 vols. Berlin, 1843–58.

Rolevinck, Werner. *De Westphalorum sive Antiquorum Saxonum Situ, Moribus, Virtutibus, et Laudibus Libri III*. Cologne, 1602.

Schannat, Johann Friedrich (ed.). *Fuldischer Lehn-Hof sive de clientela fuldensi beneficiaria nobili et equestri tractatus*. Frankfurt am Main, 1726.

Scherg, Theodor J. 'Franconica aus dem Vatican 1462–1492.' *Archivalische Zeitschrift*, n.s., 16 (1909), 1–156.

Schlecht, Joseph (ed.). 'Die Kleinen Annalen des Kilian Leib, Priors zu Rebdorf. Nach dem Codex Münch im bischöfl. Ordinariats-Archiv zu Eichstätt.' *Sammelblatt des Historischen Vereins Eichstätt* 2 (1887 [1888]), 39–68.

Schuhmann, Günther (ed.). *Stadtarchiv Ansbach*. Munich, 1956.

Schultheiß, Werner, (ed.). *Die Acht-, Verbots- und Fehdebücher Nürnbergs von 1285–1400. Mit einer Einführung in die Rechts- und Sozialgeschichte und das Kanzlei- und Urkundenwesen Nürnbergs im 13. und 14. Jahrhundert*. Nuremberg, 1960.

Schwarzenberg, Baron Johann of. *Ain Lied mit vorgehender anzaygung / wider das mordlaster des raubens*. 1525?

Schwarzenberg, Baron Johann of. *Das Büchlein vom Zutrinken*. Edited by Willy Scheel. Halle, 1900.

Schweitzer, C. A. 'Auszüge der Urkunden aus der Chronik des Michaelsberger Abtes Eberhard.' *Bericht des Historischen Vereins Bamberg* 17 (1854), 1–175.

Scott, Tom, and Bob Scribner (eds.). *The German Peasants' War: A History in Documents*. Translated by Tom Scott and Bob Scribner. New Jersey, 1991.

Seinsheim, Georg Ludwig von. *Kurtze Ablainung und Verantwortung / etlicher unbeständiger unerfindlicher schmählicher Zulagen / Die Wilhelm von Grumbach / und seine Zugewandte*

Selected bibliography

/ *Ihme von Seinßheim / inn den im Truck außgangen Büchern / So inn der Einnam der Vestung Grimmenstein / Anno 1567 gefunden / zugemessen worden.* (1568) 1590.

Spangenberg, Cyriacus. *Hennebergische Chronica: Der uralten löblichen Grafen und Fürsten zu Henneberg, Genealogia, Stamm-Baum und Historia, ihrer Ankunfft, Lob und denckwürdigen Tathen, Geschichten und Sachen wahre und gründliche Beschreibung.* Edited by Christoph Albrecht Erck. Meiningen, 1755.

Stamm, Heide (ed.). *Das Turnierbuch des Ludwig von Eyb (cgm 961). Edition und Untersuchung mit einem Anhang: Die Turnierchronik des Jörg Rugen (Textabdruck).* Stuttgart, 1986.

Stein, Friedrich (ed.). *Monumenta Suinfurtensia historica inde ab anno DCCXCI usque ad annum MDC: Denkmäler der Schweinfurter Geschichte bis zum Ende des 16. Jahrhunderts.* Schweinfurt, 1875.

Thiel, Matthias (ed.). *Archiv der Freiherren Stromer von Reichenbach auf Burg Grünsberg.* Part 1, *Urkunden.* Neustadt a.d. Aisch, 1972.

Trithemius, Johannes. *Annales Hirsaugienses.* Vol. II. St Gallen, 1690.

Ulmschneider, Helgard (ed.). *Götz von Berlichingen: Mein Fehd und Handlung.* Sigmaringen, 1981.

Unser Friderichen Freyherren von Schwartzenberg und zu Hohenlandsperg diser zeit Wirtembergischen Obervogts zu Schorndorf / warhafftiger bericht und gegenschrifft / auff Ludwigs der sich von Hutten und einen ritter nennt ausschreiben zum andern mal im druck ausgangen / im angang / mittel / ende / und durchaus erlogen (sovil er des wider und zusein vermeint) dann er sich auch sonst abermals in vil stucken selbst zum höchsten und mer verletzt / dann verantwort hat. 1535.

'Urkunden und Aktenprodukte im Königlichen Archive zu Nürnberg das Hochgräfliche Geschlecht Giech betreffend.' *Jb.Mfr.* 9 (1839), 99–106.

Venetianische Depeschen vom Kaiserhof (Dispacci di Germania). Vol. III. Edited by Gustav Turba. Vienna, 1895.

Verhandlungen zwischen der Stadt Nürnberg und der fränkischen Ritterschaft wegen Christoph von Giech und Contz Schott. Nuremberg, 1500.

Vogel, Wilhelm (ed.). *Des Ritters Ludwig von Eyb des Aelteren Aufzeichnung über das kaiserliche Landgericht des Burggrafthums Nürnberg.* Erlangen, 1867.

Volkert, Wilhelm (ed.). *Schloßarchiv Sandersdorf.* Munich, 1962.

Weech, Friedrich von (ed.). 'Das Reissbuch anno 1504: Die Vorbereitungen der Kurpfalz zum bairischen Erbfolgekriege.' *ZGO* 26 (1874), 137–264.

Weinrich, Lorenz (ed.). *Quellen zur Verfassungsgeschichte des Römisch-Deutschen Reiches im Spätmittelalter (1250–1500).* Darmstadt, 1893.

Weiss, Johann Gustav. 'Freiherrlich Rüdt'sches Archiv zu Bödigheim.' *ZGO* 50 (1896), m32–m46.

Wendehorst, Alfred (ed.). *Urkundenbuch der Marienkapelle am Markt zu Würzburg 1317–1530.* Würzburg, 1974.

Widemann, Joseph (ed.). *Urkunden der Benediktiner-Abtei St. Stephan in Würzburg. Ergänzungsheft.* Erlangen, 1983.

Wittmann, Pius (ed.). *Monumenta Castellana: Urkundenbuch zur Geschichte des fränkischen Dynastengeschlechtes der Grafen und Herren zu Castell, 1057–1546.* Munich, 1890.

Zeumer, Karl (ed.). *Quellensammlung zur Geschichte der deutschen Reichsverfassung in Mittelalter und Neuzeit.* Tübingen, 1907.

Selected bibliography

SECONDARY LITERATURE

Abel, Wilhelm. *Geschichte der deutschen Landwirtschaft vom frühen Mittelalter bis zum 19. Jahrhundert.* 2nd edn. Stuttgart, 1967.

Abel, Wilhelm. *Agricultural Fluctuations in Europe: From the Thirteenth to the Twentieth Centuries.* Translated by Olive Ordish. London, 1980.

Abel, Wilhelm. *Strukturen und Krisen der spätmittelalterlichen Wirtschaft.* Stuttgart, 1980.

Adelmann von Adelmannsfelden, Graf Georg Sigmund. *Das Geschlecht der Adelmann von Adelmannsfelden.* Ellwangen, 1948.

Algazi, Gadi. '"Sie würden hinten nach so gail": Vom sozialen Gebrauch der Fehde im späten Mittelalter.' In *Physische Gewalt: Studien zur Geschichte der Neuzeit,* ed. Thomas Lindenberger and Alf Lüdtke, 39–77. Frankfurt am Main, 1995.

Algazi, Gadi. *Herrengewalt und Gewalt der Herren im späten Mittelalter: Herrschaft, Gegenseitigkeit und Sprachgebrauch.* Frankfurt am Main, 1996.

Amrhein, August. 'Reihenfolge der Mitglieder des adeligen Domstifts zu Würzburg, St. Kilians-Brüder genannt, von seiner Gründung bis zur Säkularisation 742–1803.' Parts 1 and 2. *AU* 32 (1889), 1–314; 33 (1890), 1–380.

Amrhein, August. 'Gotfrid Schenk von Limpurg: Bischof von Würzburg und Herzog zu Franken 1442–1455.' Part 3. *AU* 53 (1911), 1–153.

Andermann, Kurt. *Studien zur Geschichte des pfälzischen Niederadels im Mittelalter: Eine vergleichende Untersuchung an ausgewählten Beispielen.* Speyer, 1982.

Andermann, Kurt. 'Ritter – Edelknechte – Amtleute: Aspekte pfälzischer Adelsgeschichte im späten Mittelalter, skizziert am Beispiel der Familien von Mühlhofen und von Otterbach.' *Pfälzer Heimat* 36 (1985), 1–8.

Andermann, Kurt. 'Klösterliche Grundherrschaft und niederadlige Herrschaftsbildung: Das Beispiel Amorbach.' In *Siedlungsentwicklung und Herrschaftsbildung im Hinteren Odenwald,* ed. Hermann Ehmer, 29–50. Buchen, 1988.

Andermann, Kurt. 'Grundherrschaften des spätmittelalterlichen Niederadels in Südwestdeutschland.' *Blätter für deutsche Landesgeschichte* 127 (1991), 145–90.

Andermann, Kurt. 'Zu den Einkommensverhältnissen des Kraichgauer Adels an der Wende vom Mittelalter zur Neuzeit.' In *Die Kraichgauer Ritterschaft in der frühen Neuzeit,* ed. Stefan Rhein, 65–121. Sigmaringen, 1993.

Andermann, Ulrich. *Ritterliche Gewalt und bürgerliche Selbstbehauptung: Untersuchungen zur Kriminalisierung und Bekämpfung des spätmittelalterlichen Raubrittertums am Beispiel norddeutscher Hansestädte.* Frankfurt am Main, 1991.

Andraschko, Ferdinand. *Schloß Schwarzenberg im Wandel der Zeiten: Ein Beitrag zu seiner Geschichte.* 2nd edn. Neustadt a.d. Aisch, 1967.

Andrian-Werburg, Klaus Freiherr von. 'Die niederadeligen Kemnater im Coburgischen: Zur politischen und wirtschaftlichen Existenz der mittelalterlichen adeligen Unterschicht.' *Jahrbuch der Coburger Landesstiftung* 30 (1985), 97–136.

Armstrong, C. A. J. 'Had the Burgundian Government a Policy for the Nobility?' In *Britain and the Netherlands,* ed. J. S. Bromley and E. H. Kossmann, vol. I, 9–32. Groningen, 1964.

Armstrong, C. A. J. 'La Toison d'Or et la loi des armes.' In his *England, France and Burgundy in the Fifteenth Century,* 375–81. London, 1983.

Arnold, Klaus. *Niklashausen 1476: Quellen und Untersuchungen zur sozialreligiösen Bewe-*

211

gung des Hans Behem und zur Agrarstruktur eines spätmittelalterlichen Dorfes. Baden-Baden, 1980.

Aschbach, Joseph. *Geschichte der Grafen von Wertheim von den ältesten Zeiten bis zu ihrem Erlöschen im Mannsstamme im Jahre 1556.* Frankfurt am Main, 1843.

Asmus, Herbert. 'Rechtsprobleme des mittelalterlichen Fehdewesens: Dargestellt an Hand südhannoverscher Quellen vornehmlich des Archives der Stadt Göttingen.' PhD thesis, University of Göttingen, 1951.

Aufseß, Otto Frieherr von. *Geschichte des uradelichen Aufseß'schen Geschlechtes in Franken.* Berlin, 1888.

Axtmann, Roland. 'The Formation of the Modern State: the Debate in the Social Sciences.' In *National Histories and European History*, ed. Mary Fulbrook, 21–45. London, 1993.

Bader, Karl Siegfried. 'Herrschaft und Staat im deutschen Mittelalter.' *Historisches Jahrbuch* 62–9 (1949), 618–46.

Barzel, Yoram. *Economic Analysis of Property Rights.* Cambridge, 1989.

Baum, Hans-Peter. 'Soziale Schichtung im mainfränkischen Niederadel um 1400.' *ZHF* 13 (1986), 129–48.

Baum, Hans-Peter. 'Der Lehenhof des Hochstifts Würzburg im Spätmittelalter (1303–1519): Eine rechts- und sozialgeschichtliche Studie.' 3 vols. *Habilitationsschrift*, University of Würzburg, 1990.

Berlichingen-Rossach, Friedrich Graf von. 'Ritter Conrad von Berlichingen und seine Ahnen.' *WFr* 5, no. 2 (1860), 173–202.

Beyer, Thomas. 'Zu Familienstruktur und Konnubium des niederadeligen Geschlechtes von Grumbach im Spätmittelalter.' *Zulassungsarbeit*, University of Würzburg, 1977.

Bibra, Wilhelm Freiherr von. *Beiträge zur Familien-Geschichte der Reichsfreiherrn von Bibra.* Vol. II. Munich, 1882.

Bischoff, Georges. 'Les grèves anti-seigneuriales de Ferrette: Les habitants d'un baillage du Sundgau et leur seigneur au début du xvie siècle.' *Revue d'Alsace* 105 (1979), 35–52.

Bischoff, Johannes. *Genealogie der Ministerialen von Blassenberg und Freiherren von (und zu) Guttenberg 1148–1970.* Würzburg, 1971.

Bisson, T. N. 'The "Feudal Revolution".' *Past and Present* 142 (1994), 6–42.

Bitsch, Horst. *Die Verpfändungen der Landgrafen von Hessen während des späten Mittelalters.* Göttingen, 1974.

Bittmann, Markus. *Kreditwirtschaft und Finanzierungsmethoden: Studien zu den Verhältnissen des Adels im westlichen Bodenseeraum.* Stuttgart, 1991.

Black-Michaud, Jacob. *Cohesive Force: Feud in the Mediterranean and the Middle East.* Oxford, 1975.

Blickle, Peter. *Die Revolution von 1525.* 2nd edn. Munich, 1981.

Blickle, Peter. 'Otto Brunner (1898–1982).' *Historische Zeitschrift* 236 (1983), 779–81.

Blickle, Peter. *Communal Reformation: The Quest for Salvation in Sixteenth-Century Germany.* Translated by Thomas Dunlap. New Jersey, 1992.

Boelcke, Willi A. 'Die Einkünfte Lausitzer Adelsherrschaften in Mittelalter und Neuzeit.' In *Wirtschaft, Geschichte und Wirtschaftsgeschichte: Festschrift zum 65. Geburtstag von Friedrich Lütge*, ed. Wilhelm Abel et al., 183–205. Stuttgart, 1966.

Boldt, Hans. 'Otto Brunner: Zur Theorie der Verfassungsgeschichte.' *Annali dell'Istituto storico italo-germanico in Trento* 13 (1987), 39–61.

Bonnassie, Pierre. *La Catalogne du milieu du Xe à la fin du XIe siècle: Croissance et mutations d'une société.* Vol. II. Toulouse, 1976.

Boone, James L. 'Paternal Investment and Elite Family Structure in Preindustrial States: A Case Study of Late Medieval–Early Modern Portuguese Genealogies.' *American Anthropologist* 88 (1986), 859–78.

Borgolte, Michael. 'Das soziale Ganze als Thema deutscher Mittelalterforschung vor und nach der Wende.' *Francia* 22, no. 1 (1995), 155–71.

Brady, Thomas A., Jr. *Turning Swiss: Cities and Empire, 1450–1550.* Cambridge, 1985.

Braudel, Fernand. 'On a Concept of Social History.' In his *On History,* 120–31. Translated by Sarah Matthews. London, 1980.

Braun, Hugo A. *Das Domkapitel zu Eichstätt: Von der Reformationszeit bis zur Säkularisation (1535–1806). Verfassung und Personalgeschichte.* Stuttgart, 1991.

Braun, Rainer. *Das Benediktinerkloster Michelsberg, 1015–1525: Eine Untersuchung zur Gründung, Rechtsstellung und Wirtschaftsgeschichte.* Vol. I. Kulmbach, 1978.

Brenner, Robert. 'Agrarian Class Structure and the Economic Development of Pre-Industrial Europe.' In *The Brenner Debate: Agrarian Class Structure and Economic Development in Pre-Industrial Europe,* ed. T. H. Aston and C. H. E. Philpin, 10–63. Cambridge, 1985.

Brunner, Otto. 'Beiträge zur Geschichte des Fehdewesens im spätmittelalterlichen Oesterreich.' *Jahrbuch für Landeskunde von Niederösterreich* 22 (1929), 431–507.

Brunner, Otto. 'Moderner Verfassungsbegriff und mittelalterliche Verfassungsgeschichte.' *Mitteilungen des österreichischen Instituts für Geschichtsforschung. Erg.-Band* 14 (1939), 513–28.

Brunner, Otto. *Adeliges Landleben und europäischer Geist: Leben und Werk Wolf Helmhards von Hohberg 1612–1688.* Salzburg, 1949.

Brunner, Otto. 'Inneres Gefüge des Abendlandes.' *Historia Mundi* 6 (1958), 319–85.

Brunner, Otto. *Neue Wege der Verfassungs- und Sozialgeschichte.* 3rd edn. Göttingen, 1980.

Brunner, Otto. *'Land' and Lordship: Structures of Governance in Medieval Austria.* Translated by Howard Kaminsky and James Van Horn Melton. Philadelphia, 1992.

Bulst Neithard. 'Zum Gegenstand und zur Methode von Prosopographie.' In *Medieval Lives and the Historian: Studies in Medieval Prosopography,* ed. Neithard Bulst and Jean-Philippe Genet, 1–16. Kalamazoo, 1986.

Bürger, Sven-Uwe. 'Burg Amlishagen – Anmerkungen zur Besitzgeschichte.' *WFr* 76 (1992), 39–60.

Cannon, John. *Aristocratic Century: The Peerage of Eighteenth-Century England.* Cambridge, 1984.

Carney, T. F. 'Prosopography: Payoffs and Pitfalls.' *Phoenix* 27 (1973), 156–79.

Clanchy, Michael. 'Law and Love in the Middle Ages.' In *Disputes and Settlements: Law and Human Relations in the West,* ed. John Bossy, 47–67. Cambridge, 1983.

Cohn, Henry J. *The Government of the Rhine Palatinate in the Fifteenth Century.* Oxford, 1965.

Conrads, Norbert. 'Tradition und Modernität im adligen Bildungsprogramm der Frühen Neuzeit.' In *Ständische Gesellschaft und soziale Mobilität,* ed. Winfried Schulze, 389–403. Munich, 1988.

Crailsheim, Sigmund Freiherr von. *Die Reichsfreiherrn von Crailsheim.* Vol. II. Munich, 1905.

Selected bibliography

Dannenbauer, Heinz. *Die Entstehung des Territoriums der Reichsstadt Nürnberg.* Stuttgart, 1928.

Decker, Klaus Peter. 'Klientel und Konkurrenz: Die ritterschaftliche Familie von Hutten und die Grafen von Hanau und von Ysenburg.' *Hessisches Jahrbuch für Landesgeschichte* 38 (1988), 23–48.

Deeg, Dietrich. *Die Herrschaft der Herren von Heideck: Eine Studie zu hochadeliger Familien- und Besitzgeschichte.* Neustadt a.d. Aisch, 1968.

Demandt, Karl E. *Der Personenstaat der Landgrafschaft Hessen im Mittelalter: Ein 'Staatshandbuch' Hessens vom Ende des 12. bis zum Anfang des 16. Jahrhunderts.* 2 vols. Marburg, 1981.

Diefenbacher, Michael. 'Stadt und Adel – Das Beispiel Nürnberg.' *ZGO* 141 (1993), 51–69.

Dipper, Christof. 'Otto Brunner aus der Sicht der frühneuzeitlichen Historiographie.' *Annali dell'Istituto storico italo-germanico in Trento* 13 (1987), 73–96.

Dirlmeier, Ulf. 'Merkmale des sozialen Aufstiegs und der Zuordnung zur Führungsschicht in süddeutschen Städten des Spätmittelalters.' In *Pforzheim im Mittelalter: Studien zur Geschichte einer landesherrlichen Stadt,* ed. Hans-Peter Becht, 77–106. Sigmaringen, 1983.

Dobeneck, Alban Freiherr von. 'Geschichte des ausgestorbenen Geschlechtes der von Sparneck.' Parts 1 and 2. *AO* 22, no. 3 (1905), 1–65; 23, no. 1 (1906), 1–56.

Dobeneck, Alban Freiherr von. *Geschichte der Familie von Dobeneck.* Schöneberg-Berlin, 1906.

Dobeneck, Alban Freiherr von. 'Die Geschichte des ausgestorbenen Geschlechts von Kotzau.' *AO* 24, no. 1 (1909), 1–111.

Dobeneck, Alban Freiherr von. 'Zur Geschichte des erloschenen Geschlechtes der Rabensteiner von Doehlau.' *AO* 25, no. 3 (1914), 37–145.

Donati, Claudio. *L'idea di nobiltà in Italia: Secoli XIV–XVIII.* Bari, 1988.

Droege, Georg. 'Spätmittelalterliche Staatsfinanzen in Westdeutschland.' In *Öffentliche Finanzen und privates Kapital im späten Mittelalter und in der ersten Hälfte des 19. Jahrhunderts,* ed. Hermann Kellenbenz, 5–13. Stuttgart, 1971.

Duby, Georges. *The Three Orders: Feudal Society Imagined.* Translated by Arthur Goldhammer. Chicago, 1980.

Durchhardt, Heinz. 'Reichsritterschaft und Reichskammergericht.' *ZHF* 5 (1978), 315–37.

Eiermann, Adolf. *Lazarus von Schwendi, Freiherr von Hohenlandsberg: Ein deutscher Feldoberst und Staatsmann des XVI. Jahrhunderts.* Freiburg, 1904.

Elias, Norbert. *The Civilizing Process.* Translated by Edmund Jephcott. Oxford, 1994.

Endres, Rudolf. 'Der Bauernkrieg in Franken.' *Blätter für deutsche Landesgeschichte* 109 (1973), 31–68.

Endres, Rudolf. 'Adelige Lebensformen in Franken zur Zeit des Bauernkrieges.' *Neujahrsblätter der Gesellschaft für fränkische Geschichte* 35 (1974), 5–43.

Endres, Rudolf. 'Die wirtschaftlichen Grundlagen des niederen Adels in der frühen Neuzeit.' *JffL* 36 (1976), 215–37.

Endres, Rudolf. 'Franken.' In *Der deutsche Bauernkrieg,* ed. Horst Buszello, Peter Blickle, and Rudolf Endres, 134–53. Paderborn, 1984.

Selected bibliography

Endres, Rudolf. *Adel in der Frühen Neuzeit.* Munich, 1993.

Engel, Wilhelm, Walter Janssen, and Hellmut Kunstmann. *Die Burgen Frankenberg über Uffenheim.* Neustadt a.d. Aisch, 1984.

Ernst, Fritz. *Eberhard im Bart: Die Politik eines deutschen Landesherrn am Ende des Mittelalters.* 1933. Reprint, Darmstadt, 1970.

Eyb, Eberhard Freiherr von. *Das reichsritterliche Geschlecht der Freiherren von Eyb.* Neustadt a.d. Aisch, 1984.

Falke, Johannes. 'Die Finanzwirthschaft im Kurfürstenthum Sachsen um das Jahr 1470.' *Mittheilungen des Königlich Sächsischen Vereins für Erforschung und Erhaltung vaterländischer Geschichts- und Kunstdenkmale* 20 (1870), 78–106.

Fäth, Günter. 'Der Grundbesitz der Voite von Salzburg im 14. und 15. Jahrhundert.' *Zulassungsarbeit,* University of Würzburg, 1976.

Feldbauer, Peter. 'Rangprobleme und Konnubium österreichischer Landherrenfamilien.' *ZbLG* 35 (1972), 571–90.

Fellner, Robert. *Die fränkische Ritterschaft von 1495–1524.* Berlin, 1905.

Fischer, Adolf. *Geschichte des Hauses Hohenlohe.* 2 vols. 1866–71. Reprint, Schwäbisch Hall, 1991.

Fleckenstein, Josef. 'Die Entstehung des niederen Adels und das Rittertum.' In *Herrschaft und Stand: Untersuchungen zur Sozialgeschichte im 13. Jahrhundert,* ed. Josef Fleckenstein, 17–39. Göttingen, 1977.

Fossier, Robert. 'Seigneurs et seigneuries au Moyen Age.' In *Seigneurs et seigneuries au Moyen Age,* 13–24. Paris, 1993.

Fouquet, Gerhard. 'Reichskirche und Adel: Ursachen und Mechanismen des Aufstiegs der Kraichgauer Niederadelsfamilie v. Helmstatt im Speyerer Domkapitel zu Beginn des 15. Jahrhunderts.' *ZGO* 129 (1981), 189–223.

Fouquet, Gerhard. *Das Speyerer Domkapitel im späten Mittelalter (ca. 1350–1540): Adlige Freundschaft, fürstliche Patronage und päpstliche Klientel.* 2 vols. Mainz, 1987.

Frey, Joseph. 'Die Fehde der Herren von Rosenberg auf Boxberg mit dem Schwäbischen Bund und ihre Nachwirkungen (1523–1555).' PhD thesis, University of Tübingen, 1924.

Freytag von Loringhoven, Frank Baron. *Europäische Stammtafeln: Stammtafeln zur Geschichte der europäischen Staaten.* N.s. Edited by Detlev Schwennicke. Marburg, 1980– .

Fuchshuber, Elisabeth. *Uffenheim.* Munich, 1982.

Fugger, Eberhard Graf von. *Die Seinsheim und ihre Zeit: Eine Familien- und Kulturgeschichte von 1155–1890.* Munich, 1893.

Gambetta, Diego. *The Sicilian Mafia: The Business of Private Protection.* Cambridge, Mass., 1993.

Genealogisches Handbuch des Adels. Limburg an der Lahn, 1951– .

Gluckman, Max. 'The Peace in the Feud.' In *Custom and Conflict in Africa,* 1–26. Oxford, 1963.

Goertz, Hans-Jürgen. *Pfaffenhaß und groß Geschrei: Die reformatorischen Bewegungen in Deutschland 1517–1529.* Munich, 1987.

Görner, Regina. *Raubritter: Untersuchungen zur Lage des spätmittelalterlichen Niederadels, besonders im südlichen Westfalen.* Münster in Westfalen, 1987.

Selected bibliography

Graf, Eduard, and Mathias Dietherr (eds.). *Deutsche Rechtssprichwörter.* Nördlingen, 1864.

Graf, Klaus. 'Feindbild und Vorbild: Bemerkungen zur städtischen Wahrnehmung des Adels.' *ZGO* 141 (1993), 121–54.

Grötsch, A. 'Eine blutige Ritterfehde aus dem 16. Jahrhundert (Familie Streitberg).' *Die Oberpfalz* 16 (1922), 119–20.

Guerreau, Alain. *Le féodalime: Un horizon théorique.* Paris, 1980.

Guttenberg, Erich Freiherr von. *Das Bistum Bamberg.* Part 1. Berlin, 1937.

Guttenberg, Erich Freiherr von. 'Aus Fehdezeiten (1490–1506).' In *Lebens- und Kulturbilder aud der Geschichte des fränkischen Geschlechts von Guttenberg,* ed. Wilhelm Engel, 9–45. Würzburg, 1958.

Haemmerle, Albert. *Die Canoniker der Chorherrnstifte St. Moritz, St. Peter und St. Gertrud in Augsburg bis zur Saecularisation.* N.p., 1938.

Haenle, Sigmund. 'Urkunden und Nachweise zur Geschichte des Schwanen-Ordens.' *Jb.Mfr.* 39 (1873/74), 1–178.

Hahn, Peter-Michael. *Struktur und Funktion des brandenburgischen Adels im 16. Jahrhundert.* Berlin, 1979.

Hanley, Sarah. 'Engendering the State: Family Formation and State Building in Early Modern France.' *French Historical Studies* 16 (1989), 4–27.

Harding, Robert R. *Anatomy of a Power Elite: The Provincial Governors of Early Modern France.* New Haven, 1978.

Hardtwig, Wolfgang. *Geschichtsschreibung zwischen Alteuropa und moderner Welt: Jacob Burckhardt in seiner Zeit.* Göttingen, 1974.

Hartmann, Helmut. 'Der Stiftsadel an den alten Domkapiteln zu Mainz, Trier, Bamberg und Würzburg.' *Mainzer Zeitschrift* 73, no. 4 (1978/79), 99–138.

Held, Wieland. 'Das Adelsgeschlecht der Brandenstein im 16. Jahrhundert: Seine wirtschaftliche und soziale Position im ernestinisch-sächsichen Territorialstaat.' *VSWG* 80 (1993), 175–96.

Herrmann, Max. *Albrecht von Eyb und die Frühzeit des deutschen Humanismus.* Berlin, 1893.

Hessberg, Hanns Freiherr von. 'Über die Truchsesse zu Wildberg.' *MJfGK* 10 (1958), 42–69.

Hexter, J. H. 'The Education of the Aristocracy in the Renaissance.' In his *Reappraisals in History: New Views on History and Society in Early Modern Europe,* 2nd edn, 45–70. Chicago, 1979.

Hill, J. 'Prestige and Reproductive Success in Man.' *Ethology and Sociobiology* 5 (1984), 77–95.

Hillenbrand, Eugen. 'Die Ortenauer Ritterschaft auf dem Weg zur Reichsritterschaft.' *ZGO* 137 (1989), 241–57.

Hirschmann, Gerhard. 'Johann Gottfried Biedermann zum 200. Todestag.' *Blätter für fränkische Familienkunde* 9, no. 1 (1966), 2–9.

Höfler, Constantin. 'Betrachtungen über das deutsche Städtewesen im XV. und XVI. Jahrhunderte.' *Archiv für Kunde österreichischer Geschichts-Quellen* 11 (1853), 177–229.

Hofmann, Hanns Hubert. 'Freibauern, Freidörfer, Schutz und Schirm im Fürstentum Ansbach: Studien zur Genesis der Staatlichkeit in Franken vom 15. bis 18. Jahrhundert.' *ZbLG* 23 (1960), 195–327.

Hofmann, Hanns Hubert. 'Der Adel in Franken.' In *Deutscher Adel 1430–1555*, ed. Hellmuth Rößler, 95–126. Darmstadt, 1965.

Hofmann, Karl. 'Das pfälzische Amt Boxberg zur Zeit des Bauernaufstands 1525.' *ZGO* 97 (1949), 467–97.

Hofmann, Michel. 'Die Außenbehörden des Hochstifts Bamberg und der Markgrafschaft Bayreuth.' *JffL* 3 (1937), 52–96.

Hofner, Hans. 'Zur Geschichte des vogtländischen Adels: Die Herren von Feilitzsch auf Feilitzsch.' *AO* 54 (1974), 257–317.

Holbach, Rudolf. *Stiftsgeistlichkeit im Spannungsfeld von Kirche und Welt: Studien zur Geschichte des Trierer Domkapitels und Domklerus im Spätmittelalter.* Part 2. Trier, 1982.

Holenstein, André. *Die Huldigung der Untertanen: Rechtskultur und Herrschaftsordnung (800–1800).* Stuttgart, 1991.

Honeman, Volker, and Helgard Ulmschneider. 'Eine ritterschaftliche Bibliothek des 16. Jahrhunderts: Das Verzeichnis der Bücher des Hans Pleickhard von Berlichingen (✝ 1594).' *Archiv für Geschichte des Buchwesens* 20, no. 4 (1979), 833–94.

Irsigler, Franz. 'Reinhard von Schönau und die Finanzierung der Königswahl Karls IV. im Jahre 1346: Ein Beitrag zur Geschichte der Hochfinanzbeziehungen zwischen Rhein und Maas.' In *Hochfinanz, Wirtschaftsräume, Innovationen: Festschrift für Wolfgang von Stromer*, ed. Uwe Bestmann, Franz Irsigler, and Jürgen Schneider, vol. I, 357–81. Trier, 1987.

Jackson, William H. 'The Tournament and Chivalry in German Tournament Books of the Sixteenth Century and in the Literary Works of Emperor Maximilian I.' In *The Ideals and Practice of Medieval Knighthood: Papers from the First and Second Strawberry Hill Conferences*, ed. Christopher Harper-Bill and Ruth Harvey, 49–73. Woodbridge, 1986.

Jackson, William H. 'Tournaments and the German Chivalric *renovatio*: Tournament Discipline and the Myth of Origins.' In *Chivalry in the Renaissance*, ed. Sydney Anglo, 77–91. Woodbridge, 1990.

Jäger, Berthold. *Das geistliche Fürstentum Fulda in der frühen Neuzeit: Landesherrschaft, Landstände und fürstliche Verwaltung. Ein Beitrag zur Verfassungs- und Verwaltungsgeschichte kleiner Territorien des Alten Reiches.* Marburg, 1986.

Kamann, Johann. *Die Fehde des Götz von Berlichingen mit der Reichsstadt Nürnberg und dem Hochstifte Bamberg 1512–1514.* Nuremberg, 1893.

Kanter, Erhard Waldemar. *Hans von Rechberg von Hohenrechberg: Ein Zeit- und Lebensbild.* Zurich, 1903.

Kaplan, Hillard, and Kim Hill. 'Hunting Ability and Reproductive Success among Male Ache Foragers: Preliminary Results.' *Current Anthropology* 26, no. 1 (1985), 131–3.

Kaufmann, Manfred. *Fehde und Rechtshilfe: Die Verträge brandenburgischer Landesfürsten zur Bekämpfung des Raubrittertums im 15. und 16. Jahrhundert.* Pfaffenweiler, 1993.

Keen, Maurice. 'Huizinga, Kilgour and the Decline of Chivalry.' *Medievalia et Humanistica*, n.s., 8 (1978), 1–20.

Keen, Maurice. *Chivalry.* New Haven, 1984.

Kehrer, Harold H. 'The von Sickingen and the German Princes 1262–1523.' PhD thesis, Boston University Graduate School, 1977.

Kehrer, Harold H. 'Die Familie von Sickingen und die deutschen Fürsten 1262–1523.' Parts 1 and 2. *ZGO* 127 (1979), 73–158; 129 (1981), 82–187.

Keller, Franz. 'Die Verschuldung des Hochstifts Konstanz im 14. und 15. Jahrhundert.' *Freiburger Diözesan-Archiv,* n.s., 3 (1902), 1–104.

Kerber, Dieter. *Herrschaftsmittelpunkte im Erzstift Trier: Hof und Residenz im späten Mittelalter.* Sigmaringen, 1995.

Kestler, J. B. 'Archivalische Nachrichten über die Schlacht bei Bergtheim im Jahre 1400.' *AU* 15, no. 1 (1860), 186–91.

Kisky, Wilhelm. *Die Domkapitel der geistlichen Kurfürsten in ihrer persönlichen Zusammensetzung im vierzehnten und fünfzehnten Jahrhundert.* Weimar, 1906.

Kist, Johannes. *Das Bamberger Domkapitel von 1399 bis 1556: Ein Beitrag zur Geschichte seiner Verfassung, seines Wirkens und seiner Mitglieder.* Weimar, 1943.

Klocke, Friedrich von. 'Beiträge zur Geschichte von Faustrecht und Fehdewesen in Westfalen.' *Westfälische Zeitschrift* 94 (1938), 3–56.

Kneschke, Ernst Heinrich (ed.). *Neues allgemeines deutsches Adels-Lexicon.* 9 vols. Leipzig, 1859–70.

Knittler, Herbert. 'Adel und landwirtschftliches Unternehmen im 16. und 17. Jahrhundert.' In *Adel im Wandel: Politik, Kultur, Konfession 1500–1700,* ed. Herbert Knittler, Gottfried Stangler, and Renate Zedlinger, 45–55. Vienna, 1990.

Knittler, Herbert. 'Zur Einkommensstruktur niederösterreicher Adelsherrschaften 1550–1750.' In *Adel in der Frühneuzeit: Ein regionaler Vergleich,* ed. Rudolf Endres, 99–118. Cologne, 1991.

Köberlin, Lotte. 'Die Einungsbewegung des fränkischen Adels bis zum Jahre 1494.' PhD thesis, University of Erlangen, 1924.

Köhn, Rolf. 'Einkommensquellen des Adels im ausgehenden Mittelalter, illustriert an südwestdeutschen Beispielen.' *Schriften des Vereins für Geschichte des Bodensees und seiner Umgebung* 103 (1985), 33–62.

Köhn, Rolf. 'Der Hegauer Bundschuh (Oktober 1460) – ein Aufstandsversuch in der Herrschaft Hewen gegen die Grafen von Lupfen.' *ZGO* 138 (1990), 99–141.

Köhn, Rolf. 'Die Abrechnungen der Landvögte in den österreichischen Vorlanden um 1400. Mit einer Edition des *raitregisters* Friedrichs von Hattstatt für 1399–1404.' *Blätter für deutsche Landesgeschichte* 128 (1992), 117–78.

Körner, Hans. 'Die Familie von Hutten: Genealogie und Besitz bis zum Ende des Alten Reiches.' In *Ulrich von Hutten: Ritter, Humanist, Publizist. Katalog zur Ausstellung des Landes Hessen anläßlich des 500. Geburtstages,* ed. Peter Laub, 57–78. Kassel, 1988.

Krause, Hans-Georg. 'Pfandherrschaften als verfassungsgeschichtliches Problem.' Parts 1 and 2. *Der Staat* 9 (1970), 387–404; 515–32.

Kriedte, Peter. 'Spätmittelalterliche Agrarkrise oder Krise des Feudalismus?' *Geschichte und Gesellschaft* 7 (1981), 42–68.

Krüger, Kersten. *Finanzstaat Hessen 1500–1567: Staatsbildung im Übergang vom Domänenstaat zum Steuerstaat.* Marburg, 1980.

Krüger, Kersten. 'Gerhard Oestreich und der Finanzstaat: Entstehung und Deutung eines Epochenbegriffs der frühneuzeitlichen Verfassungs- und Sozialgeschichte.' *Hessisches Jahrbuch für Landesgeschichte* 33 (1983), 333–46.

Kruse, Holger, Werner Paravicini, and Andreas Ranft (eds.). *Ritterorden und Adelsgesellschaften im spätmittelalterlichen Deutschland: Ein systematisches Verzeichnis.* Frankfurt am Main, 1991.

Kuchenbuch, Ludolf, and Bernd Michael. 'Zur Struktur und Dynamik der "feudalen" Produktionsweise im vorindustriellen Europa.' In *Feudalismus – Materialien zur Theorie und Geschichte*, ed. Ludolf Kuchenbuch and Bernd Michael, 694–761. Frankfurt am Main, 1977.

Kulenkampff, Angela. 'Einungen und Reichsstandschaft fränkischer Grafen und Herren 1402–1641.' *WFr* 45 (1971), 16–41.

Kunstmann, Hellmut. *Die Burgen der östlichen fränkischen Schweiz*. Würzburg, 1965.

Kunstmann, Hellmut. *Die Burgen der westlichen und nördlichen fränkischen Schweiz*. Part 1, *Der Südwesten: unteres Wiesenttal und Trubachtal*. Würzburg, 1971.

Landwehr, Götz. *Die Verpfändung der deutschen Reichsstädte im Mittelalter*. Cologne, 1967.

Landwehr, Götz. 'Die rechtshistorische Einordnung der Reichspfandschaften.' In *Der deutsche Territorialstaat im 14. Jahrhundert*, ed. Hans Patze, vol. I, 97–116. Sigmaringen, 1970.

Landwehr, Götz. 'Mobilisierung und Konsolidierung der Herrschaftsordnung im 14. Jahrhundert.' In *Der deutsche Territorialstaat im 14. Jahrhundert*, ed. Hans Patze, vol. II, 484–505. Sigmaringen, 1971.

Lane, Frederic Chapin. 'Economic Consequences of Organized Violence.' In *Venice and History: The Collected Papers of Frederic C. Lane*, 413–28. Baltimore, 1966.

Lang, Karl Heinrich. *Neuere Geschichte des Fürstenthums Baireuth*. Part 1, *Vom Jahr 1486 bis zum Jahr 1527*. Göttingen, 1798.

Lange-Kothe, Irmgard. 'Zur Sozialgeschichte des fürstlichen Rates in Württemberg im 15. und 16. Jahrhundert.' *VSWG* 34 (1941), 237–67.

Langendörfer, Friedhelm. 'Die Landschaden von Steinach: Zur Geschichte einer Familie des niederen Adels im Mittelalter und der frühen Neuzeit.' PhD thesis, University of Heidelberg, 1971.

Lanzinner, Maximilian. *Fürst, Räte und Landstände: Die Entstehung der Zentralbehörden in Bayern 1511–1598*. Göttingen, 1980.

Lanzinner, Maximilian. 'Der Landsberger Bund und seine Vorläufer.' In *Alternativen zur Reichsverfassung in der Frühen Neuzeit?*, ed. Volker Press and Dieter Stievermann, 65–79. Munich, 1995.

LeGates, Marlene. 'The Knights and the State in Sixteenth-Century Germany.' PhD thesis, Yale University, 1970.

LeGates, Marlene Jahss. 'The Knights and the Problem of Political Organizing in Sixteenth-Century Germany.' *Central European History* 7 (1974), 99–136.

Leinweber, Josef. *Das Hochstift Fulda vor der Reformation*. Fulda, 1972.

Leiser, Wolfgang. 'Das hohenzollerische Amt Dachsbach/Aisch bis zum Forchheimer Rezeß 1538.' *JffL* 34/35 (1975), 725–50.

Leiser, Wolfgang. 'Süddeutsche Land- und Kampfgerichte des Spätmittelalters.' *WFr* 70 (1986), 5–17.

Lenman, Bruce, and Geoffrey Parker. 'The State, the Community and the Criminal Law in Early Modern Europe.' In *Crime and the Law: The Social History of Crime in Western Europe Since 1500*, ed. V. A. C. Gatrell, Bruce Lenman, and Geoffrey Parker, 11–48. London, 1980.

Lieberich, Heinz. *Landherren und Landleute: Zur politischen Führungsschicht Baierns im Spätmittelalter*. Munich, 1964.

Linnebron, Johannes. 'Ein 50jähriger Kampf (1417–ca. 1467) um die Reform und ihr Sieg im Kloster ad sanctum Michaelem bei Bamberg.' Parts 1–6. *Studien und Mitteilungen aus dem Benediktiner- und dem Zisterzienser-Orden* 25 (1904), 252–65; 579–89; 718–29; 26 (1905), 55–68; 247–54; 534–45.

Lohmann, Eberhard. *Die Herrschaft Hirschhorn: Studien zur Herrschaftsbildung eines Rittergeschlechtes.* Darmstadt, 1986.

Looshorn, Johann. *Die Geschichte des Bisthums Bamberg.* Vol. IV, *Das Bisthum Bamberg von 1400–1556.* Munich, 1900.

Maier, A. 'Das Wiederaufleben von "Fehde" im 18. Jahrhundert.' *Zeitschrift für deutsche Wortforschung* 10 (1908/9), 181–7.

Mann, Michael. *The Sources of Social Power.* Vol. I, *A History of Power from the Beginning to A.D. 1760.* Cambridge, 1986.

Marchal, Guy P. *Sempach 1386: Von den Anfängen des Territorialstaates Luzern. Beitrag zur Frühgeschichte des Kantons Luzern. Mit einer Studie von Waltraud Hörsch: Adel im Bannkreis Österreichs.* Basel, 1986.

Marx, Karl. *Capital: A Critique of Political Economy.* Translated by Ben Fowkes. Vol. I. Harmondsworth, 1976.

Melton, Edgar. 'Comment: Hermann Aubin.' In *Paths of Continuity: Central European Historiography from the 1930s to the 1950s*, ed. Hartmut Lehmann and James Van Horn Melton, 251–61. Cambridge, 1994.

Melton, James Van Horn. 'From Folk History to Structural History: Otto Brunner (1898–1982) and the Radical-Conservative Roots of German Social History.' In *Paths of Continuity: Central European Historiography from the 1930s to the 1950s*, ed. Hartmut Lehmann and James Van Horn Melton, 263–92. Cambridge, 1994.

Merzbacher, Friedrich. 'Ein Schmählied auf Johann Freiherrn zu Schwarzenberg.' *MJfGK* 3 (1951), 288–98.

Merzbacher, Friedrich. 'Johann Freiherr zu Schwarzenberg.' *Fränkische Lebensbilder* 4 (1971), 173–85.

Midelfort, H. C. Erik. 'Adeliges Landleben und die Legitimationskrise des deutschen Adels im 16. Jahrhundert.' In *Stände und Gesellschaft im Alten Reich*, ed. Georg Schmidt, 245–64. Stuttgart, 1989.

Miller, William Ian. *Bloodtaking and Peacemaking: Feud, Law, and Society in Saga Iceland.* Chicago, 1990.

Mitteis, Heinrich. 'Land und Herrschaft: Bemerkungen zu dem gleichnamigen Buch Otto Brunners.' Parts 1 and 2. *Historische Zeitschrift* 163 (1941), 255–81; 471–89.

Mitterauer, Michael. 'Probleme der Stratifikation in mittelalterlichen Gesellschaftssystemen.' In *Theorien in der Praxis des Historikers*, ed. Jürgen Kocka, 13–43. Göttingen, 1977.

Moeglin, Jean-Marie. '"Toi, Burgrave de Nuremberg, misérable gentilhomme dont la grandeur est si récente . . .": Essai sur la conscience dynastique des Hohenzollern de Franconie au xvᵉ siècle.' *Journal des Savants* (1991), 91–131.

Moeller, Bernd. *Deutschland im Zeitalter der Reformation.* 3rd edn. Göttingen, 1988.

Molho, Anthony. *Marriage Alliance in Late Medieval Florence.* Cambridge, Mass., 1994.

Möller, Walther. *Stamm-Tafeln westdeutscher Adels-Geschlechter im Mittelalter.* 3 vols. Darmstadt, 1922–36.

Möller, Walther. *Stamm-Tafeln westdeutscher Adels-Geschlechter im Mittelalter.* N.s. 2 parts. Darmstadt, 1950–1.

Selected bibliography

Moraw, Peter. 'Landesgeschichte und Reichsgeschichte im 14. Jahrhundert.' *Jahrbuch für westdeutsche Landesgeschichte* 3 (1977), 175–91.

Moraw, Peter. 'Fürstentum, Königtum und "Reichsreform" im deutschen Spätmittelalter.' *Blätter für deutsche Landesgeschichte* 122 (1986), 117–36.

Morsel, Joseph. 'Crise? Quel crise? Remarques à propos de la prétendue crise de la noblesse allemande à la fin du Moyen Age.' *Sources. Travaux historique* 14 (1988), 17–42.

Morsel, Joseph. 'Une société politique en Franconie à la fin du Moyen Age: Les Thüngen, leurs princes, leurs pairs et leurs hommes (1275–1525).' PhD thesis, University of Paris-IV Sorbonne, 1993.

Morsel, Joseph. 'Le tournoi, mode d'éducation politique en Allemagne à la fin du Moyen Age.' In *Education, apprentissages, initiation au Moyen Age: Actes du premier colloque international de Montpellier*, vol. II, 309–31. Montpellier, 1993.

Morsel, Joseph. 'Changements anthroponymiques et sociogenèse de la noblesse en Franconie à la fin du Moyen Age.' In *Genèse médiévale de l'anthroponymie moderne*. Vol. III, *Enquêtes généalogiques et données prosopographiques*, ed. Monique Bourin and Pascal Chareille, 89–119. Tours, 1995.

Morsel, Joseph. '"Das sy sich mitt der besstenn gewarsamig schicken, das sy durch die widerwertigenn Franckenn nit nidergeworffen werdenn": Überlegungen zum sozialen Sinn der Fehdepraxis am Beispiel des spätmittelalterlichen Franken.' In *Strukturen der Gesellschaft im Mittelalter: Interdisziplinäre Mediävistik in Würzburg*, ed. Dieter Rödel and Joachim Schneider, 140–67. Wiesbaden, 1996.

Morsel, Joseph. 'Die Erfindung des Adels: Zur Soziogenese des Adels am Ende des Mittelalters – Das Beispiel Frankens.' In *Nobilitas: Funktion und Repräsentation des Adels in Alteuropa*, ed. Otto Gerhard Oexle and Werner Paravicini. Göttingen, 1996.

Muehlon, Lore. 'Johann III. von Grumbach, Bischof von Würzburg und Herzog zu Franken (1455–1466).' PhD thesis, University of Würzburg, 1935.

Muir, Edward. *Mad Blood Stirring: Vendetta & Factions in Friuli during the Renaissance.* Baltimore, 1993.

Müller, Karl Otto. 'Zur wirtschaftlichen Lage des schwäbischen Adels am Ausgang des Mittelalters.' *Zeitschrift für württembergische Landesgeschichte* 3 (1939), 285–328.

Müller, Uwe. *Die ständische Vertretung in den fränkischen Markgraftümern in der ersten Hälfte des 16. Jahrhunderts.* Neustadt a.d. Aisch, 1984.

Neitzert, Dieter. *Die Stadt Göttingen führt eine Fehde 1485/86: Untersuchung zu einer Sozial- und Wirtschaftsgeschichte von Stadt und Umland.* Hildesheim, 1992.

Neuber, Wolfgang. 'Adeliges Landleben in Österreich und die Literatur im 16. und im 17. Jahrhundert.' In *Adel im Wandel: Politik, Kultur, Konfession 1500–1700*, ed. Herbert Knittler, Gottfried Stangler, and Renate Zedlinger, 543–53. Vienna, 1990.

Neuhofer, Theodor. *Gabriel von Eyb, Fürstbischof von Eichstätt 1455–1535: Ein Lebensbild aus der Wende vom Mittelalter zur Neuzeit.* Eichstätt, 1934.

Neuschel, Kristen B. *Word of Honor: Interpreting Noble Culture in Sixteenth-Century France.* Ithaca, 1989.

Nicolet, Claude. 'Prosopographie et histoire sociale: Rome et l'Italie à l'époque républicaine.' *Annales: E.S.C.* 25 (1970), 1209–28.

Nierop, H. K. F. van. *The Nobility of Holland: From Knights to Regents, 1500–1650.* Translated by M. Ultee. Cambridge, 1993.

Selected bibliography

Obenaus, Herbert. *Recht und Verfassung der Gesellschaft mit St.Jörgenschild in Schwaben: Untersuchungen über Adel, Einung, Schiedsgericht und Fehde im fünfzehnten Jahrhundert.* Göttingen, 1961.

Oesterreicher, Paul. *Die Burg Streitberg.* Bamberg, 1819.

Oestreich, Gerhard. 'The Estates of Germany and the Formation of the State.' In his *Neostoicism and the Early Modern State*, ed. Brigitta Oestreich and H. G. Koenigsberger, 187–98. Cambridge, 1982.

Oexle, Otto Gerhard. 'Sozialgeschichte – Begriffsgeschichte – Wissenschaftsgeschichte: Anmerkungen zum Werk Otto Brunners.' *VSWG* 71 (1984), 305–41.

Orth, Elsbet. *Die Fehden der Reichsstadt Frankfurt am Main im Spätmittelalter: Fehderecht und Fehdepraxis im 14. und 15. Jahrhundert.* Wiesbaden, 1973.

Patze, Hans. 'Grundherrschaft und Fehde.' In *Die Grundherrschaft im späten Mittelalter*, ed. Hans Patze, vol. I, 263–94. Sigmaringen, 1983.

Pedlow, Gregory W. 'Marriage, Family Size, and Inheritance among Hessian Nobles, 1650–1900.' *Journal of Family History* 7 (1982), 333–52.

Perroy, Edouard. 'Social Mobility among the French *Noblesse* in the Later Middle Ages.' *Past and Present* 21 (1962), 25–38.

Peuckert, Will-Erich. *Die grosse Wende: Das apokalyptische Saeculum und Luther. Geistesgeschichte und Volkskunde.* Hamburg, 1948.

Pfeiffer, Gerhard. 'Studien zur Geschichte der fränkischen Reichsritterschaft.' *JffL* 22 (1962), 173–280.

Pfeiffer, Gerhard. 'Fürst und Land: Betrachtungen zur Bayreuther Geschichte.' *AO* 57/58 (1977/78), 7–20.

Pfeiffer, Gerhard. 'Hans Thomas von Absberg (ca. 1480?–1531).' *Fränkische Lebensbilder* 13 (1990), 17–32.

Pfeilsticker, Walther (ed.). *Neues Württembergisches Dienerbuch.* 2 vols. Stuttgart, 1957–63.

Pleticha, Eva. *Adel und Buch: Studien zur Geisteswelt des fränkischen Adels am Beispiel seiner Bibliotheken vom 15. bis zum 18. Jahrhundert.* Neustadt a.d. Aisch, 1983.

Plodeck, Karin. 'Hofstruktur und Hofzeremoniell in Brandenburg-Ansbach vom 16. bis zum 18. Jahrhundert: Zur Rolle des Herrschaftskultes im absolutistischen Gesellschafts- und Herrschaftssystem.' *Jb.Mfr* 86 (1971/72), 1–257.

Pölnitz, Sigmund Freiherr von. 'Stiftsfähigkeit und Ahnenprobe im Bistum Würzburg.' In *Herbipolis Jubilans: 1200 Jahre Bistum Würzburg. Festschrift zur Säkularfeier der Erhebung der Kiliansreliquien*, 349–55. Würzburg, 1952.

Press, Volker. 'Wilhelm von Grumbach und die deutsche Adelskrise der 1560er Jahre.' *Blätter für deutsche Landesgeschichte* 113 (1977), 396–431.

Press, Volker. *Kaiser Karl V., König Ferdinand und die Entstehung der Reichsritterschaft.* 2nd edn. Wiesbaden, 1980.

Proksch, Constance. 'Die Auseinandersetzung um den Austrag des Rechts zwischen Fürsten und Ritterschaft in Franken vom Ende des 14. bis in die Mitte des 16. Jahrhunderts.' In *Strukturen der Gesellschaft im Mittelalter: Interdisziplinäre Mediävistik in Würzburg*, ed. Dieter Rödel and Joachim Schneider, 168–95. Wiesbaden, 1996.

Pröll, Friedrich. 'Geschichte des ehemaligen markgräflich-bayreuthischen Schlosses und Amtes Osternohe und der dortigen Kirche.' *Jb.Mfr.* 50 (1903), 1–144.

Puchner, Otto. 'Zur Geschichte der Schenk von Geyern und ihres Territoriums.' In *Archiv der Freiherrn Schenk von Geyern auf Schloß Syburg*, ed. Karl Hannakam and Ludwig Veit, 1–15. Munich, 1958.

Quirin, Heinz. 'Markgraf Albrecht Achilles von Brandenburg-Ansbach als Politiker: Ein Beitrag zur Vorgeschichte des süddeutschen Städtekriegs.' *JffL* 31 (1971), 261–308.

Quirin, Heinz. 'Landesherrschaft und Adel im wettinischen Bereich während des späteren Mittelalters.' In *Festschrift für Hermann Heimpel zum 70. Geburtstag am 19. September 1971*, vol. II, 80–109. Göttingen, 1972.

Ranft, Andreas. *Adelsgesellschaften: Gruppenbildung und Genossenschaft im spätmittelalterlichen Reich.* Sigmaringen, 1994.

Rankl, Helmut. *Staatshaushalt, Stände und 'Gemeiner Nutzen' in Bayern 1500–1516.* Munich, 1976.

Rauser, Jürgen. 'Die Ahnen der Herren von Stetten 1166–1966.' *Hohenloher Historische Hefte* 17 (1967), 1–66.

Rebel, Hermann. *Peasant Classes: The Bureaucratization of Property and Family Relations under Early Habsburg Absolutism 1511–1636.* Princeton, 1983.

Rechter, Gerhard. *Das Land zwischen Aisch und Rezat: Die Kommende Virnsberg Deutschen Ordens und die Rittergüter im oberen Zenngrund.* Neustadt a.d. Aisch, 1981.

Rechter, Gerhard. 'Das Verhältnis der Reichsstädte Windsheim und Rothenburg ob der Tauber zum niederen Adel ihrer Umgebung im Spätmittelalter.' *JffL* 41 (1981), 45–87.

Rechter, Gerhard. '"difficulteten und beschwerden": Beobachtungen zum Verhältnis der kleineren Reichsstädte Frankens zum niederen Adel am Beispiel Windsheim.' In *Reichsstädte in Franken*, ed. Rainer A. Müller, 298–308. Munich, 1987.

Rechter, Gerhard. *Die Seckendorff: Quellen und Studien zur Genealogie und Besitzgeschichte.* 2 vols. Neustadt a.d. Aisch, 1987–90.

Redlich, Fritz. *The German Military Enterpriser and his Work Force: A Study in European Economic and Social History.* Vol. I. Wiesbaden, 1964.

Reinhard, Wolfgang. 'Staatsmacht als Kreditproblem: Zur Struktur und Funktion des frühneuzeitlichen Ämterhandels.' *VSWG* 61 (1974), 289–319.

Reitzenstein, Hermann Freiherr von. *Geschichte der Familie von Reitzenstein.* Vol. I. Munich, 1891.

Reitzenstein-Reuth, Hermann Freiherr von. *Geschichte der Familie von Reitzenstein.* Part 1, *Geschichte der Linie zu Wildenau.* Munich, 1882.

Reuschling, Heinzjürgen N. *Die Regierung des Hochstifts Würzburg 1495–1642: Zentralbehörden und führende Gruppen eines geistlichen Staates.* Würzburg, 1984.

Riedenauer, Erwin. 'Kontinuität und Fluktuation im Mitgliederstand der fränkischen Reichsritterschaft: Eine Grundlegung zum Problem der Adelsstruktur in Franken.' In *Gesellschaft und Herrschaft: Forschungen zu sozial- und landesgeschichtlichen Problemen vornehmlich in Bayern. Eine Festgabe für Karl Bosl zum 60. Geburtstag*, 87–152. Munich, 1969.

Ritzmann, Peter. '"Plackerey in teutschen Landen": Untersuchungen zur Fehdetätigkeit des fränkischen Adels im frühen 16. Jahrhundert und ihrer Bekämpfung durch den Schwäbischen Bund und die Reichsstadt Nürnberg, insbesondere am Beispiel des Hans Thomas von Absberg und seiner Auseinandersetzung mit den Grafen von Oettingen (1520–31).' PhD thesis, University of Munich, 1993.

Robisheaux, Thomas. *Rural Society and the Search for Order in Early Modern Germany.* Cambridge, 1989.

Rohn, Otto. 'Die Herren von Lentersheim im Mittelalter.' *Alt-Gunzenhausen* 37 (1977), 31–47.

Rohn, Otto. 'Die Herren von Lentershein. Zweiter Teil: Vom Erwerb des Schlosses Altenmuhr im Jahr 1430 bis zum Erlöschen des Stammes im Jahr 1799.' *Alt-Gunzenhausen* 38 (1979), 108–45.

Roper, Lyndal. *The Holy Household: Women and Morals in Reformation Augsburg.* Oxford, 1989.

Rösener, Werner. 'Zur Problematik des spätmittelalterlichen Raubrittertums.' In *Festschrift für Berent Schwineköper zu seinem siebzigsten Geburtstag*, ed. Helmut Maurer and Hans Patze, 469–88. Sigmaringen, 1982.

Rösener, Werner. *Agrarwirtschaft, Agrarverfassung und ländliche Gesellschaft im Mittelalter.* Munich, 1992.

Rösener, Werner. 'Adelige Herrschaft in einer alten Königslandschaft: Herrschaftsprak-tiken und Lebensformen des oberschwäbischen Adels im Spätmittelalter.' In *Politische Kultur in Oberschwaben*, ed. Peter Blickle, 119–46. Tübingen, 1993.

Rotenhan, Gottfried Freiherr von. *Die Rotenhan: Genealogie einer fränkischen Familie von 1229 bis zum Dreißigjährigen Krieg.* Neustadt a.d. Aisch, 1985.

Rotenhan, Gottfried Freiherr von. 'Streit und Fehde um die Burg Stuffenberg bei Baunach 1460/66.' *Bericht des Historischen Vereins Bamberg* 129 (1993), 75–90.

Roth, Johann Ferdinand. *Geschichte des Nuernbergischen Handels.* Vol. I. Leipzig, 1800.

Rothert, Hermann. 'Das mittelalterliche Fehdewesen in Westfalen.' *Westfälische Forschungen* 3 (1940), 145–55.

Rupprecht, Klaus. *Ritterschaftliche Herrschaftswahrung in Franken: Die Geschichte der von Guttenberg im Spätmittelalter und zu Beginn der Frühen Neuzeit.* Neustadt a.d. Aisch, 1994.

Ruser, Konrad. 'Zur Geschichte der Gesellschaften von Herren, Rittern und Knechten in Süddeutschland während des 14. Jahrhunderts.' *Zeitschrift für Württembergische Landesgeschichte* 34/35 (1975/76), 1–100.

Sabean, David Warren. *Property, Production, and Family in Neckarhausen, 1700–1870.* Cambridge, 1990.

Sablonier, Roger. *Adel im Wandel: Eine Untersuchung zur sozialen Situation des ostschweizerischen Adels um 1300.* Göttingen, 1979.

Sablonier, Roger. 'Zur wirtschaftlichen Situation des Adels im Spätmittelalter.' In *Adelige Sachkultur des Spätmittelalters*, 9–34. Vienna, 1982.

Sattler, Hans-Peter. 'Die Ritterschaft der Ortenau in der spätmittelalterlichen Wirtschaftskrise.' Parts 1–4. *Die Ortenau* 42 (1962), 220–58; 44 (1964), 22–39; 45 (1965), 32–57; 46 (1966), 32–58.

Scharold, C. G. 'Hof- und Staatshaushalt unter einigen Fürstbischöfen von Würzburg im sechzehnten Jahrhundert.' *AU* 6, no. 1 (1840), 25–67.

Schaumberg, Oskar Freiherr von. *Neuaufstellungen der Stammtafeln des uradelig fränkischen Geschlechts von Schaumberg.* Bamberg, 1953.

Scherzer, Walter. 'Siedlungs- und Wüstungsbewegung, Bevölkerungsfluktuation und Inforestierung im Bereich des Guttenberger und Irtenberger Forstes.' In Helmut

Selected bibliography

Jäger and Walter Scherzer, *Territorienbildung, Forsthoheit und Wüstungsbewegung im Waldgebiet westlich von Würzburg*, 80–235. Würzburg, 1984.

Scherzer, Walter. 'Das Henneberger Schloss und Amt Mainberg bei Schweinfurt (bis 1542).' In *Thüringische Forschungen: Festschrift für Hans Eberhardt zum 85. Geburtstag am 25. September 1993*, ed. Michael Gockel and Volker Wahl, 111–29. Cologne, 1993.

Schiera, Pierangelo. 'Otto Brunner, uno storico della crisi.' *Annali dell'Istituto storico italo-germanico in Trento* 13 (1987), 19–37.

Schindler, Norbert. 'Habitus und Herrschaft: Zum Wandel der aristokratischen Herrschaftspraxis im 16. Jahrhundert.' In his *Widerspenstige Leute: Studien zur Volkskultur in der frühen Neuzeit*, 47–77. Frankfurt am Main, 1992.

Schlitzer, Paul. 'Die Herren von Lüder: Ein Beitrag zur Ortsgeschichte von Großenlüder.' Parts 1 and 2. *Fuldaer Geschichtsblätter* 36 (1960), 178–90; 37 (1961), 65–83.

Schlosser, Friedrich Christoph. *Weltgeschichte für das deutsche Volk*. Vol. VII. Frankfurt am Main, 1847.

Schmid, Peter. *Der Gemeine Pfennig von 1495: Vorgeschichte und Entstehung, verfassungsgeschichtliche, politische und finanzielle Bedeutung*. Göttingen, 1989.

Schmitt, Richard. *Frankenberg: Besitz- und Wirtschaftsgeschichte einer reichsritterschaftlichen Herrschaft in Franken, 1528–1806 (1848)*. Ansbach, 1986.

Schmitt, Richard. 'Aus dem Zentrum des Hochstifts verdrängt: Die Herren von Hutten im Gebiet des Würzburger Bischofs.' In *Ulrich von Hutten: Ritter, Humanist, Publizist 1488–1523. Katalog zur Ausstellung des Landes Hessen anläßlich des 500. Geburtstages*, ed. Peter Laub, 103–12. Kassel, 1988.

Schneider, Joachim. 'Überregionale Integrationstendenzen im deutschen Niederadel: Zwei Briefzeitungen von 1427 und die Adelseinungen der Hussitenzeit.' In *Strukturen der Gesellschaft im Mittelalter: Interdisziplinäre Mediävistik in Würzburg*, ed. Dieter Rödel and Joachim Schneider, 115–39. Wiesbaden, 1996.

Schnell, Otto. 'Geschichte der Salzburg an der fränkischen Saale: Mit besonderer Rücksicht auf die Zeit von der Uebergabe der Burg an Bischof Heinrich von Würzburg bis auf den heutigen Tag.' *AU* 29 (1886), 1–128.

Schöler, Eugen. *Historische Familienwappen in Franken: 1860 Wappenschilde und familiengeschichtliche Notizen von Geschlechtern des Adels und der Reichsstädte in Franken*. 2nd edn. Neustadt a.d. Aisch, 1982.

Schreiner, Klaus. ' "Grundherrschaft": Entstehung und Bedeutungswandel eines geschichtswissenschaftlichen Ordnungs- und Erklärungsbegriffs.' In *Die Grundherrschaft im späten Mittelalter*, ed. Hans Patze, vol. I, 11–74. Sigmaringen, 1983.

Schubert, Ernst. *Die Landstände des Hochstifts Würzburg*. Würzburg, 1967.

Schubert, Ernst. 'Albrecht Achilles, Markgraf und Kurfürst von Brandenburg (1414–1486).' *Fränkische Lebensbilder* 4 (1971), 130–72.

Schubert, Ernst. *Einführung in die Grundprobleme der deutschen Geschichte im Spätmittelalter*. Darmstadt, 1992.

Schubert, Ernst. *Fürstliche Herrschaft und Territorium im späten Mittelalter*. Munich, 1996.

Schulte, Aloys. *Der Adel und die deutsche Kirche im Mittelalter*. 2nd edn. Stuttgart, 1922.

Schultes, Johann Adolph. *Diplomatische Geschichte des Gräflichen Hauses Henneberg*. 2 parts. Hildburghausen, 1788–91.

Schütz, Martin. 'Die Ganerbschaft vom Rothenberg in ihrer politischen, juristischen und wirtschaftlichen Bedeutung.' PhD thesis, University of Erlangen, 1924.

Selected bibliography

Schwarzenberg, Karl Fürst zu. *Geschichte des reichsständischen Hauses Schwarzenberg.* Neustadt a.d. Aisch, 1963.

Schwemmer, Wilhelm. *Burg und Amt Veldenstein-Neuhaus.* Nuremberg, 1961.

Seefried, Otto Graf. *Aus dem Stiebar-Archiv: Forschungen zur Familiengeschichte von Bauer, Bürger und Edelmann in Ober- und Mittelfranken.* Nuremberg, 1953.

Seyboth, Reinhard. *Die Markgraftümer Ansbach und Kulmbach unter der Regierung Markgraf Friedrichs des Älteren (1486–1515).* Göttingen, 1985.

Sicken, Bernhard. 'Albrecht Alcibiades von Brandenburg-Kulmbach.' *Fränkische Lebensbilder* 6 (1975), 130–60.

Sicken, Bernhard. 'Landesherrliche Einnahmen und Territorialstruktur: Die Fürstentümer Ansbach und Kulmbach zu Beginn der Neuzeit.' *JffL* 42 (1982), 153–248.

Simmel, Georg. *Soziologie: Untersuchungen über die Formen der Vergesellschaftung.* Leipzig, 1908.

Singer, Bruno. *Die Fürstenspiegel in Deutschland im Zeitalter des Humanismus und der Reformation: Bibliographische Grundlagen und ausgewählte Interpretationen: Jakob Wimpfeling, Wolfgang Seidel, Johann Sturm, Urban Rieger.* Munich, 1981.

Spielberg, Werner. 'Martin Zollner von Rothenstein und seine Sippe.' Parts 1 and 2. *Familiengeschichtliche Blätter* 15 (1917), 129–36; 167–80.

Spieß, Karl-Heinz. *Familie und Verwandtschaft im deutschen Hochadel des Spätmittelalters: 13. bis Anfang des 16. Jahrhunderts.* Stuttgart, 1993.

Sprandel, Rolf. 'Die Ritterschaft und das Hochstift Würzburg im Spätmittelalter.' *JffL* 36 (1976), 117–43.

Sprandel, Rolf. 'Die territorialen Ämter des Fürstentums Würzburg im Spätmittelalter.' *JffL* 37 (1977), 45–64.

Sprandel, Rolf. 'Mittelalterliche Verfassungs- und Sozialgeschichte vom Blickpunkt einer Landschaft: Mainfranken.' *ZHF* 7 (1980), 401–22.

Sprandel, Rolf. 'Die spätmittelalterliche Wirtschaftskonjunktur und ihre regionalen Determinanten: Forschungsüberblick und neue Perspektiven.' In *Historia Socialis et Oeconomica: Festschrift für Wolfgang Zorn zum 65. Geburtstag,* ed. Hermann Kellenbenz and Hans Pohl, 168–79. Stuttgart, 1987.

Sprandel, Rolf. *Verfassung und Gesellschaft im Mittelalter.* 4th edn. Paderborn, 1991.

Stacke, Ludwig. *Deutsche Geschichte.* Vol. I, *Von der ältesten Zeit bis zu Maximilian.* Bielefeld, 1880.

Stauber, Reinhard. 'Herzog Georg der Reiche von Niederbayern und Schwaben: Voraussetzungen und Formen landesherrlicher Expansionspolitik an der Wende vom Mittelalter zur Neuzeit.' *ZbLG* 49 (1986), 611–70.

Stauber, Reinhard. *Herzog Georg von Bayern-Landshut und seine Reichspolitik: Möglichkeiten und Grenzen reichsfürstlicher Politik im wittelsbachisch-habsburgischen Spannungsfeld zwischen 1470 und 1505.* Kallmünz, 1993.

Ste Croix, G. E. M. de. *The Class Struggle in the Ancient Greek World: From the Archaic Age to the Arab Conquests.* London, 1983.

Steinau-Steinrück, Richard von. 'Abriß aus der Geschichte des fränkischen Geschlechtes von Steinau genannt Steinrück in bezug auf seine Zugehörigkeit zu dem Hochstifte Würzburg und im besonderen auf seine Besitzungen daselbst.' *AU* 49 (1907), 1–134.

Steinmetz, Thomas. '"Conterfei etlicher Kriegshandlungen von 1523 bis in das 1527 Jar": Zu Burgendarstellungen über die "Absberger Fehde" oder den "Fränkischen

Selected bibliography

Krieg".' In *Beiträge zur Erforschung des Odenwaldes und seiner Randlandschaften, IV*, ed. Winfried Wackerfuß, 365–86. Breuberg-Neustadt, 1986.

Stetten, Freiherr von. 'Ein Fehdebrief vom Jahre 1489.' *Der deutsche Herold* 23 (1892), 114–15.

Stillfried, Rudolf Graf, and Sigmund Haenle. *Das Buch vom Schwanenorden: Ein Beitrag zu den hohenzollerischen Forschungen*. Berlin, 1881.

Stone, Lawrence. 'Prosopography.' In his *The Past and the Present Revisited*, 45–73. London, 1981.

Störmer, Wilhelm. *Miltenberg: Die Ämter Amorbach und Miltenberg des Mainzer Oberstifts als Modelle geistlicher Territorialität und Herrschaftsintensivierung*. Munich, 1979.

Störmer, Wilhelm. 'Die Rolle der höfischen Tugendbegriffe fröude, milte, êre im politischen Spannungsfeld zwischen dem Hochstift Würzburg und dem Erzstift Mainz.' *Würzburger Diözesangeschichtsblätter* 42 (1980), 1–10.

Störmer, Wilhelm. 'Grundherrschaften des höheren und niederen Adels im Main-Tauber-Raum.' In *Die Grundherrschaft im späten Mittelalter*, ed. Hans Patze, vol. II, 25–45. Sigmaringen, 1983.

Störmer, Wilhelm. 'Der Adel im herzoglichen und kurfürstlichen Bayern der Neuzeit: Fragen der adeligen Grundherrschaft und Ständemacht.' In *Adel im Wandel*, ed. Helmuth Feigl and Willibald Rosner, 47–71. Vienna, 1991.

Stromer, Wolfgang von. *Oberdeutsche Hochfinanz 1350–1450*. Part 2. Wiesbaden, 1970.

Stumpf, Andreas Sebastian. *Denkwürdigkeiten der teutschen besonders fränkischen Geschichte*. 3 parts. Erfurt and Würzburg, 1802–4.

Syme, Ronald. *The Roman Revolution*. 1939. Reprint, Oxford, 1985.

Tabacco, Giovanni. 'La dissoluzione medievale dello stato nella recente storiografia.' *Studi medievali*, 3rd ser., 1 (1960), 397–446.

Taddey, Gerhard. 'Macht und Recht im späten Mittelalter: Die Auseinandersetzungen zwischen Hohenlohe und Hessen um die Grafschaften Ziegenhain und Nidda.' *WFr* 61 (1977), 79–110.

Thumser, Matthias. *Hertnidt vom Stein (ca. 1427–1491): Bamberger Domdekan und markgräflich-brandenburgischer Rat. Karriere zwischen Kirche und Fürstendienst*. Neustadt a.d. Aisch, 1989.

Thüngen Rudolf Karl Reinhard Freiherr von. 'Zur Genealogie der Familie derer von Thüngen.' *AU* 54 (1912), 1–180.

Tilly, Charles. 'War Making and State Making as Organized Crime.' In *Bringing the State Back In*, ed. Peter B. Evans, Dietrich Rueschemeyer, and Theda Skocpol, 169–91. Cambridge, 1985.

Tilly, Charles. *Coercion, Capital, and European States, AD 990–1992*. 2nd edn. Oxford, 1992.

Trossbach, Werner. 'Das "ganze Haus" – Basiskategorie für das Verständnis der ländlichen Gesellschaft deutscher Territorien in der Frühen Neuzeit?' *Blätter für deutsche Landesgeschichte* 129 (1993), 277–314.

Turke, Paul W., and L. L. Betzig. 'Those Who Can Do: Wealth, Status, and Reproductive Success on Ifaluk.' *Ethology and Sociobiology* 6 (1985), 79–87.

Ulmschneider, Helgard. *Götz von Berlichingen: Ein adeliges Leben der deutschen Renaissance*. Sigmaringen, 1974.

Selected bibliography

Vice, Roy L. 'The German Peasants' War of 1525 and its Aftermath in Rothenburg ob der Tauber and Würzburg.' PhD thesis, University of Chicago, 1984.

Voigt, Johannes. *Markgraf Albrecht Alcibiades von Brandenburg-Kulmbach.* 2 vols. Berlin, 1852.

Wackerfuß, Winfried. *Kultur-, Wirtschafts- und Sozialgeschichte des Odenwaldes im 15. Jahrhundert: Die ältesten Rechnungen für die Grafen von Wertheim in der Herrschaft Breuberg (1409–1484).* Breuberg-Neustadt, 1991.

Wagner, Friedrich. 'Nürnbergische Geheimschrift im 15. und zu Anfang des 16. Jahrhunderts.' *Archivalische Zeitschrift* 9 (1884), 14–62.

Waldenfels, Otto Freiherr von. *Die Freiherrn von Waldenfels: Stammfolgen mit urkundlichen Belegen.* 5 vols. Munich, 1952–70.

Weber, August. 'Das Amt Haselstein.' *Fuldaer Geschichtsblätter* 32 (1956), 8–11.

Weber, Karl von. 'Ueber Turniere und Kampfspiele.' *Archiv für die sächsische Geschichte* 4 (1866), 337–84.

Weinfurter, Stefan. 'Herzog, Adel und Reformation: Bayern im Übergang vom Mittelalter zur Neuzeit.' *ZHF* 10 (1983), 1–39.

Wendehorst, Alfred. *Das Bistum Würzburg.* Parts 2 and 3. Berlin, 1969–78.

Wendehorst, Alfred, and Gerhard Rechter. 'Ein Geldverleiher im spätmittelalterlichen Franken: Philipp von Seckendorff-Gutend.' In *Hochfinanz, Wirtschaftsräume, Innovationen: Festschrift für Wolfgang von Stromer,* ed. Uwe Bestmann, Franz Irsigler, and Jürgen Schneider, vol. I, 487–529. Trier, 1987.

White, Stephen D. 'Feuding and Peace-making in the Touraine around the Year 1100.' *Traditio* 42 (1986), 195–263.

Wiesflecker, Hermann. *Kaiser Maximilian I.: Das Reich, Österreich und Europa an der Wende zur Neuzeit.* Vol. V, *Der Kaiser und seine Umwelt: Hof, Staat, Wirtschaft, Gesellschaft und Kultur.* Vienna, 1986.

Wilhelm, H. 'Die Edeln von und zum Absberg: Ein Beitrag zur fränkischen Geschichte.' *Alt-Gunzenhausen* 8 (1931), 3–197

Wilmowsky, Hubertus von. 'Die Geschichte der Ritterschaft Buchenau von ihren Anfängen bis zum Wiener Kongreß.' *Fuldaer Geschichtsblätter* 40 (1964), 1–47.

Wolf, Franz Nikolaus. 'Geschichtliche Beschreibung der Burg Hohenburg ob der Werrn.' *AU* 6, no. 2 (1840), 83–114.

Wood, James B. *The Nobility of the 'Election' of Bayeux, 1463–1666: Continuity through Change.* Princeton, 1980.

Wunder, Gerd. 'Die Ritter von Vellberg.' In *Vellberg in Geschichte und Gegenwart,* ed. Hansmartin Decker-Hauff, vol. I, *Darstellungen,* 129–96. Sigmaringen, 1984.

Würdinger, Joseph. *Kriegsgeschichte von Bayern, Franken, Pfalz und Schwaben von 1347 bis 1506.* 2 vols. Munich, 1868.

Zeißner, Sebastian. 'Dr. Kilian von Bibra: Dompropst von Würzburg (ca. 1426–1494).' *MJfGK* 2 (1950), 78–121.

Zeißner, Sebastian. 'Zwei Mitarbeiter des Fürstbischofs Rudolf von Scherenberg.' *MJfGK* 3 (1951), 127–38.

Zeißner, Sebastian. *Rudolf II. von Scherenberg: Fürstbischof von Würzburg 1466–1495.* 2nd edn. Würzburg, 1952.

Zeißner, Sebastian. 'Beiträge zur Geschichte mainfränkischer Burgen.' *MJfGK* 6 (1954), 106–28.

Index

Abel, Wilhelm, 53
Absberg, Dr Georg von, 58
Absberg, Hans von, 58
Absberg, Hans Christoph von, 58
Absberg, Hans Georg von, 58
Absberg, Hans Thomas von, 76, 138
Absberg, Paul von, 100, 108–9
advocacy, 107
Affalterbach, battle of (1502), 33
Albrecht VI, duke of Austria (1424–63), 61
Albrecht IV, duke of Bavaria (1465–1508), 31
Albrecht V, duke of Bavaria (1550–79), 143–4
Albrecht (Achilles), margrave of Brandenburg
    (1440), and elector of Brandenburg
    (1470–86), 16, 17, 20–2, 40, 65, 94, 96–9,
    119, 126–7, 128
Albrecht (Alcibiades), margrave of Brandenburg
    (1541–57), 143
Altenmuhr, castle, 58
Andermann, Kurt, 54
Ansbach, 32
Aquinas, Thomas, 5
Aufseß, Eukarius von, 57
Aufseß, Konrad von, 99
Augsburg, Peace of, 143
August, elector of Saxony, 145

Baum, Hans-Peter, 59, 77, 83, 90
Bavaria, princely council of, 40
Bayreuth, governorship, 95
Bergtheim, battle of (1400), 89
Berlichingen, Götz von, 100–1, 123
Berlichingen, Hans Pleickhard von, 123
Bibra, noble family, 48
Blickle, Peter, 55
Boone, James L., 77
Bramberg, governorship, 73, 74
Brandenburg, margraves of
    debts, 50–3
    princely council of, 40
    Territorial Court 97
Brunner, Otto
    interpretation of the feud, 4–7, 86, 87, 103–4
    criticisms of, 7–9, 104–5, 108

and 'Land', 6–7
and 'Old Europe', 4–7
Buchenau, Engelhard von, 94–5
Bullenheim, 106
Burckhardt, Jakob, 4
Burghausen, 114
Buttendorf, Georg von, 58

Cannon, John, 63
Castell, count Friedrich of, 18, 94
Castell, count Wilhelm of, 94
cathedral chapters, 81–2
cavalcades, 106
Charles V, King of the Romans (1519–31), and
    Holy Roman Emperor (1519–56/8), 34, 39,
    141, 145
chevauchées, 106
cities, feuds and, 26–34, 75–6, 107–8
Cohn, Henry J., 44
Cologne, 119–20
Common Penny, 92–3, 129–31, 141
Commynes, Philippe de, 112
continuity, of noble families, 83
councils, princely, see Bavaria, Brandenburg,
    Württemberg, Würzburg
Councillor, office of, 39–40
Crailsheim, Georg von, 112–13
Crailsheim, Marx von, 113
Crailsheim, Wolf von, 51, 59
Creusen, governorship, 95
crisis, agrarian, 53–4, 58

Derrer, Wilhelm, 28, 31
dowries, 66

Ebern, governorship, 73
Eberstein, Mangold von, 76
Egloffstein, Hans von, 91
Ehenheim, Georg von, 37
Ehenheim, Michael von, 37
Ehingen, Jörg von, 61
Eltmann, 70
endogamy, among European nobilities, 62–4
Erasmus, Desiderius, 82

229

Eschenau, 27
Esel, noble family, 59
Eyb, Anna von, 64
Eyb, Hans von, 64
Eyb, Hans Christoph von, 52, 59
Eyb, Ludwig von, 59, 129
Eyb, Martin von, 65
Eyb, Veit Asmus von, 59
Eyb, noble family, 63

Ferdinand, archduke of Austria, King of the
    Romans (1531–58), and Holy Roman
    Emperor (1558–64), 34, 141–2, 145
feudalism, 92
fiefs
    free knightly, 89
    ignoble, 89
    lordship and, 90
    superior, 90–2, 96
Franck, Sebastian, 2
Friedrich I, margrave of Brandenburg (1414),
    and elector of Brandenburg (1417–40), 65,
    93
Friedrich IV, margrave of Brandenburg
    (1486–1515), 22, 25, 31–3, 41, 57, 64, 113
Fries, Lorenz, 45, 69–70, 87, 109, 119
Fuchs von Bimbach, Adam, 72, 74
Fuchs von Bimbach, Christina, 70–1, 74
Fuchs von Bimbach, Christoph, 69–73, 87–8,
    98–9, 111
Fuchs von Bimbach, Dietrich (I), 70–1, 74
Fuchs von Bimbach, Dietrich (II), 70–1, 74
Fuchs von Bimbach, Elisabeth, 70–1, 74
Fuchs von Bimbach, Georg, 70–2, 74
Fuchs von Bimbach, Georg, 58 n. 119
Fuchs von Bimbach, Hans, 69–71, 73, 99
Fuchs von Bimbach, Hans Dietrich, 58 n. 119
Fuchs von Bimbach, Heinrich (I), 70–1, 74
Fuchs von Bimbach, Heinrich (II), 70–1, 73, 74
Fuchs von Bimbach, Heinrich (III), 69–71, 73,
    99–100, 109
Fuchs von Bimbach, Thomas, 70–2, 74
Fuchs von Bimbach zu Leuzendorf, Andreas, 73,
    74
Fuchs von Bimbach zu Leuzendorf, Christoph,
    72–4
Fuchs von Bimbach zu Leuzendorf, Jakob, 73, 74
Fuchs von Bimbach, noble family, 55
Fuchs von Preppach, Christoph, 71–2
Fuchs von Preppach, Georg, 71
Fuchs von Wonfurt, Georg, 59
Fürstenforst, castle, 19, 21, 22–3, 24, 25, 47

Gebsattel, Georg von, 97–8
Gebürg, nobility in the, 84
Gemünden, governorship 73

Georg, duke of Bavaria (1479–1503), 21, 31, 57,
    113
Georg, margrave of Brandenburg (1527–43), 40,
    51
Georg von Schaumberg, prince-bishop of
    Bamberg (1459–75), 69, 87, 97–100
Gerolzhofen, 132
Giech, Christoph von, 26–35, 57, 115
Giengen, battle of (1462), 98
Gotha, 145
Gottfried Schenk von Limpurg, prince-bishop of
    Würzburg (1443–55), 94, 97
Gottschalk, Friedrich, 3
Gottsmann, Albrecht, 137
Gottsmann, Wolf, 25, 137
governorships, district, 41–2
Gracious Pact, The, 97–8, 126 n. 21, 127
Grumbach, Wilhelm von, 143–5
Guttenberg, Apel von, 114
Guttenberg, Christoph von, 113
Guttenberg, Georg von, 47
Guttenberg, Moritz von, 113–14, 115
Guttenberg, Philipp von, 56–7, 113–14
Guttenberg, castle, 113–14
Guttenberg, noble family, 47, 113–15, 128

Hahn, Peter-Michael, 44
Hallerndorf, castle, 58
Haslach, castle, 16, 19, 20, 22
Haßfurt, governorship, 71
Henneberg, count Wilhelm (III) of, 108
Henneberg, count Wilhelm (IV) of, 139
Herbolzheim, 49
Heßberg, Darius von, 114–15
Heßberg, Sigmund von, 59
Heßberg, Wolf von, 59
Hetzelsdorf, Christoph von, 75
Hewen, lordship, 49
Hirschhorn, noble family, 88
Hutten, Ludwig von, 106
Hutten, Ulrich von, 1–2, 112, 136
Hutten, noble family, 55, 58–9

Imperial Chamber Court, 129, 139
Imperial Regiment, 139
inheritance, partible, nobles and, 37, 81, 109

Johann von Grumbach, prince-bishop of
    Würzburg (1455–66), 97–100, 109
Johann von Egloffstein, prince-bishop of
    Würzburg (1400–11), 89
Johann Friedrich II, duke of Saxony-Gotha
    (1554–66, d. 1595), 144

Kasimir, margrave of Brandenburg (1515–27), 33
Kehrer, Harold H., 47, 119

Kitzingen, governorship, 65
Knighthood, Franconian and Imperial, 30, 93, 129–46
Knights' Revolt, The, 120
Konrad von Thüngen, prince-bishop of Würzburg (1519–40), 82

Landsberg, Union of, 143, 145
Landshut, 114
Landwehr, Götz, 45
Langheim, monastery, 132
Lauffenburg, castle, 25
Leagues, noble (pre-1495), 123–7, 135
Leib, Kilian, 108–9
Leineck, Ludwig von, 95
Lentersheim, Konrad von, 58
Lentersheim, Sigmund von, 17
Lentersheim, Wilhelm von, 17
lineage, noble, the, 37
lordship, 102–4, 107, 109–11, 117–20
Lorenz von Bibra, prince-bishop of Würzburg (1495–1519), 82
Ludwig IX, duke of Bavaria (1450–79), 97, 128
Lupfen, counts of, 49

Maidburg, count Michael of, 65
Marienberg, castle, 39
Marktleugast, governorship, 47
Marschall von Ostheim, Moritz, 51
Marshal, office of, 39
Marx, Karl, 66
Master of the Household, office of, 39
Maximilian I, King of the Romans (1486), and Holy Roman Emperor (1508–1519), 25, 30, 32, 92, 120, 141
Maximilian II, King of the Romans (1562), and Holy Roman Emperor (1564–76), 122, 144–5
Melchior Zobel von Giebelstadt, prince-bishop of Würzburg (1544–58), 38–9, 65, 143
Merklin, Balthasar, 141
Montesquieu, Charles de Secondat, baron de, 29
Moraw, Peter, 119
Mühlberg, battle of (1547), 144
Müller, Uwe, 50–2

Neuhaus, castle, 59, 114–15
Neustetter genannt Stürmer, Sebastian von, 59
Niederhaide, marches of, 87
Niedernscheinfeld, village, 106
Nördlingen, 21
Nothafft, noble family, 59
Nuremberg, 26–34, 108

offices, *see* Councillor, Marshal, Master of the Household

Oestreich, Gerhard, 66
Oettingen, count Joachim of, 138
Ölhafen, Sixt, 29
Otto II of Mosbach, duke, count of the Upper Palatinate (1461–99), 21, 137

Peace, Perpetual General, The, 129, 139
Peasants' War, 105, 140
Philipp, Count Palatine and elector (1476–1508), 31
Pirckheimer, Willibald, 29, 32
Plassenburg, castle, 114
Pledge, The (*Pfandschaft*), 44–50
princes, German
    debts, 43–4, 50–3
    income, 43–4
    protection and safeguard (*Schutz und Schirm*), 103–6, 108, 110–11, 128, 142
    proximity to rule, paradigm of, 38, 64–7, 96, 117

Rain, Georg von, 110
Rechberg, Wilhelm von, 65
Redwitz, Ernst von, 140
Redwitz, Hans von, 95
Redwitz, Martin Wolf von, 59
rents, feudal, 53–5
Robisheaux, Thomas, 24
Rolevinck, Werner, 3
Rosenberg, Albrecht von, 34
Rosenberg, Konrad von, 52
Rösener, Werner, interpretation of the feud, 9–11, 85
Rotenhan, Hans von, 97
Rotenhan, Dr Sebastian von, 133 n. 58
Rothenberg, castle and co-heirship (*Ganerbschaft*), 26, 137–8, 140
Rudolf von Scherenberg, prince-bishop of Würzburg (1466–95), 48, 70, 126
Rüdt von Bödigheim, Georg, 100
Runding, castle, 59
Ruprecht of the Palatinate, archbishop-elector of Cologne (1463–78), 50

Sablonier, Roger, 77
Schaumberg, Georg von, 77–8
Schaumberg, Willibald von, 129
Schaumberg, noble family, 77
Schenk von Schenkenstein, noble family, 54
Schirnding, noble family, 46
Schlosser, Friedrich Christoph, 3
Schlüsselfeld, governorship, 22
Schmalkaldic League, 34
Schott, Konrad, 26–35, 51, 100, 115
Schott, Lutz, 26
Schott, Valentin, 100–1
Schütz von Hagenbach, Karl, 75

231

Index

Schwarzach, 49
Schwarzenberg, baron Friedrich of, 106
Schwarzenberg, baron Johann (I) of, 106
Schwarzenberg, baron Johann (called 'the Strong'), 133, 135
Schwarzenberg, baron Sigmund of, 98, 107
Schweinfurt, 108, 129–30, 131, 138–9, 141
Schwendi, Lazarus von, 122–3, 145
Seckendorff, Anna von, 64
Seckendorff, Anstand von, 58 n. 119
Seckendorff, Kilian von, 110
Seckendorff, Lamprecht von, 49, 98–9, 109
Seckendorff-Aberdar, Hans von, 40–1, 64
Seckendorff, noble family, 63–4
Seinsheim, Erkinger von, 107
Seinsheim, Georg Ludwig von, 144
Sendelfeld, village, 108
Seßlach, governorship, 73
sheep-farming, nobles and, 56–7
Sickingen, Franz von, 119–20, 138–9, 144
Sickingen, Philipp von 50
Sickingen, Swicker von, 119
Sickingen, noble family, 47–8
Sigmund, duke of Tyrol (1439), and archduke of Austria (1477–90), 61, 118
Sigmund, margrave of Brandenburg (1486–95), 22
Society of the Clasp, 124
Society of Counts, Barons, Knights and Valets, 124
Society of the Griffin, 123–4
Society of St George, 124
state
 domain, the, 66
 finance, the, 66, 120
 tax, the, 66
Stein, castle, 21
Stein, Christoph von, 137
Stettfeld, village, 98–9, 109
Strasbourg, cathedral chapter of, 82
stratification, social, among the nobility, 36–8, 60–1, 95, 96, 111–12, 120–21
Streitberg, castle and governorship, 95
Streitberg, Eberhard von, 95
Streitberg, Georg von, 95
Streitberg, Paul von, 95
Stuffenberg, governorship, 98
Stühlingen, lordship, 49
Suarez, Francisco, 5
Swabian League, 32–3, 138–40, 141

Theres, monastery, 99
Thüngen, Adam von, 64, 105
Thüngen, noble family, 96
Thüngfeld, Georg von, 59
Tilly, Charles, 120
tournaments, 36, 83–4
Trier, archbishopric, 120, 138
Trithemius, Johannes, 2
Türkensteuer, nobles and, 141

Unterhohenried, castle, 59

vassalage, multiple, 92–4, 96
vendetta, 8
Veringen, 118
Vestenberg, Eukarius von, 17–24
Vestenberg, Hans von, 16
Vestenberg, Kaspar von, 18–24, 107
Vestenberg, Konrad von, 20–3
Vestenberg, Lienhard von, 17
Vestenberg, Magdalena von, 17
Vestenberg, Margaretha von, 16
Vestenberg, Philipp von, 25
Vestenberg, Veit von, 16–26, 47, 107, 112–13
Vogelsburg, castle, 59
Vogler, Georg, 40
Voit von Salzburg, noble family, 48 n. 64
Vorderfrankenberg, lordship and castle, 58

Wallburg, castle, town, and governorship, 69–70
Werdenberg, counts of, 118
Wertheim, count Michael of, 141
Widmann, Matthias (alias von Kemnat), 2
Wimpfeling, Jakob, 81
Windsheim, 33
Wirsberg, Konrad von, 57
Worms, 119
Worms, Imperial Diet of (1495), 129
Württemberg, princely council of, 40
Würzburg
 Aulic Court, 125
 Court of Fiefs, 59, 77, 83, 90
 princely council of, 40
 Territorial Court, 125

Zabelstein, governorship, 100
Zimmern, count Froben Christoph of, 2–3, 32
Zwernitz, governorship, 95

232

CAMBRIDGE STUDIES IN EARLY MODERN HISTORY

*The Old World and the New**
J. H. ELLIOTT
*The Army of Flanders and the Spanish Road, 1567–1659: The Logistics of Spanish Victory and Defeat in the Low Countries Wars**
GEOFFREY PARKER
*Richelieu and Olivares**
J. H. ELLIOTT
Society and Religious Toleration in Hamburg 1529–1819
JOACHIM WHALEY
*Absolutism and Society in Seventeenth-Century France: State Power and Provincial Aristocracy in Languedoc**
WILLIAM BEIK
Renaissance and Revolt: Essays in the Intellectual and Social History of Modern France
J. H. M. SALMON
Louis XIV and the Origins of the Dutch War
PAUL SONNINO
*The Princes of Orange: The Stadholders in the Dutch Republic**
HERBERT H. ROWEN
Frontiers of Heresy: The Spanish Inquisition from the Basque Lands to Sicily
WILLIAM MONTER
Rome in the Age of Enlightenment: The Post-Tridentine Syndrome and the Ancien Régime
HANNS GROSS
The Cost of Empire: The Finances of the Kingdom of Naples during the Period of Spanish Rule
ANTONIO CALABRIA
Lille and the Dutch Revolt: Urban Stability in an Era of Revolution
ROBERT S. DUPLESSIS
The Armada of Flanders: Spanish Maritime Policy and European War, 1568–1668
R. A. STRADLING
The Continuity of Feudal Power: The Caracciolo di Brienza in Spanish Naples
TOMMASO ASTARITA
After the Deluge: Poland and the Second Northern War 1655–1660
ROBERT FROST
The Nobility of Holland: From Knights to Regents, 1500–1650
H. F. K. VAN NIEROP
Classes, Estates and Order in Early Modern Brittany
JAMES B. COLLINS
Early Modern Democracy in the Grisons: Social Order and Political Language in a Swiss Mountain Canton, 1470–1620
RANDOLPH C. HEAD
War, State and Society in Württemberg, 1677–1793
PETER H. WILSON
From Madrid to Purgatory: The Art and Craft of Dying in Sixteenth-Century Spain
CARLOS M. N. EIRE

The Reformation and Rural Society: The Parishes of Brandenburg-Ansbach-Kulmbach, 1528–1603
  C. SCOTT DIXON
Labour, Science and Technology in France, 1500–1620
  HENRY HELLER
The King's Army: Warfare, Soldiers, and Society during the Wars of Religion in France, 1562–1576
  JAMES B. WOOD
Spanish Naval Power, 1589–1665: Reconstruction and Defeat
  DAVID GOODMAN
State and Nobility in Early Modern Germany: The Knightly Feud in Franconia, 1440–1567
  HILLAY ZMORA
The Quest for Compromise: Peace-Makers in Counter-Reformation Vienna
  HOWARD LOUTHAN

Titles available in paperback marked with an asterisk*

The following titles are now out of print:
French Finances, 1770–1795: From Business to Bureaucracy
  J. F. BOSHER
Chronicle into History: An Essay in the Interpretation of History in Florentine Fourteenth-Century Chronicles
  LOUIS GREEN
France and the Estates General of 1614
  J. MICHAEL HAYDEN
Reform and Revolution in Mainz, 1743–1803
  T. C. W. BLANNING
Altopascio: A Study in Tuscan Society 1587–1784
  FRANK MCARDLE
Gunpowder and Galleys: Changing Technology and Mediterranean Warfare at Sea in the Sixteenth Century
  JOHN FRANCIS GUILMARTIN JR
The State, War and Peace: Spanish Political Thought in the Renaissance 1516–1559
  J. A. FERNÁNDEZ-SANTAMARIA
Calvinist Preaching and Iconoclasm in the Netherlands, 1544–1569
  PHYLLIS MACK CREW
The Kingdom of Valencia in the Seventeenth Century
  JAMES CASEY
Filippo Strozzi and the Medici: Favor and Finance in Sixteenth-Century Florence and Rome
  MELISSA MERIAM BULLARD
Rouen during the Wars of Religion
  PHILIP BENEDICT
The Emperor and his Chancellor: A Study of the Imperial Chancellery under Gattinara
  JOHN M. HEADLEY
The Military Organisation of a Renaissance State: Venice c. 1400–1617
  M. E. MALLETT AND J. R. HALE

Neostoicism and the Early Modern State
  GERHARD OESTREICH
Prussian Society and the German Order: An Aristocratic Corporation in Crisis c. 1410–1466
  MICHAEL BURLEIGH
The Changing Face of Empire: Charles V, Philip II and Habsburg Authority, 1552–1559
  M. J. RODRÍGUEZ-SALGADO
Turning Swiss: Cities and Empire 1450–1550
  THOMAS A. BRADY JR
Neighbourhood and Community in Paris
  DAVID GARRIOCH
The Duke of Anjou and the Politique Struggle during the Wars of Religion
  MACK P. HOLT